I FOUND THIS
FUNNY

MY FAVORITE
PIECES OF HUMOR

and

SOME THAT MAY NOT BE FUNNY AT ALL

Edited by

JUDD APATOW

McSWEENEY'S BOOKS
SAN FRANCISCO

www.mcsweeneys.net

ISBN: 978-1-934781-90-6

THE PROCEEDS FROM THIS BOOK
GO TO 826 NATIONAL

All proceeds from *I Found This Funny* will go directly to fund the free youth writing programs offered by 826 National.

826 National is a nonprofit tutoring, writing, and publishing organization with locations in eight cities across the country. Our goal is to assist students ages six to eighteen with their writing skills, and to help teachers get their classes excited about writing. In 2002, our first center, 826 Valencia, opened its doors in San Francisco. Due to overwhelming interest from others around the country, our tutoring and mentorship model has been duplicated in seven other cities: Ann Arbor, Boston, Chicago, Los Angeles, New York, Seattle, and Washington, D.C.

Our services are structured around the understanding that great leaps in learning can happen with one-on-one attention, and that strong writing skills are fundamental to future success. With this in mind, we provide drop-in tutoring, after-school workshops, in-school tutoring, help for English-language learners, and assistance with student publications. All of our programs are challenging and enjoyable, and ultimately strengthen each student's power to express ideas effectively, creatively, confidently, and in his or her individual voice.

For more information, please visit 826NATIONAL.ORG

CONTENTS

JUDD APATOW

Introduction

I don't remember how I learned to read. Who taught me to read? Was it my mother? We always had a lot of books around. Dr. Seuss. *Curious George.* That book about the strange animal with the spots he could take off and juggle. Lately I have been teaching my seven-year-old daughter how to read and it is hard. Someone must have put some serious hours in with me. I wish I remembered any of those moments. It must have been my mom and not some faceless Montessori teacher. I'll go with Mom. For some reason I think I picked it up really fast because if it was a long difficult road I feel like I would remember that.

I say that because my adult reading life has not been a long easy road. It took a long time before I got excited about literature and reading in general. As an adolescent I liked to read. At first only books about the Marx Brothers. Steve Martin's book of humor, *Cruel Shoes.* I remember reading the Albert Goldman book, *Ladies and Gentleman, Lenny Bruce*, in seventh grade and it had a major impact on me. It made the world of comedy I dreamed about three-dimensional and potentially obtainable (hopefully without the heroin use). The book had such an impact on me that I cut out all of the photographs in it and made a complicated, graphic book report on it. I do not think a book report was even assigned. Then my English teacher promptly "lost" it. For years I thought he was so impressed with my report that he literally stole it so he could have it for himself. He was dead to me after that, which was tough because he was the "cool" English teacher. The one who put on Beatles records and discussed the lyrics with you. The one who would say "shit" a few times a year without shame or regret. Still, dead to me.

And then Stephen King came into my life. In the junior-high years that was all I read, one right after the other. *The Dead Zone, Cujo, Firestarter.* He cranked them out one after the other. Ridiculously enjoyable books being released to the world at such a torrid pace that one would think the man would have had to be on cocaine.

But sadly, that is where my curiosity ended. Other than a brief moment in college where I believed my mind had been blown open and literature suddenly made sense to me (*Candide's* in the house, bitches!), I did not pursue it at all. I wrote jokes; I did stand-up comedy. That was my obsession. But I was always limited in my perspective. I became a decent writer because I could mimic the comics I was getting paid to write for, but my own act had no unique perspective. I was kind of funny, but forgettable to everyone, even myself.

I slogged on for a period of years, doing pretty well in Hollywood, but one does not always need to be the cream to rise in that world. I had a major shift after working with the director Jake Kasdan on Paul Feig's creation, *Freaks and Geeks.* I was directing and had written an episode that contained a scene where one of the geeks goes home alone after school and cheers himself up from his lonely life by watching Garry Shandling on *The Dinah Shore Show.* As the geek eats grilled cheese sandwiches and cake, like I had always done, the great Who song "I'm the One" plays as he blissfully escapes his frustrating life and laughs his tits off to a stand-up comedian's jokes. After I edited it, Jake Kasdan said, "That is the most personal scene you have ever made, and it's also the best."

It occurred to me that he was correct, and that I needed to find the courage to share my inner world with people through my work. I had always thought my life was pretty boring, but as I slowly brought that boring world into my writing, people connected more with the stories I was telling.

Freaks and Geeks was cancelled, and so was my next show, *Undeclared.* My wife Leslie was pregnant with our second child, so I decided to take a year off to rest and catch up on an education I abandoned during college due to lack of funds and interest. I was going to take a reading year.

So the question was—where to start? There are a lot of books out there if you've never read anything but *The Stand* your previous thirty years. I had spent some time with Owen Wilson, and he recommended a few books. One was Frederick Exley's *A Fan's Notes* and the other was Saul Bellow's *Seize the Day.* He also recommended F. Scott Fitzgerald's *The Pat Hobby Stories*, one of which is included in this collection. They are hilarious and insightful short stories about a washed-up screenwriter in Hollywood. After several films that did not perform at the box office, I related. But it also led me to suck it up and read *The Great Gatsby* finally. And then I was off. At some point I bought a book called *You've Got to Read This*, which contained the favorite stories of a bunch of famous short story writers. That collection introduced me to James Agee, whose story "A Mother's Tale" was in that collection.

And so it went: I would read a collection of short stories and then find an article about the author, see who their influences were and then get those books. I mainly read short stories due to my short attention span. Not only did I mainly read short stories, I always checked out the table of contents and mainly read the shortest stories in any book first. And usually only. I gave up on a lot of books. I still have not done *Moby Dick* or Tolstoy. I can't say I ever will, unless I have a long hospital stay and while I am in the hospital I am not too medicated or in too much pain to read.

Becoming even semiliterate had an immediate effect on my writing. The courage to dig deep and reveal inspired me to take chances and look at parts of myself I had tried to avoid through workaholism and masturbation. I became a better writer, and suddenly my cult status gave way to people actually going to the movies to see my work. All because the honesty in a book like Dave Eggers's *A Heartbreaking Work of Staggering Genius* made me think, "maybe I could write a scene about the time I got wigged out having sex with my wife when she was very pregnant. Maybe I could have Leslie's character, Debbie, say to Paul Rudd's character, 'Just because you don't yell doesn't mean you are not mean.'" I had found my voice.

In a way, this collection was inspired by *You've Got to Read This*. In that collection, Tobias Wolff wrote an introductory essay to the story "Cathedral" by Raymond Carver. So I thought, "Who is Tobias Wolff?" And then I read *This Boy's Life.*

I was so grateful for all of those recommendations and collections. This book contains my recommendations. It mainly focuses on what I am most interested in—humor. But several of the pieces are not at all funny, but I could not resist putting them in because they mean so much to me.

I made a point of including writing from all disciplines—short stories, poetry, essays, humor writing, journalism, memoir, cartoons, sketches, and even television pilots. I think it's the ultimate airplane book, bathroom book, or what one reads while waiting for a friend to come out of an appointment that you have no interest in.

I want to thank everyone at 826 National for inspiring me to get off my ass and attempt to do something for someone other than myself. I am fascinated by Dave Eggers's giving nature. He truly seems to believe in what he does and enjoys it. I am trying to follow his example, except I do it mainly out of survivor's guilt and a deeply hidden fear that God does exist and will punish me if I don't do things like take six months to find enough pieces to fill this book. The work 826 National does is very important, and I encourage all of you to go to their website and learn more about it. One day I may even do it myself. It has something to do with tutoring kids in English, I think. I don't know if they will allow anyone to learn about math.

I also would like to thank Lisa Yadavaia and Christopher Monks, who read a thousand short stories to help me locate pieces for this book, and I am sorry that I only read 10 percent of the stories you said were great and asked me to read. I get tired when I read and fall asleep quickly. And I ran out of time. Hopefully we can do a Part Two.

And finally, I would also like to thank all of the writers who allowed us to use their work. Most donated their pieces for free, except the dead ones, who all demanded payment (true!). In a way, this book allows me to trick myself into believing that I have collaborated with these people I admire in some way, and that feels good, and also makes me feel a little cocky.

Usually in these introductions the author makes a quick, kind, insightful mention of all the pieces in the book and why they were chosen, but there are too many and I am tired and want to watch the Barry Levinson movie about Doctor Kevorkian now. I pray to God that when I send this to Dave he doesn't make me rewrite it. I am not a very good writer of prose. I don't know enough words. That is why I make my actors do a lot of improv.

Have fun reading! And if you are reading this on an iPad, you are a douchebag. That was the best I could think of. I promise to punch that one up for the second printing.

Always remember—"The most important person in the world is you. It's you, and you hardly even know you! Reading is fundamental!"

Editor's Note: I am well aware that significantly more than three pieces in this book are not funny. Well, they're funny to me, but I don't want to start a big debate about the definition of funny. So please accept my apologies if you were desperately seeking a humorous escape from the pain and frustration of your day. If you open up to the wrong page you might not get it. To be honest, one third of this book might be depressing. I was in a strange place when I picked these pieces. If you really need a laugh, go straight to the cartoons. And skip James Agee till you can handle the hard stuff.

JAMES AGEE

A Mother's Tale

The calf ran up the hill as fast as he could and stopped sharp. "Mama!" he cried, all out of breath. "What is it! What are they *doing*! Where are they *going*!"

Other spring calves came galloping, too.

They all were looking up at her and awaiting her explanation, but she looked out over their excited eyes. As she watched the mysterious and majestic thing they had never seen before, her own eyes became even more than ordinarily still, and during the considerable moment before she answered, she scarcely heard their urgent questioning.

Far out along the autumn plain, beneath the sloping light, an immense drove of cattle moved eastward. They went at a walk, not very fast, but faster than they could imaginably enjoy. Those in front were compelled by those behind; those at the rear, with few exceptions, did their best to keep up; those who were locked within the herd could no more help moving than the particles inside a falling rock. Men on horses rode ahead, and alongside, and behind, or spurred their horses intensely back and forth, keeping the pace steady, and the herd in shape; and from man to man a dog sped back and forth incessantly as a shuttle, barking, incessantly, in a hysterical voice. Now and then one of the men shouted fiercely, and this like the shrieking of the dogs was tinily audible above a low and awesome sound which seemed to come not from the multitude of hooves but from the center of the world, and above the sporadic bawlings and bellowings of the herd.

From the hillside this tumult was so distant that it only made more delicate the prodigious silence in which the earth and sky were held; and, from the hill, the sight was as modest as its sound. The herd was virtually hidden in the dust it raised, and could be known, in general, only by the horns which pricked this flat sunlit dust like little briars. In one place a twist of the air revealed the trembling fabric of many backs; but it was only along the near edge of the mass that individual animals were discernible, small in a driven frieze, walking fast, stumbling and recovering, tossing their armed heads, or opening their skulls heavenward in one of those cries which reached the hillside long after the jaws were shut.

From where she watched, the mother could not be sure whether there were any she recognized. She knew that among them there must be a son of hers; she had not seen him since some previous spring, and she would not be seeing him again. Then the cries of the young ones impinged on her bemusement:

"Where are they going?"

She looked into their ignorant eyes.

"Away," she said.

"Where?" they cried. "Where? Where?" her own son cried again.

She wondered what to say.

"On a long journey."

"But where *to?*" they shouted. "*Yes,* where *to?*" her son exclaimed, and she could see that he was losing his patience with her, as he always did when he felt she was evasive.

"I'm not sure," she said.

Their silence was so cold that she was unable to avoid their eyes for long.

"Well, not *really* sure. Because, you see," she said in her most reasonable tone, "I've never seen it with my own eyes, and that's the only way to *be* sure; *isn't* it."

They just kept looking at her. She could see no way out.

"But I've *heard* about it," she said with shallow cheerfulness, "from those who *have* seen it, and I don't suppose there's any good reason to doubt them."

She looked away over them again, and for all their interest in what she was about to tell them, her eyes so changed that they turned and looked, too.

The herd, which had been moving broadside to them, was being turned away, so slowly that like the turning of stars it could not quite be seen from one moment to the next; yet soon it was moving directly away from them, and even during the little while she spoke and they all watched after it, it steadily and very noticeably diminished, and the sounds of it as well.

"It happens always about this time of year," she said quietly while they watched. "Nearly all the men and horses leave, and go into the North and the West."

"Out on the range," her son said, and by his voice she knew what enchantment the idea already held for him.

"Yes," she said, "out on the range." And trying, impossibly, to imagine the range, they were touched by the breath of grandeur.

"And then before long," she continued, "everyone has been found, and brought into one place; and then . . . what you see happens. All of them.

"Sometimes when the wind is right," she said more quietly, "you can hear them coming long before you can see them. It isn't even like a sound, at first. It's more as if something were moving far under the ground. It makes you uneasy. You wonder, why, what in the world can *that* be! Then you remember what it is and then you can really hear it. And then finally, there they all are."

She could see this did not interest them at all.

"But where are they *going?*" one asked, a little impatiently.

"I'm coming to that," she said; and she let them wait. Then she spoke slowly but casually.

"They are on their way to a railroad."

There, she thought; that's for the look you all gave me when I said I wasn't sure. She waited for them to ask; they waited for her to explain.

"A railroad," she told them, "is great hard bars of metal lying side by side, or so they tell me, and they go on and on over the ground as far as the eye can see. And great wagons run on the metal bars on wheels, like wagon wheels but smaller, and these wheels are made of solid metal too. The wagons are much bigger than any wagon you've ever seen, as big as, big as sheds, they say, and they are pulled along on the iron bars by a terrible huge dark machine, with a loud scream."

"Big as *sheds?*" one of the calves said skeptically.

"Big *enough*, anyway," the mother said. "I told you I've never seen it myself. But those wagons are so big that several of us can get inside at once. And that's exactly what happens."

Suddenly she became very quiet, for she felt that somehow, she could not imagine just how, she had said altogether too much.

"Well, *what* happens," her son wanted to know. "What do you mean, *happens.*"

She always tried hard to be a reasonably modern mother. It was probably better, she felt, to go on, than to leave them all full of imaginings and mystification. Besides, there was really nothing at all awful about what happened... if only one could know *why.*

"Well," she said, "it's nothing much, really. They just—why, when they all finally *get* there, why there are all the great cars waiting in a long line, and the big dark machine is up ahead... smoke comes out of it, they say... and... well, then, they just put us into the wagons, just as many as will fit in each wagon, and when everybody is in, why..." She hesitated, for again, though she couldn't be sure why, she was uneasy.

"Why then," her son said, "the train takes them away."

Hearing that word, she felt a flinching of the heart. Where had he picked it up, she wondered, and she gave him a shy and curious glance. Oh dear, she thought. I should never have even *begun* to explain. "Yes," she said, "when everybody is safely in, they slide the doors shut."

They were all silent for a little while. Then one of them asked thoughtfully, "Are they taking them somewhere they don't want to go?"

"Oh, I don't think so," the mother said. "I imagine it's very nice."

"*I* want to go," she heard her son say with ardor. "I want to go right now," he cried. "Can I, Mama? *Can* I? *Please?*" And looking into his eyes, she was overwhelmed by sadness.

"Silly thing," she said, "there'll be time enough for that when you're grown up. But what I very much hope," she went on, "is that instead of being chosen to go out on the range and to make the long journey, you will grow up to be very strong and bright so they will decide that you may stay here at home with Mother. And you, too," she added, speaking to the other little males; but she could not honestly wish this for any but her own, least of all for the eldest, strongest, and most proud, for she knew how few are chosen.

She could see that what she said was not received with enthusiasm.

"But I want to go," her son said.

"Why?" she asked. "I don't think any of you realize that it's a great *honor* to be chosen to stay. A great privilege. Why, it's just the most ordinary ones are taken out onto the range. But only the very pick are chosen to stay here at home. If you want to go out on the range," she said in hurried and happy inspiration, "all you have to do is be ordinary and careless and silly. If you want to have even a chance to be chosen to stay, you have to try to be stronger and bigger and braver and brighter than anyone else, and that takes *hard work. Every day.* Do you see?" And she looked happily and hopefully from one to another. "Besides," she added, aware that they were not won over, "I'm told it's a very rough life out there, and the men are unkind."

"Don't you see," she said again; and she pretended to speak to all of them, but it was only to her son. But he only looked at her. "Why do you want me to stay home?" he asked flatly; in their silence she knew the others were asking the same question.

"Because it's safe here," she said before she knew better; and realized she had put it in the most unfortunate way possible. "Not safe, not just that," she fumbled. "I mean . . . because here we *know* what happens, and what's going to happen, and there's never any doubt about it, never any reason to wonder, to worry. Don't you see? It's just *Home,*" and she put a smile on the word, "where we all know each other and are happy and well."

They were so merely quiet, looking back at her, that she felt they were neither won over nor alienated. Then she knew of her son that he, anyhow, was most certainly not persuaded, for he asked the question she most dreaded: "Where do they go on the train?" And hearing him, she knew that she would stop at nothing to bring that curiosity and eagerness, and that tendency toward skepticism, within safe bounds.

"Nobody knows," she said, and she added, in just the tone she knew would most sharply engage them, "Not for sure, anyway."

"What do you mean, *not for sure,*" her son cried. And the oldest, biggest calf repeated the question, his voice cracking.

The mother deliberately kept silence as she gazed out over the plain, and while she was silent they all heard the last they would ever hear of all those who were going away: one last great cry, as faint almost as a breath; the infinitesimal jabbing vituperation of the dog; the solemn muttering of the earth.

"Well," she said, after even this sound was entirely lost, "there was one who came back." Their instant, trustful eyes were too much for her. She added, "Or so they say."

They gathered a little more closely around her, for now she spoke very quietly.

"It was my great-grandmother who told me," she said. "She was told it by *her* great-grandmother, who claimed she saw it with her own eyes, though of course I can't vouch for that. Because of course I wasn't even dreamed of then; and Great-grandmother was so very, very old, you see, that you couldn't always be sure she knew quite *what* she was saying."

Now that she began to remember it more clearly, she was sorry she had committed herself to telling it. "Yes," she said, "the story is, there was one, *just* one, who ever came back, and he told what happened on the train, and where the train went and what happened after. He told it all in a rush, they say, the last things first and every which way, but as it was finally sorted out and gotten into order by those who heard it and those they told it to, this is more or less what happened:

"He said that after the men had gotten just as many of us as they could into the car he was in, so that their sides pressed tightly together and nobody could lie down, they slid the door shut with a startling rattle and a bang, and then there was a sudden jerk, so strong they might have fallen except that they were packed so closely together, and the car began to move. But after it had moved only a little way, it stopped as suddenly as it had started, so that they all nearly fell down again. You see, they were just moving up the next car that was joined on behind, to put more of us into it. He could see it all between the boards of the car, because the boards were built a little apart from each other, to let in air."

Car, her son said again to himself. Now he would never forget the word.

"He said that then, for the first time in his life, he became very badly frightened, he didn't know why. But he was sure, at that moment, that there was something dreadfully to be afraid of. The others felt this same great fear. They called out loudly to those who were being put into the car behind, and the others called back, but it was no use; those who were getting aboard were between narrow white fences and then were walking up a narrow slope and the men kept jabbing them as they do when they are in an unkind humor, and there was no way to go but on into the car. There was no way to get out of the car, either: he tried, with all his might, and he was the one nearest the door.

"After the next car behind was full, and the door was shut, the train jerked forward again, and stopped again, and they put more of us into still another car, and so on, and on, until all the starting and stopping no longer frightened anybody; it was just something uncomfortable that was never going to stop, and they began instead to realize how hungry and thirsty they were. But there was no food and no water, so they just had to put up with this; and about the time they became resigned to going without their suppers (for now it was almost dark), they heard a sudden and terrible scream which frightened them even more deeply than anything had frightened them before, and the train began to move again, and they braced their legs once more for the jolt when it would stop, but this time, instead of stopping, it began to go fast, and then even faster, so fast that the ground nearby slid past like a flooded creek, and the whole country, he claimed, began to move too, turning slowly around a far mountain as if it were all one great wheel. And then there was a strange kind of disturbance inside the car, he said, or even inside his very bones. He felt as if everything in him was *falling*, as if he had been filled full of a heavy liquid that all wanted to flow one way, and all the others were leaning as he was leaning, away from this queer heaviness that was trying to pull them over, and then just as suddenly this leaning heaviness was gone and they nearly fell again before they could stop leaning against it. He could never understand what this was, but it too happened so many times that they all got used to it, just as they got used to seeing the country turn like a slow wheel, and just as they got used to the long cruel screams of the engine, and the steady iron noise beneath them which made the cold darkness so fearsome, and the hunger and the thirst and the continual standing up, and the moving on and on and on as if they would never stop."

"*Didn't* they ever stop?" one asked.

"Once in a great while," she replied. "Each time they did," she said, "he thought, 'Oh, now *at last*! *At last* we can get out and stretch our tired legs and lie down! *At last* we'll be given food and water!' But they never let them out. And they never gave them food or water. They never even cleaned up under them. They had to stand in their manure and in the water they made."

"Why did the train stop?" her son asked; and with somber gratification she saw that he was taking all this very much to heart.

"He could never understand why," she said. "Sometimes men would walk up and down alongside the cars, and the more nervous and the more trustful of us would call out; but they were only looking around, they never seemed to do anything. Sometimes he could see many houses and bigger buildings together where people lived. Sometimes it was far out in the country and after they had stood still for a long time they would hear a little noise which quickly became louder, and then became suddenly a noise so loud it stopped their breathing, and during this noise something black would go by, very close, and so fast it couldn't be seen. And then it was gone as suddenly as it had appeared, and the noise became small, and then in the silence their train would start up again.

"Once, he tells us, something very strange happened. They were standing still, and cars of a very different kind began to move slowly past. These cars were not red, but black, with many glass windows like those in a house; and he says they were as full of human beings as the car he was in was full of our kind. And one of these people looked into his eyes and smiled, as if he liked him, or as if he knew only too well how hard the journey was.

"So by his account it happens to them, too," she said, with a certain pleased vindictiveness. "Only they were sitting down at their ease, not standing. And the one who smiled was eating."

She was still, trying to think of something; she couldn't quite grasp the thought.

"But didn't they *ever* let them out?" her son asked.

The oldest calf jeered. "Of *course* they did. He came back, didn't he? How would he ever come back if he didn't get out?"

"They didn't let them out," she said, "for a long, long time."

"How long?"

"So long, and he was so tired, he could never quite be sure. But he said that it turned from night to day and from day to night and back again several times over, with the train moving nearly all of this time, and that when it finally stopped, early one morning, they were all so tired and so discouraged that they hardly even noticed any longer, let alone felt any hope that anything would change for them, ever again; and then all of a sudden men came up and put up a wide walk and unbarred the door and slid it open, and it was the most wonderful and happy moment of his life when he saw the door open, and walked into the open air with all his joints trembling, and drank the water and ate the delicious food they had ready for him; it was worth the whole terrible journey."

Now that these scenes came clear before her, there was a faraway shining in her eyes, and her voice, too, had something in it of the faraway.

"When they had eaten and drunk all they could hold they lifted up their heads and looked around, and everything they saw made them happy. Even the trains made them cheerful now, for now they were no longer afraid of them. And though these trains were forever breaking to pieces and joining again with other broken pieces, with shufflings and clashings and rude cries, they hardly paid them attention any more, they were so pleased to be in their new home, and so surprised and delighted to find they were among thousands upon thousands of strangers of their own kind, all lifting up their voices in peacefulness and thanksgiving, and they were so wonderstruck by all they could see, it was so beautiful and so grand.

"For he has told us that now they lived among fences as white as bone, so many, and so spiderishly complicated, and shining so pure, that there's no use trying even to hint at the beauty and the splendor of it to anyone who knows only the pitiful little outfittings of a ranch. Beyond these mazy fences, through the dark and bright smoke which continually turned along the sunlight, dark buildings stood shoulder to shoulder in a wall as huge and proud as mountains. All through the air, all the time, there was an iron humming like the humming of the iron bar after it has been struck to tell the men it is time to eat, and in all the air, all the time, there was that same strange kind of iron strength which makes the silence before lightning so different from all other silence.

"Once for a little while the wind shifted and blew over them straight from the great buildings, and it brought a strange and very powerful smell which confused and disturbed them. He could never quite describe this smell, but he has told us it was unlike anything he had ever known before. It smelled like old fire, he said, and old blood and fear and darkness and sorrow and most terrible and brutal force and something else, something in it that made him want to run away. This sudden uneasiness and this wish to run away swept through every one of them, he tells us, so that they were all moved at once as restlessly as so many leaves in a wind, and there was great worry in their voices. But soon the leaders among them concluded that it was simply the way men must smell when there are a great many of them living together. Those dark buildings must be crowded very full of men, they decided, probably as many thousands of them, indoors, as there were of us, outdoors; so it was no wonder their smell was so strong and, to our kind, so unpleasant. Besides, it was so clear now in every other way that men were not as we had always supposed, but were doing everything they knew how to make us comfortable and happy, that we ought to just put up with their smell, which after all they couldn't help, any more than we could help our own. Very likely men didn't like the way we smelled, any more than we liked theirs. They passed along these ideas to the others, and soon everyone felt more calm, and then the wind changed again, and the fierce smell no longer came to them, and the smell of their own kind was back again, very strong of course, in such a crowd, but ever so homey and comforting, and everyone felt easy again.

"They were fed and watered so generously, and treated so well, and the majesty and the loveliness of this place where they had all come to rest was so far beyond anything they had ever known or dreamed of, that many of the simple and ignorant, whose memories were short, began to wonder whether that whole difficult journey, or even their whole lives up to now, had ever really been. Hadn't it all been just shadows, they murmured, just a bad dream?

"Even the sharp ones, who knew very well it had all really happened, began to figure that everything up to now had been made so full of pain only so that all they had come to now might seem all the sweeter and the more glorious. Some of the oldest and deepest were even of a mind that all the puzzle and tribulation of the journey had been sent us as a kind of harsh trying or proving of our worthiness; and that it was entirely fitting and proper that we could earn our way through to such rewards as these, only through suffering, and through being patient under pain which was beyond our understanding; and that now at the last, to those who had borne all things well, all things were made known: for the mystery of suffering stood revealed in joy. And now as they looked back over all that was past, all their sorrows and bewilderments seemed so little and so fleeting that, from the simplest among them even to the most wise, they could feel only the kind of amused pity we feel toward the very young when, with the first thing that hurts them or they are forbidden, they are sure there is nothing kind or fair in all creation, and carry on accordingly, raving and grieving as if their hearts would break."

She glanced among them with an indulgent smile, hoping the little lesson would sink home. They seemed interested but somewhat dazed. I'm talking way over their heads, she realized. But by now she herself was too deeply absorbed in her story to modify it much. *Let* it be, she thought, a little impatient; it's over *my* head, for that matter.

"They had hardly before this even wondered that they were alive," she went on, "and now all of a sudden they felt they understood *why* they were. This made them very happy, but they were still only beginning to enjoy this new wisdom when quite a new and different kind of restiveness ran among them. Before they quite knew it they were all moving once again, and now they realized that they were being moved, once more, by men, toward still some other place and purpose they could not know. But during these last hours they had been so well that now they felt no uneasiness, but all moved forward calm and sure toward better things still to come; he has told us that he no longer felt as if he were being driven, even as it became clear that they were going toward the shade of those great buildings, but guided.

"He was guided between fences which stood ever more and more narrowly near each other, among companions who were pressed ever more and more closely against one another; and now as he felt their warmth against him it was not uncomfortable, and his pleasure in it was not through any need to be close among others through anxiousness, but was a new kind of strong and gentle delight, at being so very close, so deeply of his own kind, that it seemed as if the very breath and heartbeat of each one were being exchanged through all that multitude, and each was another, and others were each, and each was a multitude, and the multitude was one. And quieted and made mild within this melting, they now entered the cold shadow cast by the buildings, and now with every step the smell of the buildings grew stronger, and in the darkening air the glittering of the fences was ever more queer.

"And now as they were pressed ever more intimately together he could see ahead of him a narrow gate, and he was strongly pressed upon from either side and from behind, and went in eagerly, and now he was between two fences so narrowly set that he brushed either fence with either flank, and walked alone, seeing just one other ahead of him, and knowing of just one other behind him, and for a moment the strange thought came to him, that the one ahead was his father, and that the one behind was the son he had never begotten.

"And now the light was so changed that he knew he must have come inside one of the gloomy and enormous buildings, and the smell was so much stronger that it seemed almost to burn his nostrils, and the swell and the somber new light blended together and became some other thing again, beyond his describing to us except to say that the whole air beat with it like one immense heart and it was as if the beating of this heart were pure violence infinitely manifolded upon violence: so that the uneasy feeling stirred in him again that it would be wise to turn around and run out of this place just as fast and as far as ever he could go. This he heard, as if he were telling it to himself at the top of his voice, but it came from somewhere so deep and so dark inside him that he could only hear the shouting of it as less than a whisper, as just a hot and chilling breath, and he scarcely heeded it, there was so much else to attend to.

"For as he walked along in this sudden and complete loneliness, he tells us, this wonderful knowledge of being one with all his race meant less and less to him, and in its place came something still more wonderful: he knew what it was to be himself alone, a creature separate and different from any other, who had never been before, and would never be again. He could feel this in his whole weight as he walked, and in each foot as he put it down and gave his weight to it and moved above it, and in every muscle as he moved, and it was a pride which lifted him up and made him feel large, and a pleasure which pierced him through. And as he began with such wondering delight to be aware of his own exact singleness in this world, he also began to understand (or so he thought) just why these fences were set so very narrow, and just why he was walking all by himself. It stole over him, he tells us, like the feeling of a slow cool wind, that he was being guided toward some still more wonderful reward or revealing, up ahead, which he could not of course imagine, but he was sure it was being held in store for him alone.

"Just then the one ahead of him fell down with a great sigh, and was so quickly taken out of the way that he did not even have to shift the order of his hooves as he walked on. The sudden fall and the sound of that sigh dismayed him, though, and something within him told him that it would be wise to look up: and there he saw Him.

"A little bridge ran crosswise above the fences. He stood on this bridge with His feet as wide apart as He could set them. He wore spattered trousers, but from the belt up He was naked and as wet as rain. Both arms were raised high above His head and in both hands He held an enormous Hammer. With a grunt which was hardly like the voice of a human being, and with all His strength, He brought this Hammer down into the forehead of our friend: who, in a blinding blazing, heard from his own mouth the beginning of a gasping sigh; then there was only darkness."

Oh, this is *enough!* it's *enough!* she cried out within herself, seeing their terrible young eyes. How *could* she have been so foolish as to tell so much!

"What happened then?" she heard, in the voice of the oldest calf, and she was horrified. This shining in their eyes: was it only excitement? no pity? no fear?

"What happened?" two others asked.

Very well, she said to herself. I've gone so far; now I'll go the rest of the way. She decided not to soften it, either. She'd teach them a lesson they wouldn't forget in a hurry.

"Very well," she was surprised to hear herself say aloud.

"How long he lay in this darkness he couldn't know, but when he began to come out of it, all he knew was the most unspeakably dreadful pain. He was upside down and very slowly swinging and turning, for he was hanging by the tendons of his heels from great frightful hooks, and he has told us that the feeling was as if his hide were being torn from him inch by inch, in one piece.

And then as he became more clearly aware he found that this was exactly what was happening. Knives would sliver and slice along both flanks, between the hide and the living flesh; then there was a moment of most precious relief; then red hands seized his hide and there was a jerking of the hide and a tearing of tissue which it was almost as terrible to hear as to feel, turning his whole body and the poor head at the bottom of it; and then the knives again.

"It was so far beyond anything he had ever known unnatural and amazing that he hung there through several more such slicings and jerkings and tearings before he was fully able to take it all in: then, with a scream, and a supreme straining of all his strength, he tore himself from the hooks and collapsed sprawling to the floor and, scrambling right to his feet, charged the men with the knives. For just a moment they were so astonished and so terrified they could not move. Then they moved faster than he had ever known men could—and so did all the other men who chanced to be in his way. He ran down a glowing floor of blood and down endless corridors which were hung with the bleeding carcasses of our kind and with bleeding fragments of carcasses, among blood-clothed men who carried bleeding weapons, and out of that vast room into the open, and over and through one fence after another, shoving aside many an astounded stranger and shouting out warnings as he ran, and away up the railroad toward the West.

"How he ever managed to get away, and how he ever found his way home, we can only try to guess. It's told that he scarcely knew, himself, by the time he came to this part of his story. He was impatient with those who interrupted him to ask about that, he had so much more important things to tell them, and by then he was so exhausted and so far gone that he could say nothing very clear about the little he did know. But we can realize that he must have had really tremendous strength, otherwise he couldn't have outlived the Hammer; and that strength such as his—which we simply don't see these days, it's of the olden time—is capable of things our own strongest and bravest would sicken to dream of. But there was something even stronger than his strength. There was his righteous fury, which nothing could stand up against, which brought him out of that fearful place. And there was his high and burning and heroic purpose, to keep him safe along the way, and to guide him home, and to keep the breath of life in him until he could warn us. He did manage to tell us that he just followed the railroad, but how he chose one among the many which branched out from that place, he couldn't say. He told us, too, that from time to time he recognized shapes of mountains and other landmarks, from his journey by train, all reappearing backward and with a changed look and hard to see, too (for he was shrewd enough to travel mostly at night), but still recognizable. But that isn't enough to account for it. For he has told us, too, that he simply knew the way; that he didn't hesitate one moment in choosing the right line of railroad, or even think of it as choosing; and that the landmarks didn't really guide him, but just made him the more sure of what he was already sure of; and that whenever he *did* encounter human beings— and during the later stages of his journey, when he began to doubt he would live to tell us, he traveled day and night—they never so much as moved to make him trouble, but stopped dead in their tracks, and their jaws fell open.

"And surely we can't wonder that their jaws fell open. I'm sure yours would, if you had seen him as he arrived, and I'm very glad I wasn't there to see it, either, even though it is said to be the greatest and most momentous day of all the days that ever were or shall be. For we have the testimony of eyewitnesses, how he looked, and it is only too vivid, even to hear of. He came up out of the East as much staggering as galloping (for by now he was so worn out by pain and exertion and loss of blood that he could hardly stay upright), and his heels were so piteously torn by the hooks that his hooves doubled under more often than not, and in his broken forehead the mark of the Hammer was like the socket for a third eye.

"He came to the meadow where the great trees made shade over the water. 'Bring them all together!' he cried out, as soon as he could find breath. 'All!' Then he drank; and then he began to speak to those who were already there: for as soon as he saw himself in the water it was as clear to him as it was to those who watched him that there was no time left to send for the others. His hide was all gone from his head and his neck and his forelegs and his chest and most of one side and a part of the other side. It was flung backward from his naked muscles by the wind of his running, and now it lay around him in the dust like a ragged garment. They say there is no imagining how terrible and in some way how grand the eyeball is when the skin has been taken entirely from around it: his eyes, which were bare in this way, also burned with pain, and with the final energies of his life, and with his desperate concern to warn us while he could; and he rolled his eyes wildly while he talked, or looked piercingly from one to another of the listeners, interrupting himself to cry out, '*Believe* me! Oh, *believe* me!' for it had evidently never occurred to him that he might not be believed, and must make this last great effort, in addition to all he had gone through for us, to *make* himself believed; so that he groaned with sorrow and with rage and railed at them without tact or mercy for their slowness to believe.

"He had scarcely what you could call a voice left, but with this relic of a voice he shouted and bellowed and bullied us and insulted us, in the agony of his concern. While he talked he bled from the mouth, and the mingled blood and saliva hung from his chin like the beard of a goat.

"Some say that with his naked face, and his savage eyes, and that beard and the hide lying off his bare shoulders like shabby clothing, he looked almost human. But others feel this is an irreverence even to think; and others that it is a poor compliment to pay the one who told us, at such cost to himself, the true ultimate purpose of Man. Some did not believe he had ever come from our ranch in the first place, and of course he was so different from us in appearance and even in his voice, and so changed from what he might ever have looked or sounded like before, that nobody could recognize him for sure, though some were sure they did. Others suspected that he had been sent among us with his story for some mischievous and cruel purpose, and the fact that they could not imagine what this purpose might be made them, naturally, all the more suspicious. Some believed he was actually a man, trying—and none too successfully, they said—to disguise himself as one of us; and again the fact that they could not imagine why a man would do this made them all the more uneasy. There were quite a few who doubted that anyone who could get into such bad condition as he was in was fit even to give reliable information, let alone advice, to those in good health. And some whispered, even while he spoke, that he had turned lunatic; and many came to believe this. It wasn't only that his story was so fantastic; there was good reason to wonder, many felt, whether anybody in his right mind would go to such trouble for others. But even those who did not believe him listened intently, out of curiosity to hear so wild a tale, and out of the respect it is only proper to show any creature who is in the last agony.

"What he told, was what I have just told you. But his purpose was away beyond just the telling. When they asked questions, no matter how curious or suspicious or idle or foolish, he learned, toward the last, to answer them with all the patience he could and in all the detail he could remember. He even invited them to examine his wounded heels and the pulsing wound in his head as closely as they pleased. He even begged them to, for he knew that before everything else, he must be believed. For unless we could believe him, wherever could we find any reason, or enough courage, to do the hard and dreadful things he told us we must do!

"It was only these things he cared about. Only for these, he came back."

Now clearly remembering what these things were, she felt her whole being quail. She looked at the young ones quickly, and as quickly looked away.

"While he talked," she went on, "and our ancestors listened, men came quietly among us; one of them shot him. Whether he was shot in kindness or to silence him is an endlessly disputed question which will probably never be settled. Whether, even, he died of the shot, or through his own great pain and weariness (for his eyes, they say, were glazing for some time before the men came), we will never be sure. Some suppose even that he may have died of his sorrow and his concern for us. Others feel that he had quite enough to die of, without that. All these things are tangled and lost in the disputes of those who love to theorize and to argue. There is no arguing about his dying words, though; they were very clearly remembered:

"*'Tell them! Believe!'*"

After a while her son asked, "What did he tell them to do?"

She avoided his eyes. "There's a great deal of disagreement about that, too," she said after a moment. "You see, he was so very tired."

They were silent.

"So tired," she said, "some think that toward the end, he really must have been out of his mind."

"Why?" asked her son.

"Because he was so tired out and so badly hurt."

They looked at her mistrustfully.

"And because of what he told us to do."

"What did he tell us to do?" her son asked again.

Her throat felt dry. "Just… things you can hardly bear even to think of. That's all."

They waited.

"Well, *what?*" her son asked in a cold, accusing voice.

"'*Each one is himself,*'" she said shyly. "'*Not of the herd. Himself alone.*' That's one."

"What else?"

"'*Obey nobody. Depend on none.*'"

"What else?"

She found that she was moved. "'*Break down the fences,*'" she said less shyly. "'*Tell everybody, everywhere.*'"

"Where?"

"Everywhere. You see, he thought there must be ever so many more of us than we had ever known."

They were silent. "What else?" her son asked.

"'*For if even a few do not hear me, or disbelieve me, we are all betrayed.*'"

"Betrayed?"

"He meant, doing as men want us to. Not for ourselves, or the good of each other."

They were puzzled.

"Because, you see, he felt there was no other way." Again her voice altered: "'*All who are put on the range are put onto trains. All who are put onto trains meet The Man With The Hammer. All who stay home are kept there to breed others to go onto the range, and so betray themselves and their kind and their children forever.*'

"'*We are brought into this life only to be victims; and there is no other way for us unless we save ourselves.*'

"Do you understand?"

Still they were puzzled, she saw; and no wonder, poor things. But now the ancient lines rang in her memory, terrible and brave. They made her somehow proud. She began actually to want to say them.

"'*Never be taken,*'" she said. "'*Never be driven. Let those who can, kill Man. Let those who cannot, avoid him.*'"

She looked around at them.

"What else?" her son asked, and in his voice there was a rising valor.

She looked straight into his eyes. "*Kill the yearlings,*'" she said very gently. "'*Kill the calves.*'"

She saw the valor leave his eyes.

"Kill us?"

She nodded, "'*So long as Man holds dominion over us,*'" she said. And in dread and amazement she heard herself add, "'*Bear no young.*'"

With this they all looked at her at once in such a way that she loved her child, and all these others, as never before; and there dilated within her such a sorrowful and marveling grandeur that for a moment she was nothing except her own inward whisper, "Why, *I* am one alone. And of the herd, too. Both at once. All one."

Her son's voice brought her back: "Did they do what he told them to?"

The oldest one scoffed, "Would we be here, if they had?"

"They say some did," the mother replied. "Some tried. Not all."

"What did the men do to them?" another asked.

"I don't know," she said. "It was such a very long time ago."

"Do you believe it?" asked the oldest calf.

"There are some who believe it," she said.

"Do *you?*"

"I'm told that far back in the wildest corners of the range there are some of us, mostly very, very old ones, who have never been taken. It's said that they meet, every so often, to talk and just to think together about the heroism and the terror of two sublime Beings, The One Who Came Back, and The Man With The Hammer. Even here at home, some of the old ones, and some of us who are just old-fashioned, believe it, or parts of it anyway. I know there are some who say that a hollow at the center of the forehead—a sort of shadow of the Hammer's blow—is a sign of very special ability. And I remember how Great-grandmother used to sing an old, pious song, let's see now, yes, 'Be not like dumb-driven cattle, be a hero in the strife.' But there aren't many. Not anymore."

"Do *you* believe it?" the oldest calf insisted; and now she was touched to realize that every one of them, from the oldest to the youngest, needed very badly to be sure about that.

"Of course not, silly," she said; and all at once she was overcome by a most curious shyness, for it occurred to her that in the course of time, this young thing might be bred to her. "It's just an old, old legend." With a tender little laugh she added, lightly, "We use it to frighten children with."

By now the light was long on the plain and the herd was only a fume of gold near the horizon. Behind it, dung steamed, and dust sank gently to the shattered ground. She looked far away for a moment, wondering. Something—it was like a forgotten word on the tip of the tongue. She felt the sudden chill of the late afternoon and she wondered what she had been wondering about. "Come, children," she said briskly, "it's high time for supper." And she turned away; they followed.

The trouble was, her son was thinking, you could never trust her. If she said a thing was so, she was probably just trying to get her way with you. If she said a thing wasn't so, it probably was so. But you never could be sure. Not without seeing for yourself. I'm going to go, he told himself; I don't care *what* she wants. And if it isn't so, why then I'll live on the range and make the great journey and find out what *is* so. And if what she told was true, why then I'll know ahead of time and the one *I* will charge is The Man With The Hammer. I'll put Him and His Hammer out of the way forever, and that will make me an even better hero than The One Who Came Back.

So, when his mother glanced at him in concern, not quite daring to ask her question, he gave her his most docile smile, and snuggled his head against her, and she was comforted.

The littlest and youngest of them was doing double skips in his efforts to keep up with her. Now that he wouldn't be interrupting her, and none of the big ones would hear and make fun of him, he shyly whispered his question, so warmly moistly ticklish that she felt as if he were licking her ear.

"What is it, darling?" she asked, bending down.

"What's a train?"

JONATHAN AMES

No Contact, Asshole!

The summer of 1990 was a bad one. It should have been a good one but it was a bad one. I've pulled a lot of stunts in my day, mostly of the sick sexual variety, but that summer I reached a new low. Or a new high. It was so low it was high, if you know what I mean.

I was twenty-six and a single parent. My son was four. He smelled good all the time, the way little kids do.

So my son was real cute. Red hair, blue eyes, ivory skin. Full of love. I had him for the whole summer.

We stayed with my parents in New Jersey. I needed their help with looking after my son for such a long stretch. Because I was a writer and made my living driving a taxi, I could just take off, so I did—all of July and August.

About two mornings each week, I'd go to the library to try to write from nine to twelve, and my mother would look after my son. I felt guilty about those three hours, but I needed to work a little.

Around week five, I started to come unhinged. I had no social life, I was playing with my son twelve hours a day in the humid Jersey weather, and on the two mornings I went to the library my writing was lousy. Also, my father was still working back then, so he was tormented and insane and we

---

This essay was originally published in Jonathan Ames's book I Love You More Than You Know.

weren't getting along. So, like I said, I was coming unhinged, which means I had to do something, take action. And taking action usually means hurting myself.

So one day my son was taking a nap and I was looking at the local free throwaway newspaper and I spotted a curious ad in the classifieds: a dominatrix with a transsexual assistant was offering $100 one-hour sessions. What the hell was this doing in a throwaway newspaper in suburban New Jersey?

Naturally, I called the number.

A youngish sounding woman answered the phone. "What do you want?" she said.

"I'm calling about your ad," I said in a whispery voice.

"Yeah, so? You want a session, faggot?"

She was already in character. "Yes," I said.

"When do you want to see me, faggot?"

I told her what time I could get together and the girl laid down the law. She said she'd meet me the next day at 11 a.m. at T.G.I. Friday's, just off the local highway. I was to stand at the bar and have a pack of unopened Marlboro cigarettes in my hand. If she didn't like the looks of me, she'd turn right around. If I passed inspection, she'd come over to me and ask for a cigarette. I wasn't to give her one, but follow her out to her car, where she'd blindfold me and drive me to her house. It was all very noir, metaphorically and otherwise.

"Do I have to be blindfolded?" I asked.

"You think I'm going to let a freak like you know where I live?" She was very mean on the phone, but I figured she was just being professional. A professional dominatrix, that is. They're supposed to be mean.

The next day I was at the T.G.I. Friday's by 10:50 with a pack of Marlboros. My mother thought I was at the library. I should've been with my son. I'm a terrible person.

The place had just opened when I got there. I ordered a coffee. At eleven she walked in—very short, maybe five-one, brunette, pretty, early twenties, jeans and a halter top, sunglasses. We played the cigarette game, then out to her car. My heart was explosive. She didn't have a blindfold but sunglasses that were taped over.

"I don't want a cop stopping me because he sees that I have a faggot like

34

you blindfolded," she explained. If I was lucky, she'd kill me fast and dump my body in the Meadowlands. My poor parents; my poor son.

I kept trying to peer out the bottom of the sunglasses to see where I was being taken to be murdered. Despite my nervousness, I asked her a lot of questions. She was pretty forthcoming. I've always been good with Q&A.

She was Italian-Catholic. Ever since she was a teenager she had gotten off on dominating men, especially since all men were assholes. Her high school boyfriend was her transsexual assistant; she had been feminizing him for a few years, feeding him hormone pills, making him dress like a girl, and, though he resisted at first, he was now happy with his transformation. Eventually they'd have his penis cut off and they'd be lesbian lovers.

The whole thing was so sick it was thrilling. She and this guy were actually living out a dream that millions—well, maybe thousands—of perverts wanted. And I had found her in a throwaway newspaper!

She told me that when she and her boy/girlfriend had enough money saved they were going to move to New York and open a first-class dungeon. Then from the dungeon they'd get enough money for his sex-change operation.

I got all this in a twenty-minute car ride, which I think involved her driving around in circles in case I was peering out the bottom of the glasses. I felt like James Bond being kidnapped.

We pulled into a driveway; she took me by the hand and led me into a house, which I could perceive from the bottom of my glasses. Then we went down some stairs and she removed my glasses. We were in a carpeted basement room which was just about empty—there was a radio, a futon mattress, and a big box with S&M paraphernalia. A pole ran from the floor to the ceiling and all the walls were mirrored. I gave her the hundred bucks. Then she slapped me and led me to the pole. She took some rope from her S&M box and she tied my wrists behind my back and around the pole. She slapped me again and then she left me alone in the room. It was nearly 11:30. I'd told my mother I'd meet her at 12:30 at the lake where we took my son swimming. I was going to be late!

She left me tied to that pole for ten minutes. I imagined this was part of the torture, but I thought it was a rip-off, so I managed to free myself, just like James Bond. I tried the door. It was locked. I could have busted it down, but I didn't: My James Bondness only went so far. Then she came into the room dressed in black bra, panties, stockings, boots—usual dominatrix garb—and slapped me for slipping my bonds. Her slaps stung but weren't bad. Then she put the radio on, WPLJ. I had been listening to that station my whole life, but never in the basement of a dominatrix.

"What are you into?" she asked. "Want me to flog you?"

"Can I kiss your breasts?" I asked. She looked pretty in her bra.

"No contact, asshole," she said, and then she slapped me again—contact!—and looked at me like I was crazy. But I didn't want to be flogged. I wanted to nurse on her breasts and maybe lick her pussy. I wasn't an S&M nut; I was just a nut. My perversion is that I try everything once, even if I'm not into it.

Then her tranny boyfriend—a tall, slender brunette wearing a negligee—came in and gave me a wide-eyed north/south. I wasn't bad-looking back then and so I think he was attracted to me.

The girl had the tranny undress me, and then they conferred in the corner while I stood there naked.

Then the tranny came over and started rubbing against me, trying to slow-dance with me to the music coming from the radio, and I didn't mind—he was a pretty good-looking girl. And I knew what was going on: I was being tossed to the tranny-slave like a piece of meat and the girl was getting off on watching it.

Then the tranny stopped dancing, got a strawberry-flavored condom from the S&M box, and knelt down in front of me to give me a blow job. He rolled the sugar-coated condom on me and before he took me in his mouth, the girl came over and slapped me violently. It hurt. The other slaps had been warm-ups. She went to do it again, but I caught her wrist this time and bent her arm behind her back. She was a little thing, even in her black boots. The tranny just stayed on his knees, wide-eyed. I held the girl's arm behind her back and slow-danced her from behind. My penis, in the condom, pressed against her ass. That vicious slap had done something to me, turned me into Robert Mitchum. The girl didn't say anything; I think she was stunned. Maybe she liked having the tables turned. The tranny watched and smiled. Poor nutty slave. He was going to lose his dick someday.

Well, after that, things got a little sordid. An unlit candle—in lieu of a dildo—somehow entered the picture and the three of us tolled around on that futon. At some point the girl did flog me two or three times, but I let her— I'm not an ungenerous lover and I had to build her esteem back up after I had manhandled her.

Then it ended the way things usually end: Somebody gets a paper towel and you wish you had never been born. The tranny said to me, "I hope you'll see us again. You're beautiful."

I got dressed and the girl made me put the sunglasses back on. She drove me to T.G.I. Friday's in five minutes, confirming my suspicions about the circular method she had used on the way over. She dropped me off and didn't say good-bye. It was a sunny day. One shouldn't do such things on sunny days. I don't know how the perverts in California live with themselves.

I got to the swimming hole fifteen minutes late. My mother assumed that I had been working well in the library.

I took my son into the water and we were quickly joined by several other four-year-olds. I was the only dad around and so I was like a pied piper for the kids. They were crawling all over me, playing and splashing. At some point, my son was really bouncing on my back and it hurt and for a moment I wondered why and then I remembered. My brief flogging had bruised me.

To be able to live with myself, I had immediately, upon getting into my car at T.G.I. Friday's, blocked from my mind the lurid scene I had just engaged in, but then with my son bouncing on my bruises I couldn't forget what had happened and I felt wildly ashamed. In retrospect it doesn't seem so terrible—so I cavorted with a dominatrix and a pre-op transsexual. What harm, really, was done? Isn't it a sort of funny story all these years later? Time softens everything, I guess. But in that moment, I was disgusted that my beautiful son should come in contact with those bruises. Why am I like this? I thought. What is wrong with me? I hated myself, but I had to *love him.*

So I kept playing in the water. To keep going and not lose my mind, I had to pretend that I was a good person—the generous pied piper. It was the only way to cope, and it seemed to work—my son and all the other children were laughing and happy, and my mother sat in her beach chair proud of her son and her grandchild. I played with the children for hours. It was a beautiful day.

JUDD APATOW

How I Got Kicked Out of High School
A Freaks and Geeks Diary

Garry Shandling looks white as a ghost. I've just been brought to my room at Cedars-Sinai Medical Center after having back surgery. He is visiting me. I ask Garry what's the matter. He says they just took a dead man out of the room next to mine. What is going on? How did I get here? I was happy and healthy a year and a half ago. Oh, now I remember—I developed and ran a show for network television. Wait, it's all coming back to me. Thank God I kept that diary.

Oct. 16, 1998: Dear Diary, I am in New York writing a pilot for the Fox network called *Sick in the Head*. It's about a very young therapist with no life experience. The president of Fox, Peter Roth, is a great guy. He loves the show. Got a call from my old friend Paul Feig today. He said he wrote a television pilot and he's sending it to me. There is nothing worse than reading your friends' scripts. They are always terrible. Then I'm stuck trying to think of something nice to say. "Hey, it's really... good that you wrote this. The only way to become a better writer is to write, write, write." I'll just tell him I'm busy with my pilot and give him some notes.

Oct. 18: I can't believe it, Paul's script is great. It's called *Freaks and Geeks* and it's

---

This piece first appeared in the Los Angeles Times *on April 23, 2000.*

about a brother and sister in Michigan in 1980. The boy is a geek, the girl is a burnout. It's very real and funny. It would be so nice to see a high school show on television that doesn't star a bunch of models like all of those shows on the WB. I told Paul it was "pretty good" so he wouldn't get cocky and show it to anybody else, then I sent it to DreamWorks. I'm sure they'll buy it.

Nov. 10: Bad news. My manager told me that Peter Roth is going to be fired and Doug Herzog from Comedy Central will replace him at Fox. Nevertheless, I had to talk with Peter on the phone today about *Sick in the Head.* It felt like a scene from *Goodfellas* where everyone knows a guy is about to be killed but they eat dinner with him anyway. Fortunately, Doug Herzog is a good guy. He's buddies with my manager, so this could turn out to be a good thing.

Dec. 18: We sent *Freaks and Geeks* to all the networks. Scott Sassa and Don Ohlmeyer at NBC both love it. Rob Dwek, a VP at Fox, told me they were passing because "Who wants to watch a show about a bunch of losers?" I told him they are "underdogs" and that he probably didn't like the script because he was one of the guys who used to beat up those kids. He laughed without denying it.

Jan. 20, 1999: NBC green-lit the *Freaks and Geeks* pilot. We taped "Sick in the Head." It could not have gone better. Doug Herzog loved it. I pressed him for a midseason order, but he said, "Judd, it went well, but it was the first pilot taping I have ever been to so I have nothing to judge it against." He is the president of the Fox network.

Feb. 9: Paul, our director Jake Kasdan, and myself are working on the rewrite of *Freaks and Geeks.* We are very tough on the script. I have never seen anyone in as much pain as Paul as we go through this process. Regardless, his revision pages are hilarious. He is too naïve about television to be a hackneyed writer. He claims to have never seen *Fast Times at Ridgemont High.*

Feb. 24: Casting. We hold sessions around the United States and Canada searching for "normal"-looking kids. TV has become so looks-obsessed that this choice is actually considered original. *Friends* made TV executives believe that funny people can be gorgeous, too. That show is the exception. Most beautiful people never develop a funny bone as a defense mechanism because good looks and breasts usually are enough. I long for the days when Jack Klugman was the biggest comedy star in America.

March 1: Scott Sassa approved all of our casting. We were ready for a fight, but he really gets the show. We are having a perfect experience with NBC.

March 20: Garth Ancier, the president of the WB network, has been hired as the new president of programming for NBC. We heard he saw the show and didn't "get it." He tells me he went to private school in Connecticut and doesn't relate to the blue-collar, Midwestern public school setting. Then over the weekend he showed it to some friends who went bananas for it, so now he is on board. My lower back is beginning to give me some trouble. I need to call the chiropractor.

May 6: Rumor has it that our show is going to be picked up. They are talking about putting us on either Sunday or Wednesday nights. Just as long as we don't get put on Saturday nights at 8 o'clock, the death slot.

May 16: NBC has ordered thirteen episodes of *Freaks and Geeks*. It will air on Saturday nights at 8 o'clock. I think we can do well there. A lot of people in their thirties who have young kids will be home, and that is our target audience. NBC says they will nurture us, and that it is a good slot because there is less pressure to deliver ratings. Besides, we are up against the one-hundredth year of *Cops* and *Early Edition*. How can we not do well?

    Sick in the Head didn't get picked up. When I asked Doug Herzog why he didn't order my show, he said, "Nobody here loved it." I got kinda mad and said, "Well, if you picked up anything good I wouldn't feel so bad." He said, "Judd, ninety percent of everything fails. Don't worry, I'll probably be fired in a year anyway."

May 18: At the network announcements, Paul introduced himself to Garth, who declared, "Deliver the goods or you'll wind up like this guy." Then he pointed to a man standing next to him. They both laughed. Paul didn't know who "that guy" was, but it scared the hell out of him.

June 5: Writing with the staff has begun. Our dream is to make a show about high school that feels like it was written by Garry Shandling or James Brooks. We spend every day sharing the highs and lows of our high school experiences. Paul is a bottomless pit of geek stories. He tells us about being afraid to take showers in gym class, about wearing a denim jumpsuit to school because the guy at the store in the mall told him it would make him look cool, and about his fear of French kissing. He has enough stories for thirty seasons.

Aug. 19: Shooting has begun. Can't wait to get on the air. NBC has informed us that they are going to put us on in mid-September and then take us off for three or four weeks for baseball and then relaunch us in October. There was some discussion about whether or not it would be more effective to just start in October and not have an interruption, but they say it's good because we'll get two big launches and promos on the World Series. Sounds good to me.

Sept. 17: The reviews came in. Every single review was a rave. It's weird. *Time* magazine called us "the best fall drama aimed at any demographic." *Rolling Stone* called us "stunningly funny and moving." At lunch, Paul read the reviews to the cast and crew. Everyone cheered. This is fun!

Sept. 26: The first show aired last night. The ratings were very strong. Eleven share. Scott Sassa called me at home to congratulate me. There is already talk about moving us. For the first time in my life I feel like I am part of something that might really take off.

Oct. 3: The second show aired last night. Our ratings dropped like a rock from last week. They say it's partly because our lead-in in several major markets was the low-rated *Latino Heritage Awards*. The promo people think they made a mistake switching from "review-driven" ads to an ad which told the story of the show. NBC tells us not to worry. They are still excited. Being on Saturday really does take off the pressure. Well, we're off till after the World Series.

Oct. 31: We returned to the air last night. Eight share. We are in big trouble. To hear the ratings you have to call this recording at NBC. The woman who records the voice is supposedly emotionless as she reads off the overnight numbers, but she always sounds disappointed when she says, *"Freaks and Geeks,* eight share." I feel like I'm letting her down.

Nov. 14: Scott Sassa calls and tells me that he is taking *Freaks and Geeks* off during November sweeps, and then moving it to Mondays at eight starting in January. This is a big opportunity for us. He says they will give us a major relaunch. Our main competition is the new Jennifer Love Hewitt show and *7th Heaven* on the WB. We could do well there.

I'm a little worried about being off the air for eight weeks, but Scott says a major relaunch will solve that. The only catch is that we are almost finished shooting our original thirteen episodes. We need NBC to pick up the back nine episodes so we don't have to shut down. Scott says he'll think about it.

Nov. 19: Garth Ancier takes me out to lunch to discuss creative issues concerning *Freaks and Geeks*. He would like the kids to have more victories. I tell him that the point of the program is to show how our characters survive the obstacles of high school with their compassion and senses of humor intact. Surviving is a victory. I say, "I just want the work to be truthful." He replies, "Why do you want it to be truthful? It's TV." I ask him about NBC's upcoming "Y2K" disaster movie. "Are you worried that the film might contribute to a panic on New Year's?" He jokes, "I hope there is a panic. That would mean somebody watched the show."

Dec. 9: Scott decides to pick up more episodes. One more episode. It is the shortest back-end order in television history. It feels strange because they are giving us this amazing opportunity on Monday nights, but they seem to have no faith that we can succeed. I'm starting to think they really like the show and don't have the heart to kill it. My back really hurts when I drive.

Jan. 1, 2000: The year-end reviews came in. *Time* magazine said we were the best series on network television. *Entertainment Weekly* and *TV Guide* put us on their top 10 lists. Hopefully that type of press reminds NBC that we are the type of show that deserves time to find its audience. I haven't heard them say the word "nurture" in quite a while.

Jan. 10: Tonight's our first airing on Monday night. Scott Sassa says if we get an eight share, his shoe size, he will order four more new episodes. I've never heard a man so vocal about his shoe size being an eight. It's hard to complain when someone sets the bar so low. I was feeling good about our chances, but

ABC moved *Who Wants to Be a Millionaire* against us. That show is like an assassin. I hope people get bored with it before it kills every good show on TV.

Jan. 11: They are not getting bored with it. It got over a twenty share. We did an eight share, exactly. Scott made good on his word and ordered four more. I'm sure he wishes he had bigger feet. I'd be excited about next week, but we are going up against Dick Clark's *American Music Awards.* How are we supposed to grab viewers when our show opens with a group of geeks discussing deadly peanut allergies and their show opens with Britney Spears revealing her belly?

Jan. 19: Today I found myself wondering if I should create a really smart, hilarious show that just happens to be about hot models.

Feb. 1: Our best episode, the one about the geeks finally getting a chance to pick sides in gym class, is preempted in several major markets due to the tragic Alaska Airlines crash. Our time slot is filled with local news coverage of the crash, which consists solely of a single shot of a pitch-dark ocean. Next week our competition is the Mary Tyler Moore reunion movie. NBC says it is a different audience but Paul thinks everyone will watch just to see what they look like. My chiropractor says if my back doesn't feel better soon I should see a doctor.

Feb. 8: Paul was right. Mary held us down while Rhoda kneed us in the face. America loves reunions, no matter how awful. It reminded me of the Harlem Globetrotters on *Gilligan's Island* and those *Honeymooners* episodes they shot when they were all over seventy. I must admit I flipped over during our commercials and had a hard time switching back. I tell Paul that we should assume there is no second season and that we should focus on making the shows great because they will be on cable forever. We hold back none of our good ideas for next year.

Feb. 9: Garth calls. He tells us he's taking us off the air for February sweeps. "You don't want to go up against all those event shows." We will disappear for four weeks and then relaunch for the third time. Garth promises us he'll let the final eight episodes run straight through till May. If we could just be on for a few months without interruption, I know our ratings would improve.

March 8: We return next week, but NBC isn't running many promos. Leno did a joke a few weeks ago where he said we were canceled, and now I think America believes it. I send Scott a note, but it is hard to demand more promo time when you are the lowest-rated show on the network. Scott tells my manager they are putting all their promo muscle behind their two new shows: *Daddio* and *God, the Devil and Bob.* They are very excited about *Daddio.*

March 12: We only received two minutes and ten seconds of prime-time promo this past week. *God, the Devil and Bob* received over eleven minutes. We get our asses handed to us by a film called *Satan's School for Girls* starring Shannen Doherty.

March 14: The Museum of Television & Radio honored us as part of the William Paley Festival. We were one of only three new shows selected. The other two were *The West Wing* and *Once and Again.* During the Q&A someone asks whether or not the show is too dark. I reply, "Sometimes I think that's true, but last week on *ER* someone stabbed Kellie Martin in the face and America loved it." It was fun meeting our fans. If we do not get a second season, it was a great way for our cast to remember their experience with our show. I pray none of them wind up on *E! True Hollywood Story.*

March 19: Paul Feig's mother passes away. She was very healthy. It is a complete surprise.

March 21: It's over. We were on last night, we received an eight share, and we were canceled by noon. It's such a shocker because they paid for six episodes that they are choosing not to air. How can that make financial sense? We were only on twelve out of twenty-six weeks. After I hear the news, Garth calls. I am half-crying, half-screaming as I rant at him for ten minutes. He listens calmly. He's very apologetic. He's clearly made hundreds of cancellation calls in his life and does it very well. By the end of the call, he has turned me around to the point where I am asking him if he's mad at me. I have to call Paul and tell him the news. He is at a meeting working out his late mother's financial affairs. It is a bad week. I finished the day seeing a back doctor about my injured disc. He says I'll need surgery over the summer and gives me forty Vicodins. I feel like Chevy Chase.

March 23: Paul's mom's funeral was today. All of the NBC executives who truly cared about the show and did the day-to-day work attended. It was a nice gesture, but I must admit it felt good to see them cry. It was especially sad because our cast of kids was there and they didn't just lose a show, they lost a home. We grieved for Paul's mom, and because the show is about Paul's family, we grieved for the show. Paul's eulogy was heartfelt, very moving, and often hilarious. It's been an honor working with Paul. He truly is one of the most talented people in town. The worst part about a show ending is that many of your intimate relationships end as well. I will miss Paul the most.

March 24: Scott Sassa calls. He says he was a big fan of the show, but should have canceled us in January. I am grateful to them for allowing us to make *Freaks and Geeks* without any creative interference. If there wasn't so much chaos in network television with viewer erosion and the Web coming over the hill, maybe they would have let us hang in there a little longer. Regardless, I do not consider our show to be merely eighteen episodes long. I feel like I made eighteen really good movies. Unfortunately there is no way to see them right now.

The worst part of this experience is being replaced by *Dateline*, a show I find truly evil. It is the prediction of Paddy Chayefsky's brilliant film *Network* come to terrifying fruition. These entertainment programs milk human tragedies such as Columbine for all they're worth while wearing the disguise of a news show. They think we don't notice that their show is basically a new version of *A Current Affair*, because Jane Pauley is cute and Stone Phillips wears nice sweaters. At least we tried to put something positive into the world.

March 28: Daddio is a big hit.

March 29: God, the Devil and Bob is canceled.

March 30: Doug Herzog "resigned" last week.

April 1: Dateline fills our spot with an episode about flammable mattresses. With almost no promo, they receive an eleven share.

April 14: I am sitting in my hospital room after spending five hours in postop listening to people moan as they wake up after their operations. They kept telling me my room wasn't clean yet. Apparently Cedars isn't much different than the Hyatt Hotel. It is hard to find closure. I did the best work I've ever done. I received the best reviews I've ever received. It was the lowest-rated show on NBC. Did it fail because of scheduling? Did it fail because we went out of our way to not be like all the other "successful" teen shows? I don't know. All I do know is I'm glad I'm not the dead guy they rolled out of the room next to me.

I think I'll take the summer off and see if I can convince Paul to develop a new show for next season. I hope this article doesn't make NBC too mad to work with me. Well... that guy at ABC seems nice.

AMY BLOOM

Love Is Not a Pie

In the middle of the eulogy at my mother's boring and heart-breaking funeral, I began to think about calling off the wedding. August 21 did not seem like a good date, John Wescott did not seem like a good person to marry, and I couldn't see myself in the long white silk gown Mrs. Wescott had offered me. We had gotten engaged at Christmas, while my mother was starting to die; she died in May, earlier than we had expected. When the minister said, "She was a rare spirit, full of the kind of bravery and joy which inspires others," I stared at the pale blue ceiling and thought, "My mother would not have wanted me to spend my life with this man." He had asked me if I wanted him to come to the funeral from Boston, and I said no. And so he didn't, respecting my autonomy and so forth. I think he should have known that I was just being considerate.

After the funeral, we took the little box of ashes back to the house and entertained everybody who came by to pay their respects. Lots of my father's law school colleagues, a few of his former students, my uncle Steve and his new wife, my cousins (whom my sister Lizzie and I always referred to as Thing One and Thing Two), friends from the old neighborhood, before my mother's sculptures started selling, her art world friends, her sisters, some of my friends from high school, some people I used to babysit for, my best friend from college, some friends of Lizzie's, a lot of people I didn't recognize. I'd been living away from home for a long time, first at college, now at law school.

My sister, my father, and I worked the room. And everyone who came in my father embraced. It didn't matter whether they started to pat him on the back or shake his hand, he pulled them to him and hugged them so hard I saw people's feet lift right off the floor. Lizzie and I took the more passive route, letting people do whatever they wanted to us, patting, stroking, embracing, cupping our faces in their hands.

My father was in the middle of squeezing Mrs. Ellis, our cleaning lady, when he saw Mr. DeCuervo come in, still carrying his suitcase. He about dropped Mrs. Ellis and went charging over to Mr. DeCuervo, wrapped his arms around him, and the two of them moaned and rocked together in a passionate, musicless waltz. My sister and I sat down on the couch, pressed against each other, watching our father cry all over his friend, our mother's lover.

When I was eleven and Lizzie was eight, her last naked summer, Mr. De-Cuervo and his daughter, Gisela, who was just about to turn eight, spent part of the summer with us at the cabin in Maine. The cabin was from the Spencer side, my father's side of the family, and he and my uncle Steve were co-owners. We went there every July (colder water, better weather), and they came in August. My father felt about his brother the way we felt about our cousins, so we would only overlap for lunch on the last day of our stay.

That July, the DeCuervos came, but without Mrs. DeCuervo, who had to go visit a sick someone in Argentina, where they were from. That was okay with us. Mrs. DeCuervo was a professional mother, a type that made my sister and me very uncomfortable. She told us to wash the berries before we ate them, to rest after lunch, to put on more suntan lotion, to make our beds. She was a nice lady, she was just always in our way. My mother had a few very basic summer rules: don't eat food with mold or insects on it; don't swim alone; don't even think about waking your mother before 8 a.m. unless you are fatally injured or ill. That was about it, but Mrs. DeCuervo was always amending and adding to the list, one apologetic eye on our mother, who was pleasant and friendly as usual and did things the way she always did. She made it pretty clear that if we were cowed by the likes of Mrs. DeCuervo, we were on our own. They got divorced when Gisela was a sophomore at Mount Holyoke.

We liked pretty, docile Gisela, and bullied her a little bit, and liked her even more because she didn't squeal on us, on me in particular. We liked her father, too. We saw the two of them, sometimes the three of them, at occasional picnics and lesser holidays. He always complimented us, never made stupid jokes at our expense, and brought us unusual, perfect little presents. Silver barrettes for me the summer I was letting my hair grow out from my pixie cut; a leather bookmark for Lizzie, who learned to read when she was three. My mother would stand behind us as we unwrapped the gifts, smiling and shaking her head at his extravagance.

When they drove up, we were all sitting on the porch. Mr. DeCuervo got out first, his curly brown hair making him look like a giant dandelion, with his yellow T-shirt and brown jeans. Gisela looked just like him, her long, curly brown hair caught up in a bun, wisps flying around her tanned little face. As they walked toward us, she took his hand and I felt a rush of warmth for her, for showing how much she loved her daddy, like I loved mine, and for showing that she was a little afraid of us, of me, probably. People weren't often frightened of Lizzie; she never left her books long enough to bother anyone.

My parents came down from the porch; my big father, in his faded blue trunks, drooping below his belly, his freckled back pink and moist in the sun, as it was every summer. The sun caught the red hair on his head and shoulders and chest, and he shone. The Spencers were half-Viking, he said. My mother was wearing her summer outfit, a black two-piece bathing suit. I don't remember her ever wearing a different suit. At night, she'd add one of my father's shirts and wrap it around her like a kimono. Some years, she looked great in her suit, waist nipped in, skin smooth and tan; other years, her skin looked burnt and crumpled, and the suit was too big in some places and too small in others. Those years, she smoked too much and went out on the porch to cough. But that summer the suit fit beautifully, and when she jumped off the porch into my father's arms, he whirled her around and let her black hair whip his face while he smiled and smiled.

They both hugged Mr. DeCuervo and Gisela; my mother took her flowered suitcase and my father took his duffel bag and they led them into the cabin.

The cabin was our palace; Lizzie and I would say very grandly, "We're going to the cabin for the summer, come visit us there, if it's okay with your parents." And we loved it and loved to act as though it was nothing special, when we knew, really, that it was magnificent. The pines and birches came right down to the lake, with just a thin lacing of mossy rocks before you got to the smooth, cold water, and little gray fish swam around the splintery dock and through our legs, or out of reach of our oars when we took out the old blue rowboat.

The cabin itself was three bedrooms and a tiny kitchen and a living room that took up half the house. The two small bedrooms had big beds with pastel chenille spreads; yellow with red roses in my parents' room, white with blue pansies in the other. The kids' room was much bigger, like a dormitory, with three sets of bunk beds, each with its own mismatched sheets and pillowcases. The pillows were always a little damp and smelled like salt and pine, and mine smelled of Ma Griffe as well, because I used to sleep with my mother's scarf tucked under it. The shower was outside, with a thin green plastic curtain around it, but there was a regular bathroom inside, next to my parents' room.

Mr. DeCuervo and Gisela fit into our routine as though they'd been coming to the cabin for years, instead of just last summer. We had the kind of summer cabin routine that stays with you forever as a model of leisure, of life being enjoyed. We'd get up early, listening to the birds screaming and trilling, and make ourselves some breakfast; cereal or toast if the parents were up, cake or cold spaghetti or marshmallows if they were still asleep. My mother got up first, usually. She'd make a cup of coffee and brush and braid our hair and set us loose. If we were going exploring, she'd put three sandwiches and three pieces of fruit in a bag, with an army blanket. Otherwise, she'd just wave to us as we headed down to the lake.

We'd come back at lunchtime and eat whatever was around and then go out to the lake or the forest, or down the road to see if the townie kids were in a mood to play with us. I don't know what the grown-ups did all day; sometimes they'd come out to swim for a while, and sometimes we'd find my mother in the shed she used for a studio. But when we came back at five or six, they all seemed happy and relaxed, drinking gin and tonics on the porch, watching us run toward the house. It was the most beautiful time.

At night, after dinner, the fathers would wash up and my mother would sit on the porch, smoking a cigarette, listening to Aretha Franklin or Billie Holiday or Sam Cooke, and after a little while she'd stub out her cigarette and the four of us would dance. We'd twist and lindy and jitterbug and stomp, all of us copying my mother. And pretty soon the daddies would drift in with their dish towels and their beers, and they'd lean in the doorway and watch. My mother would turn first to my father, always to him, first.

"What about it, Danny? Care to dance?" And she'd put her hand on his shoulder and he'd smile, tossing his dish towel to Mr. DeCuervo, resting his beer on the floor. My father would lumber along gamely, shuffling his feet and smiling. Sometimes he'd wave his arms around and pretend to be a fish or a bear while my mother swung her body easily and dreamily, sliding through the music. They'd always lindy together to Fats Domino. That was my father's favorite, and then he'd sit down, puffing a little.

My mother would stand there, snapping her fingers, shifting back and forth.

"Gaucho, you dance with her, before I have a coronary," said my father.

Mr. DeCuervo's real name was Bolivar, which I didn't know until Lizzie told me after the funeral. We always called him Mr. DeCuervo because we felt embarrassed to call him by a nickname.

So Mr. DeCuervo would shrug gracefully and toss the two dish towels back to my father. And then he'd bop toward my mother, his face still turned toward my father.

"We'll go running tomorrow, Dan, get you back into shape so you can dance all night."

"What do you mean, 'back'? I've been exactly this same svelte shape for twenty years. Why fix it if it ain't broke?"

And they all laughed, and Mr. DeCuervo and my mother rolled their eyes at each other, and my mother walked over and kissed my father where the sweat was beading up at his temples. The she took Mr. DeCuervo's hand and they walked to the center of the living room.

When she and my father danced, my sister and I giggled and interfered and treated it like a family badminton game in which they were the core players but we were welcome participants. When she danced with Mr. DeCuervo, we'd sit on the porch swing or lean on the windowsill and watch, not even looking at each other.

They only danced the fast dances, and they danced as though they'd been waiting all their lives for each song. My mother's movements got deeper and smoother, and Mr. DeCuervo suddenly came alive, as though a spotlight had hit him. My father danced the way he was, warm, noisy, teasing, a little overpowering; but Mr. DeCuervo, who was usually quiet and thoughtful and serious, became a different man when he danced with my mother. His dancing was light and happy and soulful, edging up on my mother, turning her, matching her every step. They would smile at all of us, in turn, and then face each other, too transported to smile.

"Dance with Daddy some more," my sister said, speaking for all three of us. They had left us too far behind.

My mother blew Lizzie a kiss. "Okay, sweetheart."

She turned to both men, laughing, and said, "That message was certainly loud and clear. Let's take a little break, Gauch, and get these monkeys to bed. It's getting late, girls."

And the three of them shepherded the three of us through the bedtime rituals, moving us in and out of the kitchen for milk, the bathroom for teeth, toilet, calamine lotion, and finally to our big bedroom. We slept in our underwear and T-shirts, which impressed Gisela.

"No pajamas?" she had said the first night.

"Not necessary," I said smugly.

We would lie there after they kissed us, listening to our parents talk and crack peanuts and snap cards; they played gin and poker while they listened to Dinah Washington and Odetta.

One night, I woke up around midnight and crossed the living room to get some water in the kitchen and see if there was any strawberry shortcake left. I saw my mother and Mr. DeCuervo hugging, and I remember being surprised, and puzzled. I had seen movies; if you hugged someone like you'd never let them go, surely you were supposed to be kissing, too. It wasn't a Mommy-Daddy hug, partly because their hugs were defined by the fact that my father was eight inches taller and a hundred pounds heavier than my mother. These two looked all wrong to me; embraces were a big pink-and-orange man enveloping a small, lean, black-and-white woman who gazed up at him. My mother and Mr. DeCuervo looked like sister and brother, standing cheek-to-cheek, with their broad shoulders and long, tanned, bare legs. My mother's hands were under Mr. DeCuervo's white T-shirt.

She must have felt my eyes on her, because she opened hers slowly.

"Oh, honey, you startled us. Mr. DeCuervo and I were just saying good night. Do you want me to tuck you in after you go to the bathroom?" Not quite a bribe, certainly a reminder that I was more important to her than he was. They had moved apart so quickly and smoothly I couldn't even remember how they had looked together. I nodded to my mother; what I had seen was already being transformed into a standard good-night embrace, the kind my mother gave to all of her close friends.

When I came back from the bathroom, Mr. DeCuervo had disappeared and my mother was waiting, looking out at the moon. She walked me to the bedroom and kissed me, first on my forehead, then on my lips.

"Sleep well, pumpkin pie. See you in the morning."

"Will you make blueberry pancakes tomorrow?" It seemed like a good time to ask.

"We'll see. Go to sleep."

"Please, Mommy."

"Okay, we'll have a blueberry morning. Go to sleep now. Good night, nurse." And she watched me for a moment from the doorway, and then she was gone.

My father got up at five to go fishing with some men at the other side of the lake. Every Saturday in July he'd go off with a big red bandanna tied over his bald spot, his Mets T-shirt, and his tackle box, and he'd fish until around three. Mr. DeCuervo said that he'd clean them, cook them, and eat them, but he wouldn't spend a day with a bunch of guys in baseball caps and white socks to catch them.

I woke up smelling coffee and butter. Gisela and Lizzie were already out of bed, and I was aggrieved; I was the one who had asked for the pancakes, and they were probably all eaten by now.

Mr. DeCuervo and Lizzie were sitting at the table, finishing their pancakes. My mother and Gisela were sitting on the blue couch in the living room while my mother brushed Gisela's hair. She was brushing it more gently than she brushed mine, not slapping her on the shoulder to make her sit still. Gisela didn't wiggle, and she didn't scream when my mother hit a knot.

I was getting ready to be mad when my mother winked at me over Gisela's head and said, "There's a stack of pancakes for you on top of the stove, bunny. Gauch, would you please lift them for Ellen? The plate's probably hot."

Mr. DeCuervo handed me my pancakes, which were huge brown wheels studded with smashed purpley berries; he put my fork and knife on top of a folded paper towel and patted my cheek. His hand smelled like coffee and cinnamon. He knew what I liked and pushed the butter and the honey and the syrup toward me.

"Juice?" he said.

I nodded, trying to watch him when he wasn't looking; he didn't seem like the man I thought I saw in the moonlight, giving my mother a funny hug.

"Great pancakes, Lila," he said.

"Great, Mom." I didn't want to be outclassed by the DeCuervos' habitual good manners. Gisela remembered her "please" and "thank you" for every little thing.

My mother smiled and put a barrette in Gisela's hair. It was starting to get warm, so I swallowed my pancakes and kicked Lizzie to get her attention.

"Let's go," I said.

"Wash your face, then go," my mother said.

I stuck my face under the kitchen tap, and my mother and Mr. DeCuervo laughed. Triumphantly, I led the two little girls out of the house, snatching our towels off the line as we ran down to the water, suddenly filled with longing for the lake.

"Last one in's a fart," I screamed, cannonballing off the end of the dock. I hit the cold blue water, shattering its surface. Lizzie and Gisela jumped in beside me, and we played water games until my father drove up in the pickup with a bucket of fish. He waved to us and told us we'd be eating fish for the next two days, and we groaned and held our noses as he went into the cabin, laughing.

There was a string of sunny days like that one: swimming, fishing with Daddy off the dock, eating peanut butter and jelly sandwiches in the rowboat, drinking Orange Crush on the porch swing.

And then it rained for a week. We woke up the first rainy morning, listening to it tap and dance on the roof. My mother stuck her head into our bedroom.

"It's monsoon weather, honeys. How about cocoa and cinnamon toast?"

We pulled on our overalls and sweaters and went into the kitchen, where my mother had already laid our mugs and plates. She was engaged in her rainy-day ritual: making sangria. First she poured the orange juice out of the big white plastic pitcher into three empty peanut butter jars. Then she started chopping up all the oranges, lemons, and limes we had in the house. She let me pour the brandy over the fruit, Gisela threw in the sugar, and Lizzie came up for air long enough to pour the big bottle of red wine over everything. I cannot imagine drinking anything else on rainy days.

My mother went out onto the porch for her morning cigarette, and when my father came down, he joined her while we played Go Fish; I could see them snuggling on the wicker settee. A few minutes later Mr. DeCuervo came down, looked out to the porch, and picked up an old magazine and started reading.

We decided to play Monopoly in our room since the grown-ups didn't want to entertain us. After two hours, in which I rotted in jail and Lizzie forgot to charge rent, little Gisela beat us and the three of us went back to the kitchen for a snack. Rainy days were basically a series of snacks, more and less elaborate, punctuated by board games, card games, and whining. We drank soda and juice all day, ate cheese, bananas, cookies, bologna, graham crackers, Jiffy popcorn, hard-boiled eggs. The grown-ups ate cheese and crackers and drank sangria.

The daddies were reading in the two big armchairs, my mother had gone off to her room to sketch, and we were getting bored. When my mother came downstairs for a cigarette, I was writing my name in the honey that had spilled on the kitchen table, and Gisela and Lizzie were pulling the stuffing out of the hole in the bottom of the blue couch.

"Jesus Christ, Ellen, get your hands out of the goddamn honey. Liz, Gisela, that's absolutely unacceptable, you know that. Leave the poor couch alone. If you're so damn stir-crazy, go outside and dance in the rain."

The two men looked up, slowly focusing, as if from a great distance.

"Lila, really..." said my father.

"Lila, it's pouring. We'll keep an eye on them now," said Mr. DeCuervo.

"Right. Like you were." My mother was grinning.

"Can we, Mommy, can we go in the rain? Can we take off our clothes and go in the rain?"

"Sure, go naked, there's no point in getting your clothes wet and no point in suits. There's not likely to be a big crowd in the yard."

We raced to the porch before my mother could get rational, stripped, and ran whooping into the rain, leaping off the porch onto the muddy lawn, shouting and feeling superior to every child in Maine who had to stay indoors.

We played Goddesses-in-the-Rain, which consisted of caressing our bodies and screaming the names of everyone we knew, and we played ring-around-the-rosy and tag and red light/green light and catch, all deliciously slippery and surreal in the sheets of gray rain. Our parents watched us from the porch.

When we finally came in, thrilled with ourselves and the extent to which we were completely, profoundly wet, in every pore, they bundled us up and told us to dry our hair and get ready for dinner.

My mother brushed our hair, and then she made spaghetti sauce while my father made a salad and Mr. DeCuervo made a strawberry tart, piling the berries into a huge, red, shiny pyramid in the center of the pastry. We were in heaven. The grown-ups were laughing a lot, sipping their rosy drinks, tossing vegetables back and forth.

After dinner, my mother took us into the living room to dance, and then the power went off.

"Shit," said my father in the kitchen.

"Double shit," said Mr. DeCuervo, and we heard them stumbling around in the dark, laughing and cursing, until they came in with two flashlights.

"The cavalry is here, ladies," said Daddy, bowing to us all, twirling his flashlight.

"American and Argentine divisions, señora y señoritas."

I had never heard Mr. DeCuervo speak Spanish before, not even that little bit.

"Well then, I know I'm safe—from the bad guys, anyway. On the other hand..." My mother laughed, and the daddies put their arms around each other and they laughed too.

"On the other hand, what? What, Mommy?" I tugged at her the way I did when I was afraid of losing her in a big department store.

"Nothing, honey. Mommy was just being silly. Let's get ready for bed, munchkins. Then you can all talk for a while. We're shut down for the night, I'm sure."

The daddies accompanied us to the bathroom and whispered that we could skip everything except peeing, since there was no electricity. The two of them kissed us goodnight, my father's mustache tickling, Mr. DeCuervo's hand sliding over my cheek. My mother came into the room a moment later, and her face was as smooth and warm as a velvet cushion. We didn't stay awake for long. The rain dance and the eating and the storm had worn us out.

It was still dark when I woke up, but the rain had stopped and the power had returned and the light was burning in our hallway. It made me feel very grown-up and responsible, getting out of bed and going around the house, turning out the lights that no one else knew were on; I was conserving electricity.

I went into the bathroom and was squeezed by stomach cramps, probably from all the burnt popcorn kernels I had eaten. I sat on the toilet for a long time, watching a brown spider crawl along the wall; I'd knock him down and then watch him climb back up again, toward the towels. My cramps were better but not gone, so I decided to wake my mother. My father would have been more sympathetic, but he was the heavier sleeper, and by the time he understood what I was telling him, my mother would have her bathrobe on and be massaging my stomach kindly, though without the excited concern I felt was my due as a victim of an illness.

I walked down to my parents' room, turning the hall light back on. I pushed open the creaky door and saw my mother spooned up against my father's back, as she always was, and Mr. DeCuervo spooned up against her, his arm over the covers, his other hand resting on the top of her head.

I stood and looked and then backed out of the bedroom. They hadn't moved, the three of them breathing deeply, in unison. What was that, I thought, what did I see? I wanted to go back and take another look, to see it again, to make it disappear, to watch them carefully, until I understood.

My cramps were gone. I went back to my own bed, staring at Lizzie and Gisela, who looked in their sleep like little girl-versions of the two men I had just seen. Just sleeping, I thought, the grown-ups were just sleeping. Maybe Mr. DeCuervo's bed had collapsed, like ours did two summers ago. Or maybe it got wet in the storm. I thought I would never be able to fall asleep, but the next thing I remember is waking up to more rain and Lizzie and Gisela begging my mother to take us to the movies in town. We went to see *The Sound of Music*, which had been playing at the Bijou for about ten years.

I don't remember much else about the summer; all of the images run together. We went on swimming and fishing and taking the rowboat out for little adventures, and when the DeCuervos left I hugged Gisela but wasn't going to hug him, until he whispered in my ear, "Next year we'll bring up a motor boat and I'll teach you how to water ski," and then I hugged him very hard and my mother put her hand on my head lightly, giving benediction.

The next summer, I went off to camp in July and wasn't there when the DeCuervos came. Lizzie said they had a good time without me. Then they couldn't come for a couple of summers in a row, and by the time they came again, Gisela and Lizzie were at camp with me in New Hampshire; the four grown-ups spent about a week together, and later I heard my father say that another vacation with Elvira DeCuervo would kill him, or he'd kill her. My mother said she wasn't so bad.

We saw them a little less after that. They came, Gisela and Mr. DeCuervo, to my high school graduation, to my mother's opening in Boston, to my father's fiftieth birthday party, and then Lizzie's graduation. When my mother went down to New York she'd have dinner with the three of them, she said, but sometimes her plans would change and they'd have to substitute lunch for dinner.

Gisela couldn't come to the funeral. She was in Argentina for the year, working with the architectural firm that Mr. DeCuervo's father had started.

After all the mourners left, Mr. DeCuervo gave us a sympathetic note from Gisela, with a beautiful pen-and-ink of our mother inside it. The two men went into the living room and took out a bottle of Scotch and two glasses. It was like we weren't there; they put on Billie Holiday singing "Embraceable You," and they got down to serious drinking and grieving. Lizzie and I went into the kitchen and decided to eat everything sweet that people had brought over: brownies, strudel, pfeffernüesse, sweet potato pie, Mrs. Ellis's chocolate cake with chocolate mousse in the middle. We laid out two plates and two mugs of milk and got to it.

Lizzie said, "You know, when I was home in April, he called every day." She jerked her head toward the living room.

I couldn't tell if she approved or disapproved, and I didn't know what I thought about it either.

"She called him Bolivar."

"What? She always called him Gaucho, and so we didn't call him anything."

"I know, but she called him Bolivar. I heard her talking to him every fucking day, El, she called him Bolivar."

Tears were running down Lizzie's face, and I wished my mother was there to pat her soft fuzzy hair and keep her from choking on her tears. I held her hand across the table, still holding my fork in my other hand. I could feel my mother looking at me, smiling and narrowing her eyes a little, the way she did when I was balking. I dropped the fork onto my plate and went over and hugged Lizzie, who leaned into me as though her spine had collapsed.

"I asked her about it after the third call," she said into my shoulder.

"What'd she say?" I straightened Lizzie up so I could hear her.

"She said, 'Of course he calls at noon. He knows that's when I'm feeling strongest.' And I told her that's not what I meant, that I hadn't known they were so close."

"You said that?"

"Yeah. And she said, 'Honey, nobody loves me more than Bolivar.' And I didn't know what to say, so I just sat there feeling like, 'Do I really want to hear this?' and then she fell asleep."

"So what do you think?"

"I don't know. I was getting ready to ask her again— "

"You're amazing, Lizzie," I interrupted. She really is, she's so quiet, but she goes and has conversations I can't even imagine having.

"But I didn't have to ask because she brought it up herself, the next day after he called. She got off the phone, looking just so exhausted, she was sweating but she was smiling. She was staring out at the crab apple trees in the yard, and she said, 'There were apple trees in bloom when I met Bolivar, and the trees were right where the sculpture needed to be in the courtyard, and so he offered to get rid of the trees and I said that seemed arrogant and he said that they'd replant them. So I said, "Okay," and he said, "What's so bad about arrogance?" And the first time he and Daddy met, the two of them drank Scotch and watched soccer while I made dinner. And then they washed up, just like at the cabin. And when the two of them are in the room together and you two girls are with us, I know that I am living in a state of grace.'"

"She said that? She said 'in a state of grace'? Mommy said that?"

"Yes, Ellen. Christ, what do you think, I'm making up interesting death-bed statements?" Lizzie hates to be interrupted, especially by me.

"Sorry. Go on."

"Anyway, we were talking and I sort of asked what were we actually talking about. I mean, close friends or very close friends, and she just laughed. You know how she'd look at us like she knew exactly where we were going when we said we were going to a friend's house for the afternoon but we were really going to drink Boone's Farm and skinny-dip at the quarry? Well, she looked just like that and she took my hand. Her hand was so light, El. And she said that the three of them loved each other, each differently, and that they were both amazing men, each special, each deserving love and appreciation. She said that she thought Daddy was the most wonderful husband a woman could have and that she was very glad we had him as a father. And I asked her how she could do it, love them both, and how they could stand it. And she said, 'Love is not a pie, honey. I love you and Ellen differently because you are different people, wonderful people, but not at all the same. And so who I am with each of you is different, unique to us. I didn't choose between you. And it's the same way with Daddy and Bolivar. People think that it can't be that way, but it can. You just have to find the right people.' And then she shut her eyes for the afternoon. Your eyes are bugging out, El."

"Well, Jesus, I guess so. I mean, I knew—"

"You knew? And you didn't tell me?"

"You were eight or something, Lizzie, what was I supposed to say? I didn't even know what I knew then."

"So what did you know?" Lizzie was very serious. It was a real breach of our rules not to have shared inside dirt about our parents, especially our mother; we were always trying to figure her out.

I didn't know how to tell her about the three of them; that was even less normal than her having an affair with Mr. DeCuervo with Daddy's permission. I couldn't even think of the words to describe what I'd seen, so I just said, "I saw Mommy and Mr. DeCuervo kissing one night after we were in bed."

"Really? Where was Daddy?"

"I don't know. But wherever he was, obviously he knew what was going on. I mean, that's what Mommy was telling you, right? That Daddy knew and that it was okay with him."

"Yeah. Jesus."

I went back to my chair and sat down. We were halfway through the strudel when the two men came in. They were drunk but not incoherent. They just weren't their normal selves, but I guess we weren't either, with our eyes puffy and red and all this destroyed food around us.

"Beautiful girls," Mr. DeCuervo said to my father. They were hanging in the doorway, one on each side.

"They are, they really are. And smart, couldn't find smarter girls."

My father went on and on about how smart we were. Lizzie and I just looked at each other, embarrassed but not displeased.

"Ellen has Lila's mouth," Mr. DeCuervo said. "You have your mother's mouth, with the right side going up a little more than the left. Exquisite."

My father was nodding his head, like this was the greatest truth ever told. And Daddy turned to Lizzie and said, "And you have your mother's eyes. Since the day you were born and I looked right into them, I thought, 'My God, she's got Lila's eyes, but blue, not green.'"

And Mr. DeCuervo was nodding away, of course. I wondered if they were going to do a complete autopsy, but they stopped.

My father came over to the table and put one hand on each of us. "You girls made your mother incredibly happy. There was nothing she ever created that gave her more pride and joy than you two. And she thought that you were both so special..." He started crying, and Mr. DeCuervo put an arm around his waist and picked up for him.

"She did, she had two big pictures of you in her studio, nothing else. And you know, she expected us all to grieve, but you know how much she wanted you to enjoy, too. To enjoy everything, every meal, every drink, every sunrise, every kiss..." He started crying too.

"We're gonna lie down for a while, girls. Maybe later we'll have dinner or something." My father kissed us both, wet and rough, and the two of them went down the hall.

Lizzie and I looked at each other again.

"Wanna get drunk?" I said.

"No, I don't think so. I guess I'll go lie down for a while too, unless you want company." She looked like she was about to fall asleep standing up, so I shook my head. I was planning on calling John anyway.

Lizzie came over and hugged me, hard, and I hugged her back and brushed the chocolate crumbs out of her hair.

Sitting alone in the kitchen, I thought about John, about telling him about my mother and her affair and how the two men were sacked out in my parents' bed, probably snoring. And I could hear John's silence and I knew he would think my father must not have really loved my mother if he'd let her go with another man; or that my mother must have been a real bitch, forcing my father to tolerate an affair "right in his own home," John would think, maybe even say. I thought I ought to call him before I got myself completely enraged over a conversation that hadn't taken place. Lizzie would say I was projecting anyway.

I called, and John was very sweet, asking how I was feeling, how the memorial service had gone, how my father was. And I told him all that and then I knew I couldn't tell him the rest and that I couldn't marry a man I couldn't tell this story to.

"I'm so sorry, Ellen," he said. "You must be very upset. What a difficult day for you."

I realize that was a perfectly normal response, it just was all wrong for me. I didn't come from a normal family, I wasn't ready to get normal.

I felt terrible, hurting John, but I couldn't marry him just because I didn't want to hurt him, so I said, "And that's not the worst of it, John. I can't marry you, I really can't. I know this is pretty hard to listen to over the phone..." I couldn't think what else to say.

"Ellen, let's talk about this when you get back to Boston. I know what kind of strain you must be under. I had the feeling that you were unhappy about some of Mother's ideas. We can work something out when you get back."

"I know you think this is because of my mother's death, and it is, but not the way you think. John, I just can't marry you. I'm not going to wear your mother's dress and I'm not going to marry you and I'm very sorry."

He was quiet for a long time, and then he said, "I don't understand, Ellen. We've already ordered the invitations." And I knew that I was right. If he had said, "Fuck this, I'm coming to see you tonight," or even, "I don't know what you're talking about, but I want to marry you anyway," I'd probably have changed my mind before I got off the phone. But as it was, I said good-bye sort of quietly and hung up the phone.

It was like two funerals in one day. I sat at the table, poking the cake into little shapes and then knocking them over. My mother would have sent me out for a walk. I'd started clearing the stuff away when my father and Mr. DeCuervo appeared, looking more together.

"How about some gin rummy, El?" my father said.

"If you're up for it," said Mr. DeCuervo.

"Okay," I said. "I just broke up with John Wescott."

"Oh?"

I couldn't tell which one spoke.

"I told him that I didn't think we'd make each other happy."

Which was what I had meant to say.

My father hugged me and said, "I'm sorry that it's hard for you. You did the right thing." Then he turned to Mr. DeCuervo and said, "Did she know how to call them, or what? Your mother knew that you weren't going to marry that guy."

"She was almost always right, Dan."

"Almost always, not quite," said my father, and the two of them laughed at some private joke and shook hands like a pair of old boxers.

"So, you deal," my father said, leaning back in his chair.

"Penny a point," said Mr. DeCuervo.

RAYMOND CARVER

Elephant

I knew it was a mistake to let my brother have the money. I didn't need anybody else owing me. But when he called and said he couldn't make the payment on his house, what could I do? I'd never been inside his house—he lived
a thousand miles away in California; I'd never even *seen* his house—but I didn't
want him to lose it. He cried over the phone and said he was losing everything
he'd worked for. He said he'd pay me back. February, he said. Maybe sooner.
No later, anyway, than March. He said his income-tax refund was on the way.
Plus, he said, he had a little investment that would mature in February. He
acted secretive about the investment thing, so I didn't press for details.

"Trust me on this," he said. "I won't let you down."

He'd lost his job last July, when the company he worked for, a fiberglass-
insulation plant, decided to lay off two hundred employees. He'd been living
on his unemployment since then, but now the unemployment was gone, and
his savings were gone, too. And he didn't have health insurance any longer.
When his job went, the insurance went. His wife, who was ten years older,
was diabetic and needed treatment. He'd had to sell the other car—her car,
an old station wagon—and a week ago he'd pawned his TV. He told me hurt
his back carrying the TV up and down the street where the pawnshops did
business. He went from place to place, he said, trying to get the best offer.
Somebody finally gave him a hundred dollars for it, this big Sony TV. He told

me about the TV, and then about throwing his back out, as if this ought to cinch it with me, unless I had a stone in place of a heart.

"I've gone belly-up," he said. "But you can help me pull out of it."

"How much?" I said.

"Five hundred. I could use more, sure, who couldn't?" he said. "But I want to be realistic. I can pay back five hundred. More than that, I'll tell you the truth, I'm not so sure. Brother, I hate to ask. But you're my last resort. Irma Jean and I are going to be on the street before long. I won't let you down," he said. That's what he said. Those were his exact words.

We talked a little more—mostly about our mother and her problems—but, to make a long story short, I sent him the money. I had to. I felt I had to, at any rate—which amounts to the same thing. I wrote him a letter when I sent the check and said he should pay the money back to our mother, who lived in the same town he lived in and who was poor and greedy. I'd been mailing checks to her every month, rain or shine, for three years. But I was thinking that if he paid her the money he owed me it might take me off the hook there and let me breathe for a while. I wouldn't have to worry on that score for a couple of months, anyway. Also, and this is the truth, I though maybe he'd be more likely to pay her, since they lived right there in the same town and he saw her from time to time. All I was doing was trying to cover myself some way. The thing is, he might have the best intentions of paying me back, but things happen sometimes. Things get in the way of best intentions. Out of sight, out of mind, as they say. But he wouldn't stiff his own mother. Nobody would do that.

I spent hours writing letters, trying to make sure everybody knew what could be expected and what was required. I even phoned out there to my mother several times, trying to explain it to her. But she was suspicious over the whole deal. I went through it with her on the phone step by step, but she was still suspicious. I told her the money that was supposed to come from me on the first of March and on the first of April would instead come from Billy, who owed the money to me. She'd get her money, and she didn't have to worry. The only difference was that Billy would pay it to her those two months instead of me. He'd pay her the money I'd normally be sending to her, but instead of him mailing it to me and then me having to turn around and send it to her, he'd pay it to her directly. On any account, she didn't have to worry. She'd get her money, but for those two months it'd come from him—from the money he owed me. My God, I don't know how much I spent on phone calls. And I wish I had fifty cents for every letter I wrote, telling him what I'd told her and telling her what to expect from him—that sort of thing.

But my mother didn't trust Billy. "What if he can't come up with it?" she said to me over the phone. "What then? He's in bad shape, and I'm sorry for him," she said. "But, son, what I want to know is, what if he isn't able to pay me? What if he can't? Then what?

"Then I'll pay you myself," I said. "Just like always. If he doesn't pay you, I'll pay you. But he'll pay you. Don't worry. He says he will, and he will."

"I don't want to worry," she said. "But I worry anyway. I worry about my boys and after that I worry about myself. I never thought I'd see one of my boys in this shape. I'm just glad your dad isn't alive to see it."

In three months my brother gave her fifty dollars of what he owed me and was supposed to pay to her. Or maybe it was seventy-five dollars he gave her. There are conflicting stories—two conflicting stories, his and hers. But that's all he paid her of the five hundred—fifty dollars or else seventy-five dollars, according to whose story you want to listen to. I had to make up the rest to her. I had to keep shelling out, same as always. My brother was finished. That's what he told me—that he was finished—when I called to see what was up, after my mother had phoned, looking for her money.

My mother said, "I made the mailman go back and check inside his truck, to see if your letter might have fallen down behind the seat. Then I went around and asked the neighbors did they get any of my mail by mistake. I'm going crazy with worry about this situation, honey." Then she said, "What's a mother supposed to think?" Who was looking out for her best interests in this business? She wanted to know that, and she wanted to know when she could expect her money.

So that's when I got on the phone to my brother to see if this was just a simple delay or a full-fledged collapse. But, according to Billy, he was a goner. He was absolutely done for. He was putting his house on the market immediately. He just hoped he hadn't waited too long to try and move it. And there wasn't anything left inside the house that he could sell. He'd sold off everything except the kitchen table and chairs. "I wish I could sell my blood," he said. "But who'd buy it? With my luck, I probably have an incurable disease." And, naturally, the investment thing hadn't worked out. When I asked him about it over the phone, all he said was that it hadn't materialized. His tax refund didn't make it either—the I.R.S. had some kind of lien on his return. "When it rains, it pours," he said. "I'm sorry, brother. I didn't mean for this to happen."

"I understand," I said. And I did. But it didn't make it any easier. Anyway, one thing and the other, I didn't get my money from him, and neither did my mother. I had to keep on sending her money every month.

I was sore, yes. Who wouldn't be? My heart went out to him, and I wished trouble hadn't knocked on his door. But my own back was against the wall now. At least, though, whatever happens to him from here on, he won't come back to me for more money—seeing as how he still owes me. Nobody would do that to you. That's how I figured anyway. But that's how little I knew.

I kept my nose to the grindstone. I got up early every morning and went to work and worked hard all day. When I came home I plopped into the big chair and just sat there. I was so tired it took me a while to get around to unlacing my shoes. Then I just went on sitting there. I was too tired to even get up and turn on the TV.

I was sorry about my brother's troubles. But I had troubles of my own. In addition to my mother, I had several other people on my payroll. I had a former wife I was sending money to every month. I had to do that. I didn't want to, but the court said I had to. And I had a daughter with two kids in Bellingham, and I had to send her something every month. Her kids had to eat, didn't they? She was living with a swine who wouldn't even *look* for work, a guy who couldn't hold a job if they handed him one. The time or two he did find something, he overslept, or his car broke down on the way in to work, or else he'd just be let go, no explanations, and that was that.

Once, long ago, when I used to think like a man about these things, I threatened to kill that guy. But that's neither here nor there. Besides, I was drinking in those days. In any case, the bastard is still hanging around.

My daughter would write these letters and say how they were living on oatmeal, she and her kids. (I guess he was starving, too, but she knew better than to mention that guy's name in her letters to me.) She'd tell me that if I could just carry her until summer, things would pick up for her. Things would turn around for her, she was sure, in the summer. If nothing else worked out—but she was sure it would; she had several irons in the fire—she could always get a job in the fish cannery that was not far from where she lived. She'd wear rubber boots and rubber clothes and gloves and pack salmon into cans. Or else she might sell root beer from a vending stand beside the road to people who lined up in their cars at the border, waiting to get into Canada. People sitting in their cars in the middle of summer were going to be thirsty, right? They were going to be crying out for cold drinks. Anyway, one thing or the other, whatever line of work she decided on, she'd do fine in the summer. She just had to make it until then, and that's where I came in.

My daughter said she knew she had to change her life. She wanted to stand on her own two feet like everyone else. She wanted to quit looking at herself as a victim. "I'm not a victim," she said to me over the phone one night. "I'm just a young woman with two kids and a son-of-a-bitch bum who lives with me. No different from lots of other women. I'm not afraid of hard work. Just give me a chance. That's all I ask of the world." She said she could do without for herself. But until her break came, until opportunity knocked, it was the kids she worried about. The kids were always asking her when Grandpop was going to visit, she said. Right this minute they were drawing pictures of the swing sets and swimming pool at the motel I'd stayed in when I'd visited a year ago. But summer was the thing, she said. If she could make it until summer, her troubles would be over. Things would change then—she knew they would. And with a little help from me she could make it. "I don't know what I'd do without you, Dad." That's what she said. It nearly broke my heart. Sure I had to help her. I was glad to be even halfway in a position to help her. I had a job, didn't I? Compared to her and everyone else in my family, I had it made. Compared to the rest, I lived on Easy Street.

I sent the money she asked for. I sent money every time she asked. And then I told her I thought it'd be simpler if I just sent a sum of money, not a whole lot, but money even so, on the first of each month. It would be money she could count on, and it would be *her* money, no one else's—her and the kids'. That's what I hoped for, anyway. I wished there was some way I could be sure the bastard who lived with her couldn't get his hands on so much as an orange or a piece of bread that my money bought. But I couldn't. I just had to go ahead and send the money and stop worrying about whether he'd soon be tucking into a plate of my eggs and biscuits.

My mother and my daughter and my former wife. That's three people on the payroll right there, not counting my brother. But my son needed money, too. After he graduated from high school, he packed his things, left his mother's house, and went to a college back East. A college in New Hampshire, of all places. Who's ever heard of New Hampshire? But he was the first kid in the family, on either side of the family, to even *want* to go to college, so everybody thought it was a good idea. I thought so, too, at first. How'd I know it was going to wind up costing me an arm and a leg? He borrowed left and right from the banks to keep himself going. He didn't want to have to work a job and go to school at the same time. That's what he said. And, sure, I guess I can understand it. In a way, I can even sympathize. Who likes to work? I don't. But after he'd borrowed everything he could, everything in sight, including enough to finance a junior year in Germany, I had to begin sending him money, and a lot of it. When, finally, I said I couldn't send any more, he wrote back and said if that was the case, if that was really the way I felt, he was going to deal drugs or else rob a bank—whatever he had to do to get money to live on. I'd be luck if he wasn't shot or sent to prison.

I wrote back and said I'd changed my mind and I could send him a little more after all. What else could I do? I didn't want his blood on my hands. I didn't want to think of my kid being packed off to prison, or something even worse. I had plenty on my conscience as it was.

That's four people, right? Not counting my brother, who wasn't a regular yet. I was going crazy with it. I worried night and day. I couldn't sleep over it. I was paying out nearly as much money every month as I was bringing in. You don't have to be a genius, or know anything about economics, to understand that this state of affairs couldn't keep on. I had to get a loan to keep up my end of things. That was another monthly payment.

So I started cutting back. I had to quit eating out, for instance. Since I lived alone, eating out was something I liked to do, but it became a thing of the past. And I had to watch myself when it came to thinking about movies. I couldn't buy clothes or get my teeth fixed. The car was falling apart. I needed new shoes, but forget it.

Once in a while I'd get fed up with it and write letters to all of them, threatening to change my name and telling them I was going to quit my job. I'd tell them I was planning a move to Australia. And the thing was, I was serious when I'd say that about Australia, even though I didn't know the first thing about Australia. I just knew it was on the other side of the world, and that's where I wanted to be.

But when it came right down to it, none of them really believed I'd go to Australia. They had me, and they knew it. They knew I was desperate, and they were sorry and they said so. But they counted on it all blowing over before the first of the month, when I had to sit down and make out the checks.

After one of my letters where I talked about moving to Australia, my mother wrote that she didn't want to be a burden any longer. Just as soon as the swelling went down in her legs, she said, she was going out to look for work. She was seventy-five years old, but maybe she could go back to waitressing, she said. I wrote her back and told her not to be silly. I said I was glad I could help her. And I was. I was glad I could help. I just needed to win the lottery.

My daughter knew Australia was just a way of saying to everybody that I'd had it. She knew I needed a break and something to cheer me up. So she wrote that she was going to leave her kids with somebody and take the cannery job when the season rolled around. She was young and strong, she said. She thought she could work the twelve-to-fourteen-hour-a-day shifts, seven days a week, no problem. She'd just have to tell herself she could do it, get herself psyched up for it, and her body would listen. She just had to line up the right kind of babysitter. That'd be the big thing. It was going to require a special kind of sitter, seeing as how the hours would be long and the kids were hyper to begin with, because of all the Popsicles and Tootsie Rolls, M&Ms, and the like that they put away every day. It's the stuff kids like to eat, right? Anyway, she thought she could find the right person if she kept looking. But she had to buy the boots and clothes for the work, and that's where I could help.

My son wrote that he was sorry for his part in things and thought he and I would both be better off if he ended it once and for all. For one thing, he'd discovered he was allergic to cocaine. It made his eyes steam and affected his breathing, he said. This meant he couldn't test the drugs in the transactions he'd need to make. So, before it could even begin, his career as a drug dealer was over. No, he said, better a bullet in the temple and end it all right here. Or maybe hanging. That would save him the trouble of borrowing a gun. And save us the price of bullets. That's actually what he said in his letter, if you can believe it. He enclosed a picture of himself that somebody had taken last summer when he was in the study-abroad program in Germany. He was standing under a big tree with thick limbs hanging down a few feet over his head. In the picture, he wasn't smiling.

My former wife didn't have anything to say on the matter. She didn't have to. She knew she'd get her money the first of each month, even if it had to come all the way from Sydney. If she didn't get it, she just had to pick up the phone and call her lawyer.

This is where things stood when my brother called one Sunday afternoon in early May. I had the windows open, and a nice breeze moved through the house. The radio was playing. The hillside behind the house was in bloom. But I began to sweat when I heard his voice on the line. I hadn't heard from him since the dispute over the five hundred, so I couldn't believe he was going to try and touch me for more money now. But I began to sweat anyway. He asked how things stood with me, and I launched into the payroll thing and all. I talked about oatmeal, cocaine, fish canneries, suicide, bank jobs, and how I couldn't go to the movies or eat out. I said I had a hole in my shoe. I talked about the payments that went on and on to my former wife. He knew all about this, of course. He knew everything I was telling him. Still, he said he was sorry to hear it. I kept talking. It was his dime. But as he talked I started thinking, *How are you going to pay for this call, Billy?* Then it came to me that *I* was going to pay for it. It was only a matter of minutes, or seconds, until it was all decided.

I looked out the window. The sky was blue, with a few white clouds in it. Some birds clung to a telephone wire. I wiped my face on my sleeve. I didn't know what else I could say. So I suddenly stopped talking and just stared out the window at the mountains, and waited. And that's when my brother said,

"I hate to ask you this, but—" When he said that, my heart did this sinking thing. And then he went ahead and asked.

This time it was a thousand. A thousand! He was worse off than when he'd called that other time. He let me have some details. The bill collectors were at the door—the door! he said—and the windows rattled, the house shook, when they hammered with their fists. *Blam, blam, blam*, he said. There was no place to hide from them. His house was about to be pulled out from under him. "Help me, brother," he said.

Where was I going to raise a thousand dollars? I took a good grip on the receiver, turned away from the window, and said, "But you didn't pay me back the last time your borrowed money. What about that?"

"I didn't?" he said, acting surprised. "I guess I thought I had. I wanted to, anyway. I tried to, so help me God."

"You were supposed to pay that money to Mom," I said. "But you didn't. I had to keep giving her money every month, same as always. There's no end to it, Billy. Listen, I take one step forward and I go two steps back. I'm going under. You're all going under, and you're pulling me down with you."

"I paid her *some* of it," he said. "I did pay her a little. Just for the record," he said, "I paid her something."

"She said you gave her fifty dollars and that was all."

"No," he said, "I gave her seventy-five. She forgot about the other twenty-five. I was over there one afternoon, and I gave her two tens and a five. I gave her some cash, and she just forgot about it. Her memory's going. Look," he said, "I promise I'll be good for it this time, I swear to God. Add up what I still owe you and add it to this money here I'm trying to borrow, and I'll send you a check. We'll exchange checks. Hold on to my check for two months, that's all I'm asking. I'll be out of the woods in two months' time. Then you'll have your money. July first, I promise, no later, and this time I *can* swear to it. We're in the process of selling this little piece of property that Irma Jean inherited a while back from her uncle. It's as good as sold. The deal has closed. It's just a question now of working out a couple of minor details and signing the papers. Plus, I've got this job lined up. It's definite. I'll have to drive fifty miles round trip every day, but that's no problem—hell, no. I'd drive a hundred and fifty if I had to, and be glad to do it. I'm saying I'll have money in the bank in two months' time. You'll get your money, all of it, by July first, and you can count on it."

"Billy, I love you," I said. "But I've got a load to carry. I'm carrying a very heavy load these days, in case you didn't know."

"That's why I won't let you down on this," he said. "You have my word of honor. You can trust me on this absolutely. I promise you my check will be good in two months, no later. Two months is all I'm asking for. Brother, I don't know where else to turn. You're my last hope."

I did it, sure. To my surprise, I still had some credit with the bank, so I borrowed the money, and I sent it to him. Our checks crossed in the mail. I stuck a thumbtack through his check and put it up on the kitchen wall next to the calendar and the picture of my son standing under that tree. And then I waited.

I kept waiting. My brother wrote and asked me not to cash the check on the day we'd agreed to. Please wait a while longer is what he said. Some things had come up. The job he'd been promised had fallen through at the last minute. That was one thing that came up. And that little piece of property belonging to his wife hadn't sold after all. At the last minute, she'd had a change of heart about selling it. It had been in her family for generations. What could he do? It was her land, and she wouldn't listen to reason, he said.

My daughter telephoned around this time to say that somebody had broken into her trailer and ripped her off. Everything in the trailer. Every stick of furniture was gone when she came home from work after her first night at the cannery. There wasn't even a chair left for her to sit down on. Her bed had been stolen, too. They were going to have to sleep on the floor like gypsies, she said.

"Where was what's-his-name when this happened?" I said.

She said he'd been out looking for work earlier in the day. She guessed he was with friends. Actually, she didn't know his whereabouts at the time of the crime, or even right now, for that matter. "I hope he's at the bottom of the river," she said. The kids had been with the sitter when the ripoff happened. But, anyway, if she could just borrow enough from me to buy some second-hand furniture she'd pay me back, she said, when she got her first check. If she had some money from me before the end of the week—I could wire it, maybe—she could pick up some essentials. "Somebody's violated my space," she said. "I feel like I've been raped."

My son wrote from New Hampshire that it was essential he go back to Europe. His life hung in the balance, he said. He was graduating at the end of summer session, but he couldn't stand to live in America a day longer after that. This was a materialist society, and he simply couldn't take it anymore. People over here, in the U.S., couldn't hold a conversation unless *money* figured in it some way, and he was sick of it. He wasn't a Yuppie, and didn't want to become a Yuppie. That wasn't his thing. He'd get out of my hair, he said, if he could just borrow enough from me, this one last time, to buy a ticket to Germany.

I didn't hear anything from my former wife. I didn't have to. We both knew how things stood there.

My mother wrote that she was having to do without support hose and wasn't able to have her hair tinted. She'd thought this would be the year she could put some money back for the rainy days ahead, but it wasn't working out that way. She could see it wasn't in the cards. "How are you?" she wanted to know. "How's everybody else? I hope you're okay."

I put more checks in the mail. Then I held my breath and waited.

While I was waiting, I had this dream one night. Two dreams, really. I dreamt them on the same night. In the first dream, my dad was alive once more, and he was giving me a ride on his shoulders. I was this little kid, maybe five or six years old. *Get up here*, he said, and he took me by the hands and swung me onto his shoulders. I was high off the ground, but I wasn't afraid. He was holding on to me. We were holding on to each other. Then he began to move down the sidewalk. I brought my hands up from his shoulders and put them around his forehead. *Don't muss my hair*, he said. *You can let go*, he said, *I've got you. You won't fall.* When he said that, I became aware of the strong grip of his hands around my ankles. Then I did let go. I turned loose and held my arms out on either side of me. I kept them out there like that for balance. My dad went on walking while I rode on his shoulders. I pretended he was an elephant. I don't know where we were going. Maybe we were going to the store, or else to the park so he could push me in the swing.

I woke up then, got out of bed, and used the bathroom. It was starting to get light out, and it was only an hour or so until I had to get up. I thought about making coffee and getting dressed. But then I decided to go back to bed. I didn't plan to sleep, though. I thought I'd just lie there for a while with my hands behind my neck and watch it turn light out and maybe think about my dad a little, since I hadn't thought about him in a long time. He just wasn't a part of my life any longer, waking or sleeping. Anyway, I got back in bed. But it couldn't have been more than a minute before I fell asleep once more, and when I did I got into this other dream. My former wife was in it, though she wasn't my former wife in the dream. She was still my wife. My kids were in it, too. They were little, and they were eating potato chips. In my dream, I thought I could smell the potato chips and hear them being eaten. We were on a blanket, and we were close to some water. There was a sense of satisfaction and well-being in the dream. Then, suddenly, I found myself in the company of some other people—people I didn't know—and the next thing that happened was that I was kicking the window out of my son's car and threatening his life, as I did once, a long time ago. He was inside the car as my shoe smashed through the glass. That's when my eyes flew open, and I woke up. The alarm was going off. I reached over and pushed the switch and lay there for a few minutes more, my heart racing. In the second dream, some-body had offered me some whiskey, and I drank it. Drinking that whiskey was the thing that scared me. That was the worst thing that could have happened. That was rock bottom. Compared to that, everything else was a picnic. I lay there for a minute longer, trying to calm down. Then I got up.

I made coffee and sat at the kitchen table in front of the window. I pushed my cup back and forth in little circles on the table and began to think seriously about Australia again. And then, all of a sudden, I could imagine how it must have sounded to my family when I'd threatened them with a move to Australia. They would have been shocked at first, and even a little scared. Then, because they knew me, they'd probably started laughing. Now, thinking about their laughter, I had to laugh, too. *Ha, ha, ha.* That was exactly the sound I made there at the table—*ha, ha, ha*—as if I'd read somewhere how to laugh.

What was it I planned to do in Australia, anyway? The truth was, I wouldn't be going there any more than I'd be going to Timbuktu, the moon, or the North Pole. Hell, I didn't want to go to Australia. But once I understood this, once I understood I wouldn't be going there—or anywhere else, for that matter—

I began to feel better. I lit another cigarette and poured some more coffee. There wasn't any milk for the coffee, but I didn't care. I could skip having milk in my coffee for a day and it wouldn't kill me. Pretty soon I packed the lunch and filled the thermos and put the thermos in the lunch pail. Then I went outside.

It was a fine morning. The sun lay over the mountains behind the town, and a flock of birds was moving from one part of the valley to another. I didn't bother to lock the door. I remembered what had happened to my daughter, but decided I didn't have anything worth stealing anyway. There was nothing in the house I couldn't live without. I had the TV, but I was sick of watching TV. They'd be doing me a favor if they broke in and took it off my hands.

I felt pretty good, all things considered, and I decided to walk to work. It wasn't all that far, and I had time to spare. I'd save a little gas, sure, but that wasn't the main consideration. It was summer, after all, and before long summer would be over. Summer, I couldn't help thinking, had been the time everybody's luck had been going to change.

I started walking alongside the road, and it was then, for some reason, I began to think about my son. I wished him well, wherever he was. If he'd made it back to Germany by now—and he should have—I hoped he was happy. He hadn't written yet to give me his address, but I was sure I'd hear something before long. And my daughter, God love her and keep her. I hoped she was doing okay. I decided to write her a letter that evening and tell her I was rooting for her. My mother was alive and more or less in good health, and I felt lucky there, too. If all went well, I'd have her for several more years.

Birds were calling, and some cars passed me on the highway. Good luck to you, too, brother, I thought. I hope your ship comes in. Pay me back when you get it. And my former wife, the woman I used to love so much. She was alive, and she was well, too—so far as I knew, anyway. I wished her happiness. When all was said and done, I decided things could be a lot worse. Just now, of course, things were hard for everyone. People's luck had gone south on them was all. But things were bound to change soon. Things would pick up in the fall maybe. There was lots to hope for.

I kept on walking. Then I began to whistle. I felt I had the right to whistle if I wanted to. I let my arms swing as I walked. But the lunch pail kept throwing me off balance. I had sandwiches, an apple, and some cookies in there, not to mention the thermos. I stopped in front of Smitty's, an old café that had gravel in the parking area and boards over the windows. The place had been boarded up for as long as I could remember. I decided to put the lunch pail down for a minute. I did that, and then I raised my arms—raised them up level with my shoulders. I was standing there like that, like a goof, when somebody tooted a car horn and pulled off the highway into the parking area. I picked up my lunch pail and went over to the car. It was a guy I knew from work whose name was George. He reached over and opened the door on the passenger's side. "Hey, get in, buddy," he said.

"Hello, George," I said. I got in and shut the door, and the car sped off, throwing gravel from under the tires.

"I saw you," George said. "Yeah, I did, I saw you. You're in training for something, but I don't know what." He looked at me and then looked at the road again. He was going fast. "You always walk down the road with your arms out like that?" He laughed—*ha, ha, ha*—and stepped on the gas.

"Sometimes," I said. "It depends, I guess. Actually, I was standing," I said. I lit a cigarette and leaned back in the seat.

"So what's new?" George said. He put a cigar in his mouth, but he didn't light it.

"Nothing's new," I said. "What's new with you?"

George shrugged. Then he grinned. He was going very fast now. Wind buffeted the car and whistled by outside the windows. He was driving as if we were late for work. But we weren't late. We had lots of time, and I told him so.

Nevertheless, he cranked it up. We passed the turnoff and kept going. We were moving by then, heading straight toward the mountains. He took the cigar out of his mouth and put it in his shirt pocket. "I borrowed some money and had this baby overhauled," he said. Then he said he wanted me to see something. He punched it and gave it everything he could. I fastened my seat belt and held on.

"*Go*," I said. "What are you waiting for, George?" And that's when we really flew. Wind howled outside the windows. He had it floored, and we were going flat out. We streaked down that road in his big unpaid-for car.

Ocean Avenue

If you can still see how you could once have loved a person, you are still in love; an extinct love is always wholly incredible. One day not too long ago, in Laguna Beach, California, an architect named Bobby Lazar went downtown to have a cup of coffee at Café Zinc with his friend Albert Wong and Albert's new wife, Dawn (who had, very sensibly, retained her maiden name). Albert and Dawn were still in that period of total astonishment that follows a wedding, grinning at each other like two people who have survived an air crash without a scratch, touching one another frequently, lucky to be alive. Lazar was not a cynical man and he wished them well, but he had also been lonely for a long time, and their happiness was making him a little sick. Albert had brought along a copy of *Science*, in which he had recently published some work on the String Theory, and it was as Lazar looked up from Al's name and abbreviations in the journal's table of contents that he saw Suzette, in her exercise clothes, coming toward the café from across the street, looking like she weighed about seventy-five pounds.

She was always too thin, though at the time of their closest acquaintance he had thought he liked a woman with bony shoulders. She had a bony back, too, he suddenly remembered, like a marimba, as well as a pointed, bony nose and chin, and she was always—but *always*—on a diet, even though she had a naturally small appetite and danced aerobically or ran five miles every day. Her face looked hollowed and somehow mutated, as do the faces of most women who get too much exercise, but there was a sheen on her brow and a mad, aerobic glimmer in her eye. She'd permed her hair since he last saw her, and it flew out around her head in two square feet of golden Pre-Raphaelite rotini—the lily maid of Astolat on an endorphin high. A friend had once said she was the kind of woman who causes automobile accidents when she walks down the street, and, as a matter of fact, as she stepped up onto the patio of the café a man passing on his bicycle made the mistake of following her with his eyes for a moment and nearly rode into the open door of a parked car.

"Isn't that Suzette?" Al said. Albert was, as it happened, the only one of his friends after the judgment who refused to behave as though Suzette had never existed, and he was always asking after her in his pointed, physicistic manner, one skeptical eyebrow raised. Needless to say, Lazar did not like to be reminded. In the course of their affair, he knew, he had been terribly erratic, by turns tightfisted and profligate, glum and overeager, unsociable and socially aflutter, full of both flattery and glib invective—a shithead, in short— and, to his credit, he was afraid that he had treated Suzette very badly. It may have been this repressed consciousness, more than anything else, that led him to tell himself, when he first saw her again, that he did not love her anymore.

"Uh-oh," said Dawn, after she remembered who Suzette was.

"I have nothing to be afraid of," Lazar said. As she passed, he called out, "Suzette?" He felt curiously invulnerable to her still evident charms, and uttered her name with the lightness and faint derision of someone on a crowded airplane signaling to an attractive but slightly elderly stewardess. "Hey, Suze!"

She was wearing a Walkman, however, with the earphones turned up very loud, and she floated past on a swell of Chaka Kahn and Rufus.

"Didn't she hear you?" said Albert, looking surprised.

"No, Dr. Five Useful Non-Implications of the String Theory, she did not," Lazar said. "She was wearing *ear*phones."

"I think she was ignoring you." Albert turned to his bride and duly consulted her. "Didn't she look like she heard him? Didn't her face kind of blink?"

"There she is, Bobby," said Dawn, pointing toward the entrance of the café. As it was a beautiful December morning, they were sitting out on the patio, and Lazar had his back to the Zinc. "Waiting on line."

He felt that he did not actually desire to speak to her but that Albert and Dawn's presence forced him into it somehow. A certain tyranny of intouchness holds sway in that part of the world—a compulsion to behave always as though one is still in therapy but making real progress, and the rules of enlightened behavior seemed to dictate that he not sneak away from the table with his head under a newspaper—as he might have done if alone—and go home to watch the Weather Channel or Home Shopping Network for three hours with a twelve-pack of Mexican beer and the phone off the hook. He turned around in his chair and looked at Suzette more closely. She had on one of those glittering, opalescent Intergalactic Amazon leotard-and-tights combinations that seem to be made of cavorite or adamantium and do not so much cling to a woman's body as seal her off from gamma rays and lethal stardust. Lazar pronounced her name again, more loudly, calling out across the sunny patio. She looked even thinner from behind.

"Oh. Bobby," she said, removing the headphones but keeping her place in the coffee line.

"Hello, Suze," he said. They nodded pleasantly to one another, and that might have been it right there. After a second or two she dipped her head semi-apologetically, smiled an irritated smile, and put the earphones—"earbuds," he recalled, was the nauseous term—back into her ears.

"She looks great," Lazar said magnanimously to Albert and Dawn, keeping his eyes on Suzette.

"She looks so thin, so drawn," said Dawn, who, frankly, could have stood to drop about fifteen pounds.

"She looks fine to me," said Al. "I'd say she looks better than ever."

"I know you would," Lazar snapped. "You'd say it just to bug me."

He was a little irritated himself now. The memory of their last few days together had returned to him, despite all his heroic efforts over the past months to repress it utterly. He thought of the weekend following that bad review of their restaurant in *Times* (they'd had a Balearic restaurant called Ibiza, in San Clemente)—a review in which the critic had singled out his distressed-stucco interior and Suzette's Majorcan paella, in particular, for censure. Since these were precisely the two points around which, in the course of opening the restaurant, they had constructed their most idiotic and horrible arguments, the unfavorable notice hit their already shaky relationship like a dumdum bullet, and Suzette went a little nuts. She didn't show up at home or at Ibiza all the next day—so that poor hypersensitive little José had to do all the cooking—but instead disappeared into the haunts of physical culture. She worked out at the gym, went to Zahava's class, had her body waxed, and then, to top it all off, rode her bicycle all the way to El Toro and back. When she finally came home she was in a mighty hormonal rage and suffered under the delusion that she could lift a thousand pounds and chew her way through vanadium steel. She claimed that Lazar had bankrupted her, among other outrageous and untrue assertions, and he went out for a beer to escape from her. By the time he returned, several hours later, she had moved out, taking with her *only his belongings*, as though she had come to see some fundamental inequity in their relationship—such as their having been switched at birth—and were attempting in this way to rectify it.

This loss, though painful, he would have been willing to suffer if it hadn't included his collection of William Powelliana, which was then at its peak and contained everything from the checkered wingtips Powell wore in *The Kennel Club Murder Case* to Powell's personal copy of the shooting script for *Life with Father* to a 1934 letter from Dashiell Hammett congratulating Powell on his interpretation of Nick Charles, which Lazar had managed to obtain from a Powell grand-nephew only minutes before the epistolary buzzards from the University of Texas tried to snap it up. Suzette sold the entire collection, at far less than its value, to that awful Kelso McNair, up in Lawndale, who only annexed it to his vast empire of Myrna Loy memorabilia and locked it away in his vault. In retaliation Lazar went down the next morning to their safe-deposit box at Dana Point, removed all six of Suzette's 1958 and '59 Barbie Dolls, and sold them to a collectibles store up in Orange for not quite four thousand dollars, at which point she brought the first suit against him.

"Why is your face turning so red, Bobby?" said Dawn, who must have been all of twenty-two.

"Oh!" he said, not bothering even to sound sincere. "I just remembered I have an appointment."

"See you, Bobby," said Al.

"See you," he said, but he did not stand up.

"You don't have to keep looking at her, anyway," Al continued reasonably. "You can just look out at Ocean Avenue here, or at my lovely new wife—hi, sweetie—and act as though Suzette's not there."

"I know," Lazar said, smiling at Dawn, then returning his eyes immediately to Suzette. "But I'd like to talk to her. No, really."

So saying, he rose from his chair and walked, as nonchalantly as he could, toward her. He had always been awkward about crossing public space, and could not do it without feeling somehow cheesy and hucksterish, as though he were crossing a makeshift dais in a Legion Hall to accept a diploma from a bogus school of real estate; he worried that his pants were too tight across the seat, that his gait was hitched and dorky, that his hands swung chimpishly at his sides. Suzette was next in line now and studying the menu, even though he could have predicted, still, exactly what she would order: a decaf au lait and a wedge of frittata with two little cups of cucumber salsa. He came up behind her and tapped her on the shoulder; the taps were intended to be devil-may-care and friendly, but of course he overdid them and they came off as brusque importunities of a man with a bone to pick. Suzette turned around looking more irritated than ever, and when she saw who it was, her dazzling green eyes grew tight little furrows at their corners.

"How are you?" said Lazar, daring to leave his hand on her shoulder, where, as though it were approaching c, very quickly it seemed to acquire a great deal of mass. He was so conscious of his hand on her damp, solid shoulder that he missed her first few words, and finally had to withdraw it, blushing.

"... great. Everything's really swell," Suzette was saying, looking down at the place on her shoulder where his hand had just been. Had he laid a freshly boned breast of raw chicken there and then taken it away her expression could not have been more bemused. She turned away, "Hi, Norris," she said to the lesbian woman behind the counter. "Just an espresso."

"On a diet?" Lazar said, feeling his smile tighten.

"Not hungry," she said. "You've gained a few pounds."

"You could be right," he said, and patted his stomach. Since he had thrown Suzette's Borg bathroom scale onto the scrap heap along with her other belongings (thus leaving the apartment all but empty), he had no idea of how much he weighed, and, frankly, as he put it to himself, smiling all the while at his ex-lover, he did not give a rat's ass. "I probably did. You look thinner than ever, really, Suze."

"Here's your espresso," said Norris, smiling oddly at Lazar, as though they were old friends, and he was confused, until he remembered that right after Suzette left him he'd run into this Norris at a party in Bluebird Canyon, and they'd had a short, bitter, drunken conversation about what it felt like when a woman left you, and Lazar impressed her by declaring, sagely, that it felt as though you'd arrived home to find that your dearest and most precious belongings in the world had been sold to a man from Lawndale.

"What about that money you owe me?" he said. The question was halfway out of his mouth before he realized it, and although he appended a hasty ha-ha at the finish, his jaw was clenched and he must have looked as if he was about to slug her.

"Whoa!" said Suzette, stepping neatly around him. "I'm getting out of here, Bobby. Goodbye." She tucked her chin against her chest, dipped her head, and slipped out the door, as though ducking into a rainstorm.

"Wait!" he said. "Suzette!"

She turned toward him as he came out onto the patio, her shoulders squared, and held him at bay with her cup of espresso coffee.

"I don't have to reckon with you anymore, Bobby Lazar," she said. "Colleen says I've already reckoned with you enough." Colleen was Suzette's therapist. They had seen her together for a while, and Lazar was both scornful and afraid of her and her lingoistic advice.

"I'm sorry," he said. "I'll try to be, um, yielding. I'll yield. I promise. I just—I don't know. How about let's sit down?"

He turned to the table where he'd left Albert, Dawn, and his cup of coffee, and discovered that his friends had stood up and were collecting their shopping bags, putting on their sweaters.

"Are you going?" he said.

"If you two are getting back together," said Albert, "this whole place is going. It's all over. It's the Big One."

"Albert!" said Dawn.

"You're a sick man, Bob," said Albert. He shook Lazar's hand and grinned.

"You're sick, and you like sick women."

Lazar cursed him, kissed Dawn on both cheeks, and laughed a reckless laugh.

"Is he drunk or something?" he heard Dawn say before they were out of earshot, and, indeed, as he returned to Suzette's table the world seemed suddenly more stressful and gay, the sky more tinged at its edges with violet.

"Is that Al's new wife?" said Suzette. She waved to them as they headed down the street. "She's pretty, but she needs to work on her thighs."

"I think Al's been working on them," he said.

"Shush," said Suzette.

They sat back and looked at each other warily and with pleasure. The circumstances under which they parted had been so strained and unfriendly and terminal that to find themselves sitting, just like that, at a bright café over two cups of black coffee seemed as thrilling as if they were violating some powerful taboo. They had been warned, begged, and even ordered to stay away from each other by everyone, from their shrinks to their parents to the bench of Orange County itself; yet here they were, in plain view, smiling and smiling. A lot of things had been lacking in their relationship, but unfortunately mutual physical attraction was not one of them, and Lazar could feel that hoary old devouring serpent uncoiling deep in its Darwinian cave.

"It's nice to see you," said Suzette.

"You look pretty," he said. "I like what you've done with your hair. You look like a Millais."

"Thank you," she said, a little tonelessly; she was not quite ready to listen to all his prattle again. She pursed her lips and looked at him in a manner almost surgical, as though about to administer a precise blow with a very small axe. She said, "*Song of the Thin Man* was on last week."

"I know," he said. He was impressed, and oddly touched. "That's pretty daring of you to mention that. Considering."

She set down her coffee cup, firmly, and he caught the flicker of her right biceps. "You got more than I got," she said. "You got six thousand dollars! I got five thousand four hundred and ninety five. I don't owe you anything."

"I only got four thousand, remember?" he said. He felt himself blushing. "That came out, well, in court—don't you remember? I—well. I lied."

"That's right," she said slowly. She rolled her eyes and bit her lip, remembering. "You lied. Four thousand. They were worth twice that."

"A lot of them were missing hair or limbs," he said.

"You pig!" She gave her head a monosyllabic shake, and the golden curls rustled like a dress. Since she had at one time been known to call him a pig with delicacy and tenderness, this did not immediately alarm Lazar. "You sold my dolls," she said, dreamily, though of course she knew this perfectly well, and had known it for quite some time. Only now, he could see, it was all coming back to her, the memory of the cruel things they had said, the tired, leering faces of the lawyers, of the acerbic envoi of the county judge dismissing all their suits and countersuits, of the day they had met for the last time in the empty building that had been their restaurant, amid the bare fixtures, the exposed wires, the crumbs of plaster on the floor; of the rancor that from the first had been the constant flower of their love. "You sold their things, too," she remembered. "All of their gowns and pumps and little swimwear."

"I was just trying to get back at you."

"For what? For making sure I at least got something out of all the time I wasted on you?"

"Take it easy, Suze."

"And then to lie about how much you got for them? Four thousand dollars!"

"At first my lawyers instructed me to lie about it," he lied.

"Kravitz! DiMartino! Those sleazy, lizardy, shystery old fat guys! Oh, you pigs!"

Now she was on her feet, and everyone out on the patio had turned with great interest to regard them. He realized, or, rather, remembered, that he had strayed into dangerous territory here, that Suzette had a passion for making scenes in restaurants. This is how it was, said a voice within Lazar—a gloomy, condemnatory voice—this is what you've been missing. He saw the odd angle at which she was holding her cup of coffee, and he hoped against hope that she did not intend to splash his face with espresso. She was one of those women who like to hurl beverages.

"Don't tell me," he said, despite himself, his voice coated with the most unctuous sarcasm, "you're *reckoning* with me again."

You could see her consulting with herself about trajectories and wind shear and beverage velocity and other such technical considerations—collecting all the necessary data, and courage—and then she let fly. The cup sailed past Lazar's head, and he just had time to begin a tolerant, superior smile, and to uncurl partially the middle finger of his right hand, before the cup bounced off the low wall beside him and ricocheted into his face.

Suzette looked startled for a moment, registering this as one registers an ace in tennis or golf, and then laughed the happy laugh of a lucky shot. As the unmerciful people on the patio applauded—oh, but that made Lazar angry—Suzette turned on her heel and, wearing a maddening smile, strode balletically off the patio of the café, out into the middle of Ocean Avenue. Lazar scrambled up from his chair and went after her, cold coffee running in thin fingers down his cheeks. Neither of them bothered to look where they were going; they trusted, in those last couple of seconds before he caught her and kissed her hollow cheek, that they would not be met by some hurtling bus or other accident.

DAN CHAON

I Demand to Know Where
You're Taking Me

Cheryl woke in the middle of the night and she could hear the macaw talking to himself—or laughing, rather, as if it had just heard a good joke. "Haw haw haw!" it went. "Haw haw haw": A perfect imitation of her brother-in-law, Wendell, that forced, ironic guffaw.

She sat up in bed and the sound stopped. Perhaps she had imagined it? Her husband, Tobe, was still soundly asleep next to her, but this didn't mean anything. He had always been an abnormally heavy sleeper, a snorer, and lately he had been drinking more before bed—he'd been upset ever since Wendell had gone to prison.

And she, too, was upset, anxious. She sat there, silent, her heart quickened, listening. Had the children been awakened by it? She waited, in the way she had when they were infants. Back then, her brain would jump awake. Was that a baby crying?

No, there was nothing. The house was quiet.

The bird, the macaw, was named Wild Bill. She had never especially liked animals, had never wanted one in her home, but what could be done? Wild Bill had arrived on the same day that Tobe and his other brothers, Carlin and Randy, had pulled into the driveway with a moving van full of Wendell's possessions. She'd stood there, watching as item after item was carried into the house, where it would remain, in temporary but indefinite storage. In the basement, shrouded in tarps, was Wendell's furniture: couch, kitchen set, bed, piano. There were his boxes of books and miscellaneous items, she didn't know what. She hadn't asked. The only thing that she wouldn't allow were Wendell's shotguns. These were being kept at Carlin's place.

It might not have bothered her so much if it had not been for Wild Bill, who remained a constant reminder of Wendell's presence in her home. As she suspected, the bird's day-to-day care had fallen to her. It was she who made sure that Wild Bill had food and water, and it was she who cleaned away the excrement-splashed newspaper at the bottom of his cage.

But despite the fact that she was his primary caretaker, Wild Bill didn't seem to like her very much. Mostly, he ignored her—as if she were some kind of *wife*, a negligible figure whom he expected to serve him. He seemed to like the children best, and of course they were very attached to him as well. They liked to show him off to their friends, and to repeat his funny sayings. He liked to ride on their shoulders, edging sideways, lifting his wings lightly, for balance.

Occasionally, as they walked around with him, he would laugh in that horrible way. "Haw haw haw!" he would squawk, and the children loved it.

But she herself was often uncomfortable with the things Wild Bill said. For example, he frequently said, "Hello, Sexy," to their eight-year-old daughter, Jodie. There was something lewd in the macaw's voice, Cheryl felt, a suggestiveness she found troubling. She didn't think it was appropriate for a child to hear herself called "sexy," especially since Jodie seemed to respond, blushing—flattered.

"Hello, Sexy," was, of course, one of Wendell's sayings, along with "Good God, Baby!" and "Smell my feet!" both of which were also part of Wild Bill's main repertoire. They had subsequently become catch-phrases for her children. She'd hear Evan, their six-year-old, out in the yard, shouting, "Good God, Baby!" and then mimicking that laugh. And even Tobe had picked up on the sophomoric retort, "Smell my feet!" It bothered her more than she could explain. It was silly, but it sickened her, conjuring up a morbid fascination with human stink, something vulgar and tiring. They repeated it and repeated it until finally, one night at dinner, she'd actually slammed her hand down on the table. "Stop it!" she cried. "I can't stand it anymore. It's ruining my appetite!"

And they sat there, suppressing guilty grins. Looking down at their plates. How delicate she was! How ladylike! How prudish!

But there was something else about the phrase, something she couldn't mention. It was a detail from the series of rapes that had occurred in their part of the state. The assaulted women had been attacked in their homes, blindfolded, a knife pressed against their skin. The first thing the attacker did was to force the women to kneel down and lick his bare feet. Then he moved on to more brutal things.

These were the crimes that Wendell had been convicted of, three months before. He had been convicted of only three of the six rapes he was accused of, but it was generally assumed that they had all been perpetrated by the same person. He was serving a sentence of no less than twenty-five years in prison, though his case was now beginning the process of appeals. He swore that he was innocent.

And they believed him—his family, all of them. They were all determined that Wendell would be exonerated, but it was especially important to Tobe, for Tobe had been Wendell's lawyer. Wendell had insisted upon it—"Who else could defend me better than my brother?" he'd said—and Tobe had finally given in, had defended Wendell in court, despite the fact that he was a specialist in family law, despite the fact that he had no experience as a criminal attorney. It was a "no-brainer" Tobe had said at the time. "No jury would believe it for a second." She had listened, nodding, as Tobe called the case flimsy, "a travesty," he said, "a bumbled investigation."

And so it was a blow when the jury, after deliberating for over a week, returned a guilty verdict. Tobe had actually let out a small cry, had put his hands over his face, and he was still in a kind of dizzied state. He believed now that if he had only recused himself, Wendell would have been acquitted. It had affected him, it had made him strange and moody and distant. It frightened her—this new, filmy look in his eyes, the drinking, the way he would wander around the house, muttering to himself.

She felt a sort of hitch in her throat, a hitch in her brain. Here he was, laughing with Jodie and Evan, his eyes bright with amusement as she slammed her hand down. She didn't understand it. When the bird croaked, "Smell my feet," didn't Tobe make the same associations that she did? Didn't he cringe? Didn't he have the same doubts?

Apparently not. She tried to make eye contact with him, to plead her case in an exchange of gazes, but he would have none of it. He smirked into his hand, as if he was one of the children.

And maybe she was over-reacting. A parrot! It was such a minor thing, wasn't it? Perhaps not worth bringing up, not worth its potential for argument. He stretched out in bed beside her and she continued to read her book, aware of the heaviness emanating from him, aware that his mind was going over and over some detail once again, retracing it, pacing around its circumference. In the past few months, it had become increasingly difficult to read him—his mood shifts, his reactions, his silences.

Once, shortly after the trial had concluded, she had tried to talk to him about it. "It's not your fault," she had told him. "You did the best you could."

She had been surprised at the way his eyes had narrowed, by the flare of anger, of pure scorn, which had never before been directed at her. "Oh, really?" he said acidly. "Whose fault is it, then? That an innocent man went to prison?" He glared at her, witheringly, and she took a step back. "Listen, Cheryl," he'd said. "You might not understand this, but this is my brother we're talking about. My little brother. Greeting card sentiments are not a fucking comfort to me." And he'd turned and walked away from her.

He'd later apologized, of course. "Don't ever talk to me that way again," she'd said, "I won't stand for it." And he agreed, nodding vigorously, he had been out of line, he was under a lot of stress and had taken it out on her. But in truth, an unspoken rift had remained between them in the months since. There was something about him, she thought, that she didn't recognize, something she hadn't seen before.

Cheryl had always tried to avoid the subject of Tobe's brothers. He was close to them, and she respected that. Both of Tobe's parents had died before Cheryl met him—the mother of breast cancer when Tobe was sixteen, the father a little more than a decade later, of cirrhosis— and this had knit them together.

They were close in an old-fashioned way, like brothers in westerns or gangster films, touching in a way, though when she had first met them she never imagined what it would be like once they became fixtures in her life.

In the beginning, she had liked the idea of moving back to Cheyenne, Wyoming, where Tobe had grown up. The state, and the way Tobe had described it, had seemed romantic to her. He had come back to set up a small law office, with his specialty in family court. She had a degree in educational administration, and was able, without much trouble, to find a job as a guidance counselor at a local high school.

It had seemed like a good plan at the time. Her own family was scattered: A sister in Vancouver; a half-sister in Chicago, where Cheryl had grown up; her father, in Florida, was remarried to a woman about Cheryl's age, and had a four-year-old son, whom she could hardly think of as a brother; her mother, now divorced for a third time, lived alone on a houseboat near San Diego. She rarely saw or spoke to any of them, and the truth was that when they'd first moved to Cheyenne she had been captivated by the notion of a kind of homely happiness—family and neighbors and garden, all the mundane middle-class clichés, she knew, but it had secretly thrilled her. They had been happy for quite a while. It was true that she found Tobe's family a little backward. But at the time, they had seemed like mere curiosities, who made sweet, smart Tobe even sweeter and smarter, to have grown up in such an environment.

She thought of this again as the usual Friday night family gathering convened at their house, now sans Wendell, now weighed with gloom and concern, but still willing to drink beer and play cards or Monopoly and talk drunkenly into the night. She thought back because almost ten years had now passed, and she still felt like a stranger among them. When the children had been younger, it was easier to ignore, but now it seemed more and more obvious. She didn't belong.

She had never had any major disagreements with Tobe's family, but there had developed, she felt, a kind of unspoken animosity, perhaps simple indifference. To Carlin, the second-oldest, Cheryl was, and would always remain, merely his brother's wife. Carlin was a policeman, crew-cutted, ruddy, with the face of a bully, and Cheryl couldn't ever remember having much of a conversation with him. To Carlin, she imagined, she was just another of the women-folk, like his wife, Karissa, with whom she was often left alone. Karissa was a horrid little mouse of a woman with small, judgmental eyes. She hovered over the brothers as they ate and didn't sit down until she was certain everyone was served; then she hopped up quickly to offer a second helping or clear a soiled plate. There were times, when Karissa was performing her duties, that she regarded Cheryl with a glare of pure, self-righteous hatred. Though of course, Karissa was always "nice"—they would talk about children, or food, and Karissa would sometimes offer compliments. "I see you've lost weight," she'd say, or: "Your hair looks much better, now that you've got it cut!"

Cheryl might have liked Tobe's next brother, Randy—he was a gentle soul, she thought, but he was also a rather heavy drinker, probably an alcoholic. She'd had several conversations with Randy that had ended with him weeping, brushing his hand "accidentally" across the small of her back or her thigh; wanting to hug. She had long ago stopped participating in the Friday night card games, but Randy still sought her out, wherever she was trying to be unobtrusive. "Hey, Cheryl," he said, earnestly pressing his shoulder against the door frame. "Why don't you come and drink a beer with us?" He gave her his sad grin. "Are you being anti-social again?"

"I'm just enjoying my book," she said. She lifted it so he could see the cover, and he read aloud in a kind of dramatized way.

"*The House of Mirth*," he pronounced. "What is it? Jokes?" he said hopefully.

"Not really," she said. "It's about society life in old turn-of-the-century New York."

"Ah," he said. "You and Wendell could probably have a conversation about that. He always hated New York!"

She nodded. No doubt Wendell would have read *House of Mirth*, and would have an opinion of it which he would offer to her in his squinting, lopsided way. He had surprised her, at first, with his intelligence, which he masked behind a kind of exaggerated folksiness and that haw-hawing laugh. But the truth was, Wendell read widely, and he could talk seriously about any number of subjects if he wanted. She and Wendell had shared a love of books and music—he had once stunned her by sitting down at his piano and playing

Debussy, then Gershwin, then an old Hank Williams song, which he sang along with in a modest, reedy tenor. There were times when it had seemed as if they could have been friends—and then, without warning, he would turn on her. He would tell her a racist joke, just to offend her; he would call her "politically correct" and would goad her with his far-right opinions, the usual stuff—gun control, feminism, welfare. He would get a certain look in his eyes, sometimes right in the middle of talking, a calculating, shuttered expression would flicker across his face. It gave her the creeps, perhaps even more now than before, and she put her hand to her mouth as Randy stood, still wavering, briefly unsteady, in the doorway. In the living room, Tobe and Carlin suddenly burst into laughter, and Randy's eyes shifted.

"I miss him," Randy said, after they had both been silently thoughtful for what seemed like a long while; he looked at her softly, as if she too had been having fond memories of Wendell. "I really miss him bad. I mean, it's like this family is cursed or something. You know?"

"No," she said, but not so gently that Randy would want to be patted or otherwise physically comforted. "It will be all right," she said firmly. "I honestly believe everything will turn out for the best."

She gave Randy a hopeful smile, but she couldn't help but think of the way Wendell would roll his eyes when Randy left the room to get another beer. "He's pathetic, isn't he?" Wendell had said, a few weeks before he was arrested. And he'd lowered his eyes, giving her that look. "I'll bet you didn't know you were marrying into white trash, did you?" he said, grinning in a way that made her uncomfortable. "Poor Cheryl!" he said. "Tobe fakes it really well, but he's still a stinky-footed redneck at heart. You know that, don't you?"

What was there to say? She was not, as Wendell seemed to think, from a background of privilege—her father had owned a dry-cleaning store. But at the same time, she had been comfortably sheltered. None of her relatives lived in squalor, or went to prison, or drank themselves daily into oblivion. She'd never known a man who got into fistfights at bars, as Tobe's father apparently had. She had never been inside a home as filthy as the one in which Randy lived.

But it struck her now that the trial was over, now that Randy stood, teary and boozy in her bedroom doorway. These men had been her husband's childhood companions—his brothers. He loved them. He *loved* them, more deeply than she could imagine. When they were together, laughing and drinking, she could feel an ache opening inside her. If he had to make a choice, who would he pick? Them or her?

In private, Tobe used to laugh about them. They were "characters," he said. He said, "You're so patient, putting up with all of their bullshit." And he kissed her, thankfully.

At the same time, he told her other stories. He spoke of a time when he was being abused by a group of high school bullies. Randy and Carlin had caught the boys after school, one by one, and "beat the living shit out of them." They had never bothered Tobe again.

He talked about Randy throwing himself into their mother's grave, as the casket was lowered, screaming "Mommy! Mommy!" and how the other brothers had to haul him out of the ground. He talked about how, at eleven or twelve, he was feeding the infant Wendell out of baby-food jars, changing his diapers. "After Mom got cancer, I practically raised Wendell," he told her once, proudly. "She was so depressed—I just remember her laying on the couch and telling me what to do. She wanted to do it herself, but she couldn't. It wasn't easy, you know. I was in high school, and I wanted to be out partying with the other kids, but I had to watch out for Wendell. He was a sickly kid. That's what I remember most. Taking care of him. He was only six when Mom finally died. It's weird. I probably wouldn't have even gone to college if I hadn't had to spend all that time at home. I didn't have anything to do but study."

The story had touched her, when they'd first started dating. Tobe was not—had never been—a very emotional or forthcoming person, and she'd felt she discovered a secret part of him. Was it vain to feel a kind of claim over these feelings of Tobe's? To take a proprietary interest in his inner life, to think: *I am the only one he can really talk to?* Perhaps it was, but they'd had what she thought of as a rather successful marriage, up until the time of Wendell's conviction. There had been an easy, friendly camaraderie between them; they made love often enough; they both loved their children. They were normally happy.

But now—what? What was it? She didn't know. She couldn't tell what was going on in his head.

Winter was coming. It was late October, and all the forecasts predicted cold, months of ice and darkness. Having grown up in Chicago, she knew that this shouldn't bother her, but it did. She dreaded it, for it always brought her into a constant state of pre-depressive gloom, something Scandinavian and lugubrious, which she had never liked about herself. Already, she could feel the edges of it. She sat in her office, in the high school, and she could see the distant mountains out the window, growing paler and less majestic until they looked almost translucent, like oddly shaped thunderheads fading into the colorless sky. A haze settled over the city. College Placement Exam scores were lower than usual. A heavy snow was expected.

And Tobe was gone more than usual now, working late at night, preparing for Wendell's appeal. They had hired a new lawyer, one more experienced as a defense attorney, but there were still things Tobe needed to do. He would come home very late at night.

She hoped that he wasn't drinking too much but she suspected that he was. She had been trying not to pay attention, but she smelled alcohol on him nearly every night he came to bed; she saw the progress of the cases of beer in the refrigerator, the way they were depleted and replaced. "What's wrong?" she thought, waiting up for him, waiting for the sound of his car in the driveway. She was alone in the kitchen, making herself some tea, thinking, when Wild Bill spoke from his cage.

"Stupid cunt," he said.

She turned abruptly. She was certain that she heard the words distinctly. She froze, with the kettle in her hand over the burner, and when she faced him, Wild Bill cocked his head at her, fixing her with his bird eye. The skin around his eye was bare, whitish wrinkled flesh, which reminded her of an old alcoholic. He watched her warily, clicking his claws along the perch. Then he said, thoughtfully: "Hello, Sexy."

She reached into the cage and extracted Wild Bill's food bowl. He was watching, and she very slowly walked to the trash can. "Bad bird!" she said. She dumped it out—the peanuts and pumpkin seeds and bits of fruit that she'd prepared for him. "Bad!" she said again. Then she put the empty food bowl back into the cage. "There," she said. "See how you like that!" And she closed the cage with a snap, aware that she was trembly with anger.

It was Wendell's voice, of course: his words. The bird was merely mimicking, merely a conduit. It was Wendell, she thought, and she thought of telling Tobe; she was wide awake when he finally came home and slid into bed, her heart was beating heavily, but she just lay there as he slipped under the covers—he smelled of liquor, whiskey, she thought. He was already asleep when she touched him.

Maybe it didn't mean anything: Filthy words didn't make someone a rapist. After all, Tobe was a lawyer, and he believed that Wendell was innocent. Carlin was a policeman, and he believed it too. Were they so blinded by love that they couldn't see it?

Or was she jumping to conclusions? She had always felt that there was something immoral about criticizing someone's relatives, dividing them from those they loved, asking them to take sides. Such a person was her father's second wife, a woman of infinite nastiness and suspicion, full of mean, insidious comments about her step-daughters. Cheryl had seen the evil in this, the damage it could do.

And so she had chosen to say nothing as Wendell's possessions were loaded into her house, she had chosen to say nothing about the macaw, even as she grew to loathe it. How would it look, demanding that they get rid of Wendell's beloved pet, suggesting that the bird somehow implicated Wendell's guilt? No one else seemed to have heard Wild Bill's foul sayings, and perhaps the bird wouldn't repeat them, now that she'd punished him. She had a sense of her own tenuous standing as a member of the family. They were still cautious of her. In a few brief moves, she could easily isolate herself—the bitchy city girl, the snob, the troublemaker. Even if Tobe didn't think this, his family would. She could imagine the way Karissa would use such stuff against her, that perky martyr smile as Wild Bill was remanded to her care, even though she was allergic to bird feathers. "I'll make do," Karissa would say. And she would cough, pointedly, daintily, into her hand.

Cheryl could see clearly where that road would lead.

*   *   *

But she couldn't help thinking about it. Wendell was everywhere—not only in the sayings of Wild Bill, but in the notes and papers Tobe brought home with him from the office, in the broody melancholy he trailed behind him when he was up late, pacing the house. In the various duties she found herself performing for Wendell's sake—reviewing her own brief testimony at the trial, at Tobe's request; going with Tobe to the new lawyer's office on a Saturday morning.

Sitting in the office, she didn't know why she had agreed to come along. The lawyer whom Tobe had chosen to replace him, Jerry Wasserman, was a transplanted Chicagoan who seemed even more out of place in Cheyenne than she did, despite the fact that he wore cowboy boots. He had a lilting, iambic voice, and was ready to discuss detail after detail. She frowned, touching her finger to her mouth as Tobe and his brothers leaned forward intently. What was she doing here?

"I'm extremely pleased by the way the appeal is shaping up," Wasserman was saying. "It's clear that the case had some setbacks, but to my mind the evidence is stronger than ever in your brother's favor." He cleared his throat. "I'd like to outline three main points for the judge, which I think will be quite—quite!—convincing."

Cheryl looked over at Karissa, who was sitting very upright in her chair, with her hands folded and her eyes wide, as if she were about to be interrogated. Carlin shifted irritably.

"I know we've talked about this before," Carlin said gruffly. "But I still can't get over the fact that the jury that convicted him was seventy-five percent female. I mean, that's something we ought to be talking about. It's just—it's just wrong, that's my feeling."

"Well," said Wasserman. "The jury selection is something we need to discuss, but it's not at the forefront of the agenda. We have to get through the appeals process first." He shuffled some papers in front of him, guiltily. "Let me turn your attention to the first page of the document I've given you, here... "

How dull he was, Cheryl thought, looking down at the first page, which had been photocopied from a law book. How could he possibly be more passionate or convincing than Tobe had been, in the first trial? Tobe had been so fervent, she thought, so certain of Wendell's innocence. But perhaps that had not been the best thing.

Maybe his confidence had worked against him. She remembered the way he had declared himself to the jury, folding his arms. "This is a case without evidence," he said. "Without *any* physical evidence!" And he had said it with such certainty that it had seemed true. The crime scenes had yielded nothing that had connected Wendell to the crimes; the attacker, whoever he was, had been extremely careful. There was no hair, no blood, no semen. The victims had been made to kneel in the bathtub as the attacker forced them to perform various degrading acts, and afterward, the attacker had left them there, turning the shower on them as he dusted and vacuumed. There wasn't a single fingerprint.

But there was this: In three of the cases, witnesses claimed to have seen Wendell's pickup parked on a street nearby. A man matching Wendell's description had been seen hurrying down the fire escape behind the apartment of one of the women.

And this: The final victim, Jenni Martinez, had been a former girlfriend of Wendell. Once, after they'd broken up, Wendell got drunk and sang loud love songs beneath her window. He'd left peaceably when the police came.

"Peaceably!" Tobe noted. These were the actions of a romantic, not a rapist! Besides which, Wendell had an alibi for the night the Martinez girl was raped. He'd been at Cheryl and Tobe's house, playing cards, and he'd slept that night on their sofa. In order for him to have committed the crime, he'd have had to feign sleep, sneaking out from under the bedding Cheryl had arranged for him on the living room sofa, without being noticed. Then, he'd have had to sneak back into the house, returning in the early morning so that Cheryl would discover him when she woke up. She had testified: He was on the couch, the blankets twisted around him, snoring softly. She was easily awakened; she felt sure that she would have heard if he'd left in the middle of the night. It was, Tobe told the jury, "a highly improbable, almost fantastical version of events."

But the jury had believed Jenni Martinez, who was certain that she'd recognized his voice. His laugh. They had believed the prosecutor, who had pointed out that there had been no more such rapes since Jenni Martinez had identified Wendell. After Wendell's arrest, the string of assaults had ceased.

After a moment, she tried to tune back in to what Feldman was saying. She ought to be paying attention. For Tobe's sake, she ought to be trying to examining the possibility of Wendell's innocence more rationally, without bias. She read the words carefully, one by one. But what she saw was Wendell's face, the way he'd looked as one of the assaulted women had testified: Bored, passive, even vaguely amused as the woman had tremulously, with great emotion, recounted her tale.

Whatever.

That night, Tobe was once again in his study, working, as she sat on the couch, watching television. He came out a couple of times, waving to her vaguely as he walked through the living room, toward the kitchen, toward the refrigerator, another beer.

She waited up. But when he finally came into the bedroom he seemed annoyed that she was still awake, and he took off his clothes silently, turning off the light before he slipped into bed, a distance emanating from him. She pressed her breasts against his back, her arms wrapped around him, but he was still. She rubbed her feet against his, and he let out a slow, uninterested breath.

"What are you thinking about?" she said, and he shifted his legs.

"I don't know," he said. "Thinking about Wendell again, I suppose."

"It will be all right," she said, though she felt the weight of her own dishonesty settle over her. "I know it." She smoothed her hand across his hair.

"You're not a lawyer," he said. "You don't know how badly flawed the legal system is."

"Well," she said.

"It's a joke," he said. "I mean, the prosecutor didn't prove his case. All he did was parade a bunch of victims across the stage. How can you compete with that? It's all drama."

"Yes," she said. She kissed the back of his neck, but he was already drifting into sleep, or pretending to. He shrugged against her arms, nuzzling into his pillow.

*   *   *

One of the things that had always secretly bothered her about Wendell was his resemblance to Tobe. He was a younger, and—yes, admit it—sexier version of her husband. The shoulders, the legs; the small hardness of her husband's mouth that she had loved was even better on Wendell's face, that sly shift of his grey eyes, which Wendell knew was attractive, while Tobe did not. Tobe tended toward pudginess, while Wendell was lean, while Wendell worked on mail-order machines, which brought out the muscles of his stomach. In the summer, coming in from playing basketball with Tobe in the driveway, Wendell had almost stunned her, and she recalled her high school infatuation with a certain athletic shape of the male body. She watched as he bent his naked torso toward the open refrigerator, looking for something to drink. He looked up at her, his eyes slanted cautiously as he lifted a can of grape soda to his lips.

Stupid cunt. It gave her a nasty jolt, because that was what his look said—a brief but steady look that was so full of leering scorn that her shy fascination with his muscled stomach seemed suddenly dirty, even dangerous. She had felt herself blushing with embarrassment.

She had not said anything to Tobe about it. There was nothing to say, really. Wendell hadn't *done* anything, and in fact he was always polite when he spoke to her, even when he was confronting her with his "beliefs." He would go into some tirade about some issue that he held dear—gun control, or affirmative action, etc.—and then he would turn to Cheryl, smiling: "Of course, I suppose there are differences of opinion," he would say, almost courtly. She remembered him looking at her once, during one of these discussions, his eyes glinting with some withheld emotion. "I wish I could think like you, Cheryl," he said. "I guess I'm just a cynic, but I don't believe that people are good, deep down. Maybe that's my problem." Later, Tobe told her not to take him seriously. "He's young," Tobe would say, rolling his eyes. "I don't know where he comes up with this asinine stuff. But he's got a good heart, you know."

Could she disagree? Could she say, no, he's actually a deeply hateful person?

But the feeling didn't go away. Instead, as the first snow came in early November, she was aware of a growing unease. With Daylight Savings Time, she woke in darkness, and when she went downstairs to make coffee, she could sense Wild Bill's silent, malevolent presence. He ruffled his feathers when she turned on the light, cocking his head so he could stare at her with the dark bead of his eye. By that time, she and Tobe had visited Wendell in prison, once, and Tobe was making regular, weekly phone calls to him. On Jodie's birthday, Wendell had sent a handmade card, a striking, pen-and-ink drawing of a spotted leopard in a jungle, the twisted vines above him spelling out "Happy Birthday, Sweet Jodie." It was, she had to admit, quite beautiful, and must have taken him a long time. But why a leopard? Why was it crouched as if hunting, its tail a snake-like whip? There was a moment, going through the mail, when she'd seen Jodie's name written in Wendell's careful, spiked cursive, that she'd almost thrown the letter away.

There was another small incident that week. They were sitting at dinner. She had just finished serving up a casserole she'd made, which reminded her, nostalgically, of her childhood. She set Evan's plate in front of him and he sniffed at the steam that rose from it.

"Mmmm," he said. "Smells like pussy."

"Evan!" she said. Her heart shrank, and she flinched again when she glanced at Tobe, who had his hand over his mouth, trying to hold back a laugh. He widened his eyes at her.

"Evan, where on earth did you hear something like that?" she said, and she knew that her voice was too confrontational, because the boy looked around guiltily.

"That's what Wild Bill says, when I give him his food," Evan said. He shrugged, uncertainly. "Wild Bill says it."

"Well, son," Tobe said. He had recovered his composure, and gave Evan a serious face.

"That's not a nice thing to say. That's not something that Wild Bill should be saying, either."

"Why not?" Evan said. And Cheryl had opened her mouth to speak, but then thought better of it. She would do more damage than good, she thought.

"It's just something that sounds rude," she said at last.

"Dad," Evan said. "What does 'pussy' mean?"

Cheryl and Tobe exchanged glances.

"It means a cat," Tobe said, and Evan's face creased with puzzlement for a moment.

"Oh," Evan said at last. Tobe looked over at her, and shrugged.

Later, after the children were asleep, Tobe said, "I'm really sorry, honey."

"Yes," she said. She was in bed, trying hard to read a novel, though she felt too unsettled. She watched as he chuckled, shaking his head. "Good God!" He said with amused exasperation. "Wendell can be such an asshole. I thought I would die when Evan said that."

After a moment, he sat down on the bed and put his fingers through his hair. "That stupid *Playboy* stuff," he said. "We're lucky the bird didn't testify."

He meant this as a joke, and so she smiled. Oh, Tobe, she thought, for she could feel, even then, his affection for his younger brother. He was already making an anecdote to tell to Carlin and Randy, who would find it hilarious. She closed her eyes as Tobe put the back of his fingers to her earlobe, stroking.

"Poor baby," he said. "What's wrong? You seem really depressed lately."

After a moment, she shrugged. "I don't know," she said. "I guess I am."

"I'm sorry," he said. "I know I've been really distracted, with Wendell and everything."

She watched as he sipped thoughtfully from the glass of beer he'd brought with him. Soon, he would disappear into his office, with the papers he had to prepare for tomorrow.

"It's not you," she said, after a moment. "Maybe it's the weather," she said.

"Yeah," Tobe said. He gave her a puzzled look. For he knew that there was a time when she would have told him, she would have plunged ahead, carefully but deliberately, until she had made her points. That was what he had expected.

But now she didn't elaborate. Something—she couldn't say what—made her withdraw, and instead she smiled for him. "It's okay," she said.

Wild Bill had begun to molt. He would pull out his own feathers, distractedly, and soon his grey, naked flesh was prominently visible in patches. His body was similar to the Cornish game hens she occasionally prepared, only different in that he was alive, and not fully plucked. The molting, or something else, made him cranky, and as Thanksgiving approached, he was sullen and almost wholly silent, at least to her. There were times, alone with him in the kitchen, that she would try to make believe that he was just a bird, that nothing was wrong. She would turn on the television, to distract her, and Wild Bill would listen, absorbing every line of dialogue.

They were alone again together, she and Wild Bill, when Wendell called. It was the second day in less than two weeks that she'd called in sick to work, that she'd stayed in bed, dozing, until well past eleven. She was sitting at the kitchen table, brooding over a cup of tea, a little guilty because she was not really ill. Wild Bill had been peaceful, half-asleep, but he ruffled his feathers and clicked his beak as she answered the phone.

At first, when he spoke, there was simply an unnerving sense of dislocation. He used to call her, from time to time, especially when she and Tobe were first married. "Hey," he'd say, "How's it going?" and then a long silence would unravel after she said, "Fine," the sound of Wendell thinking, moistening his lips, shaping unspoken words with his tongue. He was young back then, barely twenty when she was pregnant with Jodie, and she used to expect his calls, even look forward to them, listening as he hesitantly began to tell her about a book he'd read, or asking her to listen as he played the piano, the tiny sound blurred through the phone line.

This was what she thought of at first, this long ago time when he was still just a kid, a boy with, she suspected, a kind of crush on her. This was what she thought of when he said, "Cheryl?" hesitantly, and it took her a moment to calibrate her mind, to span the time and events of the last eight years and realize that here he was now, a convicted rapist, calling her from prison. "Cheryl?" he said, and she stood over the dirty dishes in the sink, a single Lucky Charm stuck to the side of one of the children's cereal bowls.

"Wendell?" she said, and she was aware of a kind of watery dread filling her up—her mouth, her nose, her eyes. "Where are you?" she said, and he let out a short laugh.

"I'm in jail," he said. "Where did you think?"

"Oh," she said, and she heard his breath through the phone line, could picture the booth where he was sitting, the little room that they'd sat in when they'd visited, the elementary school colors, the mural of a rearing mustang with mountains and lightning behind it.

"So," he said. "How's it going?"

"It's going fine," she said—perhaps a bit too stiffly. "Are you calling for Tobe? Because he's at his office... "

"No," Wendell said, and he was silent for a moment, maybe offended at her tone. She could sense his expression tightening, and when he spoke again there was something hooded in his voice. "Actually," he said, "I was calling for you."

"For me?" she said, and her insides contracted. She couldn't imagine how this would be allowed—that he'd have such freedom with the phone—and it alarmed her. "Why would you want to talk to me?" she said, and her voice was both artificially breezy and strained. "I... I can't do anything for you."

Silence again. She put her hand into the soapy water of the sink and began to rub the silverware with her sponge, her hands working as his presence descended into her kitchen.

"I've just been thinking about you," he said, in the same hooded, almost sinuous way. "I was... thinking about how we used to talk, you know, when you and Tobe first moved back to Cheyenne. I used to think that you knew me better than anybody else. Did you know that? Because you're smart. You're a lot smarter than Tobe, you know, and the rest of them—Randy, Carlin, that stupid... moron, Karissa. Jesus! I used to think, *What is she doing here? What is she doing in this family?* I guess that's why I've always felt weirdly close to you. You were the one person—" he said, and she waited for him to finish his sentence, but he didn't. He seemed to loom close, a voice from nearby, floating above her, and she could feel her throat constricting. What? she thought, and she had an image of Jenni Martinez, her wrists bound, tears leaking from her blindfold. He would have spoken to her this way, soft, insidious, as if he were regretfully blaming her for his own emotions.

"Wendell," she said, and tried to think of what to say. "I think... it must be very hard for you right now. But I don't know that... I'm really the person. I certainly don't think that I'm the *one* person, as you say. Maybe you should talk to Tobe?"

"*No*," he said, suddenly and insistently. "You just don't understand, Cheryl. You don't know what it's like—in a place like this. It doesn't take you long to sort out what's real and what's not, and to know—the right person to talk to. Good God!" he said, and it made her stiffen because he sounded so much like Wild Bill. "I remember so much," he said. "I keep thinking about how I used to give you shit all the time, teasing you, and you were just so... calm, you know. Beautiful and calm. I remember you said once that you thought the difference between us was that you really believed that people were good at heart, and I didn't. Do you remember? And I think about that. It was something I needed to listen to, and I didn't listen."

She drew breath—because she *did* remember—and she saw now clearly the way he had paused, the stern, shuttered stare as he looked at her, the way he would seek her out on those Friday party nights, watching and grinning, hoping to get her angry. Her hands clenched as she thought of the long, intense way he would listen when she argued with him. She worked with high school boys who behaved this way all the time—why hadn't she seen? "Wendell," she said. "I'm sorry, but... " And she thought of the way she used to gently turn away certain boys—*I don't like you in that way. I just want to be friends...* It was ridiculous, she thought, and wondered if she should just hang up the phone. How was it possible that they could let him call her like this, unmonitored? She was free to hang up, of course, that's what the authorities assumed. But she didn't. "I'm sorry," she said again. "Wendell, I think... I think... "

"No," he said. "Don't say anything. I know I shouldn't say this stuff to you. Because Tobe's my brother, and I *do* love him, even if he's a shitty lawyer. But I just wanted to hear your voice. I mean, I never would have said anything to you if it wasn't for being here and thinking—I can't help it—thinking that things would be different for me if we'd... if something had happened, and you weren't married. It could have been really different for me."

"No," she said, and felt a vaguely nauseous, surreal wavering passing through the room. A bank of clouds uncovered the sun for a moment, and the light altered. Wild Bill edged his clawed toes along his perch. "Listen, Wendell. You shouldn't do this. You were right to keep this to yourself, these feelings. People think these things all the time, it's natural. But we don't act on them, do you see? We don't—"

She paused, pursing her lips, and he let out another short laugh. There was a raggedness that sent a shudder across her.

"Act!" he said. "Jesus Christ, Cheryl, there's no *acting* on anything. You don't think I'm fooling myself into thinking this appeal is going to amount to anything, do you? I'm stuck here, you know that. For all intents and purposes, I'm not going to see you again for twenty years—if I even live that long. I just—I wanted to talk to you. I guess I was wondering if, considering the situation, if I called you sometimes. Just to talk. We can set... boundaries, you know, if you want. But I just wanted to hear your voice. I think about you all the time," he said. "Day and night."

She had been silent for a long time while he spoke, recoiling in her mind from the urgency of his voice and yet listening steadily. Now that he had paused, she knew that she should say something. She could summon up the part of herself that was like a guidance counselor at school, quick and steady, explaining to students that they had been expelled, that their behavior was inappropriate, that their SAT scores did not recommend college, that thoughts of suicide were often a natural part of adolescence but should not be dwelled upon. She opened her mouth, but this calm voice did not come to her, and instead she merely held the phone, limp and damp against her ear.

"I'll call you again," he said. "I love you," he said, and she heard him hang up.

In the silence of her kitchen, she could hear the sound of her pulse in her ears. It was surreal, she thought, and she crossed her hands over her breasts, holding herself. For a moment, she considered picking up the phone and calling Tobe at his office. But she didn't. She had to get her thoughts together.

She gazed out the window uncertainly. It was snowing hard now; thick white flakes drifted along with the last leaves of the trees. Something about Wendell's voice, she thought restlessly, and the fuzzy lights of distant cars seemed to shudder in the blur of steady snow. Her hands were shaking, and after a time, she got up and turned on the television, flicking through some channels: a game show, a talk show, an old black-and-white movie.

She could see him now very clearly, as a young man, the years after they'd first moved back to Wyoming—the way he would come over to their house, lolling around on the couch in his stocking feet, entertaining the infant Jodie as Cheryl made dinner, his eyes following her. And the stupid debates they used to have, the calculated nastiness of his attacks on her, the way his gaze would settle on her when he would play piano and sing to them. Wasn't that the way boys acted when they were trying not to be in love? Could she really have been so unaware, and yet have still played into it? *What is she doing in this family?* Wendell had said. She tried to think again, but something hard and knuckled had settled itself in her stomach. "My God," she said. "What am I going to do?" Wild Bill turned his head from the television, cocking his head thoughtfully, his eyes sharp and observant.

"Well?" she said to him. "What *am* I going to do?"

He said nothing. He looked at her for a little longer, then lifted his pathetic, molting wings, giving them a shake. "What a world, what a world," he said, mournfully.

This made her smile. It was not something she'd heard him say before, but she recognized it as a quote from *The Wizard of Oz,* which Wendell used to recite sometimes. It was what the Wicked Witch of the West said when she melted away, and a heaviness settled over her as she remembered him reciting it, clowning around during one of the times when they were just making conversation—when he wasn't trying to goad her. There were those times, she thought. Times when they might have been friends. "Yes," she said to Wild Bill. "What a world."

"Whatever," Wild Bill said; but he seemed to respond to her voice, or to the words that she spoke, because he gave a sudden flutter and dropped from his perch onto the table—which he would sometimes do for the children, but never for her, not even when she was eating fruit. She watched as he waddled cautiously toward her, his claws clicking lightly. She would have scolded the children: *Don't let that bird on the table, don't feed him from the table,* but she held out a bit of toast crust, and he edged forward.

"It's not going to work," she told Wild Bill, as he nipped the piece of toast from her fingers. "It's not," she said, and Wild Bill observed her sternly, swallowing her bread. He opened his beak, his small black tongue working.

"What?" she said, as if he could advise her, but he merely cocked his head.

"Stupid cunt," he said gently, decisively, and her hand froze over her piece of toast, recoiling from the bit of crust that she'd been breaking off from him. She watched the bird's mouth open again, the black tongue, and a shudder ran through her.

"No!" she said. "No! Bad!" She felt her heart contract, the weight hanging over her suddenly breaking, and she caught Wild Bill in her hands. She meant to put him back in his cage, to throw him in, without food or water, but when her hands closed over his body he bit her, hard. His beak closed over the flesh of her finger and he held on when she screamed; he clutched at her forearm with his claws when she tried to pull back, and she struck at him as he flapped his wings, her finger still clutched hard in his beak.

"You piece of filth!" she cried. Tears came to her eyes as she tried to shake loose, but he kept his beak clenched, and his claws raked her arm. He was squawking angrily, small feathers flying off him, still molting as he beat his wings against her, the soundtrack of some old movie swelling melodramatically from the television. She slapped his body against the frame of the kitchen door, and he let loose for a moment before biting down again on her other hand. "Bastard!" she screamed, and she didn't even remember opening the door until the cold air hit her. She struck him hard with the flat of her hand, flailing at him, and he fell to the snow-dusted cement of the back porch, fluttering. "Smell my feet!" he rasped, and she watched as he stumbled through the air, wavering upward until he lit upon the bare branch of an elm tree in their back yard. His bright colors stood out against the grey sky, and he looked down on her vindictively. He lifted his back feathers and let a dollop of shit fall to the ground. After a moment, she closed the back door on him.

It took a long time for him to die. She didn't know what she was thinking as she sat there at the kitchen table, her hands tightened against one another. She couldn't hear what he was saying, but he flew repeatedly against the window, his wings beating thickly against the glass. She could hear his body thump softly, like a snowball, the tap of his beak. She didn't know how many times. It became simply a kind of emphasis to the rattle of the wind, to the sound of television that she was trying to stare at.

She was trying to think, and even as Wild Bill tapped against the glass, she felt that some decision was coming to her—that some firm resolve was closing its grip over her even as Wild Bill grew quiet. He tapped his beak against the glass, and when she looked she could see him cocking his eye at her, a blank black bead peering in at her—she couldn't tell whether he was pleading or filled with hatred. He said nothing, just stared as she folded her arms tightly in front of her, pressing her forearms against her breasts. She was trying to think, trying to imagine Tobe's face as he came home from work, the way he would smile at her and she would of course smile back, the way he would look into her eyes, long and hard, inscrutably, the way Wild Bill was staring at her now. "Are you okay?" he would say, and he wouldn't notice that Wild Bill was gone, not until later. "I don't know," she would say. "I don't know what happened to him."

The rich lady on television was being kidnapped, as Wild Bill slapped his wings once more, weakly, against the window. Cheryl watched intently, though the action on the screen seemed meaningless. "How dare you!" the rich lady cried, as she was hustled along a corridor. Cheryl stared at the screen as a thuggish actor pushed the elegant woman forward.

"I demand to know where you're taking me," the elegant woman said desperately, and when Cheryl looked up Wild Bill had fallen away from his grip on the windowsill.

"You'll know soon enough, lady," the thug said. "You'll know soon enough."

HUGLEIKUR DAGSSON

Selected Drawings

ANDRE DUBUS

All the Time in the World

In college, LuAnn was mirthful and romantic, an attractive girl with black hair and dark skin and eyes. She majored in American Studies, and her discipline kept her on the dean's list. Her last name was Arceneaux; her mother's maiden name was Voorhies, and both families had come to Maine from Canada. Her parents and sister and brother and LuAnn often gestured with their hands as they talked. Old relatives in Canada spoke French.

LuAnn's college years seemed a fulfillment of her adolescence; she lived with impunity in a dormitory in Boston, with both girls and boys, with drinking and marijuana and cocaine; at the same time, she remained under the aegis of her parents. They were in a small town three hours north by bus; she went there on a few weekends, and during school vacations, and in summer. She was the middle child, between a married sister and a brother in high school. Her parents were proud of her work, they enjoyed her company, and they knew or pretended they knew as little about her life with friends as they had when she lived at home and walked a mile to school. In summer during college she was a lifeguard at a lake with a public beach. She saved some money and her parents paid her tuition and gave her a small allowance when she lived in the dormitory. They were neither strict nor lenient; they trusted her and, at home, she was like a young woman of their own generation: she drank and smoked with them, and on Sundays went to Mass with them and her brother. She went to

Sunday Mass in Boston, too, and sometimes at noon on weekdays in the university chapel, and sitting in the pew she felt she was at home: that here, among strangers, she was all of herself, and only herself, forgiven and loved.

This was a time in America when courting had given way to passion, and passion burned without vision; this led to much postcoital intimacy, people revealing themselves to each other after they were lovers, and often they were frightened or appalled by what they heard as they were lying naked on a bed. Passion became smoke and left burned grass and earth on the sheets. The couple put on their clothes, fought for a few months, or tried with sincere and confessional negotiation to bring back love's blinding heat, then parted from each other and waited for someone else. While LuAnn was in college, she did not understand all of this, though she was beginning to, and she did not expect her parents to understand any of it. She secretly took birth control pills and, when she was at home, returned from dates early enough to keep at bay her parents' fears. At Mass she received Communion, her conscience set free by the mores of her contemporaries and the efficacy of the Pill. When her parents spoke of drugs and promiscuity among young people, she turned to them an innocent face. This period of enjoying adult pleasures and at times suffering their results, while still living with her parents as a grown child, would end with the commencement she yearned for, strove for, and dreaded.

When it came, she found an apartment in Boston and a job with an insurance company. She worked in public relations. June that year was lovely, and some days she took a sandwich and cookies and fruit to work, and ate lunch at the Public Garden so she could sit in the sun among trees and grass. For the first time in her life she wore a dress or skirt and blouse five days a week, and this alone made her feel that she had indeed graduated to adult life. So did the work: she was assistant to a woman in her forties, and she liked the woman and learned quickly. She liked having an office and a desk with a telephone and typewriter on it. She was proud of her use of the telephone. Until now a telephone had been something she held while talking with friends and lovers and her family. At work she called people she did not know and spoke clearly in a low voice.

The office was large, with many women and men at desks, and she learned their names, and presented to them an amiability she assumed upon entering the building. Often she felt that her smiles, and her feigned interest in people's anecdotes about commuting and complaints about colds, were an implicit and draining part of her job. A decade later she would know that spending time with people and being unable either to speak from her heart or to listen with it was an imperceptible bleeding of her spirit.

Always in the office she felt that she was two people at once. She believed that the one who performed at the desk and chatted with other workers was the woman she would become as she matured, and the one she concealed was a girl destined to atrophy and become a memory. The woman LuAnn worked for was an intense, voluble blonde who colored her hair and was cynical, humorous, and twice divorced. When she spoke of money, it was with love, even passion; LuAnn saw money as currency to buy things with and pay bills, not an acquisition to accumulate and compound, and she felt like a lamb among wolves. The woman had a lover, and seemed happy.

LuAnn appreciated the practical function of insurance and bought a small policy on her own life, naming her parents as beneficiaries; she considered it a partial payment of her first child's tuition. But after nearly a year with the insurance company, on a Saturday afternoon while she was walking in Boston, wearing jeans and boots and a sweatshirt and feeling the sun on her face and hair, she admitted to herself that insurance bored her. Soon she was working for a small publisher. She earned less money but felt she was closer to the light she had sometimes lived in during college, had received from teachers and books and other students and often her own work. Now she was trying to sell literature, the human attempt to make truth palpable and delightful. There was, of course, always talk of money; but here, where only seven people worked and book sales were at best modest, money's end was much like its end in her own life: to keep things going. She was the publicity director and had neither assistants nor a secretary. She worked with energy and was not bored; still, there were times each day when she watched herself, and listened to herself, and the LuAnn Arceneaux she had known all her life wanted to say aloud: *Fuck* this; and to laugh.

She had lovers, one at a time; this had been happening since she was seventeen. After each one, when her sorrow passed and she was again resilient, she hoped for the next love; and her unspoken hope, even to herself, was that her next love would be her true and final one. She needed a name for what she was doing with this succession of men, and what she was doing was not clear. They were not affairs. An affair had a concrete parameter: the absence of all but physical love; or one of the lovers was married; or both of them were; or people from different continents met on a plane flying to a city they would never visit again; something hot and sudden like that. What LuAnn was doing was more complicated, and sometimes she called it naked dating: you went out to dinner, bared your soul and body, and in the morning went home to shower and dress for work. But she needed a word whose connotation was serious and deep, so she used the word everyone else used, and called it a relationship. It was not an engagement, or marriage; it was entered without vows or promises, but existed from one day to the next. Some people who were veterans of many relationships stopped using the word, and said things like: *I'm seeing Harry* and *Bill and I are fucking.*

The men saw marriage as something that might happen, but not till they were well into their thirties. One, a tall, blond, curly-haired administrator at the insurance company, spoke of money; he believed a man should not marry until paying bills was no longer a struggle, until he was investing money that would grow and grow, and LuAnn saw money growing like trees, tulips, wild grass, and vines. When she loved this man, she deceived herself and believed him. When she no longer loved him, she knew he was lying to her and to himself as well. Money had become a lie to justify his compromise of the tenderness and joy in his soul; these came forth when he was with her. At work he was ambitious and cold, spoke of precedent and the bottom line, and sometimes in the office she had to see him naked in her mind in order to see him at all.

One man she briefly loved, a sound engineer who wrote poems, regarded children as spiteful ingrates, fatherhood as bad for blood pressure, and monogamy as absurd. The other men she loved talked about marriage as a young and untried soldier might talk of war: sometimes they believed they could do it, and survive as well; sometimes they were afraid they could not; but it remained an abstraction that would only become concrete with the call to arms, the sound of drums and horns and marching feet. She knew with each man that the drumroll of pregnancy would terrify him; that even the gentlest—the vegetarian math teacher who would not kill the mice that shared his apartment—would gratefully drive her to an abortion clinic and tenderly hold her hand while she opened her legs. She knew this so deeply in her heart that it was hidden from her; it lay in the dark, along with her knowledge that she would die.

But her flesh knew the truth, and told her that time and love were in her body, not in a man's brain. In her body a man ejaculated, and the plastic in her uterus allowed him to see time as a line rising into his future, a line his lovemaking would not bend toward the curve of her body, the circle of love and time that was her womb and heart. So she loved from one day to the next, blinded herself to the years ahead, until hope was tired legs climbing a steep hill, until hope could no longer move upward or even stand aching in one flat and solid place. Then words came to her, and she said them to men, with derision, with anger, and with pain so deep that soon she could not say them at all, but only weep and, through the blur of tears, look at her lover's angry and chastened eyes. The last of her lovers before she met her final one was a carpenter with Greek blood, with dark skin she loved to see and touch; one night while they ate dinner in his kitchen, he called commitment "the c word." LuAnn was twenty-eight then. She rose from her chair, set down her glass of wine, and contained a scream while she pointed at him and said in a low voice: "You're not a man. You're a boy. You all are. You're all getting milk through the fence. You're a thief. But you don't have balls enough to take the cow."

This was in late winter, and she entered a period of abstinence, which meant that she stopped dating. When men asked her out, she said she needed to be alone for a while, that she was not ready for a relationship. It was not the truth. She wanted love, but she did not want her search for it to begin in someone's bed. She had been reared by both parents to know that concupiscence was at the center of male attention; she learned it soon enough anyway in the arms of frenzied boys. In high school she also learned that her passion was not engendered by a boy, but was part of her, as her blood and spirit were, and then she knew the words and actions she used to keep boys out of her body were also containing her own fire, so it would not spread through her flesh until its time. Knowing its time was not simple, and that is why she stopped dating after leaving the carpenter sitting at his table, glaring at her, his breath fast, his chest puffed with words that did not come soon enough for LuAnn to hear. She walked home on lighted sidewalks with gray snow banked on their curbs, and she did not cry. For months she went to movies and restaurants with women. On several weekends she drove to her parents' house, where going to sleep in her room and waking in it made her see clearly the years she had lived in Boston; made her feel that, since her graduation from college, only time and the age of her body had advanced, while she had stood on one plane, repeating the words and actions she regarded as her life.

On a Sunday morning in summer, she put on a pink dress and white high-heeled shoes and, carrying a purse, walked in warm sunlight to the ten o'clock Mass. The church was large and crowded. She did not know this yet, but she would in her thirties: the hot purity of her passion kept her in the Church. When she loved, she loved with her flesh, and to her it was fitting and right, and did not need absolving by a priest. So she had never abandoned the Eucharist; without it, she felt the Mass, and all of the Church, would be only ideas she could get at home from books; and, because of it, she overlooked what was bureaucratic or picayune about the Church. Abortion was none of these; it was in the air like war. She hoped never to conceive a child she did not want, and she could not imagine giving death to a life in her womb. At the time for Communion she stepped into the line of people going to receive the mystery she had loved since childhood. A woman with gray hair was giving the Hosts; she took a white disk from the chalice, held it before her face, and said: "The Body of Christ." LuAnn said: "Amen," and the woman placed it in her palms and LuAnn put it in her mouth, and for perhaps six minutes then, walking back to her pew and kneeling, she felt in harmony with the entire and timeless universe. This came to her every Sunday, and never at work; sometimes she could achieve it if she drove out of the city on a sunlit day and walked alone on a trail in woods, or on the shore of a lake.

After Mass she lingered on the church steps till she was alone. Few cars passed, and scattered people walked or jogged on the sidewalk and a boy on a skateboard clattered by. She descended, sliding her hand down the smooth stone wall. A few paces from the steps, she turned her face up to the sun; then the heel of her left shoe snapped, and her ankle and knee gave way: she gained her balance and raised her foot and removed the broken shoe, then the other one. Her purse in one hand and her shoes in the other, she went to the steps and sat and looked at the heel hanging at an angle from one tiny nail whose mates were bent, silver in the sunlight. A shadow moved over her feet and up her legs and she looked at polished brown loafers and a wooden cane with a shining brass tip, and a man's legs in jeans, then up at his face: he had a trimmed brown beard and blue eyes and was smiling; his hair was brown and touched the collar of his navy blue shirt. His chest was broad, his waist was thick and bulged over his belt, and his bare arms were large; he said: "I could try to fix it."

"With what?"

He blushed and said: "It was just a way of talking to you."

"I know."

"Would you like brunch?"

"Will they let me in barefoot?"

"When they see the shoe."

He held out his hand, and she took it and stood; her brow was the height of his chin. They told each other their names; he was Ted Briggs. They walked, and the concrete was warm under her bare feet. She told him he had a pretty cane, and asked him why.

"Artillery, in the war. A place called Khe Sanh."

"I know about Khe Sanh."

He looked at her.

"You do?"

"Yes."

"Good," he said.

"Why?"

"You were very young then."

"So were you."

"Nineteen."

"I was twelve."

"So how do you know about Khe Sanh?"

"I took a couple of courses. It's the best way to go to war."

He smiled and said: "I believe it."

At a shaded corner they stopped to cross the street and he held her elbow as she stepped down from the curb. She knew he was doing this because of the filth and broken glass, and that he wanted to touch her, and she liked the feel of his hand. She liked the gentle depth of his voice, and his walk; his right knee appeared inflexible, but he walked smoothly. It was his eyes she loved; she could see sorrow in them, something old he had lived with, and something vibrant and solid, too. She felt motion in him, and she wanted to touch it. He was a lawyer; he liked to read and he liked movies and deep-sea fishing. On their left, cars stopped for a red light; he glanced at her, caught her gazing at his profile, and she said: "It was bad, wasn't it?"

He stopped and looked down at her.

"Yes. I was a corpsman. You know, the nurse, the EMT—" She nodded. "With the Marines. I got hurt in my twelfth month. Ten years later I started dealing with the eleven and a half months before that."

"How's it going?"

"Better. My knee won't bend, but my head is clear in the morning."

They walked; his hand with the cane was close to her left arm, and she could feel the air between their hands and wrists and forearms and biceps, a space with friction in it, and she veered slightly closer so their skin nearly touched. They reached the street where she lived and turned onto it, facing the sun, and she did not tell him this was her street. On the first block was the restaurant; she had walked or driven past it but had not been inside. He held the door for her and she went into the dark cool air and softened lights, the smells of bacon and liquor. She was on a carpet now, and she could see the shapes of people at tables, and hear low voices; then he moved to her right side, lightly placed his hand on her forearm, and guided her to a booth. They ordered: a Bloody Mary for her and orange juice for him, and cantaloupes and omelettes and Canadian bacon with English muffins. When their drinks came, she lit a cigarette and said: "I drink. I smoke. I eat everything."

"I go to meetings. I'm in my sixth year without a drink. My second without smoking." His hand came midway across the table. "But I'd love a hit off yours."

She gave him the cigarette, her fingers sliding under his. She left her hand there, waited for his fingers again, and got them, his knuckles beneath hers, and she paused for a moment before squeezing the cigarette and withdrawing her hand. She said: "Doesn't cheating make you miss it more?"

"Oh, I'm always missing something."

"Drinking?"

"Only being able to. Or thinking I was."

"Nothing horrible has ever happened to me."

"I hope nothing does."

"I suppose if I live long enough something will."

"If you don't live long enough, *that* would be horrible. Are you seeing anyone?"

"No. Are you?"

"No. I'm waiting. I limp. I get frightened suddenly, when there's no reason to be. I get sad too, when nothing has happened. I know its name now, and— "

"What is its name?"

"It. It's just it, and I go about my day or even my week sometimes, then it's gone. The way a fever is there, and then it isn't. I want a home with love in it, with a woman and children."

"My God," she said, and smiled, nearly laughing, her hands moving up from the table. "I don't think I've *ever* heard those words from the mouth of a man."

"I love the way you talk with your hands."

They stayed in the booth until midafternoon; he invited her to a movie that night; they stepped out of the restaurant into the bright heat, and he walked with her to the door of her apartment building, and stood holding her hand. She raised her bare heels and kissed his cheek, the hair of his beard soft on her chin, then went inside. She showered for a long time and washed her hair, and, sitting at her mirror, blew it dry. She put on a robe and slept for an hour and woke happily. She ate a sandwich and soup, and dressed and put on makeup. He lived near the church, and he walked to her building and they walked to the movie; the sun was very low, and the air was cooling. After the movie, he took her hand and held it for the four blocks to her apartment, where, standing on the sidewalk, he put his arms around her, the cane touching her right calf, and they kissed. She heard passing cars, and people talking as they walked by; then for a long time she heard only their lips and tongues, their breath, their moving arms and hands. Then she stepped away and said: "Not yet."

"That's good."

"You keep saying that."

"I keep meaning it."

He waited until she was inside both doors, and she turned and waved and he held up his hand till she was on the elevator, and she waved again as the door closed.

In her apartment she went to her closet and picked up the white shoe with the broken heel. She did not believe in fate, but she believed in gifts that came; they moved with angels and spirits in the air, were perhaps delivered by them. Her red fingernails were lovely on the white leather; her hands warmed the heel.

In the morning she woke before the clock radio started, and made the bed; tonight she would see him. In her joy was fear, too, but it was a good fear of the change coming into her life. It had already come, she knew that; but she would yield slowly to it. She felt her months alone leaving her; she was shedding a condition; it was becoming her past. Outside in the sun, walking to work, she felt she could see the souls of people in their eyes. The office was bright; she could feel air touching her skin, and the warmth of electric lights. With everyone she felt tender and humorous and patient, and happily mad. She worked hard, with good concentration, and felt this, too, molting: this trying to plunder from an empty cave a treasure for her soul. She went to lunch with two women, and ordered a steak and a beer. Her friends were amused; she said she was very hungry, and kept her silence.

What she had now was too precious and flammable to share with anyone. She knew that some night with Ted it would burst and blaze, and it would rise in her again and again, would course in her blood, burn in her face, shine in her eyes. And this time love was taking her into pain, yes, quarrels and loneliness and boiling rage; but this time there was no time, and love was taking her as far as she would go, as long as she would live, taking her strongly and bravely with this Ted Briggs, holding his pretty cane; this man who was frightened by what had happened to him, but not by the madness she knew he was feeling now. She was hungry, and she talked with her friends and waited for her steak, and for all that was coming to her: from her body, from the earth, from radiant angels poised in the air she breathed.

Your Mother and I

I told you about that, didn't I? About when your mother and I moved the world to solar energy and windpower, to hydro, all that? I never told you that? Can you hand me that cheese? No, the other one, the cheddar, right. I really thought I told you about that. What is happening to my head?

Well, we have to take the credit, your mother and I, for reducing our dependence on oil and for beginning the Age of Wind and Sun. That was pretty awesome. That name wasn't ours, though. Your Uncle Frank came up with that. He always wanted to be in a band and call it that, the Age of Wind and Sun, but he never learned guitar and couldn't sing. When he sang he *enunciated* too much, you know? He sang like he was trying to teach English to Turkish children. Turkish children with learning disabilities. It was really odd, his singing.

You're already done? Okay, here's the Monterey Jack. Just dump it in the bowl. All of it, right. It was all pretty simple, converting most of the nation's electricity. At a certain point everyone knew that we had to just suck it up and pay the money—because holy crap, it really was expensive at first!—to set up the cities to make their own power. All those solar panels and windmills on the city buildings? They weren't always there, you know. No, they weren't. Look at some pictures, honey. They just weren't. The roofs of these millions of buildings weren't being used in any real way, so I said, Hey, let's have the buildings themselves generate some or all of the power they use, and it might look pretty good, to boot—everyone loves windmills, right? Windmills are awesome. So we started in Salt Lake City and went from there.

Oh hey, can you grate that one? Just take half of that block of Muenster. Here's a bowl. Thanks. Then we do the cheddar. Cheddar has to be next. After the cheddar, pecorino. Never the other way around. Stay with me, hon. Jack, Muenster, cheddar, pecorino. It is. The only way.

Right after that was a period of much activity. Your mother and I tended to do a big project like the power conversion, and then follow it with a bunch of smaller, quicker things. So we made all the roads red. You wouldn't remember this—you weren't even born. We were all into roads then, so we had most of them painted red, most of them, especially the highways—a leathery red that looked good with just about everything, with green things and blue skies and woods of cedar and golden swamps and sugar-colored beaches. I think we were right. You like them, right? They used to be grey, the roads. Insane, right? Your mom thinks yellow would have been good, too, an ochre but sweeter. Anyway, in the same week, we got rid of school funding tied to local property taxes—can you believe they used to pull that crap?—banned bicycle shorts for everyone but professionals, and made everyone's hair shinier. That was us. Your mother and I.

That was right after our work with the lobbyists—I never told you that, either? I must be losing my mind. I never mentioned the lobbyists, about when we had them all deported? That part of it, the deportation, was your mother's idea. All I'd said was, Hey, why not ban all lobbying? Or at least ban all donations from lobbyists, and make them wear cowbells so everyone would know they were coming? And then your dear mom, who was, I think, a little tipsy at the time—we were at a bar where they had a Zima special, and you know how your mom loves her Zima—she said, How about, to make sure those bastards don't come back to Washington, have them all sent to Greenland? And wow, the idea just took off. People loved it, and Greenland welcomed them warmly; they'd apparently been looking for ways to boost their tourism. They set up some cages and a viewing area and it was a big hit.

So then we were all pumped up, to be honest. Wow, this kind of thing, the lobbyists thing especially, boy, it really made your mother horny. Matter of fact, I think you were conceived around that time. She was like some kind of tsunam—

Oh don't give me that face. What? Did I cross some line? Don't you want to know when your seed was planted? I would think you'd want to know that kind of thing. Well then. I stand corrected.

Anyway, we were on a roll, so we got rid of genocide. The main idea was to create and maintain a military force of about 20,000 troops, under the auspices of the UN, which could be deployed quickly to any part of the world within about thirty-six hours. This wouldn't be the usual blue helmets, watching the slaughter. These guys would be badass. We were sick of the civilized world sort of twiddling their thumbs while hundreds of thousands of people killed each other in Rwanda, Bosnia, way back in Armenia, on and on. Then the UN would send twelve Belgian soldiers. Nice guys, but really, you have a genocide raging in Rwanda, 800,000 dead in a month and you send *twelve Belgians*?

So we made this proposal, the UN went for it, and within a year the force was up and running. And man oh man, your mother was randy again. That's when your fecundation happened, and why we called you Johnna. I remember it now—I was wrong before. Your mother and I were actually caught in the UN bathroom, after the vote went our way. The place, all marble and brass, was full of people, and at the worst possible moment, Kofi himself walked in. He sure was surprised to see us in there, on the sink, but I have to say, he was pretty cool about it. He actually seemed to enjoy it, even watched for a minute, because there was no way we were gonna stop in the middle—

Fine. I won't do that again. It's just that it's part of the story, honey. Everything we did started with love, and ended with lust—

But you're right. That was inappropriate.

We went on a tear right after genocide, very busy. I attribute it partly to the vitamins we were on—very intense program of herbs and vitamins and protein shakes. We'd shoot out of bed and bounce around like bunnies. So that's when we covered Cleveland in ivy. You've seen pictures. We did that. Just said, Hey Cleveland, what if you were covered in ivy, all the buildings? Wouldn't that look cool, and be a big tourist attraction? And they said, "Sure." Not right away, though. You know who helped with that? Dennis

Kucinich. I used to call him "Sparky," because he was such a feisty fella. Your mom, she called him "The Kooch."

We're gonna need all three kinds of salsa, hon. Yeah, use the small bowls. Just pour it right up to the edge. Right. Your brother likes to mix it up. Me, I'm a fan of the mild.

Right after Cleveland and the ivy we made all the kids memorize poetry again. We hadn't memorized any growing up—this was the seventies and eighties, and people hadn't taught that for years—and we really found we missed it. The girls were fine with the idea, and the boys caught on when they realized it would help them get older women into bed. Around that time we banned wearing fur outside of arctic regions, flooded the market with diamonds and gold and silver to the point where none had any value, fixed the ozone hole—I could show you that; we've got it on video—and then we did the thing with the llamas. What are you doing? Sour cream in the salsa? No, no. That's just wrong, sweetie. My god.

So yeah, we put llamas everywhere. That was us. We just liked looking at them, so we bred about six million and spread them around. They weren't there before, honey. No, they weren't. Oh man, there's one now, in the backyard. Isn't it a handsome thing? Now they're as common as squirrels or deer, and you have your mom and pop to thank for that.

It's jalapeño time. Use the smaller knife. You're gonna cut the crap out of your hand. You don't want one of these. You see this scar on my thumb? Looks like a scythe, right? I got that when we were negotiating the removal of the nation's billboards. I was climbing one of them, in Kentucky actually, to start a hunger strike kind of thing, sort of silly I guess, and cut the shipdoodle out of that left thumb.

Why the billboards? Have you even see one? In books? Well, I guess I just never really liked the look of them—they just seemed so ugly and such an intrusion on the collective involuntary consciousness, a blight on the land. Vermont had outlawed them and boy, what a difference that made. So your mother and I revived Lady Bird Johnson's campaign against them, and of course 98 percent of the public was with us, so the whole thing happened pretty quickly. We had most of the billboards down within a year. Right after that, your brother Sid was conceived, and it was about time I had my tubes tied.

Give me some of that cobbler, hon. We're gonna have the peach cobbler after the main event. I just wanna get the Cool Whip on it, then stick it in the freezer for a minute. That's Frank's trick. Frank's come up with a lot of good ideas for improving frozen and refrigerated desserts. No, that's not his job, honey. Frank doesn't have a job, per se.

I guess a lot of what we did—what made so much of this possible—was eliminate the bipolar nature of so much of what passed for debate in those days. So often the media would take even the most logical idea, like private funding for all sports stadiums or having all colleges require forty hours of community service to graduate, and make it seem like there were two equally powerful sides to the argument, which was so rarely the case. A logical fallacy, is what that is. So we just got them to keep things in perspective a bit, not make everyone so crazy, polarizing every last debate. I mean, there was a time when you couldn't get a lightbulb replaced because the press would find a way to quote the sole lunatic in the world who didn't want that lightbulb replaced. So we sat them all down, all the members of the media, and we said, "Listen, we all want to have progress, we all want a world for the grandkids and all. We know we're gonna need better gas mileage on the cars, and that all the toddlers are gonna need Head Start, and we're gonna need weekly parades through every town and city to keep morale up, and we'll have to get rid of Three Strikes and mandatory minimums and the execution of retarded prisoners—and that it all has to happen sooner or later, so don't go blowing opposition to any of it out of proportion. Don't go getting everyone *inflamed*." Honestly, when lynchings were originally outlawed, you can bet the newspapers made it seem like there was some real validity to the pro-lynching side of things. You can be sure that the third paragraph of any article would have said "Not *everyone* is happy about the anti-lynching legislation. We spoke to a local resident who is not at all happy about it..." Anyway, we sat everyone down, served some carrots and onion dip, and in a couple hours your mother and I straightened all that out.

About then we had a real productive period. In about six months, we established a global minimum wage, we made it so smoke detectors could be turned off without having to rip them from the ceiling, and we got Soros to buy the Amazon, to preserve it. That was fun—he took us on his jet, beautiful thing, appointed in the smoothest cherry and teak, and they had the soda where you add the colored syrup yourself. You ever have that kind? So good, but you can't overdo it—too much syrup and you feel bloated for a week. Well, then we came home, rested up for a few days, and then we found a cure for Parkinson's. We did *so*, honey. Yes that was us. Don't you ever look through the nice scrapbook we made? You should. It's in the garage with your Uncle Frank. Are you sure he's asleep? No, don't wake him up. Hell, I guess you have to wake him up anyway, because he won't want to miss the *comida grande*.

After Parkinson's, we fixed AIDS pretty well. We didn't cure it, but we made the inhibiting drugs available worldwide, for free, as a condition of the drug companies being allowed to operate in the United States. Their profit margins were insane at the time, so they relented, made amends, and it worked out fine. That was about when we made all buildings curvier, and all cars boxier.

After AIDS and the curves, we did some work on elections. First we made them no more than two months long, publicly funded, and forced the networks to give two hours a night to the campaigns. Around when you were born, the candidates were spending about $200 million each on TV ads, because the news wasn't covering the elections for more than ninety seconds a day. It was nuts! So we fixed that, and then we perfected online and phone voting. Man, participation went through the roof. Everyone thought there was just all this apathy, when the main problem was finding your damned polling place! And all the red tape—register now, vote then, come to this elementary school, but skip work to do it—on and on. Voting on a Tuesday? Good lord. But the online voting, the voting over the phone—man, that was great, suddenly participation exploded, from about, what, 40 percent, to 88. We did that over Columbus Day weekend, I think. I remember I'd just had my hair cut very short. Yeah, like in the picture in the hallway. We called that style the Timberlake.

And that's about when your mom got all kinky again. She went out, bought this one device, it was kind of like a swing, where there was this harness and—

Fine. You don't need to know that. But the harness figures in, because that's when your mother had the idea—some of her best ideas happened when she was lying down—to make it illegal to have more than one president from the same immediate family. That was just a personal gripe she had. We'd had the Adamses and Bushes and we were about to have the Clintons and your mother just got pissed. What the fuck? she said. Are we gonna have a monarchy here or what? Are we that stupid, that we have to go to the same well every time? This isn't an Aaron Spelling casting call, this is the damned presidency! I said What about the Kennedys? And she said Screw 'em! Or maybe she didn't say that, but that was the spirit of it. She's a fiery one, your mom, a fiery furnace of—

Ahem. So yeah, she pushed that through, a constitutional amendment.

That led to another busy period. One week, we made all the cars electric and put waterslides in every elementary school. We increased average life expectancy to 164, made it illegal to manufacture or wear Cosby sweaters, and made penises better looking—more streamlined, better coloring, less hair. People, you know, were real appreciative about that. And the last thing we did, which I know I've told you about, was the program where everyone can redo one year of their childhood. For $580, you could go back to the year of your choice, and do that one again. You're not allowed to change anything, do anything differently, but you get to be there again, live the whole year, with what you know now. Oh man, that was a good idea. Everyone loved it, and it made up for all the people who were pissed when we painted Kansas purple, every last inch of it. I did the period between ten-and-a-half and eleven-and-a-half. Fifth grade. Wow, that was sweet.

Speaking of ten-year-olds, here comes your brother. And Uncle Frank! We didn't have to wake you up! *Hola hermano, tios! Esta la noche de los nachos! Si, si.* And here's your mother, descending the stairs. With her hair up. This I was particularly proud of, when I convinced your mother to wear her hair up more often. When she first did it, a week before our wedding, I was breathless, I was lifted, I felt as if I'd met her twin, and oh how I was confused. Was I cheating on my beloved with this version of her, with that long neck exposed, the hair falling in helixes, kissing her clavicles? She assured me that I was not, and that's how we got married, with her hair up—that's how we did the walk with the music and the fanfare, everything yellow and white, side by side, long even strides, she and me, your mother and I.

NORA EPHRON

What I Wish I'd Known

People have only one way to be.

Buy, don't rent.

Never marry a man you wouldn't want to be divorced from.

Don't cover a couch with anything that isn't more or less beige.

Don't buy anything that is 100 percent wool, even if it seems to be very soft and not particularly itchy when you try it on in the store.

You can't be friends with people who call after 11 p.m.

Block everyone on your instant mail.

The world's greatest babysitter burns out after two and a half years.

You never know.

The last four years of psychoanalysis are a waste of money.

The plane is not going to crash.

Anything you think is wrong with your body at the age of thirty-five you will be nostalgic for at the age of forty-five.

At the age of fifty-five you will get a saggy roll just above your waist even if you are painfully thin.

This saggy roll just above your waist will be especially visible from the back and will force you to re-evaluate half the clothes in your closet, especially the white shirts.

Write everything down.

Keep a journal.

Take more pictures.

The empty nest is underrated.

You can order more than one dessert.

You can't own too many black turtleneck sweaters.

If the shoe doesn't fit in the shoe store, it's never going to fit.

When your children are teenagers, it's important to have a dog so that someone in the house is happy to see you.

Back up your files.

Overinsure everything.

Whenever someone says the words, "Our friendship is more important than this," watch out, because it almost never is.

There's no point in making piecrust from scratch.

The reason you're waking up in the middle of the night is the second glass of wine.

The minute you decide to get divorced, go see a lawyer and file the papers.

Overtip.

Never let them know.

If only one-third of your clothes are mistakes, you're ahead of the game.

If friends ask you to be their child's guardian in case they die in a plane crash, you can say no.

There are no secrets.

Nixon and Elvis

FAYE FIORE

Picture of Elvis and Nixon Is Worth a Thousand Words

WASHINGTON—The National Archives is like a safe-deposit box for America's really important papers—the Bill of Rights, the Declaration of Independence, the $7.2 million canceled check for the purchase of Alaska, the picture of Richard Nixon and Elvis Presley shaking hands in the Oval Office.

Copies of that photo—the president in his charcoal suit, the King of Rock 'n' roll in his purple velvet cape—are requested more than just about any of the Archives' treasures, including the Constitution.

Yet the story that led to their improbable meeting on Dec. 21, 1970, is as little-known as the picture is famous. In honor of Elvis's seventy-fifth birthday last week, one of the president's men, Egil "Bud" Krogh, and one of the King's most trusted friends, Jerry Schilling, met for the first time in almost forty years at the National Archives to recount the day Elvis came to Washington. A crowd waited in the frigid cold for a seat. (Even in the imperious capital, Elvis can still pack a house.)

It wasn't the glitzy birthday party other cities threw, no giant birthday cards, all-night film festivals, or flashy displays of the white jumpsuit called "Snowflake." An Elvis exhibit at the National Portrait Gallery is more Washington's speed. As was this forum, which offered an hour-long window into a

---

This piece first appeared in the Los Angeles Times *on January 14, 2010.*

simpler time, before Watergate or terrorist attacks, when the world's most famous man asked the world's most powerful one to grant him a wish, and got it.

The story begins Dec. 19, 1970, at Schilling's home in the Hollywood
Hills. The phone rings. A voice says, "It's me."

Elvis is at the Dallas airport on his way to Los Angeles and wants Schilling to pick him up at LAX.

"Who's with you?" Schilling asks.

"Nobody," the King says.

It should be noted that Elvis was a man who almost never did anything
alone. He wanted at least five guys around him just to sit and watch TV. So
Schilling is understandably concerned, all the more so when Elvis proceeds to
recite his flight number and arrival time, which is akin to the queen doing a
load of laundry.

Schilling heads to the airport and takes Elvis to the singer's mansion on
Hillcrest Drive in Beverly Hills. The next morning, it comes out that Vernon,
Elvis's father, and Priscilla, his wife, were bugging him about how he spent his
money. This aggravated the King, so all by himself he got on the first plane going out, which happened to be bound for Washington. Things did not go well.

For starters, a "smart aleck little steward" with a mustache discovers Elvis
is carrying a gun—it was his habit to carry at least three—and informs him
he cannot bring a firearm on the airplane. Elvis, unaccustomed to being told
what to do, storms off and is chased down by the pilot: "I'm sorry, Mr. Presley,
of course you can keep your gun." Elvis and his firearm reboard.

Upon arriving in the nation's capital, Elvis decides he wants a doughnut.
While waiting for his order, he encounters some unsavory types who notice
his five big gold rings and three necklaces.

"That's some nice jewelry," one thug says.

"Yeah, and I aim to keep it," says Elvis, raising one leg of his bell bottoms
to reveal a snub-nosed revolver strapped to his right ankle.

At some point, Elvis has enough of this traveling alone stuff and heads
to Los Angeles, intent on returning to Washington with one of his Memphis
Mafia, namely Schilling.

Schilling, who first met Elvis playing football when he was twelve, is accus-
tomed to odd requests from the King. But this one is particularly weird because

Elvis is bent on going to Washington but won't say why. Still, because "you don't say no to Elvis," Schilling agrees to go, even though it means missing a day at his new job as an assistant editor at Paramount, which took him a year to get.

They book two first-class seats, but still need cash, and it's a Sunday night in 1970. No ATMs. Elvis's limousine driver, Sir Gerald, arranges for a check to be cashed at the Beverly Hilton Hotel. Schilling writes one for $500, which Elvis signs. Before they leave the house, Elvis, a history buff, takes his commemorative World War II Colt .45 revolver off the wall, bullets included, and stows it in his bag.

They cash the check and head for the airport. A small group of soldiers on leave from Vietnam for Christmas are on the same flight, and Elvis wanders back to coach to talk with one of them. Soon he is back up in first class, nudging Schilling, "Hey man, where's the $500?"

Schilling knows what's coming. Elvis is an unusually generous man. After learning that Schilling was a year old when his mother died, Elvis bought him the house in Hollywood so he would "always have a home." He still lives there today.

Okay, so Elvis is on the plane, asking for the $500.

"Elvis, we're going to Washington. That's all we've got," Schilling cautions.

"You don't understand. This man's been in Vietnam," Elvis says, then heads straight to coach and gives the soldier all their cash.

While he's back there, though, Elvis bumps into George Murphy, a song-and-dance man turned U.S. senator from California. They chat for awhile, and Elvis comes back to his seat asking for stationery, which a stewardess gets him. Elvis, who has written only three letters in his life, all while stationed with the Army in Germany, sits down to write the fourth, to the president of the United States.

"Dear Mr. President, First I would like to introduce myself. I am Elvis Presley."

In five pages, Elvis explains he loves his country and wants to give something back, and, not being "a member of the Establishment," believes he could reach some people the president can't if the president would only make him a federal agent at-large so he can help fight the war on drugs.

"Sir, I can and will be of any service that I can to help the country out…

I will be here for as long as it takes to get the credentials of a federal agent...
I would love to meet you just to say hello if you're not to [*sic*] busy. Respectfully, Elvis Presley."

He asks the president to give him a call at the Washington Hotel, Room
505, where he will be staying under the alias Jon Burrows (a part he played
in one of his movies). He provides six private numbers that any one of his
fans would have killed for, to his homes in Beverly Hills, Palm Springs, and
Memphis, as well as three lines for his manager, the Colonel.

The plane lands before dawn and they get in a limo Sir George had arranged before they left, which is a good thing because they have no money.
Elvis wants to personally deliver the letter to the White House. "I don't think
this is such a good idea," Schilling says, noting the hour.

Next scene: The limo pulls up to the northwest gate. Elvis gets out and
hands his letter to a security guard, who sizes up this guy in a cape. Schilling, realizing that in the dark Elvis looks a lot like Dracula, jumps out and
explains. The guard agrees to deliver the letter to the president. Elvis and
Schilling retire to the Washington Hotel to wait.

Early that morning, the letter finds its way to the desk of Dwight Chapin,
special assistant to the president. After a moment of head-scratching, he decides this meeting has to take place. Nixon had already tried to enlist Hollywood's help in fighting the war on drugs by approaching luminaries such as
Art Linkletter; Elvis is a definite step up.

So Chapin fires off a memo to Krogh, which Krogh dismisses as a practical joke. Deciding to play along, he calls the hotel, asks for Schilling, and is
impressed that Chapin has found someone to impersonate an Elvis lackey.

The more they talk, however, the more Krogh realizes this is no joke. He
shoots a memo to White House Chief of Staff H.R. Haldeman, suggesting
this could be a real boost for the drug war effort, which isn't going so well.

"You must be kidding," Haldeman scribbles in the margin before approv-
ing the request. The meeting is on.

Krogh, a big Elvis fan who "never went on a date without him," makes
sure he's in the room. "This is history," he thinks to himself.

White House schedulers find five minutes at 11:45 a.m. for Elvis, who, on
time for once, enters wearing tight purple velvet pants, the matching cape, a

white pointy collared shirt unbuttoned to reveal two enormous gold chains, and a belt buckle the size of Rhode Island.

At 12:30 p.m., the president meets the King. Elvis is taken by the eagles on the ceiling, and Krogh has to give him a little steer toward Nixon.

Soon, though, Elvis is pulling out pictures of his wife and baby, along with photos of assorted police and security badges he has collected over the years. The allotted five minutes pass, and they're still going, bonding over their lowly beginnings—poverty, challenging childhoods. They commiserate about the burdens of fame, what a hard gig Vegas is (which, weirdly, Nixon seems to know about). Elvis offers to help Nixon fight the war on drugs and restore respect for the flag. Nixon admires Elvis's big cuff links.

Then Elvis asks for what he's been after all along, a big gold badge to add to his collection, the thing that would make him a federal agent at-large for the Bureau of Narcotics and Dangerous Drugs. He had tried to get one from an agency head but was turned down, which is why he decided to go straight to Nixon.

"Can I be one?" Elvis asks his new friend.

"Well, federal agents at-large—we just don't have those," Nixon stammers.

"I'll look into it," Krogh promises.

Elvis is crestfallen, visibly wilted under the weight of all that gold, a man who could have anything—cars, women, houses—except the one thing he wants most.

Nixon takes one look at him and caves.

"Get him the badge."

Elvis is so excited he gives the president a big hug.

"Will you meet my friends?" he asks. Schilling and Sonny West, another of the Memphis Mafia who somehow showed up at the hotel that morning, are waiting in an outer office.

"Come on in, you guys," Elvis says cheerfully. He introduces his rather tall friends to Nixon, who sizes them up, hands on hips, and says, "You got a couple of big ones here, Elvis." They all pose for pictures.

Then it's time for gifts. Elvis pulls out the commemorative Colt 45 he had taken from his wall and carried into the White House, to the dismay of the Secret Service. ("We've got a little problem here; Elvis has brought a gun.") He presents it to Nixon.

The president moves over to a drawer of presents he keeps on the left side of his desk, its contents organized in order of increasing value: golf balls, pens, and paperweights in front, and way in the back, 16-karat gold pendants, lapel pins and brooches. Nixon peruses the drawer with Elvis peeking over his shoulder. He pulls out gifts for Schilling and West.

"You know, Mr. President, they have wives," Elvis says. Nixon goes back for more. Elvis motions to the 16-karat stuff. (Schilling's wife still has her brooch.)

It's time to go. The two men agree their meeting is best kept a secret. Nixon is sinking in the polls, Elvis is working on his comeback, and neither of their constituencies was likely to understand. The Leader of the Free World and the King of Rock 'n' Roll say their goodbyes.

For thirteen months, the secret is safe. Not a security guard or a staffer, not any of the men with whom Elvis shook hands or the women he kissed when aides took him down to the White House mess for lunch afterward breathe a word.

It wasn't until columnist Jack Anderson got hold of the galleys of a memoir by Deputy Narcotics Director John Finlator that the news broke: "Elvis Presley, the swivel-hipped singer, has been issued a federal narcotics badge."

Epilogue: Nixon resigned from office under threat of impeachment three and a half years later, on Aug. 9, 1974. When he was subsequently hospitalized with phlebitis, Elvis called to wish him well.

Elvis died at age forty-two on Aug. 16, 1977, of a heart attack; fourteen prescription drugs were found in his system. Nixon later noted in his friend's defense that those were not illegal drugs.

Schilling wrote a book, *Me and a Guy Named Elvis*.

Krogh wrote one too, but *The Day Elvis Met Nixon* is mostly pictures. He also spent four months in prison for his role in the White House plumbers scandal.

Chapin served nearly eight months and Haldeman eighteen months for their part in the Watergate coverup.

The commemorative gun is on display at the Nixon Library in Yorba Linda.

The badge, specially prepared by the Bureau of Narcotics and Dangerous Drugs with Elvis's name on it, hangs in his home in Graceland, on the Wall of Gold.

PAUL FEIG

And Now a Word from the Booth...

One day, when I was in the eleventh grade, I found out the football team was looking for a new announcer. And I was very excited.

Ever since I was little, I'd always fancied that I had a great announcer's voice. When I was seven, my dad gave me an old reel-to-reel tape recorder that quickly became my favorite possession. I'd spend afternoons talking into the mike, making up compelling in-the-field news dramas full of excitement and a testing of the human spirit.

"This is Paul Feig out in the battlefield where things look relatively calm after a... wait. What's that?"

Like all seven-year-old boys, I was very good at making the sound of (a) a bomb whistling down out of the sky, (b) that bomb exploding, (c) machine-gun fire, (d) single-shot handgun fire, (e) the rumbling of a squadron of airplanes coming into range, (f) those same airplanes dive-bombing, and (g) any other mechanical sounds that involved war, death, and destruction. At this moment that I was recording my out-in-the-battlefield drama, I was performing a combination of sounds (a) and (e).

"Oh, my God. It's a bomb. Run for your— " Sound (b).

"Oh, my God, they hit the tank! We've gotta get outta here!" Sounds (f),

---

This piece was originally published in Paul Feig's memoir, Kick Me.

(a), and (c).

"We're trapped! Quick. We've gotta get to that foxhole." Sounds (b) and (c), with a few (d)'s thrown in for added mayhem.

"Argh, they got Charlie! My leg! They got my leg!" Riff on (g).

End ominously by simply turning off the tape, simulating the destruction of the tape recorder. Let your audience ruminate on the horrors of war.

Repeat. Endlessly.

My dad's old reel-to-reel eventually led to my teenage purchase of a high-end cassette recorder and microphone, upon which I would perform my scripted radio shows in the sad privacy of my Steve Martin–poster-covered bedroom. By this time, as I was making my way through the wilds of high school, I had left the art of war to the professionals and was dabbling in two areas of sound pastiche—the detective show and Ed Sullivan impersonations. Granted, Ed Sullivan had been off the air for many years by the time I started imitating him, but since I'd heard John Byner do a funny impression of Ed on the local Canadian TV station we received in Detroit, I was convinced that I could do it, too. What I planned on doing with it was a mystery, but at that time, I somehow assumed the media were clamoring for a sixteen-year-old doing imitations of a guy my peers had no memory of.

"Right here on our show, how about a big hand for President Jimmy Carter!" I'd yell enthusiastically into the microphone, as I hunched my shoulders up in a Sullivan-esque fashion. I would then continue talking like Ed Sullivan as I moved the mike away from my mouth, saying things like, "All right, Mr. Carter, right this way," creating the impression that Ed was walking away. When the mike was as far as possible from my mouth I would go into my half-baked Jimmy Carter impression, which was simply a low-grade imitation of Dan Aykroyd's impersonation from *Saturday Night Live*. I'd talk in a Jimmy Carter–like manner, thanking Ed Sullivan as I moved the mike slowly back to my mouth, simulating the approach of our thirty-ninth president. "Well, thank you very much Mr. Sullivan. My fellow Americans, today I'd like to talk to you about… peanuts." Neither my impressions nor my material were very good, but my mike technique was outstanding. And so was my growing resolve that I belonged on the radio.

So, in my junior year, when the opportunity to be the announcer for the football team arose, I jumped at it with a gusto unseen in our school regarding anything except trying to get out the front door after the last-period bell. I marched down to the office of our vice principal, Mr. Randell, to offer up my services. Mr. Randell was a nice guy who'd received a very bad rap at our school. Not only did he have the misfortune to be our vice principal, a thankless job that invites all the abuse that students are too afraid to aim at the actual principal, but he was also cursed with the misfortune of looking vaguely froglike. In retrospect, he really didn't look like anything other than an overweight guy with small features, a large fleshy face, and an underbite. But in the hands of our perennially cruel student body, whose main goal was striking out at any and all authority figures, Mr. Randell's features all added up to the poor guy being assigned the nickname "Toad."

I sat down in Mr. Randell's office and informed him of the great fortune that was about to befall both him and the football team.

"Mr. Randell, I want to be the football announcer."

"Oh, really? Excellent. I've always thought you had a good voice, ever since I saw you perform 'The Parrot Sketch' at assembly last year. I'm quite a *Monty Python* fan, too, you know." No, I didn't know, but I have to say that the *Monty Python* comedy troupe's cool quotient took a near-fatal hit with that revelation.

"Oh, really?" I said, not wanting to let any negative energy get in the way of my being offered the announcing job. "They're the greatest."

"They certainly are," he said, chuckling to himself, his mind taking a brief trip through their repertoire. Had he been my age, I could have easily launched us into a one-hour marathon of reciting sketches word-for-word, but, since befriending the vice principal would only result in even more torment from my peers, I simply chuckled, too, and stuck to the matter at hand.

"So… is anybody else up for the job?" I asked.

"No, surprisingly. I thought we'd have a few more students interested in it," he said, a hint of sadness in his voice. "Do you know a lot about football?'

Without missing a beat, I looked him in the eye and said, "Yes."

I knew nothing about football. I mean, I knew that announcers always said stuff like, "He's at the twenty, he's at the ten, he's at the five, TOUCH-DOWN!" I could do that quite well, having loudly practiced it over and over the previous evening in my room until my father came in to tell me that he and my mother couldn't hear the television. To me, being able to describe what I was seeing on the field would be a nonstop performance of making jokes, doing funny voices, and keeping he audience rapt as I called out the action of an extra-point kick. "There's the snap. The kicker runs up and... OOOOHHH! IT'S GOOOOOOOOOOD!" What more did you need to know about football than that? Nothing. At least not in my book.

"Have you ever been an announcer at a football game before?" Mr. Randell asked.

"Whenever my father and I watch football, I do the play-by-play commentary along with the TV." It was scaring me how effortlessly the lies were coming out of my mouth. My father and I never watched football together, and on the few occasions that I would turn on a game, my "announcing" the play-by-play consisted of my simply repeating any of the announcer's phrases that seemed fun to say. Phrases like "Ooo, that's *gotta* hurt" and "Oh, brother, can you believe *that?*" were the extent to which I had ever announced a football game. But in my head, at this moment, that qualified me for a great career in the announcer's booth.

This was not a new way of thinking for me. Unfortunately.

See, ever since I was a kid, I was always convinced that if the pressure was really on, I could do anything. I always imagined a scenario in which I was being held captive by some enemy soldiers who'd have a gun at my head. One of them would say, "If you can play Mozart on this piano, right now, we won't kill you. If you can't, you're dead." And then, because it was a life-or-death situation, even though I had no idea how to play the piano, somehow I'd magically be able to play Mozart. I don't know why I thought this. Probably because there had been a lot of stories on *That's Incredible!* lately about mothers who, when their children were pinned under cars, suddenly developed superhuman strength and were able to lift the autos with one hand. So I guess I figured that if a housewife can lift a car, I could play a sonata. And at the very least, I had to be able to announce a stupid football game.

Mr. Randell gave me the job and told me my first gig was that Friday night. I left his office very excited. I foresaw great things in my future. From the Chippewa Valley Big Reds football games, it would be a straight shot to taking over for George Kell and announcing the Detroit Tigers baseball games. From there, it was a quick stroll to *Wide World of Sports*, where I would be standing in the field with Jim McKay, announcing downhill skiing as I wore my supercool yellow announcer's sportcoat with the regal WWOS patch on the breast pocket. I knew I could say "and the agony of defeat" as well as anyone else out there. Big things were on the horizon, and I owed it all to a guy named Toad.

I spent the next few days practicing in my room and in my car. I didn't bother to read any books about football because I had convinced myself that I'd have a sidekick who would take care of all the details of the game. Every sportscaster has a color commentator, and I knew they weren't just going to stick me in the booth alone. Even Mr. Randell had said there'd be people up there to help me. So what was the point of trying to fill my head with a bunch of mundane rules? Leave that stuff to the support team, I thought. I was there to entertain and enthrall.

My father was quite surprised when I told him about my new job.

"*You're* going to be a football announcer?" he asked in the same supportive tone he'd used the time I told him I wanted to ask my school's head cheerleader to the prom.

"Yeah, they gave me the job."

"But you don't know anything about football."

"Sure, I do," I said, indignant.

"Well, you sure as hell didn't learn it from me. I can't stand the game."

It was true. My whole family had a strange aversion to sports. Except for my grandmother, who was fanatical about the Tigers. She always referred to them as "my Tigers" and would sooner give up her Social Security checks than miss watching a game on TV. According to her, she was always "suffering" along with her Tigers whenever they had a bad season. I've always wondered if it was my grandmother who made professional sports so unattractive to the rest of us. It's like being around alcoholics. The more they get into booze, the less cool booze seems. Being around sports enthusiasts makes me want to push an amendment through Congress banning all professional sports from our culture. The sight of people either celebrating a victory of their local sports team or getting really upset because their team didn't win has always depressed the hell out of me. I don't begrudge anybody for getting excited about the fortunes of the team they've decided to follow. It's just when it really seems to affect their happiness and satisfaction with their lives that it makes me nervous. I've become enthused over certain playoff series and championships whenever my old Detroit teams were involved, but it was because I no longer lived in Detroit and was homesick for the Midwest. By living in Los Angeles and still rooting for Detroit, I was somehow reconnecting with my past, cheering not for the men on my team but for the place in which I grew up. And if my home team lost, especially to Los Angeles, it was as if my place of birth had failed, thus causing me to be a dud, a second-rate citizen put in his place by the bigger, hipper town in which he was now living. In these moments, sports were simply a conduit through which my self-worth passed. And so, for displaced people in this country, I can understand the allure of following your favorite sports team.

But if you're living in the town that your team's in and you're going nuts all the time, then something's gotta be missing from your life.

The night of the football game arrived. I got in my car and nervously headed over to the football field. I had spent the week imagining what my debut was going to be like. I had never been to one of my school's football games, except in my sophomore year when I spent the homecoming game standing by the fence pining over Tina Jenkins, a pretty cheerleader whom I was planning to ask to the homecoming dance on the very day *of* the homecoming dance. And on that day, the announcer's booth had been a faraway and mystical place to me, a small wooden house up at the top of the bleachers. I tried to remember what the announcer for the team had sounded like but couldn't recall ever hearing one. I remember hearing the occasional announcement of a player's name and the score, but beyond that my memory had failed me. I kept telling myself that, despite what the past announcers had done with their jobs, I was going to bring a whole new level of entertainment to the proceedings. I envisioned the people in the stands laughing uproariously at my humorous side comments. I couldn't really think of what any of these humorous side comments might be, but I was sure that in the heat of the moment, I'd be playing that crowd the same way I'd be bashing out Bach's *Goldberg Variations* if a gun were pointed at my head.

I pulled into the school parking lot, which was crowded with cars and families heading over to the field. Seeing them, I started to get a little nervous, but quickly made myself feel better with the realization that these people were all in for quite a treat. They didn't notice me now, but after the game they'd be mobbing me, shaking my hand and saying "Funny, funny stuff," and "I never enjoyed football until tonight. Thank you." The night air was cold and I hadn't worn a warm enough jacket. However, I knew that once I got up into that booth, everything would be great. I had seen the inside of an announcer's booth on an episode of *The Odd Couple*, when Oscar was doing play-by-play with Howard Cosell. The clean white room with the bank of recording and sound equipment against the back wall. The microphones mounted on stands, sitting in front of you on a white counter. The window that revealed your sound engineer, to whom you would confidently nod as you were coming to the end of a commentary so that he could deftly hit the music button just as your story reached its crescendo. I couldn't wait for the game to start and my career to be launched.

I got to the bleachers and looked up at the announcer's booth. I wasn't quite sure how to get up there. I scanned around and saw that there was a rickety wooden staircase leading up to it behind the bleachers. I took a look back at the crowds who were heading to their seats. Moms and dads and little brothers and grandfathers were all decked out in red and white with the politically incorrect logo of our school's screaming Big Red Indian emblazoned on their sweatshirts and jackets. These were the football regulars, people who came out every weekend night to watch their sons and neighbors clash on the gridiron. The world of high school sports and its supporters was as foreign to me as the backstage politics of the drama club was to these people who were now packing into the stands. Would they accept me and my new take on their world? Or would my vocal antics prove too revolutionary for them? Did they want their football straight up and sober, or had they been longing for an unorthodox messiah who would challenge the very way they enjoyed their sport? Unsure, I turned and headed up the stairs to the announcer's booth, the butterflies in my stomach doubling with each creaky wooden step I trod. Whether they were ready or not, this crowd was just minutes away from the new world order, and I was going to be standing at the helm.

I got to the top and opened the door. I was immediately shocked. The booth was nothing like the one in *The Odd Couple*. It was nothing like where the announcers sat during *Monday Night Football*. It wasn't even as nice as the shed in our backyard. It was basically a big wooden box that looked like it had been assembled by the Little Rascals. There were no lights in it, it was made entirely out of plywood and particleboard, and it had no glass windows. The counter where the mike stood was basically a couple of two-by-fours that had been nailed together and then hastily pounded into the wall. A bunch of men in their late forties and early fifties were standing around, wrapped in heavy coats and wearing aviator glasses. They all seemed to have mustaches. When they saw me, they gave me a look.

"Where the hell have you been? You're the announcer, right?" said the biggest mustache man. These guys all looked like the deer hunters who always came into my dad's store to buy bright orange clothes that were supposed to prevent them from drunkenly shooting each other out in the forest.

"Uh, yeah, Mr. Randell told me to get here at seven. I thought I was early."

"No, kid, the game *starts* at seven. Christ, I thought one of us was gonna have to announce it." He shook his head as if my misinterpretation of the time had reaffirmed everything he's ever believed about how the new generation was going to drag the country into anarchy through its stupidity and laziness. "Well, get over here so we can tell you what you've gotta do."

The guy motioned for me to sit on a metal folding chair behind the microphone. The "window" in front of the mike was simply a large, long rectangle that had been cut out of the front of the booth. The wind was blowing and it was freezing. I realized that my lack of a warm jacket was now going to result in a very uncomfortable evening. I sat down on the ancient metal folding chair and felt a shock of cold penetrate the back of my jeans and immediately freeze my ass. The mustache guys all surrounded me, leaning in over my shoulders and exhaling clouds of breath that bore the distinct scent of Dewar's and Old Milwaukee.

"Okay, here's the team's roster. Jake will be calling out the numbers of the players who make the plays. When he does, you look on the sheet, find the names if you don't know them already, and then make the announcement. You announce the tackler first and then you announce whoever assisted in the tackle. Got it?"

My head was immediately swimming. The tone of voice the guy was using was not the reassuring voice of my mother or my teachers or anyone who was planning on patiently guiding me through an unfamiliar experience. These were a bunch of older guys the likes of which I had seen on construction sites and in VFW halls, the types of guys who I imagined had beaten up hippies in the sixties, guys who supported the Vietnam War and thought the only reason we lost it was because we didn't drop the bomb on the VC. In short, the kind of guys who would have no patience for a teenage male who didn't know anything about the sport of football. I felt a hot flash of impending failure shoot up the back of my neck.

"Do you *got* it?" he repeated impatiently. I could feel him trying to prevent himself from calling me "you little sissy boy."

Completely intimidated, I nodded yes, not having a clue how anybody could ever figure out who tackled whom, let alone be able to decipher information as obtuse as who "assisted" in the tackle. But I tried to keep a positive attitude.

"And then I do all the play-by-play, too, right?" I asked.

They looked at me as if I had just announced I wanted to blow them all.

"Play-by-play? Who do you think you are? Howard goddamn Cosell?" This, of course, got a big laugh out of them all, and I immediately had the feeling these guys were quite capable of reenacting Ned Beatty's "squeal like a pig" scene from *Deliverance*. "You don't do play-by-play over the loudspeaker at a game. Jesus Christ, you'd drive everybody crazy."

The evening was getting worse by the second. I had been in the booth for less than two minutes and already I knew that I never wanted to do this again. The unpleasant, oppressive sound of the marching band drifted up through the open window in front of me, carried along on an icy wind that made my chest tense up. I felt the beginnings of uncontrollable shivering starting to take root in my torso, and I knew that speaking was going to become harder and harder.

"Man, I should've brought my coat. It's cold in here," I said, somehow hoping my discomfort would be a legitimate cause for dismissal.

"Christ Almighty, you didn't bring a *coat*?" said the main mustache guy. "Where the hell did you think you were gonna be? In some goddamn hotel suite?"

Sort of, I thought. I definitely didn't envision that I'd be in a killin' shack that some sadist had dropped on top of the bleachers.

The guys all exchanged incredulous looks, and it was quite clear that we were not going to be best friends by the end of the evening. And because of that, I didn't expect the magnanimous gesture that happened next.

"Pete, give the kid your coat."

As cold as I was, the one thing I knew, with all certainty, was that I didn't want Pete's coat. I didn't want to place anything on my body that belonged to any of these guys, let alone something they were wearing at that very moment. I felt panic rise up in me. It was the same feeling I'd had the time I went camping with a friend's family and forgot my toothbrush and his mother said, "Well, why don't you just use Dave's toothbrush? He doesn't have any germs." I was able to beg my way out of having to use Dave's toothbrush by producing a pack of Dentine chewing gum. However, tonight, Pete's coat was unfortunately inescapable.

"Oh no, that's okay. I'm not that cold," I said, trying to sound suddenly warm.

"Oh, fer Christ sake, put it on. If you start shivering, you're no good to anyone up here."

And with that, Pete, the biggest guy who had the dirtiest hair and the greasiest pants I'd seen this side of a pit-crew member at a stock car race, peeled off his plaid hunting jacket and handed it to me. There's a smell you encounter on the occasions when you get into a chain smoker's car on a rainy, humid day and see that his dog, who has just spent the last couple of hours running through a stagnant swamp, is in the backseat. Well, that was the smell I *wish* I was partaking in when Pete's coat came near my nose. In order to have a stinkier coat, Pete would had to have died and been buried in it. I felt faint, but knew I didn't really have a leg to stand on when it came to convincing these guys I was just joking about being cold. And so, like a man being handed the gun after the fifth click in a game of Russian roulette, I resignedly took Pete's jacket and put it on.

Before I could fully immerse myself in the wave of nausea that was beginning to overtake me, I saw the cheerleaders head out onto the field with an eight-foot-wide hoop that had been covered with paper. On the paper was painted "Go Big Reds" in big, poorly spaced letters. As the cheerleaders brought the hoop out, the crowd started to cheer. Two of the cheerleaders took the hoop into my school's end zone and held it up parallel to the goalpost. The other cheerleaders ran out around the hoop and started doing their uncontrol- lable kick-and-leap-into-the-air moves that cheerleaders seemed to do inces- santly. The main mustache guy poked me in the shoulder blade and pointed to the list of players.

"All right, it's time to introduce the team. Once the band does its fanfare, you welcome everyone to the game and then introduce the players. As you say each name, they'll run out and break through the hoop. Keep the pace up or it'll take too long."

More prophetic words were never spoken.

I looked down at the list of players' names.

It's here that I need to give you a small factoid about the metro Detroit area. Detroit has one of the largest Polish communities in the country. And a lot of Polish Americans went to my school. And the minute I looked at that list, I realized that every Polish kid in our school was on the football team. Sitting on the counter before me was an endless list of names, none of which were less than ten letters long and all with a definite shortage of vowels. These were names that looked more like "words" a toddler with a bucket of plas- tic consonants would construct than the proud family monikers of onetime immigrants who fought and struggled to come to our country. Names like Krymnikowski and Pfekotovsky stared out at me like a street map of Warsaw. Before I could even consult with my mustachioed cohorts, the band hit its warbly fanfare and three guys kicked my chair.

"You're on!"

I nervously clicked on the mike and said, "Ladies and gentlemen, welcome to tonight's football game." Even though I was talking into a microphone, I couldn't for the life of me hear myself over the loudspeaker. I heard the crowd cheer. I could only deduce that either they could hear me or a car had just been raffled off. "Is this on?" I asked the guys. Before I could look back at them, I heard someone in the stands yell "Yes," followed by much derisive laughter. It was then that I realized I didn't even know the name of the other team. I guess part of me had assumed that someone would have written up this kind of copy for me so that all I'd have to do was read it out loud and be amusing. I put my hand over the mike and turned to the guys. "What's the name of the other team?"

The men rolled their eyes like teenage girls, making open-mouthed faces that said in an unheard Valley Girl voice, "Oh my God, I can't believe you don't know that." The main guy recovered quickly and yelled at me, "The Cougars! The goddamn Warren High Cougars!"

I moved my hand and said into the mike, "Tonight's game is between the Warren High School Cougars and the Chippewa Valley Big Reds!" The crowd cheered again, and it was at that moment that I realized how easy it was to get a rise out of a football crowd. Momentarily energized, I continued. "And now, let's meet the players!"

The band hit another fanfare and then the snare player did a drumroll. It was all very exciting except for the fact that I now knew I had to take on that list of names. The cheerleaders tensed their grip on the hoop. I could see the players standing in the back of the end zone, lined up, waiting to hear their names, the first player setting himself to sprint forward and burst through the large paper ring. I looked back at my support team.

"Just read the list. Read it in order," the main guy said to me, with a don't-screw-this-up look on his face.

I looked at the first name on the list and dove in. "Mike Krack...eye... now...ski." And indeed, Mike Krackinowski ran up and burst through the hoop as the crowd cheered.

All except for one angry voice from the stands.

"It's Krack-*in*-owski!"

I looked out the window. Sitting two rows from the booth was a very angry mother with a large beehive hairdo wearing a Valvoline windbreaker. She was glaring at me. Her look was so intense that I was momentarily stunned. I felt a finger poke me in the ribs.

"Go on! Keep reading!"

I looked back down at the list. "Bob Stan...zow...line...insky." And out ran Bob.

"It's Stanzo-lin-*nine*-sky!" Another angry parent, this time right under the booth's window, was glaring at me. I felt another prickly wave of panic run up the back of my neck. It was the panic of being trapped, of no escape, of knowing that there was nowhere to go but down. These two names had taken me about twenty seconds to get out, and the pace of the players running out of the hoop was not at all what the inventors of the Hoop Introduction Industry had in mind when they came up with it. Just go back to the list, I told myself. Go back to the list.

"Steven Lip...ow.........rank...in........flaanski." Another player ran through the hoop. Another angry parent yelled at me. Another wave of prickly panic shot up the back of my neck.

It took me five minutes to get through the first half of the list. The crowd became a mixture of angry parents who felt I was destroying the dignity of both their football-playing sons and their families' heritages, and students who found the whole spectacle funnier by the second. The football team was staring up at the announcer's booth, the coaches were staring up at the announcer's booth, and the cheerleaders were staring up at the announcer's booth. Each name I was able to mangle brought a less enthusiastic player through the hoop. Through my mispronunciations, I was single-handedly defeating our football team more effectively than any rival school ever could. The fact that their team's announcer didn't really know who any of them were seemed to put the whole idea of their participation in organized sports on trial. Maybe they weren't as good as they thought they were. Maybe football wasn't the be-all and end-all of their lives. Whatever they were thinking, they knew that there was at least one guy in the school who couldn't care less that they could throw or catch a football, that they could run fast and dodge their way through other guys and knock their fellow players down. And that guy was now in charge of the school's sound system.

Finally, the main mustache guy said, "Oh, for fuck's sake," and grabbed the microphone. He snatched the list of names from me and started reading them off quickly. The crowd cheered at my dismissal and the football team ran en masse through the hoop and onto the field. The opposing team ran out and the referees blew their whistles. The mustache guy slammed the list down in front of me, clicked off the mike and said, "Jesus Christ, where the hell did you learn to read, anyway?"

"Uh..." I said, quite sure it wasn't the answer he wanted to hear, "at this school."

The rest of the evening was a blur. They spoon-fed me the names of the tacklers and the assistants, and I said them and froze my ass off and never got used to the horrible smell of Pete's jacket. When the game was over, no bonding had occurred between me and the Green Berets up in the booth. They gave me a look that said "don't come back" when the game was finally over, and I hastily made my way down the rickety stairs and sprinted to the safety of my car before the crowds could see me.

That Monday, I was so humiliated that I avoided Mr. Randell at every turn, sure that he had heard about my disastrous job behind the mike. And when the next Friday rolled around, I very happily stayed far away from the football field, sure that restraining orders had been issued to keep me away from the announcer's booth. I never felt more relieved in my life to not be somewhere than I did that Friday night and enjoyed an evening of *SCTV* watching and junk food eating with my next-door neighbor Craig.

The following Monday, Mr. Randell called me into his office.

"So," he said, with a very disappointed look on his face, "where were you Friday night? You missed the game."

I was shocked. I couldn't even conceive of anyone's expecting that I would have returned to the scene of my failure. And now, completely embarrassed, I just couldn't bring myself to admit to him that I assumed I had been fired.

"Uh... I thought it was gonna rain Friday night and that they were gonna call the game off, so I didn't go."

I sat there for a fifteen-minute lecture on responsibility and what it means for a man to keep his word, basically the same one my dad had given me during Little League. I nodded and looked remorseful the entire time, taking solace in the knowledge that if this was the hair shirt I would have to put on in order to never have to attend another football game again, it was well worth it. And it was still more pleasurable to wear than Pete's coat.

At the end of his tirade, he gave me a very fatherly look and shocked me by saying, "So, I can count on you to show up and announce the game again this Friday?"

I looked at the man and realized that drastic measures had to be taken to escape this Sartre-like situation that the job of being our school's football announcer had turned out to be.

"Mr. Randell," I said, apologetically, "I'm afraid I can't announce the football games anymore. Friday nights I have to go shopping with my mom."

F. SCOTT FITZGERALD

Pat Hobby and Orson Welles

I

"Who's this Welles?" Pat asked of Louie, the studio bookie. "Every time I pick up a paper they got about this Welles."

"You know, he's that beard," explained Louie.

"Sure, I know he's that beard, you couldn't miss that. But what credit's he got? What's he done to draw 150 grand a picture?" What indeed? Had he, like Pat, been in Hollywood over twenty years? Did he have credits that would knock your eye out, extending up to—well, up to five years ago when Pat's credits had begun to be few and far between?

"Listen—they don't last long," said Louie consolingly, "We've seen 'em come and we've seen 'em go. Hey, Pat?"

Yes, but meanwhile those who had toiled in the vineyard through the heat of the day were lucky to get a few weeks at three-fifty. Men who had once had wives and Filipinos and swimming pools.

"Maybe it's the beard," said Louie. "Maybe you and I should grow a beard. My father had a beard but it never got him off Grand Street."

The gift of hope had remained with Pat through his misfortunes—and the valuable alloy of his hope was proximity. Above all things, one must stick around, one must be there when the glazed, tired mind of the producer grappled with the question, "Who?" So presently Pat wandered out of the drugstore, and crossed the street to the lot that was home.

As he passed through the side entrance an unfamiliar studio policeman stood in his way.

"Everybody in the front entrance now."

"I'm Hobby, the writer," Pat said.

The Cossack was unimpressed.

"Got your card?"

"I'm between pictures. But I've got an engagement with Jack Berners."

"Front gate."

As he turned away Pat thought savagely: "Lousy Keystone Cop!" In his mind he shot it out with him. *Plunk!* the stomach. *Plunk! plunk! plunk!*

At the main entrance, too, there was a new face.

"Where's Ike?" Pat demanded.

"Ike's gone."

"Well, it's all right, I'm Pat Hobby. Ike always passes me."

"That's why he's gone," said the guardian blandly. "Who's your business with?"

Pat hesitated. He hated to disturb a producer.

"Call Jack Berners's office," he said. "Just speak to his secretary."

After a minute the man turned from the phone. "What about?" he said.

"About a picture."

He waited for an answer.

"She wants to know what picture?"

"To hell with it," said Pat disgustedly. "Look—call Louie Griebel. What's all this about?"

"Orders from Mr. Kasper," said the clerk. "Last week a visitor from Chicago fell in the wind machine—Hello. Mr. Louie Griebel?"

"I'll talk to him," said Pat, taking the phone.

"I can't do nothing, Pat," mourned Louie. "I had trouble getting my boy in this morning. Some twerp from Chicago fell in the wind machine."

"What's that got to do with me?" demanded Pat vehemently.

He walked, a little faster than his wont, along the studio wall to the point where it joined the back lot. There was a guard there but there were always people passing to and fro and he joined one of the groups. Once inside he would see Jack and have himself excepted from this absurd ban. Why, he had known this lot when the first shacks were rising on it, when this was considered the edge of the desert.

"Sorry mister, you with this party?"

"I'm in a hurry," said Pat. "I've lost my card."

"Yeah? Well, for all I know you may be a plainclothes man." He held open a copy of a photo magazine under Pat's nose, "I wouldn't let you in even if you told me you was this here Orson Welles."

II

There is an old Chaplin picture about a crowded streetcar where the entrance of one man at the rear forces another out in front. A similar image came into Pat's mind in the ensuing days whenever he thought of Orson Welles. Welles was in; Hobby was out. Never before had the studio been barred to Pat, and though Welles was on another lot it seemed as if his large body, pushing in brashly from nowhere, had edged Pat out the gate.

"Now where do you go?" Pat thought. He had worked in the other studios but they were not his. At this studio he never felt unemployed—in recent times of stress he had eaten property food on its stages, half a cold lobster during a scene from *The Divine Miss Carstairs*; he had often slept on the sets and last winter made use of a Chesterfield overcoat from the costume department. Orson Welles had no business edging him out of this. Orson Welles belonged with the rest of the snobs back in New York.

On the third day he was frantic with gloom. He had sent note after note to Jack Berners and even asked Louie to intercede—now word came that Jack had left town. There were so few friends left. Desolate, he stood in front of the automobile gate with a crowd of staring children, feeling that he had reached the end at last.

A great limousine rolled out, in the back of which Pat recognized the great overstuffed Roman face of Harold Marcus. The car rolled toward the children and, as one of them ran in front of it, slowed down. The old man spoke into the tube and the car halted. He leaned out blinking.

"Is there no policeman here?" he asked of Pat.

"No, Mr. Marcus," said Pat quickly. "There should be. I'm Pat Hobby, the writer—could you give me a lift down the street?"

It was unprecedented—it was an act of desperation—but Pat's need was great.

Mr. Marcus looked at him closely.

"Oh yes, I remember you," he said. "Get in."

He might possibly have meant get up in front with the chauffeur. Pat compromised by opening one of the little seats. Mr. Marcus was one of the most powerful men in the whole picture world. He did not occupy himself with production any longer. He spent most of his time rocking from coast to coast on fast trains, merging and launching, launching and merging, like a much-divorced woman.

"Some day those children'll get hurt."

"Yes, Mr. Marcus," agreed Pat heartily. "Mr. Marcus— "

"They ought to have a policeman there."

"Yes, Mr. Marcus. Mr. Marcus— "

"Hm-m-m!" said Mr. Marcus. "Where do you want to be dropped?"

Pat geared himself to work fast.

"Mr. Marcus, when I was your press agent— "

"I know," said Mr. Marcus. "You wanted a ten dollar a week raise."

"What a memory!" cried Pat in gladness. "What a memory! But Mr. Marcus, now I don't want anything at all."

"This is a miracle."

"I've got modest wants, see, and I've saved enough to retire."

He thrust his shoes slightly forward under a hanging blanket. The Chesterfield coat effectively concealed the rest.

"That's what I'd like," said Mr. Marcus gloomily. "A farm—with chickens. Maybe a little nine-hole course. Not even a stock ticker."

"I want to retire, but different," said Pat earnestly. "Pictures have been my life. I want to watch them grow and grow— "

Mr. Marcus groaned.

"Till they explode," he said. "Look at Fox! I cried for him." He pointed to his eyes, "Tears!"

Pat nodded very sympathetically.

"I want only one thing." From the long familiarity he went into the foreign locution. "I should go on the lot anytime. From nothing. Only to be there. Should bother nobody. Only help a little from nothing if any young person wants advice."

"See Berners," said Marcus.

"He said see you."

"Then you did want something." Marcus smiled. "All right, all right by me. Where do you get off now?"

"Could you write me a pass?" Pat pleaded. "Just a word on your card?"

"I'll look into it," said Mr. Marcus. "Just now I've got things on my mind. I'm going to a luncheon." He sighed profoundly. "They want I should meet this new Orson Welles that's in Hollywood."

Pat's heart winced. There it was again—that name, sinister and remorseless, spreading like a dark cloud over all his skies.

"Mr. Marcus," he said so sincerely that his voice trembled, "I wouldn't be surprised if Orson Welles is the biggest menace that's come to Hollywood for years. He gets 150 grand a picture and I wouldn't be surprised if he was so radical that you had to have all new equipment and start all over again like you did with sound in 1928."

"Oh my God!" groaned Mr. Marcus.

"And me," said Pat, "all I want is a pass and no money—to leave things as they are."

Mr. Marcus reached for his card case.

III

To those grouped together under the name "talent," the atmosphere of a studio is not unfailingly bright—one fluctuates too quickly between high hope and grave apprehension. Those few who decide things are happy in their work and sure that they are worthy of their hire—the rest live in a mist of doubt as to when their vast inadequacy will be disclosed.

Pat's psychology was, oddly, that of the masters, and for the most part he was unworried even though he was off salary. But there was one large fly in the ointment—for the first time in his life he began to feel a loss of identity. Due to reasons that he did not quite understand, though it might have been traced to his conversation, a number of people began to address him as "Orson."

Now, to lose one's identity is a careless thing in any case. But to lose it to an enemy, or at least to one who has become scapegoat for our misfortunes— that is a hardship. Pat was *not* Orson. Any resemblance must be faint and far-fetched and he was aware of the fact. The final effect was to make him, in that regard, something of an eccentric.

"Pat," said Joe the barber, "Orson was in here today and asked me to trim his beard."

"I hope you set fire to it," said Pat.

"I did," Joe winked at waiting customers over a hot towel. "He asked for a singe so I took it all off. Now his face is as bald as yours. In fact you look a bit alike."

This was the morning the kidding was so ubiquitous that, to avoid it, Pat lingered in Mario's bar across the street. He was not drinking—at the bar, that is, for he was down to his last thirty cents, but he refreshed himself frequently from a half-pint in his back pocket. He needed the stimulus for he had to make a touch presently and he knew that money was easier to borrow when one didn't have an air of urgent need.

His quarry, Jeff Boldini, was in an unsympathetic state of mind. He too was an artist, albeit a successful one, and a certain great lady of the screen had just burned him up by criticizing a wig he had made for her. He told the story to Pat at length and the latter waited until it was all out before broaching his request.

"No soap," said Jeff. "Hell, you never paid me back what you borrowed last month."

"But I got a job now," lied Pat. "This is just to tide me over. I start tomor-row."

"If they don't give the job to Orson Welles," said Jeff humorously.

Pat's eyes narrowed but he managed to utter a polite, borrower's laugh.

"Hold it," said Jeff. "You know I think you look like him?"

"Yeah."

"Honest. Anyhow, I could make you look like him. I could make you a beard that would be his double."

"I wouldn't be his double for fifty grand."

With his head on one side, Jeff regarded Pat.

"I could," he said. "Come on in to my chair and let me see."

"Like hell."

"Come on. I'd like to try it. You haven't got anything to do. You don't work till tomorrow."

"I don't want a beard."

"It'll come off."

"I don't want it."

"It won't cost you anything. In fact I'll be paying *you*—I'll loan you the ten smackers if you'll let me make you a beard."

Half an hour later Jeff looked at his completed work.

"It's perfect," he said. "Not only the beard but the eyes and everything."

"All right. Now take it off," said Pat moodily.

"What's the hurry? That's a fine muff. That's a work of art. We ought to put a camera on it. Too bad you're working tomorrow—they're using a dozen beards out on Sam Jones's set and one of them went to jail in a homo raid. I bet with that muff you could get the job."

It was weeks since Pat had heard the word "job" and he could not himself say how he managed to exist and eat. Jeff saw the light in his eye.

"What say? Let me drive you out there just for fun," pleaded Jeff. "I'd like to see if Sam could tell it was a phony muff."

"I'm a writer, not a ham."

"Come on! Nobody would never know you back of that. And you'd draw another ten bucks."

As they left the makeup department Jeff lingered behind a minute. On a strip of cardboard he crayoned the name Orson Welles in large block letters. And outside, without Pat's notice, he stuck it in the windshield of his car.

He did not go directly to the back lot. Instead he drove not too swiftly up the main studio street. In front of the administration building he stopped on the pretext that the engine was missing, and almost in no time a small but definitely interested crowd began to gather. But Jeff's plans did not include stopping anywhere long, so he hopped in and they started on a tour around the commissary.

"Where are we going?" demanded Pat.

He had already made one nervous attempt to tear the beard from him, but to his surprise it did not come away.

He complained of this to Jeff.

"Sure," Jeff explained. "That's made to last. You'll have to soak it off."

The car paused momentarily at the door of the commissary. Pat saw blank eyes staring at him and he stared back at them blankly from the rear seat.

"You'd think I was the only beard on the lot," he said gloomily.

"You can sympathize with Orson Welles."

"To hell with him."

This colloquy would have puzzled those without, to whom he was nothing less than the real McCoy.

Jeff drove on slowly up the street. Ahead of them a little group of men were walking—one of them, turning, saw the car and drew the attention of the others to it. Whereupon the most elderly member of the party threw up his arms in what appeared to be a defensive gesture, and plunged to the sidewalk as the car went past.

"My God, did you see that?" exclaimed Jeff. "That was Mr. Marcus."

He came to a stop. An excited man ran up and put his head in the car window.

"Mr. Welles, our Mr. Marcus has had a heart attack. Can we use your car to get him to the infirmary?"

Pat stared. Then very quickly he opened the door on the other side and dashed from the car. Not even the beard could impede his streamlined flight. The policeman at the gate, not recognizing the incarnation, tried to have words with him but Pat shook him off with the ease of a triple-threat back and never paused till he reached Mario's bar.

Three extras with beards stood at the rail, and with relief Pat merged himself into their corporate whiskers. With a trembling hand he took the hard-earned ten dollar bill from his pocket.

"Set 'em up," he cried hoarsely. "Every muff has a drink on me."

JONATHAN FRANZEN

Two Ponies

In May 1970, a few nights after National Guardsmen killed four student protesters at Kent State University, my father and my brother Tom started fighting. They weren't fighting about the Vietnam War, which both of them opposed. The fight was probably about a lot of different things at once. But the immediate issue was Tom's summer job. He was a good artist, with a meticulous nature, and my father had encouraged him (you could even say forced him) to choose a college from a short list of schools with strong programs in architecture. Tom had deliberately chosen the most distant of these schools, Rice University, and he'd just returned from his second year in Houston, where his adventures in late-sixties youth culture were pushing him toward majoring in film studies, not architecture. My father, however, had found him a plum summer job with Sverdrup & Parcel, the big engineering firm in St. Louis, whose senior partner, General Leif Sverdrup, had been an Army Corps of Engineers hero in the Philippines. It couldn't have been easy for my father, who was shy about asking favors, to pull the requisite strings at Sverdrup. But the office gestalt was hawkish and buzz-cut and generally inimical to bell-bottomed, lefty film-studies majors, and Tom didn't want to be there.

Up in the bedroom that he and I shared, the windows were open and the

---

This piece was first published in Jonathan Franzen's personal history, The Discomfort Zone.

air had the stuffy wooden house smell that came out every spring. I preferred the make-believe no-smell of air conditioning, but my mother, whose subjective experience of temperature was notably consistent with low gas and electricity bills, claimed to be a devotee of "fresh air," and the windows often stayed open until Memorial Day.

On my night table was the *Peanuts Treasury*, a large, thick hardcover compilation of daily and Sunday funnies by Charles M. Schulz. My mother had given it to me the previous Christmas, and I'd been rereading it at bedtime ever since. Like most of the nation's ten-year-olds, I had a private, intense relationship with Snoopy, the cartoon beagle. He was a solitary not-animal animal who lived among larger creatures of a different species, which was more or less my feeling in my own house. My brothers were less like siblings than like an extra, fun pair of quasi-parents. Although I had friends and was a Cub Scout in good standing, I spent a lot of time alone with talking animals. I was an obsessive rereader of A.A. Milne and the *Narnia* and *Dr. Dolittle* novels, and my involvement with my collection of stuffed animals was on the verge of becoming age-inappropriate. It was another point of kinship with Snoopy that he, too, liked animal games. He impersonated tigers and vultures and mountain lions, sharks, sea monsters, pythons, cows, piranhas, penguins, and vampire bats. He was the perfect sunny egoist, starring in his ridiculous fantasies and basking in everyone's attention. In a cartoon strip full of children, the dog was the character I recognized as a child.

Tom and my father had been talking in the living room when I went up to bed. Now, at some late and even stuffier hour, after I'd put aside the *Peanuts Treasury* and fallen asleep, Tom burst into our bedroom. He was shouting sarcastically. "You'll get over it! You'll forget about me! It'll be so much easier! You'll get over it!" My father was offstage somewhere, making large abstract sounds. My mother was right behind Tom, sobbing at his shoulder, begging him to stop, to stop. He was pulling open dresser drawers, repacking bags he'd only recently unpacked. "You think you want me here," he said, "but you'll get over it."

What about me? my mother pleaded. *What about Jon?*

"You'll get over it."

I was a small and fundamentally ridiculous person. Even if I'd dared sit up in bed, what could I have said? "Excuse me, I'm trying to sleep?" I lay still and followed the action through my eyelashes. There were further dramatic comings and goings, through some of which I may in fact have slept. Finally I heard Tom's feet pounding down the stairs and my mother's terrible cries, now nearly shrieks, receding after him: "Tom! Tom! Tom! Please! Tom!" And then the front door slammed.

Things like this had never happened in our house. The worst fight I'd ever witnessed was between my brothers on the subject of Frank Zappa, whose music Tom admired and Bob one afternoon dismissed with such patronizing disdain that Tom began to sneer at Bob's own favorite group, the Supremes, which led to bitter words. But a scene of real wailing and open rage was completely off the map. When I woke up the next morning, the memory of it already felt decades old and semi-dreamlike and unmentionable.

My father had left for work, and my mother served me breakfast without comment. The food on the table, the jingles on the radio, and the walk to school all were unremarkable; and yet everything about the day was soaked in dread. At school that week, in Miss Niblack's class, we were rehearsing our fifth-grade play. The script, which I'd written, had a large number of bit parts and one very generous role that I'd created with my own memorization abilities in mind. The action took place on a boat, involved a taciturn villain named Mr. Scuba, and lacked the most rudimentary comedy, point, or moral. Not even I, who got to do most of the talking, enjoyed being in it. Its badness—my responsibility for its badness—became a part of the day's general dread.

There was something dreadful about springtime itself. The riot of biology, the *Lord of the Flies* buzzing, the pullulating mud. After school, instead of staying outside to play, I followed my dread home and cornered my mother in our dining room. I asked her about my upcoming class performance. Would Dad be in town for it? What about Bob? Would Bob be home from college yet? And what about Tom? Would Tom be there, too? This was quite plausibly an innocent line of questioning—I was a small glutton for attention, forever turning conversations to the subject of myself—and, for a while, my mother gave me plausibly innocent answers. Then she slumped into a chair, put her face in her hands, and began to weep.

"Didn't you hear anything last night?" she said.

"No."

"You didn't hear Tom and Dad shouting? You didn't hear doors slamming?"

"No!"

She gathered me in her arms, which was probably the main thing I'd been dreading. I stood there stiffly while she hugged me. "Tom and Dad had a terrible fight," she said. "After you went to bed. They had a terrible fight, and Tom got his things and left the house, and we don't know where he went."

"Oh."

"I thought we'd hear from him today, but he hasn't called, and I'm frantic, not knowing where he is. I'm just frantic!"

I squirmed a little in her grip.

"But this has nothing to do with you," she said. "It's between him and Dad and has nothing to do with you. I'm sure Tom's sorry he won't be here to see your play. Or maybe, who knows, he'll be back by Friday and he will see it."

"Okay."

"But I don't want you telling anyone he's gone until we know where he is. Will you agree not to tell anyone?"

"Okay," I said, breaking free of her. "Can we turn the air-conditioning on?"

I was unaware of it, but an epidemic had broken out across the country. Late adolescents in suburbs like ours had suddenly gone berserk, running away to other cities to have sex and not go to college, ingesting every substance they could get their hands on, not just clashing with their parents but rejecting and annihilating everything about them. For a while, the parents were so frightened and so mystified and so ashamed that each family, especially mine, quarantined itself and suffered by itself.

When I went upstairs, my bedroom felt like an overwarm sickroom. The clearest remaining vestige of Tom was the *Don't Look Back* poster that he'd taped to a flank of his dresser where Bob Dylan's psychedelic hairstyle wouldn't always be catching my mother's censorious eye. Tom's bed, neatly made, was the bed of a kid carried off by an epidemic.

In that unsettled season, as the so-called generation gap was rending the cultural landscape, Charles Schulz's work was uniquely beloved. Fifty-five million Americans had seen *A Charlie Brown Christmas* the previous December, for a Nielsen share of better than 50 percent. The musical *You're a Good Man, Charlie Brown* was in its second sold-out year on Broadway. The astronauts of *Apollo X*, in their dress rehearsal of the first lunar landing, had christened their orbiter and landing vehicle *Charlie Brown* and *Snoopy*. Newspapers carrying *Peanuts* reached more than 150 million readers, *Peanuts* collections were all over the bestseller list, and if my own friends were any indication, there was hardly a kid's bedroom in America without a *Peanuts* wastebasket or *Peanuts* bedsheets or a *Peanuts* wall hanging. Schulz, by a luxurious margin, was the most famous living artist on the planet.

To the countercultural mind, the strip's square panels were the only square thing about it. A begoggled beagle piloting a doghouse and getting shot down by the Red Baron had the same antic valence as Yossarian paddling a dinghy to Sweden. Wouldn't the country be better off listening to Linus van Pelt than to Robert McNamara? This was the era of flower children, not flower adults. But the strip appealed to older Americans as well. It was unfailingly inoffensive (Snoopy never lifted a leg) and was set in a safe, attractive suburb where the kids, except for Pigpen, whose image Ron McKernan of the Grateful Dead pointedly embraced, were clean and well-spoken and conservatively dressed. Hippies and astronauts, the rejecting kids and the rejected grown ups, were all of one mind here.

An exception was my own household. As far as I know, my father never in his life read a comic strip, and my mother's interest in the funnies was limited to a single-panel feature called *The Girls*, whose generic middle-aged matrons, with their weight problems and stinginess and poor driving skills and weakness for department-store bargains, she found just endlessly amusing.

I didn't buy comic books, not even *Mad* magazine, but I worshipped at the altars of Warner Bros. cartoons and the funnies section of the *St. Louis Post-Dispatch*. I read the section's black-and-white page first, skipping the dramatic features like *Steve Roper* and *Juliet Jones* and glancing at *Li'l Abner* only to satisfy myself that it was still trashy and repellent. On the full-color back page I read the strips strictly in reverse order of preference, doing my best to be amused by Dagwood Bumstead's midnight snacks and struggling to ignore the fact that Tiger and Punkinhead were the kind of messy, unreflective kids whom I disliked in real life, before I treated myself to my favorite strip, *B.C.* The strip, by Johnny Hart, was caveman humor. Hart wrung hundreds of gags from the friendship between a flightless bird and a long-suffering tortoise who was constantly attempting un-turtlish feats of agility and flexibility. Debts were always paid in clams; dinner was always roast leg of something. When I was done with *B.C.*, I was done with the paper.

The comics in St. Louis's other paper, the *Globe-Democrat*, which my parents didn't take, seemed bleak and foreign to me. *Broom Hilda* and *Funky Winkerbean* and *The Family Circus* were off-putting in the manner of the kid whose partially visible underpants, which had the name CUTTAIR hand-markered on the waistband, I'd stared at throughout my family's tour of the Canadian parliament. Although *The Family Circus* was resolutely unfunny, its panels clearly were based on some actual family's humid, baby-filled home life and were aimed at an audience that recognized this life, which compelled me to posit an entire subspecies of humanity that found *The Family Circus* hilarious.

I knew very well, of course, why the *Globe-Democrat*'s cartoons were so lame: the paper that carried *Peanuts* didn't *need* any other good strips. Indeed, I would have swapped the entire *Post-Dispatch* for a daily dose of Schulz. Only *Peanuts*, the strip we didn't get, dealt with stuff that really mattered. I didn't for a minute believe that the children in *Peanuts* were really children—they were so much more emphatic and cartoonishly *real* than anybody in my own neighborhood—but I nevertheless took their stories to be dispatches from a universe of childhood more substantial and convincing than my own. Instead of playing kickball and Four Square, the way my friends and I did, the kids in *Peanuts* had real baseball teams, real football equipment, real fistfights. Their relationships with Snoopy were far richer than the chasings and bitings that constituted my own relationships with neighborhood dogs. Minor but incredible disasters, often involving new vocabulary words, befell them daily. Lucy was "blackballed by the Bluebirds." She knocked Charlie Brown's croquet ball so far that he had to call the other players from a phone booth. She gave Charlie Brown a signed document in which she swore not to pull the football away when he tried to kick it, but the "peculiar thing about this document," as she observed in the final frame, was that "it was never notarized." When Lucy smashed the bust of Beethoven on Schroeder's toy piano, it struck me as odd and funny that Schroeder had a closet full of identical replacement busts, but I accepted it as humanly possible, because Schulz had drawn it.

To the *Peanuts Treasury* I soon added two other equally strong hardcover collections, *Peanuts Revisted* and *Peanuts Classics*. A well-meaning relative once also gave me a copy of Robert Short's bestseller, *The Gospel According to Peanuts*, but it couldn't have interested me less. *Peanuts* wasn't a portal on the Gospel. It *was* my gospel.

Chapter 1, verses 1–4, of what I knew about disillusionment: Charlie Brown passes the house of the Little Red-Haired Girl, the object of his eternal fruitless longing. He sits down with Snoopy and says, "I wish I had two ponies." He imagines offering one of the ponies to the Little Red-Haired Girl, riding out into the countryside with her, and sitting down with her beneath a tree. Suddenly he's scowling at Snoopy and asking, "Why aren't you two ponies?" Snoopy, rolling his eyes, thinks: "I knew we'd get around to that."

Or Chapter 1, verses 26–32, of what I knew about the mysteries of etiquette: Linus is showing off his new wristwatch to everyone in the neighborhood. "New watch!" he says proudly to Snoopy, who, after a hesitation, licks it. Linus's hair stands on end. "YOU LICKED MY WATCH!" he cries. "It'll rust! It'll turn green! He ruined it!" Snoopy is left looking mildly puzzled and thinking, "I thought it would have been impolite not to taste it."

Or Chapter 2, verses 6–12, of what I knew about fiction: Linus is annoying Lucy, wheedling and pleading with her to read him a story. To shut him up, she grabs a book, randomly opens it, and says, "A man was born, he lived and he died. The End!" She tosses the book aside, and Linus picks it up reverently. "What a fascinating account," he says. "It almost makes you wish you had known the fellow."

The perfect silliness of stuff like this, the koan-like inscrutability, entranced me even when I was ten. But many of the more elaborate sequences, especially the ones about Charlie Brown's humiliation and loneliness, made only a generic impression on me. In a classroom spelling bee that Charlie Brown has been looking forward to, the first word he's asked to spell is "maze." With a complacent smile, he produces "M-A-Y-S." The class screams with laughter. He returns to his seat and presses his face into his desktop, and when his teacher asks him what's wrong, he yells at her and ends up in the principal's office. *Peanuts* was steeped in Schulz's awareness that for every winner in a competition there has to be a loser, if not twenty losers, or two thousand, but I personally enjoyed winning and couldn't see why so much fuss was made about the losers.

In the spring of 1970, Miss Niblack's class was studying homonyms to prepare for what she called the Homonym Spelldown. I did some desultory homonym drilling with my mother, rattling off "sleigh" for "slay" and "slough" for "slew" the way other kids roped softballs into center field. To me, the only halfway interesting question about the Spelldown was who was going to come in second. A new kid had joined our class that year, a shrimpy black-haired striver, Chris Toczko, who had it in his head that he and I were academic rivals. I was a nice enough little boy as long as you kept away from my turf. Toczko was annoyingly unaware that I, not he, by natural right, was the best student in the class. On the day of the Spelldown, he actually taunted me. He said he'd done a lot of studying and he was going to beat me. I looked down at the little pest and did not know what to say. I evidently mattered a lot more to him than he did to me.

For the Spelldown, we all stood by the blackboard, Miss Niblack calling out one half of a pair of homonyms and my classmates sitting down as soon as they had failed. Toczko was pale and trembling, but he knew his homonyms. He was the last kid standing, besides me, when Miss Niblack called out the word "liar." Toczko trembled and essayed: "L... I..." and I could see that I had beaten him. I waited impatiently while, with considerable anguish, he extracted two more letters from his marrow: "E... R?"

"I'm sorry, Chris, that's not a word," Miss Niblack said.

With a sharp laugh of triumph, not even waiting for Toczko to sit down, I stepped forward and sang out, "L-Y-R-E! *Lyre.* It's a stringed instrument."

I hadn't really doubted that I would win, but Toczko had got to me with his taunting, and my blood was up. I was the last person in class to realize that Toczko was having a meltdown. His face turned red and he began to cry, insisting angrily that "lier" was a word, it *was* a word.

I didn't care if it was a word or not. I knew my rights. However many homonyms of "liar" might exist in theory, the word Miss Niblack wanted was clearly "lyre." Toczko's tears disturbed and disappointed me, as I made quite clear by fetching the classroom dictionary and showing him that "lier" wasn't in it. This was how both Toczko and I ended up in the principal's office.

I'd never been sent down before. I was interested to learn that the principal, Mr. Barnett, had a *Webster's International Unabridged* in his office. Toczko, who barely outweighed the dictionary, used two hands to open it and roll back the pages to the "L" words. I stood at his shoulder and saw where his tiny, trembling index finger was pointing: *lier, n, one that lies (as in ambush).* Mr. Barnett immediately declared us co-winners of the Spelldown—a compromise that didn't seem quite fair to me, since I would surely have murdered Toczko if we'd gone another round. But his outburst had spooked me, and I decided it might be okay, for once, to let somebody else win.

A few months after the Homonym Spelldown, just after summer vacation started, Toczko ran out into Grant Road and was killed by a car. What little I knew then about the world's badness I knew mainly from a camping trip, some years earlier, when I'd dropped a frog into a campfire and watched it shrivel and roll down the flat side of a log. My memory of that shriveling and rolling was sui generis, distinct from my other memories. It was like a nagging, sick-making atom of rebuke in me. I felt similarly rebuked now when my mother, who knew nothing of Toczko's rivalry with me, told me that he was dead. She was weeping as she'd wept over Tom's disappearance some weeks earlier. She sat me down and made me write a letter of condolence to Toczko's mother. I was very much unaccustomed to considering the interior states of people other than myself, but it was impossible not to consider Mrs. Toczko's. Though I never met her in person, in the ensuing weeks I pictured her suffering so incessantly and vividly that I could almost see her: a tiny, trim, dark-haired woman who cried the way her son did.

"Everything I do makes me feel guilty," says Charlie Brown. He's at the beach, and he has just thrown a pebble into the water, and Linus has commented, "Nice going... it took that rock four thousand years to get to shore, and now you've thrown it back."

I felt guilty about Toczko. I felt guilty about the little frog. I felt guilty about shunning my mother's hugs when she seemed to need them most. I felt guilty about the washcloths at the bottom of the stack in the linen closet, the older, thinner washcloths that we seldom used. I felt guilty for preferring my best shooter marbles, a solid red agate and a solid yellow agate, my king and my queen, to marbles farther down my rigid marble hierarchy. I felt guilty about the board games that I didn't like to play—Uncle Wiggily, U.S. Presidential Elections, Game of the States—and sometimes, when my friends weren't around, I opened the boxes and examined the pieces in the hope of making the games feel less forgotten. I felt guilty about neglecting the stiff-limbed, scratchy-pelted Mr. Bear, who had no voice and didn't mix well with my other stuffed animals. To avoid feeling guilty about them, too, I slept with one of them per night, according to a strict weekly schedule.

We laugh at dachshunds for humping our legs, but our own species is even more self-centered in its imaginings. There's no object so Other that it can't be anthropomorphized and shanghaied into conversation with us. Some objects are more amenable than others, however. The trouble with Mr. Bear was that he was more realistically bearlike than the other animals. He had a distinct, stern, feral persona; unlike our faceless washcloths, he was assertively Other. It was no wonder I couldn't speak through him. An old shoe is easier to invest with comic personality than is, say, a photograph of Cary Grant. The blanker the slate, the more easily we can fill it with our own image.

Our visual cortexes are wired to quickly recognize faces and then quickly subtract massive amounts of detail from them, zeroing in on their essential message: Is this person happy? Angry? Fearful? Individual faces may vary greatly, but a smirk on one is a lot like a smirk on another. Smirks are conceptual, not pictorial. Our brains are like cartoonists—and cartoonists are like our brains, simplifying and exaggerating, subordinating facial detail to abstract comic concepts.

Scott McCloud, in his cartoon treatise *Understanding Comics*, argues that the image you have of yourself when you're conversing is very different from your image of the person you're conversing with. Your interlocutor may produce universal smiles and universal frowns, and they may help you to identify with him emotionally, but he also has a particular nose and particular skin and particular hair that continually remind you that he's an Other. The image you have of your own face, by contrast, is highly cartoonish. When you feel yourself smile, you imagine a cartoon of smiling, not the complete skin-and-nose-and-hair package. It's precisely the simplicity and universality of cartoon faces, the absence of Otherly particulars, that invite us to love them as we love ourselves. The most widely loved (and profitable) faces in the modern world tend to be exceptionally basic and abstract cartoons: Mickey Mouse, the Simpsons, Tintin, and—simplest of all, barely more than a circle, two dots, and a horizontal line—Charlie Brown.

Charles Schulz only ever wanted to be a cartoonist. He was born in St. Paul in 1922, the only child of a German father and a mother of Norwegian extraction. Much of the existing Schulzian literature dwells on the Charlie Brownish traumas in his early life: his skinniness and pimples, his unpopularity with girls at school, the inexplicable rejection of a batch of his drawings by his high-school yearbook, and, some years later, the rejection of his marriage proposal by the real-life Little Red-Haired Girl, Donna Mae Johnson. Schulz himself spoke of his youth in a tone close to anger. "It took me a long time to become a human being," he told an interviewer in 1987.

> *I was regarded by many as kind of sissyfied, which I resented because I really was not a sissy. I was not a tough guy, but... I was good at any sport where you threw things, or hit them, or caught them, or something like that. I hated things like swimming and tumbling and those kinds of things, so I was really not a sissy. {...But} the coaches were so intolerant and there was no program for all of us. So I never regarded myself as being much and I never regarded myself as good-looking and I never had a date in high school, because I thought, who'd want to date me? So I didn't bother.*

Schulz "didn't bother" going to art school, either—it would only have discouraged him, he said, to be around people who could draw better than he could.

On the eve of Schulz's induction into the Army, his mother died of cancer. Schulz later described the loss as a catastrophe from which he almost did not recover. During basic training he was depressed, withdrawn, and grieving. In the long run, though, the Army was good for him. He entered the service, he recalled later, as a "nothing person" and came out as a staff sergeant in charge of a machine-gun squadron. "I thought, by golly, if that isn't a man, I don't know what is," he said. "And I felt good about myself, and that lasted about eight minutes, and then I went back to where I am now."

After the war, he returned to his childhood neighborhood, lived with his father, became intensely involved in a Christian youth group, and learned to draw kids. For the rest of his life, he virtually never drew adults. He avoided adult vices—didn't drink, didn't smoke, didn't swear—and, in his work, he spent more and more time in the imagined yards and sandlots of his childhood. He was childlike, too, in the absoluteness of his scruples and inhibitions. Even after he became famous and powerful, he was reluctant to demand a more flexible layout for *Peanuts*, because he didn't think it was fair to the papers that had been his loyal customers. He also thought it was unfair to draw caricatures. ("If somebody has a big nose," he said, "I'm sure that they regret the fact that they have a big nose, and who am I to point it out in gross caricature?") His resentment of the name *Peanuts*, which his editors had given the strip in 1950, was still fresh at the end of his life. "To label something that was going to be a life's work with a name like *Peanuts* was really insulting," he told an interviewer in 1987. To the suggestion that thirty-seven years might have softened the insult, Schulz replied: "No, no. I hold a grudge, boy."

Was Schulz's comic genius the product of his psychic wounds? Certainly the middle-aged artist was a mass of resentments and phobias that seemed attributable, in turn, to early traumas. He was increasingly prone to attacks of depression and bitter loneliness ("Just the mention of a hotel makes me turn cold," he told his biographer), and when he finally broke away from his native Minnesota, he set about replicating its comforts in California, building himself an ice rink where the snack bar was called "Warm Puppy." By the 1970s, he was reluctant even to get on an airplane unless someone from his family was with him. This would seem to be a classic instance of the pathology that produces great art: wounded in his adolescence, our hero took permanent refuge in the childhood world of *Peanuts*.

But what if Schulz had chosen to become a toy salesman, rather than an artist? Would he still have lived such a withdrawn and emotionally turbulent life? I suspect not. I suspect that Schulz the toy salesman would have gutted his way through a normal life the same way he'd gutted out his military service. He would have done whatever it took to support his family—begged a Valium prescription from his doctor, had a few drinks at the hotel bar.

Schulz wasn't an artist because he suffered. He suffered because he was an artist. To keep choosing art over the comforts of a normal life—to grind out a strip every day for fifty years; to pay the very steep psychic price for this—is the opposite of damaged. It's the sort of choice that only a tower of strength and sanity can make. The reason that Schulz's early sorrows look like "sources" of his later brilliance is that he had the talent and resilience to find humor in them. Almost every young person experiences sorrows. What's distinctive about Schulz's childhood is not his suffering but the fact that he loved comics from an early age, was gifted at drawing, and had the undivided attention of two loving parents.

Every February, Schulz drew a strip about Charlie Brown's failure to get any valentines. Schroeder, in one installment, chides Violet for trying to fob off a discarded valentine on Charlie Brown several days after Valentine's Day, and Charlie Brown shoves Schroeder aside with the words "Don't interfere—I'll take it!" But the story Schulz told about his own childhood experience with valentines was very different. When he was in first grade, he said, his mother helped him make a valentine for each of his classmates, so that nobody would be offended by not getting one, but he felt too shy to put them in the box at the front of the classroom, and so he took them all home again to his mother. At first glance, this story recalls a 1957 strip in which Charlie Brown peers over a fence at a swimming pool full of happy kids and then trudges home by himself and sits in a bucket of water. But Schulz, unlike Charlie Brown, had a mother on duty—a mother to whom he chose to give his entire basket. A child deeply scarred by a failure to get valentines would probably not grow up to draw lovable strips about the pain of never getting valentines. A child like that—one thinks of R. Crumb—might instead draw a valentine box that morphs into a vulva that devours his valentines and then devours him, too.

This is not to say that the depressive and failure-ridden Charlie Brown, the selfish and sadistic Lucy, the philosophizing oddball Linus, and the obsessive Schroeder (whose Beethoven-sized ambitions are realized on a one-octave toy piano) aren't all avatars of Schulz. But his true alter ego is clearly Snoopy: the protean trickster whose freedom is founded on his confidence that he's lovable at heart, the quick-change artist who, for the sheer joy of it, can become a helicopter or a hockey player or Head Beagle and then again, in a flash, before his virtuosity has a chance to alienate you or diminish you, be the eager little dog who just wants dinner.

I never heard my father tell a joke. Sometimes he reminisced about a business colleague who ordered a "Scotch and Coke" and a "flander" fillet in a Dallas diner in July, and he could laugh at his own embarassments, his impolitic remarks at the office, his foolish mistakes on home-improvement projects; but there wasn't a silly bone in his body. He responded to other people's jokes with a wince or a grimace. As a boy, I told him a story I'd made up about a trash-hauling company cited for "fragrant violations." He shook his head, stone-faced, and said, "Not plausible."

In another archetypical *Peanuts* strip, Violet and Patty are abusing Charlie Brown in vicious stereo: "GO ON HOME! WE DON'T WANT YOU AROUND HERE!" He trudges away with his eyes on the ground, and Violet remarks, "It's a strange thing about Charlie Brown. You almost never see him laugh."

The few times he ever played catch with me, my father threw the ball like a thing he wanted to get rid of, a piece of rotten fruit, and he snatched at my return throws with an awkward pawing motion. I never saw him touch a football or a Frisbee. His two main recreations were golf and bridge, and his enjoyment of them consisted in perpetually reconfirming that he was useless at the one and unlucky at the other.

He only ever wanted not to be a child anymore. His parents were a pair of nineteenth-century Scandinavians caught up in a Hobbesian struggle to prevail in the swamps of north-central Minnesota. His popular, charismatic older brother drowned in a hunting accident when he was still a young man. His nutty and pretty and spoiled younger sister had an only daughter who died in a one-car accident when she was twenty-two. My father's parents also died in a one-car accident, but only after regaling him with prohibitions, demands, and criticisms for fifty years. He never said a harsh word about them. He never said a nice word, either.

The few childhood stories he told were about his dog, Spider, and his gang of friends in the invitingly named little town, Palisade, that his father and uncles had constructed among the swamps. The local high school was eight miles from Palisade. In order to attend, my father lived in a boardinghouse for a year and later commuted in his father's Model A. He was a social cipher, invisible after school. The most popular girl in his class, Romelle Erickson, was expected to be the valedictorian, and the school's "social crowd" was "shocked," my father told me many times, when it turned out that the "country boy," "Earl Who," had claimed the title.

When he registered at the University of Minnesota, in 1933, his father went with him and announced, at the head of the registration line, "He's going to be a civil engineer." For the rest of his life, my father was restless. In his thirties, he agonized about whether to study medicine; in his forties, he was offered a partnership in a contracting firm which, to my mother's everlasting disappointment, he wasn't bold enough to accept; in his fifties and sixties, he admonished me never to let a corporation exploit my talents. In the end, though, he spent fifty years doing exactly what his father had told him to do.

After he died, I came into a few boxes of his papers. Most of the stuff was disappointingly unrevealing, and from his early childhood there was nothing except one brown envelope in which he'd saved a thick bundle of valentines. Some of them were flimsy and unsigned, some of them were more elaborate, with crepe-paper solids or 3-D foldouts, and a few from "Margaret" were in actual envelopes; the styles ranged from backwoods Victorian to 1920s art deco. The signatures—most of them from the boys and girls his age, a few from his cousins, one from his sister—were in the crude handwriting of elementary school. The gushiest profusions came from his best friend, Walter Anderson. But there weren't any valentines from his parents, or any other cards or tokens of their love, in any of the boxes.

My mother called him "oversensitive." She meant that it was easy to hurt his feelings, but the sensitivity was physical as well. When he was young, a doctor gave him a pinprick test that showed him to be allergic to "almost everything," including wheat, milk, and tomatoes. A different doctor, whose office was at the top of five long flights of stairs, greeted him with a blood-pressure test and immediately declared him unfit to fight the Nazis. Or so my father told me, with a shrugging gesture and an odd smile (as if to say,

"What could I do?") when I asked him why he hadn't been in the war. Even as a teenager, I sensed that his social awkwardness and sensitivities had been aggravated by not serving. He came from a family of pacifist Swedes, however, and was very happy not to be a soldier. He was happy that my brothers had college deferments and good luck with the lottery. Among his war-vet colleagues, he was such an outlier on the subject of Vietnam that he didn't dare talk about it. At home, in private, he aggressively avowed that, if Tom had drawn a bad number, he personally would have driven him to Canada.

Tom was a second-born in the mold of my father. He got poison ivy so bad it was like measles. He had a mid-October birthday and was perennially the youngest kid in his classes. On his only date in high school, he was so nervous that he forgot his baseball tickets and left the car idling in the street while he ran back inside; the car rolled down the hill and punched through an asphalt curb, clearing two levels of a terraced garden, and came to rest on a neighbor's front lawn. To me, it simply added to Tom's mystique that the car was not only still drivable but entirely undamaged. Neither he nor Bob could do any wrong in my eyes. They were expert whistlers and chess players, amazing wielders of tools and pencils, and the sole suppliers of whatever anecdotes and data I was able to impress my friends with. In the margins of Tom's school copy of *A Portrait of the Artist as a Young Man*, he drew a two-hundred-page riffle-animation of a stick-figure pole-vaulter clearing a hurdle, landing on his head, and being carted away on a stretcher by stick-figure E.M.S personnel. This seemed to me a master-work of filmic art and science. But my father had told Tom: "You'd make a good architect, here are three schools to choose from." He said: "You're going to work for Sverdrup."

Tom was gone for five days before we heard from him. His call came on a Sunday after church. We were sitting on the screen porch, and my mother ran the length of the house to answer the phone. She sounded so ecstatic with relief that I felt embarrassed for her. Tom had hitchhiked back to Houston and was doing deep-fry at a Church's fried-chicken establishment, hoping to save enough money to join his best friend in Colorado. My mother kept asking him when he might come home, assuring him that he was welcome and that he wouldn't have to work at Sverdrup; but I could tell, without even hearing Tom's responses, that he wanted nothing to do with us now.

* * *

The purpose of a comic strip, Schulz liked to say, was to sell newspapers and to make people laugh. His formulation may look self-deprecating at first glance, but in fact it is an oath of loyalty. When I.B. Singer, in his Nobel address, declared that the novelist's first responsibility is to be a storyteller, he didn't say "mere storyteller," and Schulz didn't say "merely make people laugh." He was loyal to the reader who wanted something funny from the funny pages. Just about anything—protesting against world hunger; getting a laugh out of words like "nooky"; dispensing wisdom; dying—is easier than real comedy.

Schulz never stopped trying to be funny. Around 1970, though, he began to drift away from aggressive humor and into melancholy reverie. There came tedious meanderings in Snoopyland with the unhilarious bird Woodstock and the unamusing beagle Spike. Certain leaden devices, such as Marcie's insistence on calling Peppermit Patty "sir," were heavily recycled. By the late eighties, the strip had grown so quiet that younger friends of mine seemed baffled by my fandom. It didn't help that later *Peanuts* anthologies loyally reprinted so many Spike and Marcie strips. The volumes that properly showcased Schulz's genius, the three hardcover collections from the sixties, had gone out of print.

Still more harmful to Schulz's reputation were his own kitschy spinoffs. Even in the sixties, you had to fight through cloying Warm Puppy paraphernalia to reach the comedy; the cuteness levels in latter-day *Peanuts* TV specials tied my shoes in knots. What first made *Peanuts Peanuts* was cruelty and failure, and yet every *Peanuts* greeting card and tchotchke and blimp had to feature somebody's sweet, crumpled smile. Everything about the billion-dollar *Peanuts* industry argued against Schulz as an artist to be taken seriously. Far more than Disney, whose studios were churning out kitsch from the start, Schulz came to seem an icon of art's corruption by commerce, which sooner or later paints a smiling sales face on everything it touches. The fan who wants to see him as an artist sees a merchant instead. Why isn't he two ponies?

It's hard to repudiate a comic strip, however, if your memories of it are more vivid than your memories of your own life. When Charlie Brown went off to summer camp, I went along in my imagination. I heard him trying to make conversation with the fellow camper who lay in his bunk and refused to say anything but, "Shut up and leave me alone." I watched when he finally came home again and shouted to Lucy, "I'm back! I'm back!" and Lucy gave him a bored look and said, "Have you been away?"

I went to camp myself, in the summer of 1970. But aside from an alarming personal hygiene situation which seemed to have resulted from my peeing in some poison ivy, and which, for several days, I was convinced was either a fatal tumor or puberty, my camp experience paled beside Charlie Brown's. The best part of it was coming home and seeing Bob waiting for me, in his new Karmann Ghia, at the YMCA parking lot.

Tom was also home by then. He'd managed to make his way to his friend's house in Colorado, but the friend's parents weren't happy about harboring somebody else's runaway son, and so they'd sent Tom back to St. Louis. Officially, I was very excited that he was back. In truth, I was embarrassed to be around him. I was afraid that if I referred to his sickness and our quarantine, I might prompt a relapse. I wanted to live in a *Peanuts* world where rage was funny and insecurity was lovable. The littlest kid in my *Peanuts* books, Sally Brown, grew older for a while and then hit a glass ceiling and went no further. I wanted everyone in my family to get along and nothing to change; but suddenly, after Tom ran away, it was as if the five of us looked around, asked why we should be spending time together, and failed to come up with many good answers.

For the first time, in the months that followed, my parents' conflicts became audible. My father came home on cool nights to complain about the house's "chill." My mother countered that the house wasn't cold if you were *doing housework all day*. My father marched in to the dining room to adjust the thermostat and dramatically point to its "Comfort Zone," a pale-blue arc between 72 and 78 degrees. My mother said that she was *so hot*. And I decided, as always, not to voice my suspicion that the Comfort Zone referred to air-conditioning in the summer rather than heat in the winter. My father set the temperature at 72 and retreated to the den, which was situated directly above the furnace. There was then a lull, and then big explosions. No matter what corner of the house I hid myself in, I could hear my father bellowing, "LEAVE THE GOD-DAMNED THERMOSTAT ALONE!"

"Earl. I didn't touch it!"

"You did! Again!"

"I didn't think I even moved it, I just *looked* at it, I didn't mean to change it."

"Again! You monkeyed with it again! I had it set where I wanted it. And you moved it down to seventy!"

"Well, if I did somehow change it, I'm sure I didn't mean to. You'd be hot, too, if you worked all day in the kitchen."

"All I ask at the end of a long day at work is that the temperature be set in the Comfort Zone."

"Earl, it is so hot in the kitchen. You don't know, because you're never *in* here, but it is *so* hot."

"The *low end* of the Comfort Zone! Not even the middle! The low end! It is not too much to ask!"

And I wonder why "cartoonish" remains such a pejorative. It took me half my life to achieve seeing my parents as cartoons. And to become more perfectly a cartoon myself: what a victory that would be.

My father eventually applied technology to the problem of temperature. He bought a space heater to put behind his chair in the dining room, where he was bothered in winter by drafts from the bay window behind him. Like so many of his appliance purchases, the heater was a pathetically cheap little thing, a wattage hog with a stertorous fan and a grinning orange mouth which dimmed the lights and drowned out conversation and produced a burning smell every time it cycled on. When I was in high school, he bought a quieter, more expensive model. One evening my mother and I started reminiscing about the old model, caricaturing my father's temperature sensitivities, doing cartoons of the little heater's faults, the smoke and the buzzing, and my father got mad and left the table. He thought we were ganging up on him. He thought I was being cruel, and I was, but I was also forgiving him.

IAN FRAZIER

Coyote v. Acme

In the United States District Court,
Southwestern District,
Tempe, Arizona
Case No. B19294,
JUDGE JOAN KUJAVA, PRESIDING

WILE E. COYOTE, PLAINTIFF
—V.—
ACME COMPANY, DEFENDANT

Opening Statement of Mr. Harold Schoff, attorney for Mr. Coyote: My client,
Mr. Wile E. Coyote, a resident of Arizona and contiguous states, does hereby
bring suit for damages against the Acme Company, manufacturer and retail
distributor of assorted merchandise, incorporated in Delaware and doing
business in every state, district, and territory. Mr. Coyote seeks compensation
for personal injuries, loss of business income, and mental suffering caused as
a direct result of the actions and/or gross negligence of said company, under
Title 15 of the United States Code, Chapter 47, section 2072, subsection (a),
relating to product liability.

Mr. Coyote states that on eighty-five separate occasions he has purchased of the Acme Company (hereinafter, "Defendant"), through that company's mail-order department, certain products which did cause him bodily injury due to defects in manufacture or improper cautionary labelling. Sales slips made out to Mr. Coyote as proof of purchase are at present in the possession of the Court, marked Exhibit A. Such injuries sustained by Mr. Coyote have temporarily restricted his ability to make a living in his profession as predator. Mr. Coyote is self-employed and thus not eligible for Workmen's Compensation.

Mr. Coyote states that on December 13th he received of Defendant via parcel post one Acme Rocket Sled. The intention of Mr. Coyote was to use the Rocket Sled to aid him in pursuit of his prey. Upon receipt of the Rocket Sled Mr. Coyote removed it from its wooden shipping crate and, sighting his prey in the distance, activated the ignition. As Mr. Coyote gripped the handlebars, the Rocket Sled accelerated with such sudden and precipitate force as to stretch Mr. Coyote's forelimbs to a length of fifty feet. Subsequently, the rest of Mr. Coyote's body shot forward with a violent jolt, causing severe strain to his back and neck and placing him unexpectedly astride the Rocket Sled. Disappearing over the horizon at such speed as to leave a diminishing jet trail along its path, the Rocket Sled soon brought Mr. Coyote abreast of his prey. At that moment the animal he was pursuing veered sharply to the right. Mr. Coyote vigorously attempted to follow this maneuver but was unable to, due to poorly designed steering on the Rocket Sled and a faulty or nonexistent braking system. Shortly thereafter, the unchecked progress of the Rocket Sled brought it and Mr. Coyote into collision with the side of a mesa.

Paragraph One of the Report of Attending Physician (Exhibit B), prepared by Dr. Ernest Grosscup, M.D., D.O., details the multiple fractures, contusions, and tissue damage suffered by Mr. Coyote as a result of this collision. Repair of the injuries required a full bandage around the head (excluding the ears), a neck brace, and full or partial casts on all four legs.

Hampered by these injuries, Mr. Coyote was nevertheless obliged to support himself. With this in mind, he purchased of Defendant as an aid to mobility one pair of Acme Rocket Skates. When he attempted to use this product, however, he became involved in an accident remarkably similar to that which occurred with the Rocket Sled. Again, Defendant sold over the counter, without caveat, a product which attached powerful jet engines (in this case, two) to inadequate vehicles, with little or no provision for passenger safety. Encumbered by his heavy casts, Mr. Coyote lost control of the Rocket Skates soon after strapping them on, and collided with a roadside billboard so violently as to leave a hole in the shape of his full silhouette.

Mr. Coyote states that on occasions too numerous to list in this document he has suffered mishaps with explosives purchased of the Defendant: the Acme "Little Giant" Firecracker, the Acme Self-Guided Aerial Bomb, etc. (For a full listing, see the Acme Mail Order Explosives Catalogue and attached deposition, entered in evidence as Exhibit C.) Indeed, it is safe to say that not once has an explosive purchased of Defendant by Mr. Coyote performed in an expected manner. To cite just one example: At the expense of much time and personal effort, Mr. Coyote constructed around the outer rim of a butte a wooden trough beginning at the top of the butte and spiralling downward around it to some few feet above a black X painted on the desert floor. The trough was designed in such a way that a spherical explosive of the type sold by Defendant would roll easily and swiftly down to the point of detonation indicated by the X. Mr. Coyote placed a generous pile of birdseed directly on the X, and then, carrying the spherical Acme Bomb (Catalogue #78-832), climbed to the top of the butte. Mr. Coyote's prey, seeing the birdseed, approached, and Mr. Coyote proceeded to light the fuse. In an instant, the fuse burned down to the stem, causing the bomb to detonate. In addition to reducing all Mr. Coyote's careful preparations to naught, the premature detonation of Defendant's product resulted in the following disfigurements to Mr. Coyote:

1. Severe singeing of the hair on the head, neck, and muzzle.

2. Sooty discoloration.

3. Fracture of the left ear at the stem, causing the ear to dangle in the aftershock with a creaking noise.

4. Full or partial combustion of whiskers, producing kinking, frazzling, and ashy disintegration.

5. Radical widening of the eyes, due to brow and lid charring.

*   *   *

We come now to the Acme Spring-Powered Shoes. The remains of a pair of these purchased by Mr. Coyote on June 23rd are Plaintiff's Exhibit D. Selected fragments have been shipped to the metallurgical laboratories of the University of California at Santa Barbara for analysis, but to date no explanation has been found for this product's sudden and extreme malfunction. As advertised by Defendant, this product is simplicity itself: two wood-and-metal sandals, each attached to milled-steel springs of high tensile strength and compressed in a tightly coiled position by a cocking device with a lanyard release. Mr. Coyote believed that this product would enable him to pounce upon his prey in the initial moments of the chase, when swift reflexes are at a premium.

To increase the shoes' thrusting power still further, Mr. Coyote affixed them by their bottoms to the side of a large boulder. Adjacent to the boulder was a path which Mr. Coyote's prey was known to frequent. Mr. Coyote put his hind feet in the wood-and-metal sandals and crouched in readiness, his right forepaw holding firmly to the lanyard release. Within a short time Mr. Coyote's prey did indeed appear on the path coming toward him. Unsuspecting, the prey stopped near Mr. Coyote, well within range of the springs at full extension. Mr. Coyote gauged the distance with care and proceeded to pull the lanyard release.

At this point, Defendant's product should have thrust Mr. Coyote forward and away from the boulder. Instead, for reasons yet unknown, the Acme Spring-Powered Shoes thrust the boulder away from Mr. Coyote. As the intended prey looked on unharmed, Mr. Coyote hung suspended in air. Then the twin springs recoiled, bringing Mr. Coyote to a violent feet-first collision with the boulder, the full weight of his head and forequarters falling upon his lower extremities.

The force of this impact then caused the springs to rebound, whereupon Mr. Coyote was thrust skyward. A second recoil and collision followed. The boulder, meanwhile, which was roughly ovoid in shape, had begun to bounce down a hillside, the coiling and recoiling of the springs adding to its velocity. At each bounce, Mr. Coyote came into contact with the boulder, or the boulder came into contact with Mr. Coyote, or both came into contact with the ground. As the grade was a long one, this process continued for some time.

The sequence of collisions resulted in systemic physical damage to Mr. Coyote, viz., flattening of the cranium, sideways displacement of the tongue, reduction of length of legs and upper body, and compression of vertebrae from base of tail to head. Repetition of blows along a vertical axis produced a series of regular horizontal folds in Mr. Coyote's body tissues—a rare and painful condition which caused Mr. Coyote to expand upward and contract downward alternately as he walked, and to emit an off-key accordion-like wheezing with every step. The distracting and embarrassing nature of this symptom has been a major impediment to Mr. Coyote's pursuit of a normal social life.

As the Court is no doubt aware, Defendant has a virtual monopoly of manufacture and sale of goods required by Mr. Coyote's work. It is our contention that Defendant has used its market advantage to the detriment of the consumer of such specialized products as itching powder, giant kites, Burmese tiger traps, anvils, and two-hundred-foot-long rubber bands. Much as he has come to mistrust Defendant's products, Mr. Coyote has no other domestic source of supply to which to turn. One can only wonder what our trading partners in Western Europe and Japan would make of such a situation, where a giant company is allowed to victimize the consumer in the most reckless and wrongful manner over and over again.

Mr. Coyote respectfully requests that the Court regard these larger economic implications and assess punitive damages in the amount of $17 million. In addition, Mr. Coyote seeks actual damages (missed meals, medical expenses, days lost from professional occupation) of $1 million; general damages (mental suffering, injury to reputation) of $20 million; and attorney's fees of $750,000. Total damages: $38,750,000. By awarding Mr. Coyote the full amount, this Court will censure Defendant, its directors, officers, shareholders, successors, and assigns, in the only language they understand, and reaffirms the right of the individual predator to equal protection under the law.

JACK HANDEY

My First Day in Hell

My first day in Hell is drawing to a close. They don't really have a sunset here, but the fires seem to dim a bit, and the screaming gets more subdued. Most of the demons are asleep now, their pointy tails curled up around them. They look so innocent, it's hard to believe that just a few hours ago they were raping and torturing us.

The day started off at a party at the Chelsea Hotel, where some friends were daring me to do something. The next thing I knew, I was in Hell. At first, it seemed like a dream, but then I remembered that five-martini dreams are usually a lot worse.

There's a kind of customs station when you arrive here, where a skeleton in a black robe checks a big book to make sure your name's there. And as he slowly scans the pages with his bony finger you can't help thinking, Why does a skeleton need a robe? Especially since it's so hot. That's the first thing you notice about Hell, how hot it is. I know it's a cliché, but it's true. Fortunately, it's a steamy, sulfury kind of hot. Like a spa or something.

You might think that people in Hell are all nude. But that's a myth. You wear what you were last wearing on earth. For instance, I am dressed like the German U-boat captain in the movie *Das Boot*, because that's what I wore to the party. It's an easy costume, because all you really need is the hat. The bad part is, people are always asking you who you are, even in Hell. Come on! *Das Boot*!

The food here turns out to be surprisingly good. The trouble is, just about all of it is poisoned. So a few minutes after you finish eating you're doubled over in agony. The weird thing is, as soon as you recover you're ready to dig in all over again.

Despite the tasty food and warm weather, there's a dark side to Hell. For one thing, it's totally disorganized. That anything gets done down here is a miracle. You'll be herded along in one big line, then it'll separate into three lines, then the lines will all come back together again! For no apparent reason! It's crazy. You try to ask a demon a question, but he just looks at you. I don't mean to sound prejudiced, but you wonder if they even speak English.

To relieve the boredom, you can throw rocks at other people in line. They just think it was a demon. But I discovered the hard way that the demons don't like it when they're beating someone and you join in.

It's odd, but Hell can be a lonely place, even with so many people around. They all seem caught up in their own little worlds, running to and fro, wailing and tearing at their hair. You try to make conversation, but you can tell they're not listening.

A malaise set in within a couple hours of my arriving. I thought getting a job might help. It turns out I have a lot of relatives in Hell, and, using connections, I became the assistant to a demon who pulls people's teeth out. It wasn't actually a job, more of an internship. But I was eager. And at first it was kind of interesting. After a while, though, you start asking yourself: Is this what I came to Hell for, to hand different kinds of pliers to a demon? I started wondering if I should even have come to Hell at all. Maybe I should have lived my life differently, and gone to Heaven instead.

I decided I had to get away—the endless lines, the senseless whipping, the forced sing-alongs. You get tired of trying to explain that you've already been branded, or that something that big won't fit in your ear, even with a hammer. I wandered off. I needed some *me* time. I came to a cave and went inside. Maybe I would find a place to meditate, or some gold nuggets.

That's when it happened, one of those moments which could only happen in Hell. I saw Satan. Some people have been in Hell for hundreds of years and have never seen Satan, but there he was: he was shorter than I thought he'd be, but he looked pretty good. He was standing on a big rock with his reading glasses on. I think he was practicing a speech. "Hey, Satan," I yelled out, "how's it going?" I was immediately set upon by demons. I can't begin to describe the tortures they inflicted on me, because apparently they are trade secrets. Suffice it to say that, even as you endure all the pain, you find yourself thinking, Wow, how did they think of *that*?

My stitches are a little itchy, but at least the demons sewed most of my parts back on. More important, my faith in Hell as an exciting place where anything can happen has been restored.

I had better get some rest. They say the bees will be out soon and that it's hard to sleep with the constant stinging. I lost my internship, but I was told I can reapply in a hundred years. Meanwhile, I've been assigned to a construction crew. Tomorrow we're supposed to build a huge monolith, then take picks and shovels and tear it down, then beat each other to death. It sounds pointless to me, but what do I know. I'm new here.

ERNEST HEMINGWAY

The Killers

The door of Henry's lunchroom opened and two men came in. They sat down at the counter.

"What's yours?" George asked them.

"I don't know," one of the men said. "What do you want to eat, Al?"

"I don't know," said Al. "I don't know what I want to eat."

Outside it was getting dark. The streetlight came on outside the window. The two men at the counter read the menu. From the other end of the counter Nick Adams watched them. He had been talking to George when they came in.

"I'll have a roast pork tenderloin with applesauce and mashed potatoes," the first man said.

"It isn't ready yet."

"What the hell do you put it on the card for?"

"That's the dinner," George explained. "You can get that at six o'clock."

George looked at the clock on the wall behind the counter.

"It's five o'clock."

"The clock says twenty minutes past five," the second man said.

"It's twenty minutes fast."

"Oh, to hell with the clock," the first man said. "What have you got to eat?"

"I can give you any kind of sandwiches," George said. "You can have ham and eggs, bacon and eggs, liver and bacon, or a steak."

"Give me chicken croquettes with green peas and cream sauce and mashed potatoes."

"That's the dinner."

"Everything we want's the dinner, eh? That's the way you work it."

"I can give you ham and eggs, bacon and eggs, liver."

"I'll take ham and eggs," the man called Al said. He wore a derby hat and a black overcoat buttoned across the chest. His face was small and white and he had tight lips. He wore a silk muffler and gloves.

"Give me bacon and eggs," said the other man. He was about the same size as Al. Their faces were different, but they were dressed like twins. Both wore overcoats too tight for them. They sat leaning forward, their elbows on the counter.

"Got anything to drink?" Al asked.

"Silver beer, bevo, ginger ale," George said.

"I mean you got anything to drink?"

"Just those I said."

"This is a hot town," said the other. "What do they call it?"

"Summit."

"Ever hear of it?" Al asked his friend.

"No," said the friend.

"What do you do here nights?" Al asked.

"They eat the dinner," his friend said. "They all come here and eat the big dinner."

'That's right," George said.

"So you think that's right?" Al asked George.

"Sure."

"You're a pretty bright boy, aren't you?"

"Sure," said George.

"Well, you're not," said the other little man. "Is he, Al?"

"He's dumb," said Al. He turned to Nick. "What's your name?"

"Adams."

"Another bright boy," Al said. "Ain't he a bright boy, Max?"

"The town's full of bright boys," Max said.

George put the two platters, one of ham and eggs, the other of bacon and eggs, on the counter. He set down two side dishes of fried potatoes and closed the wicket into the kitchen.

"Which is yours?" he asked Al.

"Don't you remember?"

"Ham and eggs."

"Just a bright boy," Max said. He leaned forward and took the ham and eggs. Both men ate with their gloves on. George watched them eat.

"What are you looking at?" Max looked at George.

"Nothing."

"The hell you were. You were looking at me."

"Maybe the boy meant it for a joke, Max," Al said.

George laughed.

"You don't have to laugh," Max said to him. "You don't have to laugh at all, see?"

"All right," said George.

"So he thinks it's all right." Max turned to Al. "He thinks it's all right. That's a good one."

"Oh, he's a thinker," Al said. They went on eating.

"What's the bright boy's name down the counter?" Al asked Max.

"Hey, bright boy," Max said to Nick. "You go around on the other side of the counter with your boy friend."

"What's the idea?" Nick asked.

"There isn't any idea."

"You better go around, bright boy," Al said. Nick went around behind the counter.

"What's the idea?" George asked.

"None of your damn business," Al said. "Who's out in the kitchen?"

"The nigger."

"What do you mean, the nigger?"

"The nigger that cooks."

"Tell him to come in."

"What's the idea?"

"Tell him to come in."

"Where do you think you are?"

"We know damn well where we are," the man called Max said. "Do we look silly?"

"You talk silly," Al said to him. "What the hell do you argue with this kid for? Listen," he said to George, "tell the nigger to come out here."

"What are you going to do to him?"

"Nothing. Use your head, bright boy. What would we do to a nigger?"

George opened the slit that opened back into the kitchen. "Sam," he called. "Come in here a minute."

The door to the kitchen opened and the nigger came in. "What was it?" he asked. The two men at the counter took a look at him.

"All right, nigger. You stand right there," Al said.

Sam, the nigger, standing in his apron, looked at the two men sitting at the counter. "Yes, sir," he said. Al got down from his stool.

"I'm going back to the kitchen with the nigger and bright boy," he said. "Go on back to the kitchen, nigger. You go with him, bright boy." The little man walked after Nick and Sam, the cook, back into the kitchen. The door shut after them. The man called Max sat at the counter opposite George. He didn't look at George but looked in the mirror that ran along back of the counter. Henry's had been made over from a saloon into a lunch counter.

"Well, bright boy," Max said, looking into the mirror, "why don't you say something?"

"What's it all about?"

"Hey, Al," Max called, "bright boy wants to know what it's all about."

"Why don't you tell him?" Al's voice came from the kitchen.

"What do you think it's all about?"

"I don't know."

"What do you think?"

Max looked into the mirror all the time he was talking.

"I wouldn't say."

"Hey, Al, bright boy says he wouldn't say what he thinks it's all about."

"I can hear you, all right," Al said from the kitchen. He had propped open the slit that dishes passed through into the kitchen with a catsup bottle. "Listen, bright boy," he said from the kitchen to George. "Stand a little farther along the bar. You move a little to the left, Max." He was like a photographer arranging for a group picture.

"Talk to me, bright boy," Max said. "What do you think's going to happen?"

George did not say anything.

"I'll tell you," Max said. "We're going to kill a Swede. Do you know a big Swede named Ole Andreson?"

"Yes."

"He comes here to eat every night, don't he?"

"Sometimes he comes here."

"He comes here at six o'clock, don't he?"

"If he comes."

"We know all that, bright boy," Max said. "Talk about something else. Ever go to the movies?"

"Once in a while."

"You ought to go to the movies more. The movies are fine for a bright boy like you."

"What are you going to kill Ole Andreson for? What did he ever do to you?"

"He never had a chance to do anything to us. He never even seen us."

"And he's only going to see us once," Al said from the kitchen.

"What are you going to kill him for, then?" George asked.

"We're killing him for a friend. Just to oblige a friend, bright boy."

"Shut up," said Al from the kitchen. "You talk too goddam much."

"Well, I got to keep bright boy amused. Don't I, bright boy?"

"You talk too damn much," Al said. "The nigger and my bright boy are amused by themselves. I got them tied up like a couple of girl friends in the convent."

"I suppose you were in a convent."

"You never know."

"You were in a kosher convent. That's where you were."

George looked up at the clock.

"If anybody comes in you tell them the cook is off, and if they keep after it, you tell them you'll go back and cook yourself. Do you get that, bright boy?"

"All right," George said. "What you going to do with us afterward?"

"That'll depend," Max said. "That's one of those things you never know at the time."

George looked up at the clock. It was a quarter past six. The door from the street opened. A streetcar motorman came in.

"Hello, George," he said. "Can I get supper?"

"Sam's gone out," George said. "He'll be back in about half an hour."

"I'd better go up the street," the motorman said. George looked at the clock. It was twenty minutes past six.

"That was nice, bright boy," Max said. "You're a regular little gentleman."

"He knew I'd blow his head off," Al said from the kitchen.

"No," said Max. "It ain't that. Bright boy is nice. He's a nice boy. I like him."

At six fifty-five George said: "He's not coming."

Two other people had been in the lunchroom. Once George had gone out to the kitchen and made a ham-and-egg sandwich "to go" that a man wanted to take with him. Inside the kitchen he saw Al, his derby hat tipped back, sitting on a stool beside the wicket with the muzzle of a sawed-off shotgun resting on the ledge. Nick and the cook were back to back in the corner, a towel tied in each of their mouths. George had cooked the sandwich, wrapped it up in oiled paper, put it in a bag, brought it in, and the man had paid for it and gone out.

"Bright boy can do everything," Max said. "He can cook and everything. You'd make some girl a nice wife, bright boy."

"Yes?" George said. "Your friend, Ole Andreson, isn't going to come."

"We'll give him ten minutes," Max said.

Max watched the mirror and the clock. The hands of the clock marked seven o'clock, and then five minutes past seven.

"Come on, Al," said Max. "We better go. He's not coming."

"Better give him five minutes," Al said from the kitchen.

In the five minutes a man came in, and George explained that the cook was sick.

"Why the hell don't you get another cook?" the man asked. "Aren't you running a lunch counter?" He went out.

"Come on, Al," Max said.

"What about the two bright boys and the nigger?"

"They're all right."

"You think so?"

"Sure. We're through with it."

"I don't like it," said Al. "It's sloppy. You talk too much."

"Oh, what the hell," said Max. "We got to keep amused, haven't we?"

"You talk too much, all the same," Al said. He came out from the kitchen. The cut-off barrels of the shotgun made a slight bulge under the waist of his too-tight-fitting overcoat. He straightened his coat with his gloved hands.

"So long, bright boy," he said to George. "You got a lot of luck."

"That's the truth," Max said. "You ought to play the races, bright boy."

The two of them went out the door. George watched them, through the window, pass under the arc light and cross the street. In their tight overcoats and derby hats they looked like a vaudeville team. George went back through the swinging door into the kitchen and untied Nick and the cook.

"I don't want any more of that," said Sam, the cook. "I don't want any more of that."

Nick stood up. He had never had a towel in his mouth before.

"Say," he said. "What the hell?" He was trying to swagger it off.

"They were going to kill Ole Andreson," George said. "They were going to shoot him when he came in to eat."

"Ole Andreson?"

"Sure."

The cook felt the corners of his mouth with his thumbs.

"They all gone?" he asked.

"Yeah," said George. "They're gone now."

"I don't like it," said the cook. "I don't like any of it at all."

"Listen," George said to Nick. "You better go see Ole Andreson."

"All right."

"You better not have anything to do with it at all," Sam, the cook, said. "You better stay way out of it."

"Don't go if you don't want to," George said.

"Mixing up in this ain't going to get you anywhere," the cook said. "You stay out of it."

"I'll go see him," Nick said to George. "Where does he live?"

The cook turned away.

"Little boys always know what they want to do," he said.

"He lives up at Hirsch's rooming house," George said to Nick.

"I'll go up there."

Outside the arc light shone through the bare branches of a tree. Nick walked up the street beside the car tracks and turned at the next arc light down a side street. Three houses up the street was Hirsch's rooming house. Nick walked up the two steps and pushed the bell. A woman came to the door.

"Is Ole Andreson here?"

"Do you want to see him?"

"Yes, if he's in."

Nick followed the woman up a flight of stairs and back to the end of a corridor. She knocked on the door.

"Who is it?"

"It's somebody to see you, Mr. Andreson," the woman said.

"It's Nick Adams."

"Come in."

Nick opened the door and went into the room. Ole Andreson was lying on the bed with all his clothes on. He had been a heavyweight prizefighter and he was too long for the bed. He lay with his head on two pillows. He did not look at Nick.

"What was it?" he asked.

"I was up at Henry's," Nick said, "and two fellows came in and tied up me and the cook, and they said they were going to kill you."

It sounded silly when he said it. Ole Andreson said nothing.

"They put us out in the kitchen," Nick went on. "They were going to shoot you when you came in to supper."

Ole Andreson looked at the wall and did not say anything.

"George thought I better come and tell you about it."

"There isn't anything I can do about it," Ole Andreson said.

"I'll tell you what they were like."

"I don't want to know what they were like," Ole Andreson said. He looked at the wall. "Thanks for coming to tell me about it."

"That's all right."

Nick looked at the big man lying on the bed.

"Don't you want me to go and see the police?"

"No," Ole Andreson said. "That wouldn't do any good."

"Isn't there something I could do?"

"No. There ain't anything to do."

"Maybe it was just a bluff."

"No. It ain't just a bluff."

Ole Andreson rolled over toward the wall.

"The only thing is," he said, talking toward the wall, "I just can't make up my mind to go out. I been in here all day."

"Couldn't you get out of town?"

"No," Ole Andreson said. "I'm through with all that running around."

He looked at the wall.

"There ain't anything to do now."

"Couldn't you fix it up some way?"

"No. I got in wrong." He talked in the same flat voice. "There ain't anything to do. After a while I'll make up my mind to go out."

"I better go back and see George," Nick said.

"So long," said Ole Andreson. He did not look toward Nick. "Thanks for coming around."

Nick went out. As he shut the door he saw Ole Andreson with all his clothes on, lying on the bed looking at the wall.

"He's been in his room all day," the landlady said downstairs. "I guess he don't feel well. I said to him: 'Mr. Andreson, you ought to go out and take a walk on a nice fall day like this,' but he didn't feel like it."

"He doesn't want to go out."

"I'm sorry he don't feel well," the woman said. "He's an awfully nice man. He was in the ring, you know."

"I know it."

"You'd never know it except from the way his face is," the woman said. They stood talking just inside the street door. "He's just as gentle."

"Well, good night, Mrs. Hirsch," Nick said.

"I'm not Mrs. Hirsch," the woman said. "She owns the place. I just look after it for her. I'm Mrs. Bell."

"Well, good night, Mrs. Bell," Nick said.

"Good night," the woman said.

Nick walked up the dark street to the corner under the arc light, and then along the car tracks to Henry's eating house. George was inside, back of the counter.

"Did you see Ole?"

"Yes," said Nick. "He's in his room and he won't go out."

The cook opened the door from the kitchen when he heard Nick's voice.

"I don't even listen to it," he said and shut the door.

"Did you tell him about it?" George asked.

"Sure. I told him but he knows what it's all about."

"What's he going to do?"

"Nothing."

"They'll kill him."

"I guess they will."

"He must have got mixed up in something in Chicago."

"I guess so," said Nick.

"It's a hell of a thing."

"It's an awful thing," Nick said.

They did not say anything. George reached down for a towel and wiped the counter.

"I wonder what he did?" Nick said.

"Double-crossed somebody. That's what they kill them for."

"I'm going to get out of this town," Nick said.

"Yes," said George. "That's a good thing to do."

"I can't stand to think about him waiting in the room and knowing he's going to get it. It's too damned awful."

"Well," said George, "you better not think about it."

Selected Poems

ROMANTIC MOMENT

After seeing the nature documentary we walk down Canyon Road,
into the plaza of art galleries and high-end clothing stores

where the orange trees are fragrant in the summer night
and the smooth adobe walls glow fleshlike in the dark.

It is just our second date, and we sit down on a bench,
holding hands, not looking at each other,

and if I were a bull penguin right now I would lean over
and vomit softly into the mouth of my beloved

and if I were a peacock I'd flex my gluteal muscles to
erect and spread the quills of my Cinemax tail.

If she were a female walkingstick bug she might
insert her hypodermic proboscis delicately into my neck

and inject me with a rich hormonal sedative
before attaching her egg sac to my thoracic undercarriage,

and if I were a young chimpanzee I would break off a nearby treelimb
and smash all the windows in the plaza jewelry stores.

And if she was a Brazilian leopard frog she would wrap her impressive
tongue three times around my right thigh and

pummel me lightly against the surface of our pond
and I would know her feelings were sincere.

Instead we sit awhile in silence, until
she remarks that in the relative context of tortoises and iguanas,

human males seem to be actually rather expressive.
And I say that female crocodiles really don't receive

enough credit for their gentleness.
Then she suggests that it is time for us to go

do something personal, hidden and human.

JASON THE REAL

If I was a real guy,
said my friend Jason,
and I got an e-mail like that,
what would you do?

Someone had told him he was a big sexy dreamboat
and he was trying to figure out
if he should buy a sports car and a condom

or take an AlkaSeltzer and go to bed
to recover from the agitation.

You remember what that was like, don't you?
to be excited by an unexpected pleasure
that is almost immediately turned into a problem?

My friend Jason, gentle guy
with the blood galloping around inside his head
like a wild pony,

changing his shirt thirteen times;
doing the victory dance of the eligible bachelor,
combing his hair and falling over furniture.

That girl had knocked him out of focus
with her sweet words
about finding him pretty

and now he was standing on the Continental Divide
i.e., whether to remain continent or not—
But he didn't like having to decide.

It is so human to turn a freedom into pain
and it is so sweet when life

comes to teach you suffering

by giving you a choice,
and you twist and turn
in the little flames of possibility.

—But that is how you build your castle.
That is how one earns a name
like Jason the Real.

NOT RENOUNCING

I always thought that I was going to catch Elena
in the library one afternoon, and she would shove me gently backwards
into the corridor of 839.7 in the Dewey Decimal System,
where we would do it in the culdesac of 18th-century drama.

Or I thought that we would meet by chance
in a bed and breakfast on the Delaware seashore,
and B and B eachother in a helter skelter
of goosedown duvets and camomille tea.

When I flew over the high plains of Wyoming,
I dreamed of taking off her cowboy shirt
and seeing her pale skin in a field of windswept prairie grass
which kept us completely out of sight

and even in the British National Museum
I fell into a trance before the model
of the castle and the moat, the drawbridge
and the catapult, with all those moveable, moving parts.

This is the imagination of a man.
It wanes and waxes all through his life,
like a kind of tumescence. I am not bragging
and I'm not renouncing.

I stood in one garden,
looking over the fence at another.
I thought I had to change my life or give up,
but I didn't. Year after year

they kept growing into each other:
the dreamed into the real,
the real into the dreamed—the two gardens

sending their flexible, sinuous vines,
their tendrils and unbuttoning blossoms,
ceaselessly over their borders.

FRED HAD WATCHED A LOT OF KUNG FU EPISODES

so when the policeman asked
to see his driver's license, he said,
Does the wind need permission

from the hedgehog to blow?
which resulted in a search of the car,
which miraculously yielded nothing

since Fred had swallowed all the mescaline already
and was just beginning to fall in love
with the bushy caterpillar eyebrows
of the officer in question.

In those days we could identify
the fingerprints on a guitar string
by the third note of the song
broadcast from the window of a passing car,

but we couldn't tell the difference
between a personal disaster
and "having an experience,"

so Fred thought being locked up for the night
was kind of fun,
with the graffiti on the drunk-tank wall
chattering in Mandarin
and the sentient cockroaches coming out to visit
in triplicate.

Back then it wasn't a question of pleasure or pain,
It wasn't a question of getting to the top
then trying not to fall at any cost.

It was a question of staying tuned in,
one episode at a time,

said Fred to himself
as he walked home the next morning
under the spreading lotus trees on Walnut Street,
feeling Oriental.

THE LONELIEST JOB IN THE WORLD

As soon as you begin to ask the question, *Who loves me?*,
you are completely screwed, because
the next question is *How Much?*,

and then it is hundreds of hours later,
and you are still hunched over
your flow charts and abacus,

trying to decide if you have gotten enough.
This is the loneliest job in the world:
to be an accountant of the heart.

It is late at night. You are by yourself,
and all around you, you can hear
the sounds of people moving

in and out of love,
pushing the turnstiles, putting
their coins in the slots,

paying the price which is asked,
which constantly changes.
No one knows why.

LUCKY

If you are lucky in this life
you will get to help your enemy
the way I got to help my mother
when she was weakened past the point of saying no.

Into the big enamel tub,
half-filled with water
which I had made just right,
I lowered the childish skeleton she had become.

Her eyelids fluttered as I soaped and rinsed
her belly and her chest,
the sorry ruin of her flanks
and the frayed grey cloud
between her legs.

Some nights beside her bed,
book open in my lap,
while I listened to the air
move thickly in and out of her dark lungs,
my mind filled up with praise
as lush as music,

amazed at the symmetry and luck
that would offer me the chance to pay
my heavy debt of punishment and love
with love and punishment.

And once, after her bath,
I held her dripping in the uncomfortable
air between the wheelchair and the tub,
until she begged me like a child to stop,

an act of cruelty
which we both understood
as the ancient, irresistible rejoicing
of power over weakness.

If you are lucky in this life,
you will get to raise the spoon
of pristine, frosty ice cream
to the trusting creature mouth
of your old enemy

because the tastebuds at least are not broken
because there is a covenant between you
and sweet is sweet in any language.

FORTUNE

like in the Chinese restaurant, it is
the perfect forethought and timing with which
the slices of orange arrive
on a small plate with the bill.

So, while you are paying what is owed,
the sweet juice fills your mouth for free.

And the fortune cookie too
which offers you the pleasure of Breakage
and then the other pleasure of Discovery,

extracting and reading the little strip of paper
with a happiness that you maybe conceal,
the way the child you once were
is even now concealed inside you.

Maybe you will marry a red-haired woman
Maybe you are going to take a long journey
Maybe a red-haired woman will steal your car and take a long journey
Maybe you will be buried next to your mother

And when the people you are dining with
                    smile and reveal their fortunes,
and ask you to tell them your own,
you smile and tell them a lie

And they laugh and think you are weird and funny and sad
and you know that you
                    are all of those things,

But you don't tell them the truth
because you can't trust anyone,
                    and you never have:
That is your fortune.

MIRANDA JULY

Majesty

I am not the kind of person who is interested in Britain's royal family. I've visited computer chat rooms full of this type of person, and they are people with
small worlds, they don't consider the long term, they aren't concerned about
the home front; they are too busy thinking about the royal family of another
country. The royal clothes, the royal gossip, the royal sad times, especially the
sad times, of this one family. I was only interested in the boy. The older one.
At one time I didn't even know his name. If someone had shown me a picture,
I might have guessed who he was, but not his name, not his weight or his
hobbies or the names of the girls who attended that co-ed university of his. If
there were a map of the solar system, but instead of stars it showed people and
their degrees of separation, my star would be the one you had to travel the most
light-years from to get to his. You would die getting to him. You could only
hope that your grandchildren's children would get to him. But they wouldn't
know what to do; they wouldn't know how to hold him. And he would be
dead; he would be replaced by his great-grandson's beautiful strapping son.
His sons will all be beautiful and strapping royalty, and my daughters will all
be middle-aged women working for a local non-profit and spearheading their
neighborhood earthquake-preparedness groups. We come from long lines of
people destined never to meet.

All my life I have had the same dream. It's what they call reoccurring;

it always unfolds to the same conclusion. Except for on October 9, 2002. The dream began as it always does, in a low-ceilinged land where everyone is forced to crawl around on hands and knees. But this time I realized that everyone around me was having sex, it was a consequence of living horizontally. I was furious and tried to pry the couples apart with my hands, but they were stuck together like mating beetles. Then, suddenly, I saw him. Will. In the dream I recognized he was a celebrity, but I didn't know which one. I felt very embarrassed because I knew he was used to being around cute young girls and he had probably never seen anyone who looked like me before. But gradually I realized he had lifted up the back of my skirt and was nuzzling his face between my buns. He was doing this because he loved me. It was a kind of loving I had never known was possible. And then I woke up. That's how I used to end all my stories in school: *And then I woke up!* But that wasn't the end, because as I opened my eyes, a car drove by outside and it was blaring music, which usually I hate and actually I think should be illegal, but this song was so beautiful—it went like this: "All I need is a miracle, all I need is you." Which exactly matched the feeling I was having from the dream. I got out of bed and, as if I needed more evidence, I opened the *Sacramento Bee*, and there, in the World News section, was an article about Prince Charles's visit to a housing estate in Glasgow, a trip he took with his son, Prince William Arthur Philip Louis. There was a picture. He looked just as he had when nuzzling my buns, the same lovely blond confidence, the same nose.

I typed "royal family" into a dream-interpretation website, but they didn't have that in their database, so then I typed "butt" and hit "interpret," and this came back: *To see your buttocks in your dream represents your instincts and urges.* It also said: *To dream that your buttocks are misshapen suggests undeveloped or wounded aspects of your psyche.* But my butt was shaped all right, so that let me know my psyche was developed, and the first part told me to trust my instincts, to trust my butt, the butt that trusted him.

That day I carried the dream around like a full glass of water, moving gracefully so I would not lose any of it. I have a long skirt like the one he lifted, and I wore it with a new sexual feeling. I swayed in to work; I glided around the staff kitchen. My sister calls these skirts "dirndls." She means this in a derogatory way. In the afternoon she came by my office at QuakeKare to use the Xerox machine. She seemed almost surprised to see me there, as if we had bumped into each other at Kinko's. QuakeKare's mandate is to teach preparedness and support quake victims around the world. My sister likes to joke that she's practically a quake victim, because her house is such a mess.

What do you call that exactly, a dirndl? she said.

It's a skirt. You know it's a skirt.

But doesn't it seem strange that the well-tailored, flattering piece of clothing that I'm wearing is also called a skirt? Shouldn't there be a distinction?

Not everyone thinks shorter is more arousing.

Arousing? Did you just say "arousing"? Were we talking about arousal? Oh my God, I can't believe you just said that word. Say it again.

What? Arousing.

Don't say it! It's too much, it's like you said "fuck" or something.

Well, I didn't.

No. Do you think you might never fuck again? When you said Carl left you, that was the first thing that came into my mind: She will never fuck again.

Why are you like this?

What? Should I be all buttoned up, like you? Hush-hush? Is that healthier?

I'm not that buttoned up.

Well, I would love to go out on that limb with you, but I'm going to need some evidence of this unbuttonedness.

I have a lover!

But I did not say this, I did not say I am loved, I am a person worth loving, I am not dirty anywhere, ask Prince William. That night I made a list of ways to meet him in reality:

Go to his school to give a lecture on earthquake safety.
Go to the bars near his school and wait for him.

They were not mutually exclusive; they were both reasonable ways to get to know someone. People meet in bars every day, and they often have sex with people they meet in bars. My sister does this all the time, or she did when she was in college. Afterward she would call and tell me every detail of her night, not because we are close—we are not. It is because there is something wrong with her. I would almost call what she does sexual abuse, but she's my younger sister, so there must be another word for it. She's over the top. That's all I can say about her. If the top is here, where I am, she's over it, hovering over me, naked.

The next morning I woke up at six and began walking. I knew I'd never be thin, but I decided to work toward an allover firmness that would feel okay if he touched me in the dark. After I lost ten pounds, I would be ready to join a gym; until then I would just walk and walk and walk. As I moved through the neighborhood, I re-ignited the dream, reaching such a pitch of clarity that I felt I might see him around the next corner. Upon seeing him, I would put my head under his shirt and stay there forever. I could see sunlight streaming through the stripes of his rugby pullover; my world was small and smelled like man. In this way I was blinded and did not see the woman until she stepped right in front of me. She was wearing a yellow bathrobe.

Shit. Did you see a little brown dog run that way? Potato!

No.

Are you sure? Potato! He must have just run out. Potato!

I wasn't paying attention.

Well, you would have seen him. Shit. Potato!

Sorry.

Jesus. Well, if you see him, grab him and bring him back over here. He's a little brown dog, his name is Potato. Potato!

Okay.

I walked on. It was time to concentrate on meeting him; plans one and two. I've gone to other schools and discussed earthquake safety, so it wouldn't be the first time. There's a school in the neighborhood, Buckman Elementary, and every year they invite the firemen in to explain how to Stop, Drop, and Roll, and later in the day I come in and talk about earthquake safety. Sadly, there is very little you can do. You can stop, you can drop, you can jump up in the air and flap your arms, but if it's the Big One, you're better off just praying. Last year a little boy asked what made me the expert, and I was honest with him. I told him I was more afraid of earthquakes than any person I knew. You have to be honest with children. I described my reoccurring nightmare of being smothered in rubble. Do you know what "smothered" means? I acted out the word, gasping with my eyes popping out, crouching down on the carpet and clawing for air. As I recovered from the demonstration, he put his hand on my shoulder and gave me a leaf that was almost in the shape of a shark. He said it was the best one; he showed me other ones he had collected, all of them more leaf than shark. Mine was the sharkiest. I carried it home in my purse; I put it on the kitchen table; I looked at it before I went to bed. And then in the middle of the night, I got up and pushed it down the garbage disposal. I just don't have room in my life for such a thing. One question is: Do they even have earthquakes in England? If they don't, this is the wrong approach. But if they don't, I have one more reason to want to live in the palace with him rather than convincing him to move into my apartment.

Then Potato ran by. He was a little brown dog, just like the woman said. He tore past me like he was about to miss a plane. He was gone by the time I even realized it had to be Potato. But he looked joyful, and I thought: Good for him. Live the dream, Potato.

Forget the school visit. I would step into the pub. That's what they call a bar over there. I would step into the pub. I would be wearing a skirt like the one he lifted in the dream. I would see him there with his friends and bodyguards. He wouldn't notice me, he would be shining, each golden hair on his arms would be shining. I would go to the jukebox and put on "All I Need Is a Miracle." This would give me confidence. I would sit at the bar and order a drink and I would begin to tell a yarn. A yarn is the kind of story that winds people in, like yarn around two hands. I would wind them in, the other people at the counter. There would be one part of the story that involved participation, something people would be compelled to chant at key moments. I haven't thought of the story yet, but I would say, for example: "And again I knocked on the door and yelled," and then everyone at the bar would chant: "Let me in! Let me in!" Eventually, all the people around me would be chanting this, and the circle of chanters would grow as they gathered in curiosity. Soon William would wonder what all the fuss was about. He would walk over with a bemused smile. What are the commoners doing now? I would see him there, so near to me, to every part of me, but I would not stop, I would keep spinning the yarn, and the next time I knocked on the door he would shout with everyone else: "Let me in! Let me in!" And somehow this story, this amazing story that had already drafted half the English countryside, would have a punch line that called upon William alone. It would be a new kind of punch line, totally unlike "orange you glad I didn't say banana." This punch line would pull him to me, he would stand before me, and with tears in his eyes, he would beg me: "Let me in! Let me in!" And I would press his giant head against my chest, and because the yarn wasn't quite over, I would say:

Ask my breasts, my forty-six-year-old breasts.

And he would yell into them, muffled: Let me in, let me in!

And my stomach, ask my stomach.

Let me in, let me in!

Get down on your knees, Your Highness, and ask my vagina, that ugly beast.

Let me in, let me in, let me in.

The sun was collapsing with a glare that seemed prehistoric; I felt not only blinded but lost, or as if I had lost something. And again she appeared, the woman in the yellow bathrobe. This time she was in a little red car. She had not even put on her clothes; she was still wearing the robe. And she was yelling "Potato!" so desperately that she was forgetting to stick her head out the window, she was yelling into the interior of the car uselessly, as if Potato were within her, like God. Her vaulted cry was startling, a true wail. She had lost someone she loved, she feared for his safety, it was really happening, it was happening now. And I was involved, because amazingly, I had just seen Potato. I ran over to the car.

He just went that way.

What!

Down Effie Street.

Why didn't you stop him?

He was going so fast, it took me a moment to realize it was him.

It was Potato?

Yeah.

Was he injured?

No, he looked happy.

Happy? He was terrified.

As soon as she said this, I thought of how fast he was running and understood she was right. He was running in blind panic, in terror. A teenage Filipino boy walked up to the car and just stood there, the way people do when disaster strikes. We ignored him.

He went that way?

Yeah, but that was at least ten minutes ago.

Shit!

She roared off, down Effie Street. The boy stayed with me, as if we were together in this.

She lost her dog.

He nodded and glanced around, like the dog might be right nearby.

What's the reward?

I don't think there is one yet.

She has to have a reward.

This seemed crass to me, but before I could say so, the red car returned. She was driving slowly now. She rolled down her window, and I walked over with a spilled feeling inside. She was in a nightie. The yellow bathrobe had been formed into a little nest on the passenger seat, and in the nest was Potato, dead. I said I was terribly sorry. The woman responded with a look that told me I alone was responsible and she would share no words with a professional dog killer. I wondered how many other things had flown past me into death. Perhaps many. Perhaps I was flying past them, like the grim reaper, signaling the end. This would explain so much.

She drove off, and the boy and I were alone again. I was only a few blocks from my house, but it was hard to walk away. I didn't know what I would think about when I began moving again. William. Who was William? It felt perverse, almost illegal to think about him now. And exhausting. Suddenly it seemed as if our relationship took mountains of strength to maintain. She was probably burying the dog in her yard right now. I looked at the boy; he was the opposite of a prince. He had nothing. When my sister was in college, she used to sometimes take these boys home. She would call me the next morning.

I could see it in his pants, it was like half hard, so I could already tell it was big.

Please stop now.

But when he took off his pants, I almost shit on myself, I was like, Please honey, get that thing up in me, and quick!

I see.

And then he took out this tiny piece of black rope or something and tied it around his cock, and I'm like, What's that for? And he just laughed in this nasty little-boy way. And I put on these tacky panties that I just got, they have a zipper in front that goes all the way around to the back? But he didn't really like those, I guess, because he just pulled them off and told me to do myself. Have you ever heard a guy say it like that? Do yourself?

No.

Of course you haven't. Anyways, I was rubbing and rubbing and I was super wet and he's all pushing it in my face and I'm going crazy for it and then, you're not going to believe this, he jizzes all over my face. Before I even get it in. Can you believe that?

Yes.

Well, yeah, I guess so. I guess he was really young and he probably'd never seen such a white pussy before.

And then my sister paused to listen to the sound of my breath over the phone. She could hear that I was done, I had come. So she said goodbye and I said goodbye and we hung up. It is this way between us; it has always been this way. She has always taken care of me like this. If I could quietly kill her without anyone knowing, I would.

I looked at the boy; he was looking at me as if we had already agreed on something. Just by standing beside him for a minute too long, I had somehow propositioned him. I couldn't leave him without some kind of negotiation.

You could wash my car.

For how much?

Ten dollars?

For ten dollars I won't do anything.

Okay.

I opened my purse and gave him ten dollars and he walked down Effie Street toward certain death and I walked home. In the reoccurring dream, everything has already fallen down, and I'm underneath. I'm crawling, sometimes for days, under the rubble. And as I crawl, I realize that this one was the Big One. It was the earthquake that shook the whole world, and every single thing was destroyed. But this isn't the scary part. That part always comes right before I wake up. I am crawling, and then suddenly, I remember: the earthquake happened years ago. This pain, this dying, this is just normal. This is how life is. In fact, I realize, there never was an earthquake. Life is just this way, broken, and I am crazy to hope for something else.

JOHN LAHR

The Goat Boy Rises

On October 1st, the comedian Bill Hicks, after doing his twelfth gig on the David Letterman show, became the first comedy act to be censored at CBS's Ed Sullivan Theatre, where Letterman is now in residence, and where Elvis Presley was famously censored in 1956. Presley was not allowed to be shown from the waist down. Hicks was not allowed to be shown at all. It's not what's in Hicks's pants but what's in his head that scared the CBS panjandrums. Hicks, a tall thirty-one-year-old Texan with a pudgy face aged beyond its years from hard living on the road, is no motormouth vulgarian but an exhilarating comic thinker in a renegade class all his own. Until the ban, which, according to Hicks, earned him "more attention than my other eleven appearances on Letterman times one hundred," Hicks's caustic observations and mischievous cultural connections had found a wide audience in England, where he is some-thing of a cult figure. I caught up with Hicks backstage on a rainy Sunday last November at the Dominion Theatre, in London, where a record-breaking crowd of two thousand Brits was packed so tightly that they were standing three deep at the back of the dress circle to hear Hicks deliver some acid home truths about the U.S.A., which to him stands for United States of Advertising. Hicks thinks against society and insists on the importance of this intellectual

---

This profile of Bill Hicks first appeared in the New Yorker *on November 1, 1993.*

freedom as a way to inspire others to think for themselves. "To me, the comic is the guy who says 'Wait a minute' as the consensus forms," Hicks told me as we climbed the stairs to his dressing room. "He's the antithesis of the mob mentality. The comic is a flame—like Shiva the Destroyer, toppling idols no matter what they are. He keeps cutting everything back to the moment."

Even then, the talk about courting comic danger had Hicks worrying about his prospects in America. "Comedy in the States has been totally gutted," he told me when we'd settled into the dressing room. "It's commercialized. They don't have people on TV who have points of view, because that defies the status quo, and we can't have that in the totalitarian mind-control government that runs the fuckin' airwaves. I can't get a shot there. I get David Letterman a lot. I love Letterman, but every time I go on, we have tiffs over material. They love me, but his people have this fictitious mainstream audience they think they play to. It's untrue. It doesn't exist. I like doing the show, but it's almost like working a puzzle: How can I be me in the context of doing this material? The best thing I do is make connections. I connect everything. It's hard to do it in six minutes."

Hicks certainly went for broke and pronounced his real comic self in the banned Letterman performance, which he'll be reprising in New York at Caroline's Comedy Club on October 27th, and which he wrote out for me in a thirty-nine-page letter that also recounts his version of events. Hicks had to write out his set because the tape of it, which the Letterman people said they'd send three weeks ago, had not yet reached him. He doubts it ever will. But the routine, which he had prepared for a Letterman appearance a week earlier (he was bumped because the show ran long), had been, he wrote, "approved and reapproved" by a segment producer of the show. Indicating stage directions and his recollection of significant audience response, Hicks set out some of the "hot points" to which the network took exception.

You know who's really bugging me these days? These pro-lifers... (*Smattering of applause.*)
You ever look at their faces?... "I'm pro-life!" (*Here Bill makes a pinched face of hate and fear; his lips are pursed as though he's just sucked on a lemon.*) "I'm pro-life!" Boy, they look it, don't they? They just exude joie de vivre. You just want to hang with them and play Trivial Pursuit all night long. (*Audience chuckles.*)
You know what bugs me about them? If you're so pro-life, do me a favor—don't

lock arms and block medical clinics. If you're so pro-life, lock arms and block cemeter-
ies. (*Audience laughs*.)... I want to see pro-lifers at funerals opening caskets—"Get out!"
Then I'd be really impressed by their mission. (*Audience laughs and applauds*.)

I've been traveling a lot lately. I was over in Australia during Easter. It was interesting to note they celebrate Easter the same way we do—commemorating the death and
resurrection of Jesus by telling our children a giant bunny rabbit... left chocolate eggs
in the night. (*Audience laughs*.)
    Gee, I wonder why we're so messed up as a race. You know, I've read the Bible.
Can't find the words "bunny" or "chocolate" in the whole book. (*Audience laughs*.)

I think it's interesting how people act on their beliefs. A lot of Christians, for instance,
wear crosses around their necks. Nice sentiment, but do you think when Jesus comes
back, he's really going to want to look at a cross? (*Audience laughs. Bill makes a face of
pain and horror*.)
    Ow! *Maybe* that's why he hasn't shown up yet. (*As Jesus looking down from Heaven*)
"I'm not going, Dad. No, they're still wearing crosses—they totally missed the point.
When they start wearing fishes, I might go back again... No, I'm not going... Okay,
I'll tell you what—I'll go back as a bunny."

Hicks, who delivered his monologue dressed not in his usual gunslinger
black but in "bright fall colors—an outfit bought just for the show and reflec-
tive of my bright and cheerful mood," seemed to have a lot to smile about.
Letterman—who Hicks says greeted him as he sat down to talk with "Good set,
Bill! Always nice to have you drop by with an uplifting message!" and signed
off saying, "Bill, enjoy answering your mail for the next few weeks"—had been
seen to laugh. The word in the Green Room was also good. A couple of hours
later, Hicks was back in his hotel, wearing nothing but a towel, when the call
came from Robert Morton, the executive producer of the Letterman show, telling him he'd been deep-sixed. Hicks sat down on the bed. "I don't understand,
Robert. What's the problem? I thought the show went great." The following
is a condensed version of what Hicks remembers from the long conversation.
    "You killed out there," Morton said, and went on to say, according to
Hicks, that the CBS office of standards and practices felt that some of the
material was unsuitable for broadcast.
    "Ah, which material exactly did they find . . ."
    "Well, almost all of it."
    "Bob, they're so obviously jokes."

Hicks protested that he had run his routine by his sixty-three-year-old mother in Little Rock, Arkansas, and it passed the test. Morton insisted that the situation was out of his hands. He offered to set up another appearance and, according to Hicks, shouldered the blame for not having spent more time beforehand editing out the "hot points."

"Bob, they're just jokes. I don't want to be edited by you or anyone else. Why are people so afraid of jokes?"

"Bill, you've got to understand our audience."

"Your audience! Your audience is comprised of people, right? Well, I understand people, being one myself. People are who I play to every night, Bob. We get along just fine. We taped the show at five-thirty in the afternoon, and your audience had no problem with the material then. Does your audience become overly sensitive between the hours of eleven-thirty p.m. and twelve-thirty a.m.? And by the way, Bob, when I'm not performing on your show, *I'm* a member of the audience of your show. Are you saying my material is not suitable for me? This doesn't make any sense. Why do you underestimate the intelligence of your audience?"

"Bill, it's not our decision."

Morton apologized to Hicks, explaining that the show had to answer to the network, and said that he'd reschedule him soon. The conversation ended soon after that exchange, and in the intervening weeks Hicks has had no further word, he says, from Morton or Letterman. He has, however, heard indirectly from the CBS standards-and-practices office. A man who heard an interview with Hicks on the radio and was outraged over the censorship wrote to CBS to upbraid the network for not airing Hicks's set. He faxed the reply from CBS standards-and-practices to the radio station, which faxed it to Hicks's office. "It is true that Bill Hicks was taped that evening and that his performance did not air," the letter said. "What is inaccurate is that the deletion of his routine was required by CBS. In fact, although a CBS Program Practices editor works on that show, the decision was solely that of the producers of the program who decided to substitute his performance with that of another comedian. Therefore, your criticism that CBS censored the program is totally without foundation. Creative judgments must be made in the course of producing and airing any program and, while we regret that you disagreed with this one, the producers felt it necessary and that is not a decision we would override."

Hicks, who refers to the television set as Lucifer's Dream Box, is now in Lucifer's Limbo. He can't get the Letterman show to send him a tape of his performance. He can't get to the bottom of who censored him. And, as yet, he has no return date on Letterman. I called Robert Morton two weeks ago, and, when pressed, he finally grasped the nettle. He had begun by saying that the decision not to show Hicks's routine was made jointly by the Letterman show and CBS and ended up telling me that the producers of the show were solely responsible. "Ultimately, it was our decision," he said. "We're the packagers and owners of the program. It's our job to deliver a finished product to the network."

"It's been a strange little adventure for Willy," Hicks told me at the Dominion last year, referring to his American comedy career. And so it has proved—stranger, in fact, than Hicks' most maverick imaginings. The farce came full circle in the week following the Letterman debacle. A friend called Hicks to tell him about a commercial she'd seen during the Letterman show—a pro-life commercial. "The networks are delivering an audience to the advertisers," Hicks said later. "They showed their hand. They'll continue to pretend they're a hip talk show. And I'll continue to be me. As Bob Dylan said, the only way to live outside the law is to be totally honest. So I will remain lawless."

Outlaw is how Hicks was styling himself last year for the Dominion performance as he put on his black rifleman's coat and Stetson in the dressing room. When the curtain came up on his performance, Hicks was revealed in his hat, long coat, and cowboy boots, while behind him huge orange flames licked the air. Images of heat and hunting are the perfect backdrop to Hicks's kind of comic attack. He was a hostile sharpshooter taking aim at the culture's received opinions and trying to shoot them down. The British, who have an appetite for this kind of intellectual anarchy, embraced Hicks with a rare and real enthusiasm from the moment he stumbled onto the vivacious English comedy scene in November 1990, as one of eighteen comedians in "Stand Up America!," a six-week limited engagement in the West End. The next year,

Hicks was at the Edinburgh Festival, where he outclassed the native talent and won the Critics' Award. This led to his 1992 "Dangerous Tour" of Britain and Ireland, which culminated in appearances in the West End, at the Queen's Theatre, that May. The response was overwhelming, and now Hicks was doing one of the final performances of the "Relentless Tour," his second lap of honor around the British Isles in one year. Hicks was at home with the English, whose sense of irony made them more receptive to his combative humor than the credulous American public had been. "There's a greater respect for the performer," he said. "If you're onstage, people think you've earned it. In America—I'm not kidding—people bark their approval." I looked at him dubiously. "Ask around," Hicks said, and he simulated the sound. "They bark like animals. It's frightening. It's what American society has reduced people to. Ironically, in this show I call myself Goat Boy. They shouldn't be barking, they should be *baa*ing."

My first encounter with Hicks was his Gulf War routine, which had been broadcast during the postwar euphoria at the beginning of 1992 on England's Channel 4. My sixteen-year-old son, Chris, was bellowing from the living room for me to come quickly. It was midnight, and he was sprawled, laughing, on the sofa, watching Hicks at the Montreal Comedy Festival calling a massacre a massacre. "So scary, watching the news. How they built it all out of proportion. Like Iraq was ever, or could ever, under any stretch of the imagination, be any threat to us *whatsoever*. But, watching the news, you never would have got that idea. Remember how it started? They kept talking about 'the élite Republican Guard' in these hushed tones, like these guys were the bogeyman or something. 'Yeah, we're doing well now, but we have yet to face... the élite Republican Guard.' Like these guys were twelve-feet-tall desert warriors—'Never lost a battle. We shit bullets.' Well, after two months of continuous carpet bombing and not *one* reaction at all from them, they became simply 'the Republican Guard'—not nearly as élite as we may have led you to believe. And after another month of bombing they went from 'the élite Republican Guard' to 'the Republican Guard' to 'the Republicans made this shit up about there being guards out there.'

"People said, 'Uh, uh, Bill, Iraq had the fourth-largest Army in the world.' Yeah, maybe, but you know what? After the first three largest armies, there's a *real* big fuckin' drop-off. The Hare Krishnas are the fifth-largest army in the world. And they've already got our airports."

Most TV comics trade in brand-name jokes or jokes that play off physical stereotypes. They don't question their culture so much as pander to its insatiable hunger for distraction. But Hicks's mischievous flights of fantasy bring the audience back to reality with a thump. Hicks is a kind of ventriloquist of his contradictory nature, letting voices and sound effects act out both his angst and his appetites. Occasionally, the instinct for Goat Boy comes over him, and Hicks, a man of instincts, goes with it. Goat Boy is Pan, or Hicks's version of him—a randy goat "with a placid look in his eyes, completely at peace with nature"—through which he celebrates his own rampaging libido.

"I am Goat Boy," he would say in the act that night, in a grave baritone. "Come here, my little fruit basket."

"What do you want, Goat Boy?" he answered, in a coy Southern falsetto. "You big old shaggy thing."

"Ha, ha, ha, ha," Hicks growled into the microphone. "I am here to please you."

"How?"

"Tie me to your headboard. Throw your legs over my shoulders, let me roll you like a feed bag." Hicks brought the microphone close to his mouth. He snorted, slurped, and finally screamed, "Hold on to my horns!" Then, as suddenly as the impulse had come upon him, Hicks broke off the fantasy, saying, "I need professional help at this point."

The secret of Hicks's psychic survival has always been comedy. He started writing and performing his jokes as an alienated thirteen-year-old in Houston in 1975, and, by his own count, for the last five years he has been performing about two hundred and sixty-five days a year, sometimes doing as many as three two-hour gigs a night. Few contemporary comics or actors have such an opportunity to get their education in public. Hicks uses the stage time to write his material in front of an audience. "I do it all onstage, *all* of it," he said, and then began to relate how he'd started on his eccentric journey. "When I was about eleven, it dawned on me that I didn't like where I was," he said, speaking of the subdivision where he lived, which was called Nottingham

Forest; of Stratford High School, which looked like a prison and where he was bored out of his skull for four years; and of his father, who was a midrange executive with General Motors. The Hicks family lived in "strict Southern Baptist ozone." The memory still rankled. "One time a friend of mine—we were nine—runs over and goes, 'Bill, I just saw some hippies down at the store.' I go, 'No way.' He goes, 'I swear.' My dad goes, 'Get off this property! We don't swear on this property!'

"We were living the American Dream. This was the best life had to offer. But there was no life, and no creativity. My dad, for instance, plays the piano. The same song for thirty years—I think it's 'Kitten on the Keys.' I don't play the piano, but all my friends are musicians. My dad goes, 'Do they read music?' I go, 'No.' 'Well, how do they play it?' I go to the piano and I write a song. What's the difference? He can't improvise. That, to me, is the suburbs. You get to a point, and that's it—it's over."

Once he'd seized on the idea of writing jokes, Hicks closeted himself in his bedroom and went to school on comedians. He started watching Johnny Carson. "I thought he was the only comic in the world, because I never stayed up later," he said. Soon Hicks began burning the midnight oil, taping other comic acts on television. "I'd take their jokes and also write my own. I performed them around school, and what I loved was when both got equal laughs. I knew which one was me and which one I'd seen on TV the night before. I learned how to mesh these things. How to get into character. I was very, very popular and known as a comedian at school. I'd always have to have material, constantly, all day. It got to the point where my English teacher gave me five minutes to do before class. My older brother Steve encouraged me. I typed up about two pages of jokes—whimsical stuff in the Woody Allen vein, which really appealed to me—and slipped them under his door. He came in later that night and said, 'What's this?' I said, 'I dunno. I'm writing these things. They're jokes.' He couldn't believe it. 'These are funny, man. Keep doing this.' "

Hicks' first partner in comedy was Dwight Slade, with whom he formed the act Bill and Dwight in the eighth grade. A tape exists of Hicks and Slade giggling through some of their early routines, which involved pretending to be brothers with "many, many problems." "Ladies and gentlemen, the comedy sensation Dwight Slade and Bill Hicks. And here they are!" it begins, and then the two of them collapse into roars of amusement at their own vain attempts to strike adult postures while reading gags about God, sex, abortion, and parents.

The jokes illustrated Hicks' precocity, and suggested how comedy both masked and admitted the hostility that kept him sullen and virtually silent around his family. "I can remember being at dinner when Bill would come down to eat," Steve Hicks told me. "He'd sit there with his face buried in a book. Absolutely no conversation from him or to him. Nothing. Then he would go up to his room and close and lock the door. We had no idea what he was doing." Hicks' room, which had nothing on the walls but a guitar, was a cell of rebellious solitude. He kept a typewriter under his bed and hid his pages of jokes inside its case.

In 1976, there were no comedy clubs in Houston. Except for school, the only outlets for Bill and Dwight's routines were talent shows and night clubs. They scoured the paper for auditions, and often rode their bikes the seventeen miles into town and back for a tryout. That summer, when they were both fourteen, a talent agent to whom they'd sent a tape liked it enough to get them airtime on Jerry Lewis's Telethon from 2 to 2:45 a.m. Their big break posed three immediate problems: (1) they didn't have forty-five minutes of material, (2) they'd never performed as Bill and Dwight in front of a live audience, and (3) they had to tell their parents. The first two problems were surmountable, but the third proved the sticking point. Hicks's parents said no. Hicks and Slade had to cancel, explaining that they were too young to drive themselves to the job. But in 1978, when the Comedy Workshop opened on San Felipe, in Houston, they talked their way into the lineup. This time, they made the gig. To get to it, Hicks had to climb out his window, shin down the drainpipe to the garage roof, jump from the roof to the ground, and hightail it to the Catholic church behind his house, where Kevin Booth, a friend who had a car, picked him up and then drove both performers to the club. Bill and Dwight did fifteen minutes—a kind of double solo performance, each doing Woody Allen shtick without the actual give-and-take of a comedy team. "What was really funny was when my friends would come and I'd go, 'I... uh... I have trouble... trouble with women,'" Hicks said. "And my friends would go, 'No, you don't!' I'd go, 'My parents are very poor.' 'No, they're not!' They were amazed we were in this adult world. They were seventeen and could drive us there, but when they got us there we were in the adult world."

The comedy team performed five times before Slade moved to Portland, Oregon, where he still lives, working as a stand-up comic. Hicks put his anarchic energy into a hapless punk-rock group called Stress, in which he sang a song called "I'm Glad I'm Not a Hubcap (Hubcaps Don't Get Laid)." At some point in his seventeenth year, Hicks's parents took him to a psychotherapist. "There was no connection between me and my parents—none," he said. "They had no idea of who I was. They still don't get what I do. How could they have understood it fifteen years ago?" The therapist met with the family, then with Hicks. At the end of the session, the therapist took Hicks aside. "Listen, you can continue to come if you feel like it," Hicks recalled him saying. "But it's them, not you." Soon afterward, at the beginning of Hicks's senior year, his father was transferred to Little Rock, Arkansas. He and his wife left Hicks behind in the house and left him the keys to the car. Hicks began doing comedy every night. His parents thought he was studying. The comedy club put him on first, because he had to get home early. Sometimes the phone would be ringing just as he walked in the door. "The conversations were like this," Hicks said. He fell easily into his father's Southern accent: "'Where were you?' 'Library.' 'Again?'" Even after his parents left, his material was almost entirely about them.

To this day, Hicks continues to mythologize his parents and his relationship with them, in comic routines that spoof their Southern propriety. But this is only professional acrimony, and doesn't stop Hicks from thanking his parents on his record albums or turning up regularly for ritual family occasions. Hicks, like all comedians, picks at ancient wounds to keep open the soreness that feeds his laughter and to demonstrate his mastery over the past.

In 1982, Hicks's parents finally saw him perform. They had been visiting Steve in Dallas, where the family had assembled for Thanksgiving, and his parents decided to surprise him. The plan was to drive the three hours to Austin, see the show, and drive back to Dallas the same night before setting out the next day for the six-hour ride to Little Rock. Steve and his wife waited up for them but finally fell asleep around 3 a.m. At nine, their phone rang. The Hickses had been so appalled by their son's act that they'd got in their car and driven nonstop to Little Rock. "They were in a state of shock," Steve says. "They didn't say a word to each other for nine hours. They didn't even realize they'd driven through Dallas!"

At one end of Hicks's long, corridor-like dressing room at the Dominion was a window overlooking the stage. Hicks walked over and looked out at the paying customers. "It's about that time," he said. Isolation suddenly fell over him like some fog blown in by his unconscious. Showtime was approaching, and he wanted to be alone. Fifteen minutes later, he brought his aggression roaring onstage. The narrative swung into attack as Hicks, like a man driven to distraction by the media, fought his way free of its overload by momentarily becoming its exaggerated voice: "Go back to bed! America is in control again... Here... here is American Gladiators. Watch this! Shut up. Go back to bed. Here's fifty-six channels of it. Watch these pituitary retards bang their fuckin' skulls together and congratulate yourself on living in the land of freedom. Here you go, America! You are free to do as we tell you! You are free!"

Hicks worked at a tremendous rate, pounding away at the absurdities of American culture with short jabs of wit and following up with a flurry of counterpunches. "Ever notice how people who believe in creationism look really unevolved?" he said. "Their eyes real close together. Eyebrow ridges. Big, furry hands and feet. 'I believe God created me in one day.' Looks like he rushed it." Later, near the end of the evening, Hicks drew one final lesson. "The world is like a ride at an amusement park," he said. "And when you choose to go on it, you think that it's real. Because that's how powerful our minds are." A young Englishman three seats away from me shouted "Bollocks!" And, without missing a beat, completely caught up in the dialogue he was having with his audience, Hicks said, "There is a lot of denial in this ride. The ride, in fact, is made up of denial. All things work in Goat Boy's favor!" Thrilled by the improvised insight, the audience burst into applause, and then Hicks guided the rest of the show smoothly to its conclusion, which, for all its combativeness, ended on the word "peace."

* * *

Hicks came to my house the next day for tea. He was tired and a little distracted, and was wondering out loud which way to take his quirky talent.
"Once this stuff is done, it's over with—I'm not married to any of it," he said.
"Goat Boy is the only thing that really intrigues me right now. He's not Satan.
He's not Evil. He's Nature." Hicks paused and added, "I'm trying to come up
with this thing about 'Conversations with Goat Boy.'" Then, suddenly, the
interrogator and Goat Boy started a conversation at my tea table:

"You don't like America?"

"I don't *see* America. To me, there is just a rapidly decreasing wilderness."

Hicks stopped and smiled. "That is Goat Boy. There is no America. It's
just a big pavement now to him. That's the whole point. What is America
anyway—a landmass including the Philippines? There are so many different
Americas. To him, to Nature, it's just land, the earth. Indian spirit—Indians
would understand randy Pan, the Goat Boy. They'd probably have a mask and
a celebration."

My son wandered into the kitchen and lingered to eavesdrop on the conversation. At one point, he broke in. "I don't know how you have the courage
to say those things," he said. "I could never talk like that in front of people."

Hicks smiled but had no response. Saying the unsayable was just his job.
He analyzed the previous night's performance, which had been filmed for an
HBO special. (It was broadcast in September to good reviews.) "People watch
TV not to think," he said. "I'd like the opportunity to stir things up once,
and see what happens. But I've got a question. Do I even want to be part of
it anymore? Show business or art—these are choices. It's hard to get a grip on
me. It's also hard for me to have a career, because there's no archetype for what
I do. I have to create it, or uncover it." To that end, he said, he and Fallon
Woodland, a stand-up from Kansas City, were writing *The Counts of the Neth-
erworld*, a TV comedy commissioned for England's Channel 4 and set in the
collective unconscious of mankind. Hicks was doing a column for the English
satire magazine *Scallywag*. He was planning a comedy album, called *Arizona
Bay*, a narrative rant against California with his own guitar accompaniment.
Should he stay in England, where he was already a cult figure, or return to

America? He recounted a joke on the subject by his friend Barry Crimmins, another American political comedian. "'Hey, buddy,' this guy says to him after a show. 'America—love it or leave it!' And Crimmins goes, 'What? And be a victim of our foreign policy?'"

As Hicks was about to go, he said, "We are facilitators of our creative evolution. We can ignite our brains with light." The line brought back something his high-school friend Kevin Booth had told me: "Bill was the first person I ever met whose goal was to become enlightened." At various times in his life, Hicks had meditated, studied Hindu texts, gobbled hallucinogens, searched for U.F.O.s—anything to make some larger spiritual and intellectual connection. His comedy takes an audience on a journey to places in the heart where it can't or won't go without him. Through laughter, Hicks makes unacceptable ideas irresistible. He is particularly lethal because he persuades not with reason but with joy. "I believe everyone has this fuckin' poem in his heart," he said on his way out.

HUGLEIKUR DAGSSON

More Selected Drawings

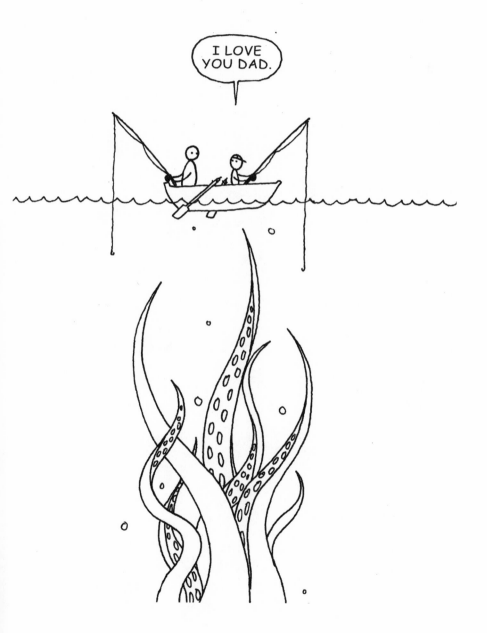

STEVE MARTIN

In the Birdcage

During the 1960s, the five-foot-high hand-painted placard in front of the Bird Cage Theater at Knott's Berry Farm read "World's Greatest Entertaiment." The missing "n" in "entertainment" was overlooked by staff, audience, and visitors for an entire decade. I worked there between the ages of eighteen and twenty-two as an actor in melodramas. Knott's Berry Farm began in the twenties, when Walter and Cordelia Knott set up a roadside berry stand. A few years later, Cordelia opened her chicken-dinner restaurant, and Walter bought pieces of a ghost town and moved the Old West buildings to his burgeoning tourist destination. Squawking peacocks roamed the grounds, and there was a little wooden chapel that played organ music while you stared at a picture of Jesus and watched his eyes magically open.

My first performances for a paying audience were at the Bird Cage, a wooden theater with a canvas roof. Inside were two hundred folding chairs on riders, arranged around a thrust Masonite stage that sat behind a patch of fake grass. A painted cutout of a birdcage, worthy of a Sotheby's folk-art auction, hung over center stage, and painted representations of drapes framed the proscenium. The actors swept the stage, raised and lowered the curtains, cleaned

This piece is taken from Steve Martin's autobiography, Born Standing Up, *originally excerpted in the* New Yorker *on October 29, 2007.*

the house of trash, and went out on the grounds pitching the show to visitors strolling around the park. I was being paid two dollars a show, twenty-five shows a week. Even in 1963, the rate was considered low.

The show consisted of a twenty-five-minute melodrama in which the audience was encouraged to cheer the hero and boo the villain. I appeared in *The Bungling Burglar*, performing the role of Hamilton Brainwood, a detective who was attracted to the provocatively named soubrette, Dimples Reardon. Fortunately, I ended up with the virtuous, heroic Angela Trueheart. The play was followed by a ten-minute "olio" segment involving two five-minute routines in which the actors did their specialties, usually songs or short comedy acts, and here I was able to work steadily on my fledgling comedy-magic act, five minutes at a time, four times a day (five on Sunday), for three years.

The Bird Cage was a normal theatrical nuthouse. Missed cues caused noisy pileups in the wings, or a missing prop left us hanging while we ad-libbed excuses to leave the stage and retrieve it. A forgotten line would hang in the air, searching for someone, anyone, to say it. The theater was run by Woody Wilson, a dead ringer for W.C. Fields, and a boozer, too, and the likable George Stuart, who, on Saturday nights, would entertain the crowd with a monologue that had them roaring. "You're from Tucson? I spent a week there one night!" Four paying customers was officially an audience, so we often did shows to resonating silence. On one of these dead afternoons, Woody Wilson peed so loudly in the echoing bathroom that it broke us up and got embarrassed laughs from our conservative family audience.

The theater was stocked with genuine characters. Ronnie Morgan, rail thin, would dress up as Lincoln and read the Gettysburg Address for local elementary schools. On a good day, he would show us young lads cheesecake photos of his wife in a leopard-skin bikini, and even at age eighteen we thought it was weird. There was Joe Carney, a blustery and funny actor, who opened the lavatory door from the top to avoid germs. Paul Shackleton was the son of a preacher and could not tolerate a swear word, but he once laughed till he cried when we sat down under a eucalyptus tree to drink our Cokes and a bird shit on my head. For days we could not look each other in the eye without breaking into uncontrollable hysterics. John Stuart, a talented tenor with a mischievous sense of humor, once secretly put talcum powder in my top hat. Onstage, whenever I popped the hat on or off, a mushroom cloud of smoke bloomed from my head, leaving me bewildered as to why the audience was laughing.

Stormie Sherk, later to become an enormously successful Christian author and proselytizer under her married name, Stormie Omartian, was beautiful, witty, bright, and filled with an engaging spirit that was not yet holy. We performed in the melodramas together, my role was either the comic or the leading man, depending on the day of the week. She wore calico dresses that complemented her strawberry-blond hair and vanilla skin. Soon we were in love and would roam around Knott's in our period costumes and find a period place to sit, mostly by the period church next to the manmade lake, where we would stare endlessly into each other's eyes. We developed a love duet for the Bird Cage in which she would sing "Gypsy Rover" while I accompanied her on my five-string banjo. When she sang the song, the lyric that affected me the most was—believe it or not—"La dee doo la dee doo dah day." We would talk of a wedding in a lilac-covered dale, and I could fill any conversational gaps with ardent recitations of poetry by Keats and Shelley, which I picked up at Santa Ana Junior College. Finally, the inevitable happened. I was a late-blooming eighteen-year-old when I had my first sexual experience, involving the virginal Stormie, a condom (swiped from my parents' drawer), and the front seat of my car, whose windows became befogged with desire.

If Stormie had said I would look good in a burgundy ball gown, I would have gone out and bought a burgundy ball gown. Instead, she suggested that I read W. Somerset Maugham's *The Razor's Edge*, a book about a quest for knowledge—universal, unquestionable knowledge. I was swept up in the book's glorification of truth-seeking, and the idea that, like a stage magician, I could have secrets possessed by only a few. Santa Ana Junior College offered no major in philosophy, so I enrolled at Long Beach State. I paid the tuition with my Bird Cage wages, aided in my second year by a dean's list scholarship ($180 a year) achieved through impassioned studying, fuelled by my "Razor's Edge" romanticism. I rented a small apartment near school, so small that its street number was 1059 ¼. Stormie eventually moved an hour north to attend UCLA, and we struggled for a while to see each other, but without the metaphor of the nineteenth century to enchant us, we realized that our real lives lay before us, and we drifted apart.

*　　*　　*

At the Bird Cage, I formed the soft primordial core of what became my comedy act. Over the three years I worked there, I strung together everything I knew: some comedy juggling, a few standard magic routines, a couple of banjo songs, and some very old jokes. My act was eclectic, and it would take ten more years for me to make sense of it. However, the opportunity to perform four or five times a day gave me confidence and poise. Even though my material had few distinguishing features, the repetition helped me lose my amateur rattle.

Catalyzed by the popularity of the folk group the Kingston Trio, small music clubs began to sprout in every unlikely venue. Shopping malls and restaurant cellars now had corner-stage showrooms that sometimes did and sometimes did not serve alcohol. There were almost no clubs dedicated to comedy—they would not exist for at least another fifteen years—so every comedian was an outsider. Having no agent or any hope of finding one, I could not audition for movies or television, or even learn where auditions were held. I didn't know about the trade papers—*Variety* or *The Hollywood Reporter*—from which I might have gathered some information. I lived in suburbia at a time when the hour-long drive to Los Angeles in my first great car—a white 1957 Chevy Bel Air, which, despite its beauty, guzzled quarts of oil and then spewed it back out in the form of white smoke—seemed like a trip across the continent in a Conestoga wagon. But the local folk clubs thrived on single acts, and their Monday nights were reserved for budding talent. Stand-up comedy felt like an open door. It was possible to assemble a few minutes of material and be onstage that week, as opposed to standing in line in the mysterious world of Hollywood, getting no response, no phone calls returned, and no opportunity to perform. On Mondays, I could tour around Orange County, visit three clubs in one night, and be onstage, live, in front of an audience. If I flopped at the Paradox in Tustin, I might succeed an hour later at the Ice House in Pasadena.

I continued to attend Long Beach State, taking Stormie-inspired courses in metaphysics, ethics, and logic. New and exhilarating words such as "epistemology," "ontology," "pragmatism," and "existentialism"—whose definitions alone were stimulating—swirled through my head and reconfigured by thinking. One semester, I was taking Philosophy of Language, Continental Rationalism (whatever that is), History of Ethics, and, to complete the group, Self-Defense, which I found especially humiliating when, one afternoon in class, I was nearly beaten up by a girl wearing boxing gloves.

A college friend lent me some comedy records. There were three by Mike Nichols and Elaine May, several by Lenny Bruce, and one by Tom Lehrer, the great song parodist. Nichols and May recorded without an audience, and I fixated on every nuance. Their comedy was sometimes created by only a subtle vocal shift: "Tell me, Dr. Schweitzer, what exactly is this *reverence for life?*" Lenny Bruce, on the records I heard, was doing mostly nonpolitical bits that were hilarious. Walden at a prison riot: "We'll meet any reasonable demands you men want! Except the vibrators!" Tom Lehrer influenced me with one bizarre joke about an individualism friend "whose name was Henry, only to give you an idea of what an individualist he was, he spelled it H-E-N-3-R-Y." Some people fall asleep at night listening to music; I fell asleep to Lenny, Tom, and Mike and Elaine. These albums broke ground and led me to a Darwinian discovery: comedy could evolve.

On campus, I experienced a life-changing moment of illumination, appropriately occurring in the bright sun. I was walking across the quad when a startling thought came to me: to implement a new concept called originality that was presenting itself in my classes in literature, poetry, and philosophy, I would have to write everything in my comedy act myself. Any line or idea with even a vague feeling of familiarity or provenance had to be expunged. There could be nothing that made the audience feel that they weren't seeing something utterly new.

This realization mortified me. I did not know how to write comedy—at all. But I did know that I would have to drop some of my best one-liners, pilfered from gag books or other people's routines, and consequently lose a major portion of my already strained act. The thought of losing all this material was depressing. After several years of working up my weak twenty minutes, I was now starting from almost zero.

I added poetry readings by T.S. Eliot and Stephen Vincent Benet to fill time, but I was desperate to invent new material. Sitting in a science class, my wandering mind searching for ideas, I stared at the periodic table of elements that hung behind the professor. That weekend, I went onstage at the Ice House and announced, "And now I would like to do a dramatic reading of the period table of elements: 'Fe... Au... He.'" That bit didn't last long.

In logic class, I opened my textbook, the last place I was expecting to find comic inspiration, and was startled to find that the author Lewis Carroll was also a logician. He wrote logic textbooks and included argument forms based on the syllogism, normally presented in logic books this way:

(1) All men are moral.
(2) Socrates is a man.
Therefore Socrates is mortal.

But Carroll's were convoluted, and they struck me as funny in a new way:

(1) Babies are illogical.
(2) Nobody is despised who can manage a crocodile.
(3) Illogical persons are despised.
Therefore babies cannot manage crocodiles.

And:

(1) No interesting poems are unpopular among people of real taste.
(2) No modern poetry is free from affectation.
(3) All your poems are on the subject of soap bubbles.
(4) No affected poetry is popular among people of real taste.
(5) Only a modern poem would be on the subject of soap bubbles.
Therefore all your poems are uninteresting.

These word games bothered and intrigued me. Appearing to be silly nonsense, on examination they were absolutely logical—yet they were still funny. Lewis Carroll's clever fancies from the nineteenth century expanded my notion of what comedy could be. I began closing my show by announcing, "I'm not going home tonight. I'm going to Bananaland, a place where only two things are true, only two things: one, all chairs are green; and, two, no chairs are green." Not at Lewis Carroll's level, but the line worked for my contemporaries, and I loved implying that the one thing I believed in was a contradiction.

*   *   *

My college roommate, Phil Carey, was an artist and a musician. He sang bass, not in a barbershop quartet but for a sophisticated chorale that favored complicated rhythms and mismatched twelve-tone arrangements. Phil's contagious enthusiasm got me excited about art, particularly the avant-garde, and we quickly noted that the campus art scene was also a great arena in which to meet girls. We loved reading magazine reports of New York galleries stuffed with Warhol's Brillo boxes and giant flowers, Lichtenstein's cartoon panels, and throngs of people dressed in black. Phil had a developed sense of humor: his cat was named Miles, and when asked if the cat was named after Miles Davis, Phil would say "No, it was 'and miles to go before I sleep.'"

Working on a college project about Charles Ives, Phil landed an interview with Aaron Copland. However, he would have to drive from Los Angeles to conduct it. I jumped at the chance to go along. In the summer of 1966—I was still twenty and proud that I would make it to New York City before I turned twenty-one—we installed a homemade cot in the back of my coughing blue windowless VW bus and drove across America without stopping. I was trying to write like E.E. Cummings, so my letters to my college girlfriend Nina, all highly romantic, goopy, and filled with references to flower and stars, read like amateur versions of his poems.

Three days after we left Los Angeles, Phil and I arrived at Copland's house, a low-slung A-frame with floor-to-ceiling windows in a dappled forest by the road. We knocked on the door, Copland answered, and over his shoulder we saw a group of men sitting in the living room wearing what looked like skimpy black thongs. He escorted us back to a flagstone patio, where I had the demanding job of turning the tape recorder on and off while Phil asked questions about Copland's creative process. We emerged a half hour later with the coveted interview and got in the car, never mentioning the men in skimpy black thongs, because, like trigonometry, we couldn't quite comprehend it.

After a detour to Cambridge, Massachusetts, to cruise the home of my idol Cummings, we drove into glorious Manhattan. Saucer-eyed, we hustled over to the Museum of Modern Art, where we saw, among the Cezannes and the Matisses, Dalí's famous painting of melting clocks, the shockingly tiny

"Persistence of Memory." We were dismayed to find that Warhol and Lichten-stein had not yet been ordained.

Before we left Cambridge, I sent this postcard to Nina:

Dear Nina,

Today, (about an hour ago) I stood in front of e.e. cummings's house at Harvard; his wife is still living there—we saw her. But the most fantastic thing was when we asked directions to Irving Street, the person we asked said to tell Mrs. Cummings hello from the Jameses! She turned out to be William James's great-granddaughter!

Then I added:

I have decided my act is going to go avant-garde. It is the only way to do what I want.

I'm not sure what I meant, but I wanted to use the lingo, and it was seductive to make these pronouncements. Through the years, I have learned that there is no harm in charging oneself up with delusions between moments of valid inspiration.

At the Ice House in Pasadena, I had met the comedian George McKelvey. George had an actual career and was quite funny. In reference to the radio's invisible crime-fighter the Shadow, he would ask, "If you could be invisible, what would you do? {long pause} Fight crime?" He was in Aspen, Colorado, during spring break, about to work a small folk club, when he broke his leg skiing. Could I fill in for him? He asked. He generously offered me all his salary—I think it was three hundred dollars for the two weeks, which would be more than I had ever earned anywhere, anytime. I was twenty-one years old when I headed for the free-wheeling ski resort.

In March of 1967, I arrived at a pre-fab house just outside Aspen. Visiting entertainers were bunked there, and after I made my way through the crunchy snow and stowed my suitcase under my bed several of us introduced ourselves. One was my co-bill, John McClure, a lanky guitarist with an acute sense of humor. Wandering in later was a pretty waitress named Linda Byers, who, I assumed, would fall for me because of my carefully designed, poetry-quoting artist's persona, but who, to my surprise, chose John, and they formed a long-term relationship. Also in the house was one of the few English comedians working in America, Jonathan Moore, who played a bagpipe to open his act, scaring the audience with its ancient howl as he entered the club from behind them. Jonathan was older than the rest of us. He had been around, wore sunglasses indoors, and had the charm of a well-spoken cynic.

The night club, the Abbey Cellar on Galena Street, was a basement in the middle of town and hard even for us to find. John and I, in order to drum up business, left little cards on the tables in the upstairs restaurant that read "Steve Martin/John McClure, Entertainment Ordinaire," which to me was hilariously funny but never seemed to be noticed as a joke.

Aspen was no place for poetry readings, and they were stripped permanently from my act. I was now doing my triptych of banjo playing, comedy, and magic. One evening at the Abbey Cellar, I had my first experience with a serious heckler who, sitting at a front table with his wife and another straight-looking couple, stood up and said, "See if you think this is funny," and threw a glass of red wine at me. The problem for him was that, at this point in the evening, the employees outnumbered the audience. A few seconds later, John McClure and the rough, tough Irish bartender appeared like centurions and escorted him out. Eventually, his friends slunk out, too. The expulsion had a downside: the audience was now smaller by two-thirds and in shock, and sat in stunned silence for the rest of my show. Later, I developed a few defensive lines to use against the unruly: "Oh, I remember when I had my first beer." And if that didn't cool them off I would use a psychological trick. I would lower my voice and continue with my act, talking almost inaudibly. The audience couldn't hear the show, and they would shut the heckler up on their own.

My experience at the Abbey Cellar was important to me, but not as important as what was going on after hours. John and I shared a room, and Linda would join us for lengthy chats. What we discussed was the new zeitgeist. I don't now how it got to this bedroom in Aspen, but it was creeping everywhere simultaneously. I didn't know its name yet but found out later that it was called Flower Power, and I was excited to learn that we were not living in the Age of Aquarius, an age when, at least astrologically, the world would be taken over by macramé. Anticorporate, individual, and freak-based, the new philosophy proposed that all we had to do was love each other, and there would be no more wars or strife. Nothing could have seemed newer or more appealing. The word "love" was being tossed around as though only we insiders knew its definition. The vast numbers of us who changed out lives around this belief proved that, yes, it is possible to fool all of the people some of the time. But any new social philosophy is good for creativity. New music was springing up, new graphics twisted and swirled as if on LSD, and an older generation was being glacially inched aside to make room for the freshly weaned new one. (The art world, always contrarian, responded to psychedelia with monochrome and minimalism.) It was fun trying to "turn" a young conservative, which was easy because our music was better. I remember trying to convince a visiting member of the Dallas Ski Club that "Yummy, Yummy, Yummy (I've Got Love in My Tummy)" was not really a good song, no matter how much he liked it. After two weeks in Aspen, I walked back to Los Angeles feeling like an anointed prophet, taking my friends aside and burping out new philosophy.

I continued to pursue my studies and half believed I might try for a doctorate in philosophy and become a teacher (teaching is, after all, a form of show business). I'm not sure what the purpose of fooling myself was, but I toyed with the idea for several semesters. I concluded that not to continue with comedy would leave a question in my mind that would nag me for the rest of my life: Could I have had a career in performing? Everything was dragging me toward the arts; even the study of modern philosophy suggested that philosophy was nonsense. A classmate, Ron Barnette, and I spend hours engaged in late-night mind-altering dialogues in laundromats and parking lots, discussing Wittgenstein, whose investigations disallowed so many types of philosophical discussions that we became convinced that the very discussion we were having was impossible. Soon I felt that a career in the irrational world of creativity not only made sense but had moral purpose.

I was living several lives at once: I was a student at Long Beach State; I still worked at the Bird Cage Theater; and at night I performed in various folk clubs with an eclectic, homemade comedy routine that was held together with wire and glue. I was still an opening act, and one of the clubs I played was Ledbetter's, a comparatively classy beer-and-wine nightspot a few blocks from UCLA that catered to the college crowd. Fats Johnson, a jovial folk-singer who dressed to kill in black suits with white ruffled shirts and wore elaborate rings on his guitar-strumming hand, often headlined the club. One night, I asked him about his philosophy of dressing for the stage. He said, firmly, "Always look better than they do."

Now that most of my work was in Westwood, Long Beach State, forty miles away, seemed like Siberia. I transferred to UCLA, so I could be closer to the action, and I took several courses there. One was an acting class, the kind that feels like prison camp and treats students like detainees who need to be broken; another was a course in television writing, which seemed practical. I also continued my studies in philosophy. I had done pretty well in symbolic logic at Long Beach, so I signed up for advanced symbolic logic at my new school. Saying that I was studying advanced symbolic logic at UCLA had a nice ring; what had been nerdy in high school now had mystique. On the first day of class, however, I discovered that UCLA used a different set of symbols from those I had learned at Long Beach. To catch up, I added Logic 101, which meant that I was studying beginning logic and advanced logic at the same time. I was overwhelmed, and shocked to find that I couldn't keep up. I abruptly changed my major to theater and, free from the workload of my logic classes, took a relaxing inhale of crisp California air. But on the exhale I realized that I was now investing in no other future but show business.

Overnight, there were dozens of new people in my life. Pot smoking was de rigueur—this being the sixties—and even though I was armed with only a comedy act that was at best hit-and-miss, I was fearless and ready to go. Among the crowd of singers and musicians whose local fame I assumed was worldwide was a sylphlike figure, a nonsinger and a nonmusician, who none-theless seemed to be regarded quite highly in this small showbiz matrix. Her name was Melissa, but her friends called her Mitzi. She was twenty-one years old, with a Katharine Hepburn beauty and a similarly willowy frame. She was intelligent, energetic, and lit from within. Her hair was ash brown, and always at the end of one of her long and slender arms was a Nikon camera with a lens the size of a can of Campbell's soup.

When her current romance withered, Mitzi and I became entwined. After several weeks of courtship, I was ready for family inspection, and she invited me to her parents' house for dinner. Mitzi's last name was Trumbo. Her father was the screenwriter Dalton Trumbo, one of the notorious Hollywood Ten, a group of writers and directors who were black-listed during the Red Scare of the late forties. During his congressional hearing, Trumbo vociferously challenged the right of his inquisitors to interrogate him, prompting a frustrated committee member to yell, "This is typical Communist tactics!" in a futile attempt to get him to shut up. It was Trumbo who wrote or co-wrote the screenplays for *Spartacus*, *Lonely Are the Brave*, *Hawaii*, *Exodus*, and *Papillon*; whose personal letters read like Swiftian essays; who had to flee to Mexico and stay for several years, writing under pseudonyms such as Sam Jackson and James Bonham in order to escape McCarthyism; and whom, at this stage in my tunnel-visioned life, I had never heard of.

From my perspective, Mitzi was a sophisticate. She had traveled. She was politically aware and had attended Reed College, in Oregon, a bastion of liberal thought. Her intelligence was informed by her family history. When I went to dinner at her home in the Hollywood Hills, I did not know that the months I would spend in this family's graces would broaden my life.

My first glimpse of Dalton Trumbo revealed an engrossed intellect—not finessing his latest screenplay but sorting the seeds and stems from a brick of pot. "Pop smokes marijuana," Mitzi explained, "with the wishful thought of cutting down on his drinking." Sometimes, from their balcony, I would see Trumbo walking laps around the perimeter of the pool. He held a small counter in one hand and clicked it every time he passed the diving board. These health walks were compromised by the cigarette he constantly held in his other hand.

Dalton Trumbo was the first raconteur I ever met. The family dinners—frequented by art dealers, actors, and artists of all kinds, including the screenwriters Hugo Butler and Ring Lardner, Jr., and the director George Roy Hill—were lively, political, and funny. I had never been in a house where conversations were held during dinner or where food was placed before me after being prepared behind closed doors. It was also the first time I ever heard swear words spoken by adults in front of their offspring. Lyndon Johnson's Vietnam bombing policy dominated the conversation, and the government's iron-fisted response to war protesters rankled the dinner guests, since the Hollywood Ten were all familiar with oppression. Trumbo had a patriarchal delivery whether he was on a rant or discussing art or slinging wit, but nothing he said was elitist—though I do remember him saying, as he spread his arms to indicate the china and silver serving ladles, "Admittedly, we do live well."

The Trumbo house was modern, built on a hillside, and extended down three floors into a ravine. The walls in the living room give me my most vivid memory of the house, for they were covered with art. Political art. I have never seen real paintings in a house, and this might have been where my own inclination toward owning pictures began. In the dining room was a William Gropper, depicting members of the House Un-American Activities Committee grotesquely outlined in fluorescent green against a murky background. There was a Raphael Soyer, as Moses Soyer, and a Jack Levine panting of Hindenburg making Hitler chancellor. These artists are obscure today but not forgotten. Gropper's art depicted politicos as porcine bullies, and Jack Levine's well-brushed social realism had a biting edge that fit the politics of the family perfectly.

One afternoon, on the way to the Trumbo house, Mitzi warned me, "Pop's in a bad mood today. He's got a screenplay due in four days and he hasn't started it yet." The screenplay was for the movie *The Fixer* starring Alan Bates. Eventually, the work got done and the movie was ready to shoot. Trumbo encouraged Mitzi to join him, and she was whisked off to Budapest. After I'd received several charming letters from her and then noticed a lag in the regularity of their arrival, Mitzi sent me a gentle and direct Dear John letter. She had been swept away by the director John Frankenheimer, who, twenty years later, tried and failed to seduce my then-wife, Victoria Tennant, whom he was directing in a movie. Mitzi was simply too alluring to be left alone in a foreign country, and I was too hormonal to be left alone in Hollywood. Incidentally, Frankenheimer died a few years ago, but it was not I who killed him.

By now I had ingratiated myself with enough folk clubs that I wondered if I could possibly support myself without the security of my steady job at Knott's Berry Farm. Bumping up against age twenty-two, I looked around the Bird Cage and saw actors who had been working there fifteen years and counting, and I knew it could be a trap for me. With some trepidation,

I gave notice. Stormie was gone, John Stuart and Paul Shackleton were gone, too, so there were no actual tearful goodbyes. Handshakes with George and Woody. Three years after I had started at the Bird Cage, I slipped away almost unnoticed.

A few years ago, after giving in to a sentimental urge to visit Knott's Berry Farm and the little theater where I got my start, I found myself in the deserted lobby of the Bird Cage, long since closed. It looked as though time had stopped the day I left. On one wall were photos from various productions, some of them including me as resident goofball. I tugged on the theater door; it was locked. I was about to give up when I remembered a back entrance to the employees only area, a clunky, oversized wooden gate that rarely locked because it was so rickety. I sneaked behind the theater and opened the door, which, for the millionth time, had failed to latch. The darkened theater flooded with sunlight, and I stepped inside and quickly shut the door. Light filtered in from the canvas roof, giving the Bird Cage a dim, golden huge. There I was, standing in a memory frozen in amber, and I experienced an overwhelming rush of sadness.

I went backstage and had a muscle memory of how to raise and lower the curtain, tying it off with a looping knot shown to me on my first day of work. I fiddled with the sole lighting rheostat, as antique as Edison. I stood on the stage and looked out at the empty theatre and was overcome by the feeling of today being pressed into yesterday. I didn't realize how much this place had meant to me.

Driving home along the Santa Ana Freeway, I was unnerved. I asked myself what it was that had made this place capable of inducing in me such a powerful nostalgic shock. The answer floated clearly into my mind, as though I had asked the question of a Magic 8 Ball: I wanted to be there again—if only for a day—indulging in high spirits and high jinks, before I turned professional, before comedy became serious.

The Jockey

The jockey came to the doorway of the dining room, then after a moment stepped to one side and stood motionless, with his back to the wall. The room was crowded, as this was the third day of the season and all the hotels in the town were full. In the dining room bouquets of August roses scattered their petals on the white table linen, and from the adjoining bar came a warm, drunken wash of voices. The jockey waited with his back to the wall and scrutinized the room with pinched, crêpy eyes. He examined the room until at last his eyes reached a table in a corner diagonally across from him, at which three men were sitting. As he watched, the jockey raised his chin and tilted his head back to one side, his dwarfed body grew rigid, and his hands stiffened so that the fingers curled inward like gray claws. Tense against the wall of the dining room, he watched and waited in this way.

He was wearing a suit of green Chinese silk that evening, tailored precisely and the size of a costume outfit for a child. The shirt was yellow, the tie striped with pastel colors. He had no hat with him and wore his hair brushed down in a stiff, wet bang on his forehead. His face was drawn, ageless, and gray. There were shadowed hollows at his temples and his mouth was set in a wiry smile. After a time he was aware that he had been seen by one of the three men he had been watching. But the jockey did not nod; he only raised his chin still higher and hooked the thumb of his tense hand in the pocket of his coat.

The three men at the corner table were a trainer, a bookie, and a rich man. The trainer was Sylvester—a large, loosely built fellow with a flushed nose and slow blue eyes. The bookie was Simmons. The rich man was the owner of a horse named Seltzer, which the jockey had ridden that afternoon. The three of them drank whiskey with soda, and a white-coated waiter had just brought on the main course of the dinner.

It was Sylvester who first saw the jockey. He looked away quickly, put down his whiskey glass, and nervously mashed the tip of his red nose with his thumb. "It's Bitsy Barlow," he said. "Standing over there across the room. Just watching us."

"Oh, the jockey," said the rich man. He was facing the wall and he half turned his head to look behind him. "Ask him over."

"God no," Sylvester said.

"He's crazy," Simmons said. The bookie's voice was flat and without inflection. He had the face of a born gambler, carefully adjusted, the expression a permanent deadlock between fear and greed.

"Well, I wouldn't call him that exactly," said Sylvester. "I've known him a long time. He was okay until about six months ago. But if he goes on like this, I can't see him lasting another year. I just can't."

"It was what happened in Miami," said Simmons.

"What?" asked the rich man.

Sylvester glanced across the room at the jockey and wet the corner of his mouth with his red, fleshy tongue. "A accident. A kid got hurt on the track. Broke a leg and a hip. He was a particular pal of Bitsy's. An Irish kid. Not a bad rider, either."

"That's a pity," said the rich man.

"Yeah. They were particular friends," Sylvester said. "You would always find him up in Bitsy's hotel room. They would be playing rummy or else lying on the floor reading the sports page together."

"Well, those things happen," said the rich man.

Simmons cut into his beefsteak. He held his fork prongs downward on the plate and carefully piled on mushrooms with the blade of his knife. "He's crazy," he repeated. "He gives me the creeps."

All the tables in the dining room were occupied. There was a party at the banquet table in the center, and green-white August moths had found their way in from the night and fluttered about the clear candle flames. Two girls wearing flannel slacks and blazers walked arm in arm across the room into the bar. From the main street outside came the echoes of holiday hysteria.

"They claim that in August Saratoga is the wealthiest town per capita in the world." Sylvester turned to the rich man. "What do you think?"

"I wouldn't know," said the rich man. "It may very well be so."

Daintily, Simmons wiped his greasy mouth with the tip of his forefinger. "How about Hollywood? And Wall Street—"

"Wait," said Sylvester. "He's decided to come over here."

The jockey had left the wall and was approaching the table in the corner. He walked with a prim strut, swinging out his legs in a half-circle with each step, his heels biting smartly into the red velvet carpet on the floor. On the way over he brushed against the elbow of a fat woman in white satin at the banquet table; he stepped back and bowed with dandified courtesy, his eyes quite closed. When he had crossed the room he drew up a chair and sat at a corner of the table, between Sylvester and the rich man, without a nod of greeting or a change in his set, gray face.

"Had dinner?" Sylvester asked.

"Some people might call it that." The jockey's voice was high, bitter, clear.

Sylvester put his knife and fork down carefully on his plate. The rich man shifted his position, turning sidewise in his chair and crossing his legs. He was dressed in twill riding pants, unpolished boots, and a shabby brown jacket—this was his outfit day and night in the racing season, although he was never seen on a horse. Simmons went on with his dinner.

"Like a spot of seltzer water?" asked Sylvester. "Or something like that?"

The jockey didn't answer. He drew a gold cigarette case from his pocket and snapped it open. Inside were a few cigarettes and a tiny gold penknife. He used the knife to cut a cigarette in half. When he had lighted his smoke he held up his hand to a waiter passing by the table. "Kentucky bourbon, please."

"Now, listen, Kid," said Sylvester.

"Don't Kid me."

"Be reasonable. You know you got to behave reasonable."

The jockey drew up the left corner of his mouth in a stiff jeer. His eyes lowered to the food spread out on the table, but instantly he looked up again. Before the rich man was a fish casserole, baked in a cream sauce and garnished with parsley. Sylvester had ordered eggs Benedict. There was asparagus, fresh buttered corn, and a side dish of wet black olives. A plate of French-fried potatoes was in the corner of the table before the jockey. He didn't look at the food again, but kept his pinched eyes on the centerpiece of full-blown lavender roses. "I don't suppose you remember a certain person by the name of McGuire," he said.

"Now, listen," said Sylvester.

The waiter brought the whiskey, and the jockey sat fondling the glass with his small, strong, callused hands. On his wrist was a gold-link bracelet that clinked against the table edge. After turning the glass between his palms, the jockey suddenly drank the whiskey neat in two hard swallows. He set down the glass sharply. "No, I don't suppose your memory is that long and extensive," he said.

"Sure enough, Bitsy," said Sylvester. "What makes you act like this? You hear from the kid today?"

"I received a letter," the jockey said. "The certain person we were speaking about was taken out from the cast on Wednesday. One leg is two inches shorter than the other one. That's all."

Sylvester clucked his tongue and shook his head. "I realize how you feel."

"Do you?" The jockey was looking at the dishes on the table. His gaze passed from the fish casserole to the corn, and finally fixed on the plate of fried potatoes. His face tightened and quickly he looked up again. A rose shattered and he picked up one of the petals, bruised it between his thumb and forefinger, and put it in his mouth.

"Well, those things happen," said the rich man.

The trainer and the bookie had finished eating, but there was food left on the serving dishes before their plates. The rich man dipped his buttery fingers in his water glass and wiped them with his napkin.

"Well," said the jockey. "Doesn't somebody want me to pass them something? Or maybe perhaps you desire to re-order. Another hunk of beefsteak, gentlemen, or—"

"Please," said Sylvester. "Be reasonable. Why don't you go on upstairs?"

"Yes, why don't I?" the jockey said.

His prim voice had risen higher and there was about it the sharp whine of hysteria.

"Why don't I go up to my god-damn room and walk around and write some letters and go to bed like a good boy? Why don't I just—" He pushed his chair back and got up. "Oh, foo," he said. "Foo to you. I want a drink."

"All I can say is it's your funeral," said Sylvester. "You know what it does to you. You know well enough."

The jockey crossed the dining room and went into the bar. He ordered a Manhattan, and Sylvester watched him stand with his heels pressed tight together, his body hard as a lead soldier's, holding his little finger out from the cocktail glass and sipping the drink slowly.

"He's crazy," said Simmons. "Like I said."

Sylvester turned to the rich man. "If he eats a lamb chop, you can see the shape of it in his stomach a hour afterward. He can't sweat things out of him any more. He's a hundred and twelve and a half. He's gained three pounds since we left Miami."

"A jockey shouldn't drink," said the rich man.

"The food don't satisfy him like it used to and he can't sweat it out. If he eats a lamb chop, you can watch it tooching out in his stomach and it don't go down."

The jockey finished his Manhattan. He swallowed, crushed the cherry in the bottom of the glass with his thumb, then pushed the glass away from him. The two girls in blazers were standing at his left, their faces turned toward each other, and at the other end of the bar two touts had started an argument about which was the highest mountain in the world. Everyone was with somebody else; there was no other person drinking alone that night. The jockey paid with a brand-new fifty-dollar bill and didn't count the change.

He walked back to the dining room and to the table at which the three men were sitting, but he did not sit down. "No, I wouldn't presume to think your memory is that extensive," he said. He was so small that the edge of the table top reached almost to his belt, and when he gripped the corner with his wiry hands he didn't have to stoop. "No, you're too busy gobbling up dinners in dining rooms. You're too—"

"Honestly," begged Sylvester. "You got to behave reasonable."

"Reasonable! Reasonable!" The jockey's gray face quivered, then set in a mean, frozen grin. He shook the table so that the plates rattled, and for a moment it seemed that he would push it over. But suddenly he stopped. His hand reached out toward the plate nearest to him and deliberately he put a few of the French-fried potatoes in his mouth. He chewed slowly, his upper lip raised, then he turned and spat out the pulpy mouthful on the smooth red carpet which covered the floor. "Libertines," he said, and his voice was thin and broken. He rolled the word in his mouth, as though it had a flavor and a substance that gratified him. "You libertines," he said again, and turned and walked with his rigid swagger out of the dining room.

Sylvester shrugged one of his loose, heavy shoulders. The rich man sopped up some water that had been spilled on the tablecloth, and they didn't speak until the waiter came to clear away.

Public Opinion

Mrs. Buckwell	Nancy Walls
Henry Buckwell	Alec Baldwin
Man	Will Ferrell
Governor	Darrell Hammond
Voice #1	David Koechner
Voice #2	Colin Quinn
Voice #3	Molly Shannon
Voice #4	Will Ferrell
Woman	Paula Pell

(OPEN ON: VT PRETAPE: MODEL—EXT. OF HOUSE WITH BEDROOM WINDOW LIGHT GOING OFF)

(SFX: CRICKET)

(VT PRETAPE (CONT'D): CUT TO: BEDROOM)

MRS. BUCKWELL
What's wrong honey, can't sleep?

This sketch was originally broadcast on Saturday Night Live *on January 20, 1996.*

                    HENRY BUCKWELL
I guess I'm just nervous about the election.

                     MRS. BUCKWELL
Don't worry, you're going to win, and be the best governor our state
ever had.

                    HENRY BUCKWELL
Thanks, sweetie.

(SFX: WINDOW BREAKING)

                     MRS. BUCKWELL
I think someone's downstairs.

                    HENRY BUCKWELL
I'll get the gun.

                     MRS. BUCKWELL
Honey, don't.

(CUT TO: LIVE. SHADOWY LIVING ROOM. HENRY BUCKWELL
STEPS OUT IN HIS BATHROBE HOLDING A GUN. THERE IS A
SHADOWY FIGURE IN THE FOREGROUND)

                    HENRY BUCKWELL
Don't move. I've got a gun.

(THE FIGURE DARTS QUICKLY. HENRY BUCKWELL FIRES THE
GUN)

(SFX: SHOTS)

(SFX: DOG YELP)

(THE LIGHTS COME UP TO REVEAL A MOTIONLESS COLLIE. A MAN
ENTERS HOLDING A LEASH)

                         MAN
Lassie!... Lassie! Oh my god, Lassie! You shot Lassie!

(MRS. BUCKWELL ENTERS IN HER NIGHTGOWN)

MRS. BUCKWELL

(SCREAMING)

No! No! You shot Lassie!

(TWO SMALL CHILDREN ENTER AND IMMEDIATELY BEGIN CRYING)

CHILD

(CRYING)

Daddy shot Lassie! Lassie's dead!

HENRY BUCKWELL

It was an accident. What the hell were you doing here anyway?

MAN

(SOBBING)

She was just trying to warn you that you had a carbon monoxide leak. And you shot her! It's Lassie.

CHILD

I hate you, Daddy!

HENRY BUCKWELL

I didn't mean to...

(CUT TO: VT: OF HEADLINES SWIRLING TOWARD SCREEN. 1) CANDIDATE BUCKWELL KILLS LASSIE 2) BUCKWELL FALLS TO SECOND IN GOVERNOR'S RACE AFTER SHOOTING LASSIE 3) LASSIE KILLER TO DEBATE GOVERNOR TONIGHT)

(MUSIC: UNDER)

(CUT TO: A PODIUM WHERE THE GOVERNOR IS FINISHING SPEAKING)

GOVERNOR

...And in conclusion, we need to get the poor people pullin' themselves up by their bootstraps or else in prison.

(SFX: APPLAUSE)

STEVE H. (V.O.) (1/4)

And now we will hear from the challenger Henry Buckwell.

(HENRY BUCKWELL STEPS UP TO THE PODIUM)

HENRY BUCKWELL

I guess I have a little more faith in people than the current governor.
I believe people want to work if given the opportunity.

VOICE #1

You shot Lassie!!!

HENRY BUCKWELL

I believe that we have created a system that excludes people of certain
races and—

VOICE #2

Shut up, Lassie killer!!!

HENRY BUCKWELL

Yes... that was an accident... but as I was saying, I envision a state
where people have the opportunity to—

VOICE #3

To kill Lassie!!!

VOICE #4

You killed Lassie, you bastard!

HENRY BUCKWELL

Listen!

(CROWD SILENCES)

HENRY BUCKWELL (CONT'D)

That was a mistake. Why can't you understand?

WOMAN

Kiss my...

HENRY BUCKWELL

(TURNS TO FACE HER)

Kiss my ass.

WOMAN

I just wanted you to kiss my baby.

(WOMAN EXITS)

VOICE #4

He cursed at a baby!

VOICE #3

He did! He swore at an infant!!!

HENRY BUCKWELL

I couldn't see who it was! I didn't know!!!

(CROWD BOOS LOUDLY)

(CUT TO: VT: OF PAPERS SPINNING. 1) LASSIE KILLER CANDI-
DATE CURSES OUT BABY 2) FIRST DOGS AND NOW BABIES
3) LASSIE KILLER/BABY CURSER TO SPEAK TONIGHT)

(MUSIC: UNDER)

(CUT TO: HENRY BUCKWELL STEPPING TOWARD PODIUM)

(FLASHES GO OFF)

(SFX: FLASH)

HENRY BUCKWELL

People, there has been confusion about some recent events. But I
come before you tonight as an American.

VOICE #4

You're a baby curser!

VOICE #1

You shot Lassie!

(CROWD STARTS BOOING AND THROWING EGGS. HENRY BUCKWELL GETS HIT IN THE BUTT WITH AN EGG. HE ABSENT-MINDEDLY REACHES BEHIND HIMSELF AND GRABS THE FLAG. HE WIPES THE EGG OFF OF HIS BUTT WITH THE FLAG)

HENRY BUCKWELL

Please, if everyone would just calm down...

(A PHOTOGRAPHER STEPS IN AND PHOTOGRAPHS HENRY BUCKWELL WIPING HIS BUTT WITH THE FLAG)

(FLASHBULB FLASHES)

(SFX: FLASH)

(CUT TO: VT: THE PICTURE FREEZES AND SUPERS ONTO A NEWSPAPER HEADLINE. 1) BUCKWELL WIPES ASS WITH FLAG 2) LASSIE ASSASSIN AND BABY SLANDERER CLEANS SELF WITH OLD GLORY AND OFFERS PROGRAM TO LOWER UNEMPLOY-MENT 4) LASSIE KILLER/BABY ATTACKER/FLAG DEFILER SPEAKS TONIGHT ON TV)

(MUSIC: UNDER)

(CUT TO: HENRY BUCKWELL STEPPING UP TO PODIUM)

HENRY BUCKWELL

Ladies and gentlemen of this great state, I come before you, a humble man who hopes only to help other people. And, yes, I've stumbled, I've shot Lassie, I've cursed at an infant, and yes, I've wiped my butt with the flag. But don't let that define me. Don't judge me. Because someday you could find yourself in a similar situation. You could kill Babe, that lovable pig.

VOICE #4

Don't talk about Babe like that.

(THEY BOO)

(THEY PELT HIM WITH EGGS)

(BUCKWELL REACHES FOR THE FLAG, DECIDES AGAINST IT,
AND GRABS A BABY FROM A NEARBY WOMAN. HE WIPES HIS
BUTT WITH THE BABY)

VOICE #1

He wiped his ass with a baby!

VOICE #3

Oh my god!

HENRY BUCKWELL

Please, you're missing my point. I just want to serve you all as governor!

VOICE #4

That'll never happen! Everyone hates you!

HENRY BUCKWELL

Then I think it's a sad day when a man can't get elected because he shot
a dog, shouted obscenities at a newborn, defiled the flag, and wiped his
ass with a baby. And I ask each of you to look beyond those things and
vote for me. You know what? I think we're gonna surprise some people.

(SFX: CROWD CHEERS)

(FREEZE OF HENRY BUCKWELL HOLDING ARMS UP VICTORI-
OUSLY)

(MATTE VT: THE FOLLOWING TEXT ON SCREEN)

VOICE OVER

And he did. For Henry Buckwell went on to receive zero percent of the
vote. While the incumbent received a hundred percent. But Henry did
go on to be governor of his own state. He put a bunch of his daughter's
dolls around a hole in the woods and served as their governor for three
years. People would often hear his voice echo through the woods as he

yelled, "I'm the governor! I'm the governor!" Henry Buckwell now delivers newspapers with a big radio taped to the front of his bicycle so he can let everyone know "who's winnin' the ballgame."

(OUT)

LORRIE MOORE

Four Calling Birds,
Three French Hens

When the cat died on Veterans Day, his ashes then packed into a cheesy pink-posied tin and placed high upon the mantel, the house seemed lonely and Aileen began to drink. She had lost all her ties to the animal world. She existed now in a solely manmade place: the couch was furless, the carpet dry and unmauled, the kitchen corner where the food dish had been no longer scabby with Mackerel Platter and hazardous for walking.

Oh, Bert!

He had been a beautiful cat.

Her friends interpreted the duration and intensity of her sorrow as a sign of displaced mourning: her grief was for something larger, more appropriate—it was the impending death of her parents; it was the son she and Jack had never had (though wasn't three-year-old Sofie cute as a zipper?); it was this whole Bosnia, Cambodia, Somalia, Dinkins, Giuliani, NAFTA thing.

No, really, it was just Bert, Aileen insisted. It was just her sweet, handsome cat, her buddy of ten years. She had been with him longer than she had with either Jack or Sofie or half her friends, and he was such a smart, funny guy—big and loyal and verbal as a dog.

"What do you mean, *verbal as a dog?*" Jack scowled.

"I swear it," she said.

"Get a grip," said Jack, eyeing her glass of blended malt. Puccini's

"Humming Chorus," the Brahms "Alto Rhapsody," and Samuel Barber's "Adagio for Strings" all murmured in succession from the stereo. He flicked it off. "You've got a daughter. There are holidays ahead. That damn cat wouldn't have shed one tear over you."

"I really don't think that's true," she said a little wildly, perhaps with too much fire and malt in her voice. She now spoke that way sometimes, insisted on things, ventured out on a limb, lived dangerously. She had already—carefully, obediently—stepped through all the stages of bereavement: anger, denial, bargaining, Häagen-Dazs, rage. Anger to rage—who said she wasn't making progress? She made a fist but hid it. She got headaches, mostly prickly ones, but sometimes the zigzag of a migraine made its way into her skull and sat like a cheap, crazy tie in her eye.

"I'm sorry," said Jack. "Maybe he would have. Fundraisers. Cards and letters. Who can say? You two were close, I know."

She ignored him. "Here," she said, pointing at her drink. "Have a little festive lift!" She sipped at the amber liquor, and it stung her chapped lips.

"Dewar's," said Jack, looking with chagrin at the bottle.

"Well," she said defensively, sitting up straight and buttoning her sweater. "I suppose you're out of sympathy with Dewar's. I suppose you're more of a *Do-ee*."

"That's right," said Jack disgustedly. "That's right! And tomorrow I'm going to wake up and find I've been edged out by Truman!" He headed angrily up the stairs, while she listened for the final clomp of his steps and the cracking slam of the door.

Poor Jack: perhaps she had put him through too much. Just last spring, there had been her bunion situation—the limping, the crutch, and the big blue shoe. Then in September, there had been Mimi Andersen's dinner party, where Jack, the only non-smoker, was made to go out on the porch while everyone else stayed inside and lit up. And *then*, there had been Aileen's one-woman performance of "the housework version of *Lysistrata*." "No Sweepie, No Kissie," Jack had called it. But it had worked. Sort of. For about two weeks. There was, finally, only so much one woman on the vast and wicked stage could do.

"I'm worried about you," said Jack in bed. "I'm being earnest here. And not in the Hemingway sense, either." He screwed up his face. "You see how

I'm talking? Things are wacko around here." Their bookcase headboard was so stacked with novels and sad memoirs, it now resembled a library carrel more than a conjugal bed.

"You're fine. I'm fine. Everybody's fine," said Aileen. She tried to find his hand under the covers, then just gave up.

"You're someplace else," he said. "Where are you?"

The birds had become emboldened, slowly reclaiming the yard, filling up the branches, cheeping hungrily in the mornings from the sills and eaves. "What is that *shrieking?*" Aileen asked. The leaves had fallen, but now jays, ravens, and house finches darkened the trees—some of them flying south, some of them staying on, pecking the hardening ground for seeds. Squirrels moved in, poking through the old apples that had dropped from the flowering crab. A possum made a home for himself under the porch, thumping and chewing. Raccoons had discovered Sofie's little gym set, and one morning Aileen looked out and saw two of them swinging on the swings. She'd wanted animal life? Here was animal life!

"Not this," she said. "None of this would be happening if Bert were still here." Bert had patrolled the place. Bert had kept things in line.

"Are you talking to me?" asked Jack.

"I guess not," she said.

"What?"

"I think we need to douse this place in repellent."

"You mean, like, bug spray?"

"Bug spray, Bugs Bunny," chanted Sofie. "Bug spray, Bugs Bunny."

"I don't know what I mean," said Aileen.

At her feminist film-critique group, they were still discussing *Cat Man*, a movie done entirely in flashback from the moment a man jumps off the ledge of an apartment building. Instead of being divided into acts or chapters, the movie was divided into floor numbers, in descending order. At the end of the movie, the handsome remembering man lands on his feet.

Oh, Bert!

One of the women in Aileen's group—Lila Conch—was angry at the movie. "I just hated the way anytime a woman character said anything of substance, she also happened to be half-naked."

Aileen sighed. "Actually, I found those parts the most true to life," she said. "They were the parts I liked the best."

The group glared at her. "Aileen," said Lila, recrossing her legs. "Go to the kitchen for us, dear, and set up the brownies and tea."

"Seriously? asked Aileen.

"Uh—yes," said Lila.

Thanksgiving came and went in a mechanical way. Aileen and Jack, with Sofie, went out to a restaurant and ordered different things, as if the three of them were strangers asserting their ornery tastes. Then they drove home. Only Sofie, who had ordered the child's Stuffed Squash, was somehow pleased, sitting in the car seat in back and singing a Thanksgiving song she'd learned at day care. "'Oh, a turkey's not a pig, you doink/He doesn't says *oink*/He says *gobble, gobble, gobble*.'" Their last truly good holiday had been Halloween, when Bert was still alive and they had dressed him up as Jack. They'd then dressed Jack as Bert, Aileen as Sofie, and Sofie as Aileen. "Now I'm you, Mommy," Sofie had said when Aileen had tied one of her kitchen aprons around her and pressed lipstick onto her mouth. Jack came up and rubbed his Magic Marker whiskers against Aileen, who giggled in her large pink footie pajamas. The only one who wasn't having that much fun was Bert himself, sporting one of Jack's ties, and pawing at it to get it off. When he didn't succeed, he gamely dragged the tie around for a while, trying to ignore it. Then, cross and humiliated, he waddled over to the corner near the piano and lay there, annoyed. Remembering this, a week later—when Bert was dying in an oxygen tent at the vet's, heart failing, fluid around his lungs (though his ears still pricked up when Aileen came to visit him; she wore her usual perfume so he would know her smell, and hand-fed him cat snacks when no one else could get him to eat)—Aileen had felt overwhelmed with sorrow and regret.

"I think you should see someone," said Jack.

"Are we talking a psychiatrist or an affair?"

"An affair, of course." Jack scowled. "An *affair*?"

I don't know." Aileen shrugged. The whiskey she'd been drinking lately had caused her joints to swell, so that now when she lifted her shoulders, they just kind of stayed like that, stiffly, up around her ears.

Jack rubbed her upper arm, as if he either loved her or was wiping something off on her sleeve. Which could it be? "Life is a long journey across a wide country," he said. "Sometimes the weather's good. Sometimes it's bad. Sometimes it's so bad, your car goes off the road."

"Really."

"Just go talk to someone," he said. "Our health plan will cover part."

"Okay," she said. "Okay. Just—no more metaphors."

She got recommendations, made lists and appointments, conducted interviews.

"I have a death-of-a-pet situation," she said. "How long does it take for you to do those?"

"I beg your pardon?"

"How long will it take you to get me over the death of my cat, and how much do you charge for it?"

Each of the psychiatrists, in turn, with their slightly different outfits, and slightly different potted plants, looked shocked.

"Look," Aileen said. "Forget Prozac. Forget Freud's abandonment of the seduction theory. Forget Jeffrey Masson—or is it *Jackie* Mason? The only thing that's going to revolutionize *this* profession is Bidding the Job!"

"I'm afraid we don't work that way," she was told again and again—until finally, at last, she found someone who did.

"I specialize in Christmas," said the psychotherapist, a man named Sidney Poe, who wore an argyle sweater vest, a crisp bowtie, shiny black oxfords, and no socks. "Christmas specials. You feel better by Christmas, or your last session's free."

"I like the sound of that," said Aileen. It was already December first. "I like the sound of that a lot."

"Good," he said, giving her a smile that, she had to admit, looked crooked and unsound. "Now, what are we dealing with here, a cat or a dog?"

"A cat," she said.

"Whoa-boy." He wrote something down, muttered, looked dismayed.

"Can I ask you a question first?" asked Aileen.

"Certainly," he said.

"Do you offer Christmas specials because of the high suicide rates around Christmas?"

"'The high suicide rates around Christmas,'" he repeated in an amused and condescending way. "It's a myth, the high suicide rates around Christmas. It's the *homicide* rate that's high. Holiday homicide. All that time the family suddenly gets to spend together, and the *ham*, that *eggnog*."

She went to Sidney Poe on Thursdays—"Advent Thursdays," she called them. She sat before him with a box of designer Kleenex on her lap, recalling Bert's finer qualities and golden moments, his great sense of humor and witty high jinks. "He used to try to talk on the phone, when I was on the phone. And once when I was looking for my keys, I said aloud 'Where're my keys?' and he came running into the room, thinking I'd said, Where's my *kitty?*"

Only once did she actually have to slap Sidney awake—lightly. Mostly, she could just clap her hands once and call his name—*Sid!*—and he would jerk upright in his psychiatrist's chair, staring wide.

"In the intensive care unit at the animal hospital," Aileen continued, "I saw a cat who'd been shot in the spine with a BB. I saw dogs recovering from jaw surgery. I saw a retriever who'd had a hip replacement come out into the lobby dragging a little cart behind him. He was so happy to see his owner. He dragged himself toward her and she knelt down and spread her arms wide to greet him. She sang out to him and cried. It was the animal version of *Porgy and Bess*." She paused for a minute. "It made me wonder what was going on in this country. It made me think we should ask ourselves, What in the hell's going on?"

"I'm afraid we're over our time," said Sidney.

The next week, she went to the mall first. She wandered in and out of the stores with their thick tinsel and treacly Muzak Christmas carols. Everywhere she went, there were little cat Christmas books, cat Christmas cards, cat Christmas wrapping paper. She hated these cats. They were boring, dopey, caricatured, interchangeable—not a patch on Bert.

"I had great hopes for Bert," she said later to Sidney. "They gave him all the procedures, all the medications—but the drugs knocked his kidneys out.

When the doctor suggested putting him to sleep, I said, 'Isn't there anything else we can do?' and you know what the doctor said? He said, 'Yes. An autopsy.' A thousand dollars later and he says, 'Yes. An autopsy.'"

"Eeeeyew," said Sid.

"A cashectomy," said Aileen. "They gave poor Bert a cashectomy!" And here she began to cry, thinking of the sweet, dire look on Bert's face in the oxygen tent, the bandaged tube in his paw, the wet fog in his eyes. It was not an animal's way to die like that, but she had subjected him to the full medical treatment, signed him up for all that metallic and fluorescent voodoo, not knowing what else to do.

"Tell me about Sofie."

Aileen sighed. Sofie was adorable. Sofie was terrific. "She's fine. She's great." Except Sofie was getting little notes sent home wither her from day care. "'Today, Sofie gave the teacher the finger—except it was her index finger.' Or 'Today, Sofie drew a mustache on her face.' Or 'Today, Sofie demanded to be called Walter.'"

"Really."

"Our last really good holiday was Halloween. I took her trick-or-treating around the neighborhood, and she was so cute. It was only by the end of the night that she began to catch on to the whole concept of it. Most of the time, she was so excited, she'd ring the bell, and when someone came to the door, she'd thrust out her bag and say, 'Look! I've got treats for you!'"

Aileen had stood waiting, down off the porches, on the sidewalk, in her big pink footie pajamas. She'd let Sofie do the talking. "I'm my mommy and my mommy's me," Sofie explained.

"I see," said the neighbors. And then they'd call and wave from the doorway. "Hello, Aileen! How are you doing?"

"We've got to focus on Christmas here," said Sidney.

"Yes," said Aileen despairingly. "We've only got one more week."

On the Thursday before Christmas, she felt flooded with memories: the field mice, the day trips, the long naps together. "He had limited notes to communicate his needs," she said. "He had his 'food' mew, and I'd follow him to his dish. He had his 'out' mew, and I'd follow him to the door. He had his 'brush' mew, and I'd go with him to the cupboard where his brush was kept.

And then he had his existential mew, where I'd follow him vaguely around the house as he wandered in and out of rooms, not knowing exactly what or why."

Sidney's eyes began to well. "I can see why you miss him," he said.

"You can?"

"Of course! But that's all I can leave you with."

"The Christmas special's up?"

"I'm afraid so," he said, standing. He reached to shake her hand. "Call me after the holiday and let me know how you feel."

"All right," she said sadly. "I will."

She went home, poured herself a drink, stood by the mantel. She picked up the pink-posied tin and shook it, afraid she might hear the muffled banging of bones, but she heard nothing. "Are you sure it's even him?" Jack asked. "With animals, they probably do mass incinerations. One scoop for cats, two for dogs."

"*Please*," she said. At least she had not buried Bert in the local pet cemetery, with its intricate gravestones and maudlin inscriptions—*Beloved Rexie: I'll be joining you soon*. Or *In memory of Muffin, who taught me to love*.

"I got the very last Christmas tree," said Jack. "It was leaning against the shed wall, with a broken high heel, and a cigarette dangling from its mouth. I thought I'd bring it home and feed it soup."

At least she had sought something more tasteful than the cemetery, sought the appropriate occasion to return him to earth and sky, get him down off the fireplace and out of the house in a meaningful way, though she'd yet to find the right day. She had let him stay on the mantel and had mourned him deeply—it was only proper. You couldn't pretend you had lost nothing. A good cat had died—you had to begin there, not let your blood freeze over. If your heart turned away at this, it would turn away at something greater, then more and more until your heart stayed averted, immobile, your imagination redistributed away from the world and back only toward the bad maps of yourself, the sour pools of your own pulse, your own tiny, mean, and pointless wants. Stop here! Begin here! Begin with Bert!

Here's to Bert!

Early Christmas morning, she woke Sofie and dressed her warmly in her snowsuit. There was a light snow on the ground and a wind blew powdery gusts around the yard. "We're going to say good-bye to Bert," said Aileen.

"Oh, Bert!" said Sofie, and she began to cry.

"No, it'll be happy!" said Aileen, feeling the pink-posied tin in her jacket pocket. "He wants to go out. Do you remember how he used to want to go out? How he would mee-ow at the door and then we would let him go?"

"Mee-ow, mee-ow," said Sofie.

"Right," said Aileen. "So that's what we're going to do now."

"Will he be with Santa Claus?"

"Yes! He'll be with Santa Claus!"

They stepped outside, down off the porch steps. Aileen pried open the tin. Inside, there was a small plastic bag and she tore that open. Inside was Bert: a pebbly ash like the sand and ground shells of a beach. Summer in December! What was Christmas if not a giant mixed metaphor? What was it about if not the mystery of interspecies love—God's for man! Love had sought a chasm to leap across and landed itself right here: the Holy Ghost among the barn animals, the teacher's pet sent to be adored and then to die. Aileen and Sofie each seized a fistful of Bert and ran around the yard, letting wind take the ash and scatter it. Chickadees flew from the trees. Frightened squirrels headed for the yard next door. In freeing Bert, perhaps they would become him a little: banish the interlopers, police the borders, then go back inside and play with the decorations, claw at the gift wrap, eat the big headless bird.

"Merry Christmas to Bert!" Sofie shouted. The tin was now empty.

"Yes, merry Christmas to Bert!" said Aileen. She shoved the tin back into her pocket. The she and Sofie raced back into the house, to get warm.

Jack was in the kitchen, standing by the stove, still in his pajamas. He was pouring orange juice and heating buns.

"Daddy, Merry Christmas to Bert!" Sofie popped open the snaps of her snowsuit.

"Yes," said Jack, turning. "Merry Christmas to Bert!" He handed Sofie some juice, then Aileen. But before she drank hers, Aileen waited for him to say something else. He cleared his throat and stepped forward. He raised his glass. His large quizzical smile said, This is a very weird family. But instead, he exclaimed, "Merry Christmas to everyone in the whole wide world!" and let it go at that.

ALICE MUNRO

Material

I don't keep up with Hugo's writing. Sometimes I see his name, in the library, on the cover of some literary journal that I don't open—I haven't opened a literary journal in a dozen years, praise God. Or I read in the paper or see on a poster—this would be in the library too, or in a bookstore—an announcement of a panel discussion at the university, with Hugo flown in to discuss the state of the novel today, or the contemporary short story, or the new nationalism in our literature. Then I think, Will people really go, will people who could be swimming or drinking or going for a walk really take themselves out to the campus to find the room and sit in rows listening to those vain quarrelsome men? Bloated, opinionated, untidy men, that is how I see them, cosseted by the academic life, the literary life, by women. People will go to hear them say that such and such a writer is not worth reading anymore, and that some writer must be read; to hear them dismiss and glorify and argue and chuckle and shock. People, I say, but I mean women, middle-aged women like me, alert and trembling, hoping to ask intelligent questions and not be ridicu-lous; soft-haired young girls awash in adoration, hoping to lock eyes with one of the men on the platform. Girls, and women too, fall in love with such men; they imagine there is power in them.

The wives of the men on the platform are not in that audience. They are buying groceries or cleaning up messes or having a drink. Their lives are concerned with food and mess and houses and cars and money. They have to remember to get the snow tires on and go to the bank and take back the beer bottles, because their husbands are such brilliant, such talented incapable men, who must be looked after for the sake of the words that will come from them. The women in the audience are married to engineers or doctors or businessmen. I know them, they are my friends. Some of them have turned to literature frivolously, it is true, but most come shyly, and with enormous transitory hope. They absorb the contempt of the men on the platform as if they deserved it; they half-believe they do deserve it, because of their houses and expensive shoes, and their husbands who read Arthur Hailey.

I am married to an engineer myself. His name is Gabriel, but he prefers the name Gabe. In this country he prefers the name Gabe. He was born in Romania; he lived there until the end of the war, when he was sixteen. He has forgotten how to speak Romanian. How can you forget, how can you forget the language of your childhood?

I used to think he was pretending to forget, because the things he had seen and lived through when he spoke that language were too terrible to remember. He told me this was not so. He told me his experience of the war was not so bad. He described the holiday uproar at school when the air-raid sirens sounded. I did not quite believe him. I required him to be an ambassador from bad times as well as distant countries. Then I thought he might not be Romanian at all, but an impostor.

This was before we were married, when he used to come and see me in the apartment on Clark Road where I lived with my little daughter, Clea. Hugo's daughter too, of course, but he had to let go of her. Hugo had grants, he travelled, he married again and his wife had three children; he divorced and married again, and his next wife, who had been his student, had three more children, the first born to her while he was still living with his second wife. In such circumstances a man can't hang on to everything. Gabriel used to stay all night sometimes on the pullout couch I had for a bed in this tiny, shabby apartment, and I would look at him sleeping and think that for all I knew he might be a German or a Russian or even of all things a Canadian faking a past and an accent to make himself interesting. He was mysterious to me. Long after he became my lover and after he became my husband he remained, remains, mysterious to me. In spite of all the things I know about him, daily and physical things. His face curves out smoothly and his eyes, set shallowly in his head, curve out too under the smooth pink lids. The wrinkles he has are traced on top of this smoothness, this impenetrable surface; they are of no consequence. His body is substantial, calm. He used to be a fine, rather lazy-looking skater. I cannot describe him without a familiar sense of capitulation. I cannot describe him. I could describe Hugo, if anybody asked me, in great detail—Hugo as he was eighteen, twenty years ago, crew-cut and skinny, with the bones of his body and even of his skull casually, precariously, joined and knitted together, so that there was something uncoordinated, unexpected about the shifting planes of his face, as well as the movements, often danger-ous, of his limbs. "He's held together by nerves," a friend of mine at college said when I first brought him around, and it was true; after that I could almost see the fiery strings.

Gabriel told me when I first knew him that he enjoyed life. He did not say that he believed in enjoying it; he said that he did. I was embarrassed for him. I never believed people who said such things and anyway, I associated this statement with gross, self-advertising, secretly unpleasantly restless men. But it seems to be the truth. He is not curious. He is able to take pleasure and give off smiles and caresses and say softly, "Why do you worry about that? It is not a problem of yours." He has forgotten the language of his childhood. His lovemaking was strange to me at first, because it was lacking in desperation. He made love without emphasis, so to speak, with no memory of sin or hope of depravity. He does not watch himself. He will never write a poem about it, never, and indeed may have forgotten it in half an hour. Such men are com-monplace, perhaps. It was only that I had not known any. I used to wonder if I would have fallen in love with him if his accent and his forgotten, nearly forgotten, past had been taken away; if he had been, say, an engineering stu-dent in my own year at college. I don't know, I can't tell. What holds anybody in a man or a woman may be something as flimsy as a Romanian accent or the calm curve of an eyelid, some half-fraudulent mystery.

No mystery of this sort about Hugo. I did not miss it, did not know about it, maybe would not have believed in it. I believed in something else, then. Not that I knew him all the way through, but the part I knew was in my blood and from time to time would give me a poison rash. None of that with Gabriel; he does not disturb me, any more than he is disturbed himself.

It was Gabriel who found me Hugo's story. We were in a bookstore, and he came to me with a large, expensive paperback, a collection of short stories. There was Hugo's name on the cover. I wondered how Gabriel had found it, what he had been doing in the fiction section of the store anyway; he never reads fiction. I wondered if he sometimes went and looked for things by Hugo. He is interested in Hugo's career as he would be interested in the career of a magician or popular singer or politician with whom he had, through me, a plausible connection, a proof of reality. I think it is because he does such anonymous work himself, work intelligible only to his own kind. He is fascinated by people who work daringly out in the public eye, without the protection of any special discipline—it must seem so, to an engineer—just trying to trust themselves, and elaborating their bag of tricks, and hoping to catch on.

"Buy it for Clea," he said.

"Isn't it a lot of money for a paperback?"

He smiled.

"There's your father's picture, your real father, and he has written this story you might like to read," I said to Clea, who was in the kitchen making toast. She is seventeen. Some days she eats toast and honey and peanut butter and Oreos, and cream cheese and chicken sandwiches and fried potatoes. If anybody comments on what she is eating or not eating, she may run upstairs and slam the door of her room.

"He looks overweight," said Clea, and put the book down. "You always said he was skinny." Her interest in her father is all from the point of view of heredity, and what genes he might have passed on to herself. Did he have a bad complexion, did he have a high I.Q., did the women in his family have big breasts?

"He was when I knew him," I said. "How was I to know what had happened to him since?"

He looked, however, very much as I would have thought he would look by now. When I saw his name in the newspaper or on a poster, I had pictured somebody much like this; I had foreseen the ways in which time and his life would have changed him. It did not surprise me that he had got fat but not bald, that he had let his hair grow wild and had grown a full, curly beard.

Pouches under his eyes, a dragged-down look to the cheeks even when he is laughing. He is laughing, into the camera. His teeth have gone from bad to worse. He hated dentists, said his father died of a heart attack in the dentist's chair. A lie, like so much else, or at least an exaggeration. He used to smile crookedly for photographs to hide the right top incisor, dead since somebody at high school pushed him into a drinking fountain. Now he doesn't care, he laughs, he bares those rotting stumps. He looks, at the same time, woebegone and cheerful. A Rabelaisian writer. Checked wool shirt open at the top to show his undershirt; he didn't use to wear one. Do you wash, Hugo? Do you have bad breath, with those teeth? Do you call your girl students fond exasperated dirty names, are there phone calls from insulted parents, does the Dean or somebody have to explain that no harm is meant, that writers are not as other men are? Probably not, probably no one minds. Outrageous writers may bounce from one blessing to another nowadays, bewildered, as permissively reared children are said to be, by excess of approval.

I have no proof. I construct somebody from this one smudgy picture, I am content with such clichés. I have not the imagination or goodwill to proceed differently; and I have noticed anyway, everybody must have noticed as we go further into middle age, how shopworn and simple, really, are the disguises, the identities if you like, that people take up. In fiction, in Hugo's business, such disguises would not do, but in life they are all we seem to want, all anybody can manage. Look at Hugo's picture, look at the undershirt, listen to what it says about him.

Hugo Johnson was born and semi-educated in the bush, and in the mining and lumbering towns of Northern Ontario. He has worked as a lumberjack, beer-slinger, counterman, telephone lineman, and sawmill foreman, and has been sporadically affiliated with various academic communities. He lives now most of the time on the side of a mountain above Vancouver, with his wife and six children.

The student wife, it seems, got stuck with all the children. What happened to Mary Frances, did she die, is she liberated, did he drive her crazy? But listen to the lies, the half-lies, the absurdities. *He lives on the side of a mountain above Vancouver.* It sounds as if he lives in a wilderness cabin, and all it means, I'm willing to bet, is that he lives in an ordinary comfortable house in North or West Vancouver, which now stretch far up the mountain. He has been *sporadically affiliated with various academic communities*. What does that mean? If it means he has taught for years, most of his adult life, at universities, that teaching at universities has been the only steady well-paid job he has ever had, why doesn't it say so? You would think he came out of the bush now and then to fling them scraps of wisdom, to give them a demonstration of what a real male *writer*, a creative *artist*, is like; you would never think he was a practicing *academic*. I don't know if he was a lumberjack or a beer-slinger or a counterman, but I do know that he was not a telephone lineman. He had a job painting telephone poles. He quit that job in the middle of the second week because the heat and the climbing made him sick. It was a broiling June, just after we had both graduated. Fair enough. The sun really did make him sick; twice he came home and vomited. I have quit jobs myself that I could not stand. The same summer I quit my job folding bandages at Victoria Hospital, because I was going mad with boredom. But if I was a writer, and was listing all my varied and colorful occupations, I don't think I would put down *bandage folder*; I don't think I would find that entirely honest.

After he quit, Hugo found a job marking Grade 12 examination papers. Why didn't he put that down? *Examination marker*. He liked marking examination papers better than he liked climbing telephone poles, and probably better than he liked lumberjacking or beer-slinging or any of those other things if he ever did them; why couldn't he put it down? *Examination marker*.

Nor has he, to my knowledge, ever been the foreman in a sawmill. He worked in his uncle's mill the summer before I met him. What he did all day was load lumber and get sworn at by the real foreman, who didn't like him because of his uncle being the boss. In the evenings, if he was not too tired, he used to walk half a mile to a little creek and play his recorder. Blackflies bothered him, but he did it anyway. He could play "Morning," from *Peer Gynt*, and some Elizabethan airs whose names I have forgotten. Except for one: "Wolsey's Wilde." I learned to play it on the piano so we could play a duet. Was that meant for Cardinal Wolsey, and what was a *wilde*, a dance? Put that down, Hugo. *Recorder player*. That would be quite all right, quite in fashion now; as I understand things, recorder-playing and such fey activities are not out of favor now, quite the contrary. Indeed, they may be more acceptable than all that lumberjacking and beer-slinging. Look at you, Hugo, your image is not only fake but out-of-date. You should have said you'd meditated for a year in the mountains of Uttar Pradesh; you should have said you'd taught Creative Drama to autistic children; you should have shaved your head, shaved your beard, put on a monk's cowl; you should have shut up, Hugo.

When I was pregnant with Clea we lived in a house on Argyle Street in Vancouver. It was such a sad, gray stucco house on the outside, in the rainy winter, that we painted the inside, all the rooms, vivid ill-chosen colors. Three walls of the bedrooms were Wedgwood blue, one was magenta. We said it was an experiment to see if color could drive anybody mad. The bathroom was a deep orange-yellow. "It's like being inside a cheese," Hugo said when we finished it. "That's right, it is," I said. "That's very good, phrase-maker." He was pleased, but not as pleased as if he'd written it. After that he said, every time he showed anybody the bathroom, "See the color? It's like being inside a cheese." Or, "It's like peeing inside a cheese." Not that I didn't do the same thing, save things up and say them over and over. Maybe I said that about peeing inside a cheese. We had many phrases in common. We both called the landlady the Green Hornet, because she had worn, the only time we had seen her, a poison-green outfit with bits of rat fur and a clutch of violets, and had given off a venomous sort of buzz. She was over seventy and she ran a downtown boardinghouse for men. Her daughter Dotty we called the harlot-in-residence. I wonder why we chose to say "harlot"; that was not, is not, a word in general use. I suppose it had a classy sound, a classy depraved sound, contrasting ironically—we were strong on irony—with Dotty herself.

She lived in a two-room apartment in the basement of the house. She was supposed to pay her mother forty-five dollars monthly rent and she told me she meant to try to make the money baby-sitting.

"I can't go out to work," she said, "on account of my nerves. My last husband, I had him six months dying down at Mother's, dying with his kidney disease, and I owe her three hundred dollars board still on that. She made me make him his eggnog with skim milk. I'm broke every day of my life. They say it's all right not having wealth if you got health, but what if you never had either one? Bronchial pneumonia from the time I was three years old.

Rheumatic fever at twelve. Sixteen I married my first husband, he was killed in a logging accident. Three miscarriages. My womb is in shreds. I use up three packs of Kotex every month. I married a dairy farmer out in the Valley and his herd got the fever. Wiped us out. That was the one who died with his kidneys. No wonder. No wonder my nerves are shot."

I am condensing. This came out at greater length and by no means dolefully, indeed with some amazement and pride, at Dotty's table. She asked me down for cups of tea, then for beer. This is life, I thought, fresh from books, classes, essays, discussions. Unlike her mother, Dotty was flat-faced, soft, doughy, fashioned for defeat, the kind of colorless puzzled woman you see carrying a shopping bag, waiting for the bus. In fact, I had seen her once on a bus downtown and not recognized her at first in her dull blue winter coat. Her rooms were full of heavy furniture salvaged from her marriage—an upright piano, overstuffed chesterfield and chairs, walnut-veneer china cabinet, and dining-room table, where we sat. In the middle of the table was a tremendous lamp, with a painted china base and a pleated dark-red silk shade, held out at an extravagant angle, like a hoop skirt.

I described it to Hugo. "That is a whorehouse lamp," I said. Afterward I wanted to be congratulated on the accuracy of this description. I told Hugo he ought to pay more attention to Dotty if he wanted to be a writer. I told him about her husbands and her womb and her collection of souvenir spoons, and he said I was welcome to look at them all by myself. He was writing a verse play.

Once when I went down to put coal on the furnace, I found Dotty in her pink chenille dressing gown saying goodbye to a man in a uniform, some sort of deliveryman or gas-station attendant. It was the middle of the afternoon. She and this man were not parting in any way that suggested either lechery or affection and I would not have understood anything about it, I would probably have thought he was some relative, if she had not begun at once a long complicated slightly drunk story about how she had got wet in the rain and had to leave her clothes at her mother's house and worn home her mother's dress which was too tight and that was why she was now in her dressing gown. She said that first Larry had caught her in it delivering some sewing he wanted her to do for his wife, and now me, and she didn't know what we would think of her. This was strange, as I had seen her in her dressing gown many times before. In the middle of her laughing and explaining, the man, who had not looked at me, not smiled or said a word or in any way backed up her story, simply ducked out the door.

"Dotty has a lover," I said to Hugo.

"You don't get out enough. You're trying to make life interesting."

The next week I watched to see if this man came back. He did not. But three other men came, and one of them came twice. They walked with their heads down, quickly, and did not have to wait at the basement door. Hugo couldn't deny it. He said it was life imitating art again, it was bound to happen, after all the fat varicose-veined whores he'd met in books. It was then we named her the harlot-in-residence and began to brag about her to our friends. They stood behind the curtains to catch a glimpse of her going in or out.

"That's not her!" they said. "Is that her? Isn't she disappointing? Doesn't she have any professional clothes?"

"Don't be so naïve," we said. "Did you think they all wore spangles and boas?"

Everybody hushed to hear her play the piano. She sang or hummed along with her playing, not steadily, but loudly, in the rather defiant, self-parodying voice people use when they are alone, or think they are alone. She sang "Yellow Rose of Texas" and "You Can't Be True, Dear."

"Whores should sing hymns."

"We'll get her to learn some."

"You're all such voyeurs. You're all so mean," said a girl named Mary Frances Shrecker, a big-boned, calm-faced girl with black braids down her back. She was married to a former mathematical prodigy, Elsworth Shrecker, who had had a breakdown. She worked as a dietician. Hugo said he could not look at her without thinking of the word *lumpen*, but he supposed she might be nourishing, like oatmeal porridge. She became his second wife. I thought she was the right wife for him, I thought she would stay forever, nourishing him, but the student evicted her.

The piano-playing was an entertainment for our friends, but disastrous on the days when Hugo was home trying to work. He was supposed to be working on his thesis but he really was writing his play. He worked in our bedroom, at a card table in front of the window, facing a board fence. When Dotty had been playing for a bit, he might come out to the kitchen and stick his face into mine and say in low, even tones of self-consciously controlled rage, "You go down and tell her to cut that out."

"You go."

"Bloody hell. She's your friend. You cultivate her. You encourage her."

"I never told her to play the piano."

"I arranged so that I could have this afternoon free. That did not just happen. I arranged it. I am at a crucial point, I am at the point where this play *lives* or *dies*. If I go down there I'm afraid I might strangle her."

"Well don't look at *me*. Don't strangle *me*. Excuse my breathing and everything."

I always did go down to the basement, of course, and knock on Dotty's door and ask her if she would mind not playing the piano now, because my husband was at home and was trying to work. I never said the word *write*, Hugo had trained me not to, that word was like a bare wire to us. Dotty apologized every time; she was scared of Hugo and respectful of his work and his intelligence. She left off playing but the trouble was she might forget, she might start again in an hour, half an hour. The possibility made me nervous and miserable. Because I was pregnant I always wanted to eat, and I would sit at the kitchen table greedily, unhappily, eating something like a warmed-up plateful of Spanish rice. Hugo felt the world was hostile to his writing; he felt not only all its human inhabitants but its noises and diversions and ordinary clutter were linked against him, maliciously, purposefully, diabolically thwarting and maiming him and keeping him from his work. And I, whose business it was to throw myself between him and the world, was failing to do so, by choice perhaps as much as ineptitude for the job. I did not believe in him. I had not understood how it would be necessary to believe in him. I believed that he was clever and talented, whatever that might mean, but I was not sure he would turn out to be a writer. He did not have the authority I thought a writer should have. He was too nervous, too touchy with everybody, too much of a show-off. I believed that writers were calm, sad people, knowing too much. I believed that there was a difference about them, some hard and shining, rare intimidating quality they had from the beginning, and

Hugo didn't have it. I thought that someday he would recognize this. Meanwhile, he lived in a world whose rewards and punishments were as strange, as hidden from me, as if he had been a lunatic. He would sit at supper, pale and disgusted; he would clench himself over the typewriter in furious paralysis when I had to get something from the bedroom, or he would leap around the living room asking me what he was (a rhinoceros who thinks he is a gazelle, Chairman Mao dancing a war dance in a dream dreamt by John Foster Dulles) and then kiss me all over the neck and throat with hungry gobbling noises. I was cut off from the source of these glad or bad moods, I did not affect them.

I teased him sourly: "Suppose after we have the baby the house is on fire and the baby and the play are both in there, which would you save?"

"Both."

"But supposing you can just save one? Never mind the baby, suppose I am in there, no, suppose I am drowning *here* and you are *here* and cannot possibly reach us both— "

"You're making it tough for me."

"I know I am. I know I am. Don't you hate me?"

"Of course I hate you." After this we might go to bed, playful, squealing, mock-fighting, excited. All our life together, the successful part of our life together, was games. We made up conversations to startle people on the bus. Once we sat in a beer parlor and he berated me for going out with other men and leaving the children alone while he was off in the bush working to support us. He pleaded with me to remember my duty as a wife and as a mother. I blew smoke in his face. People around us were looking stern and gratified. When we got outside we laughed till we had to hold each other up, against the wall. We played in bed that I was Lady Chatterley and he was Mellors.

"Where be that little rascal John Thomas?" he said thickly. "I canna find John Thomas!"

"Frightfully sorry, I think I must have swallowed him," I said, ladylike.

There was a water pump in the basement. It made a steady thumping noise. The house was on fairly low-lying ground not far from the Fraser River, and during the rainy weather the pump had to work most of the time to keep the basement from being flooded. We had a dark rainy January, as usual in

Vancouver, and this was followed by a dark rainy February. Hugo and I felt gloomy. I slept a lot of the time. Hugo couldn't sleep. He claimed it was the pump that kept him awake. He couldn't work because of it in the daytime and he couldn't sleep because of it at night. The pump had replaced Dotty's piano-playing as the thing that most enraged and depressed him in our house. Not only because of its noise, but because of the money it was costing us. Its entire cost went onto our electricity bill, though it was Dotty who lived in the basement and reaped the benefits of not being flooded. He said I should speak to Dotty and I said Dotty could not pay the expenses she already had. He said she could turn more tricks. I told him to shut up. As I became more pregnant, slower and heavier and more confined to the house, I got fonder of Dotty, used to her, less likely to store up and repeat what she said. I felt more at home with her than I did sometimes with Hugo and our friends.

All right, Hugo said, I ought to phone the landlady. I said he ought. He said he had far too much to do. The truth was we both shrank from a confrontation with the landlady, knowing in advance how she would confuse and defeat us with shrill evasive prattle.

In the middle of the night in the middle of a rainy week I woke up and wondered what had wakened me. It was the silence.

"Hugo, wake up. The pump's broken. I can't hear the pump."

"I am awake," Hugo said.

"It's still raining and the pump isn't going. It must be broken."

"No, it isn't. It's shut off. I shut it off."

I sat up and turned on the light. He was lying on his back, squinting and trying to give me a hard look at the same time.

"You didn't turn it off."

"All right, I didn't."

"You did."

"I could not stand the goddamn expense anymore. I could not stand thinking about it. I could not stand the noise, either. I haven't had any sleep in a week."

"The basement will flood."

"I'll turn it on in the morning. A few hours' peace is all I want."

"That'll be too late, it's raining torrents."

"It is not."

"You go to the window."

"It's raining. It's not raining torrents."

I turned out the light and lay down and said in a calm stern voice, "Listen to me, Hugo, you have to go and turn it on, Dotty will be flooded out."

"In the morning."

"You have to go and turn it on *now*."

"Well I'm not."

"If you're not, I am."

"No, you're not."

"I am."

But I didn't move.

"Don't be such an alarmist."

"*Hugo.*"

"Don't *cry*."

"Her stuff will be ruined."

"Best thing could happen to it. Anyway, it won't." He lay beside me stiff and wary, waiting, I suppose, for me to get out of bed, go down to the basement, and figure out how to turn the pump on. Then what would he have done? He could not have hit me, I was too pregnant. He never did hit me, unless I hit him first. He could have gone and turned it off again, and I could have turned it on, and so on; how long could that last? He could have held me down, but if I struggled he would have been afraid of hurting me. He could have sworn at me and left the house, but we had no car, and it was raining too hard for him to stay out very long. He would probably have just raged and sulked, alternately, and I could have taken a blanket and gone to sleep on the living-room couch for the rest of the night. I think that is what a woman of firm character would have done. I think that is what a woman who wanted that marriage to last would have done. But I did not do it. Instead, I said to myself that I did not know how the pump worked, I did not know where to turn it on. I said to myself that I was afraid of Hugo. I entertained the possibility that Hugo might be right, nothing would happen. But I wanted something to happen, I wanted Hugo to crash.

When I woke up, Hugo was gone and the pump was thumping as usual.

Dotty was pounding on the door at the top of the basement stairs.

"You won't believe your eyes what's down here. I'm up to my knees in water. I just put my feet out of bed and up to my knees in water. What happened? You hear the pump go off?"

"No," I said.

"I don't know what could've gone wrong, I guess it could've got overworked. I had a couple of beers before I went to bed, elst I would've known there was something wrong. I usually sleep light. But I was sleeping like the dead and I put my feet out of bed and Jesus, it's a good thing I didn't pull on the light switch at the same time, I would have been electrocuted. Everything's floating."

Nothing was floating and the water would not have come to any grown person's knees. It was about five inches deep in some places, only one or two in others, the floor being so uneven. It had soaked and stained the bottom of her chesterfield and chairs and got into the bottom of her piano. The floor tiles were loosened, the rugs soggy, the edges of her bedspread dripping, her floor heater ruined.

I got dressed and put on a pair of Hugo's boots and took a broom downstairs. I started sweeping the water toward the drain outside the door. Dotty made herself a cup of coffee in my kitchen and sat for a while on the top step watching me, going over the same monologue about having a couple of beers and sleeping more soundly than usual, not hearing the pump go off, not understanding why it should go off, if it had gone off, not knowing how she was going to explain to her mother, who would certainly make it out to be her fault and charge her. We were in luck, I saw. (We were?) Dotty's expectation and thrifty relish of misfortune made her less likely than almost anyone else would have been to investigate just what had gone wrong. After the water level went down a bit, she went into her bedroom, put on some clothes and some boots which she had to drain first, got her broom, and helped me.

"The things that don't happen to me, eh? I never get my fortune told. I've got these girlfriends that are always getting their fortune told and I say, never mind me, there's one thing I know and I know it ain't good."

I went upstairs and phoned the university, trying to get Hugo. I told them it was an emergency and they found him in the library.

"It did flood."

"What?"

"It did flood. Dotty's place is underwater."

"I turned the pump on."

"Like hell you did. This morning you turned it on."

"This morning there was a downpour and the pump couldn't handle it. That was after I turned it on."

"The pump couldn't handle it last night because the pump wasn't on last night and don't talk to me about any downpour."

"Well there was one. You were asleep."

"You have no idea what you've done, do you? You don't even stick around to look at it. I have to look. I have to cope. I have to listen to that poor woman."

"Plug your ears."

"Shut up, you filthy moral idiot."

"I'm sorry. I was kidding. I'm sorry."

"Sorry. You're bloody sorry. This is the mess you made and I told you you'd make and you're bloody sorry."

"I have to go to a seminar. I am sorry. I can't talk now, and it's no good talking to you now, I don't know what you're trying to get me to say."

"I'm just trying to get you to *realize*."

"All right, I realize. Though I still think it happened this morning."

"You don't realize. You never realize."

"You dramatize."

"*I* dramatize!"

Our luck held. Dotty's mother was not so likely as Dotty to do without explanations and it was, after all, her floor tiles and wallboard that were ruined. But Dotty's mother was sick, the cold wet weather had undermined her too, and she was taken to hospital with pneumonia that very morning. Dotty went to live in her mother's house, to look after the boarders. The basement had a disgusting, moldy smell. We moved out too, a short time later. Just before Clea was born we took over a house in North Vancouver, belonging to some friends who had gone to England. The quarrel between us subsided in the excitement of moving; it was never really resolved. We did not move much from the positions we had taken on the phone. I said you don't realize, you never realize, and he said, what do you want me to say? Why do you make such a fuss over this, he asked reasonably. Anybody might wonder. Long after I was away from him, I wondered too. I could have turned on the pump, as I have said, taking responsibility for both of us, as a patient realistic woman, a really married woman, would have done, as I am sure Mary Frances would have done, did, many times, during the ten years she lasted. Or I could have told Dotty the truth, though she was not a very good choice to receive such information. I could have told somebody, if I thought it was that important, pushed Hugo out into the unpleasant world and let him taste trouble. But I didn't, I was not able fully to protect or expose him, only to flog him with blame, desperate sometimes, feeling I would claw his head open to pour my vision into it, my notion of what had to be understood. What presumptuousness, what cowardice, what bad faith. Unavoidable. "You have a problem of incompatibility," the marriage counsellor said to us a while later. We laughed till we cried in the dreary municipal hall of the building in North Vancouver where the marriage counseling was dispensed. That is our problem, we said to each other, what a relief to know it, incompatibility.

I did not read Hugo's story that night. I left it with Clea and she as it turned out did not read it either. I read it the next afternoon. I got home about two o'clock from the girls' private school where I have a part-time job teaching history. I made tea as I usually do and sat down in the kitchen to enjoy the hour before the boys, Gabriel's sons, get home from school. I saw the book still lying on top of the refrigerator and I took it down and read Hugo's story.

The story is about Dotty. Of course, she has been changed in some un-important ways and the main incident concerning her has been invented, or grafted on from some other reality. But the lamp is there, and the pink chenille dressing gown. And something about Dotty that I had forgotten: When you were talking she would listen with her mouth slightly open, nodding, then she would chime in on the last word of your sentence with you. A touching and irritating habit. She was in such a hurry to agree, she hoped to understand. Hugo has remembered this, and when did Hugo ever talk to Dotty?

That doesn't matter. What matters is that this story of Hugo's is a very good story, as far as I can tell, and I think I can tell. How honest this is and how lovely, I had to say as I read. I had to admit. I was moved by Hugo's story; I was, I am, glad of it, and I am not moved by tricks. Or if I am, they have to be good tricks. Lovely tricks, honest tricks. There is Dotty, lifted out of life and held in light, suspended in the marvelous clear jelly that Hugo has spent all his life learning how to make. It is an act of magic, there is no getting around it; it is an act, you might say, of a special, unsparing, unsentimental love. A fine and lucky benevolence. Dotty was a lucky person, people who understand and value this act might say (not everybody, of course, does understand and value this act); she was lucky to live in that basement for a few months and eventually to have this done to her, though she doesn't know what has been done and wouldn't care for it, probably, if she did know. She has passed into Art. It doesn't happen to everybody.

Don't be offended. Ironical objections are a habit with me. I am half-ashamed of them. I respect what has been done. I respect the intention and the effort and the result. Accept my thanks.

I did think that I would write a letter to Hugo. All the time I was preparing dinner, and eating it, and talking to Gabriel and the children, I was thinking of a letter. I was thinking I would tell him how strange it was for me to realize that we shared, still shared, the same bank of memory, and that what was all scraps and oddments, useless baggage, for me, was ripe and usable, a paying investment, for him. Also I wanted to apologize, in some not-outright way, for not having believed he would be a writer. Acknowledgment, not apology; that was what I owed him. A few graceful, a few grateful, phrases.

At the same time, at dinner, looking at my husband Gabriel, I decided that he and Hugo are not really so unalike. Both of them have managed something. Both of them have decided what to do about everything they run across in this world, what attitude to take, how to ignore or use things. In their limited and precarious ways they both have authority. They are not *at the mercy*. Or think they are not. I can't blame them for making whatever arrangements they can make.

After the boys had gone to bed and Gabriel and Clea had settled to watch television, I found a pen and got the paper in front of me, to write my letter, and my hand jumped. I began to write short jabbing sentences that I had never planned:

This is not enough, Hugo. You think it is, but it isn't. You are mistaken, Hugo.

That is not an argument to send through the mail.

I do blame them. I envy and despise.

Gabriel came into the kitchen before he went to bed, and saw me sitting with a pile of test papers and my marking pencils. He might have meant to talk to me, to ask me to have coffee, or a drink, with him, but he respected my unhappiness as he always does; he respected the pretense that I was not unhappy but preoccupied, burdened with these test papers; he left me alone to get over it.

FLANNERY O'CONNOR

Good Country People

Besides the neutral expression that she wore when she as alone, Mrs. Freeman had two others, forward and reverse, that she used for all her human dealings. Her forward expression was steady and driving like the advance of a heavy truck. Her eyes never swerved to left or right but turned as the story turned as if they followed a yellow line down the center of it. She seldom used the other expression because it was not often necessary for her to retract a statement, but when she did, her face came to a complete stop, there was an almost imperceptible movement of her black eyes, during which they seemed to be receding, and then the observer would see that Mrs. Freeman, though she might stand there as real as several grain sacks thrown on top of each other, was no longer there in spirit. As for getting anything across to her when this was the case, Mrs. Hopewell had given it up. She might talk her head off. Mrs. Freeman could never be brought to admit herself wrong on any point. She would stand there and if she could be brought to say anything, it was something like, "Well, I wouldn't of said it was and I wouldn't of said it wasn't," or letting her gaze range over the top kitchen shelf where there was an assortment of dusty bottles, she might remark, "I see you ain't ate many of them figs you put up last summer."

They carried on their most important business in the kitchen at breakfast. Every morning Mrs. Hopewell got up at seven o'clock and lit her gas heater and Joy's. Joy was her daughter, a large blonde girl who had an artificial leg.

Mrs. Hopewell thought of her as a child though she was thirty-two years old and highly educated. Joy would get up while her mother was eating and lumber into the bathroom and slam the door, and before long, Mrs. Freeman would arrive at the back door. Joy would hear her mother call, "Come on in," and then they would talk for a while in low voices that were indistinguishable in the bathroom. By the time Joy came in, they had usually finished the weather report and were on one or the other of Mrs. Freeman's daughters, Glynese or Carramae, Joy called them Glycerin and Caramel. Glynese, a redhead, was eighteen and had many admirers; Carramae, a blonde, was only fifteen but already married and pregnant. She could not keep anything in her stomach. Every morning Mrs. Freeman told Mrs. Hopewell how many times she had vomited since the last report.

Mrs. Hopewell liked to tell people that Glynese and Carramae were two of the finest girls she knew and that Mrs. Freeman was a *lady* and that she was never ashamed to take her anywhere or introduce her to anybody they might meet. Then she would tell how she had happened to hire the Freemans in the first place and how they were a godsend to her and how she had had them four years. The reason for her keeping them so long was that they were not trash. They were good country people. She had telephoned the man whose name they had given as a reference and he had told her that Mr. Freeman was a good farmer, but that his wife was the nosiest woman ever to walk the earth. "She's got to be into everything," the man said "If she don't get there before the dust settles, you can bet she's dead, that's all. She'll want to know all your business. I can stand him real good," he had said, "but me nor my wife neither could have stood that woman one more minute on this place." That had put Mrs. Hopewell off for a few days.

She had hired them in the end because there were no other applicants but she had made up her mind beforehand exactly how she would handle the woman. Since she was the type who had to be into everything then. Mrs. Hopewell had decided, she would not only let her be into everything, she would *see to it* that she was into everything—she would give her the responsibility of everything, she would put her in charge. Mrs. Hopewell had no bad qualities of her own, but she was able to use other people's in such a constructive way that she never felt the lack. She had hired the Freemans and she had kept them four years.

Nothing is perfect. This was one of Mrs. Hopewell's favorite sayings. Another was: that is life! And still another, the most important, was: well, other people have their opinions too. She would make these statements, usually at the table, in a tone of gentle insistence as if no one held them but her, and the large hulking Joy, whose constant outrage had obliterated every expression from her face, would stare just a little to the side of her, her eyes icy blue, with the look of someone who has achieved blindness by an act of will and means to keep it.

When Mrs. Hopewell said to Mrs. Freeman that life was like that, Mrs. Freeman would say, "I always said so myself." Nothing had been arrived at by anyone that had not first been arrived at by her. She was quicker than Mr. Freeman. When Mrs. Hopewell said to her after they had been on the place a while, "You know, you're the wheel behind the wheel," and winked, Mrs. Freeman had said, "I know it. I've always been quick. It's some that are quicker than others."

"Everybody is different," Mrs. Hopewell said.

"Yes, most people is," Mrs. Freeman said.

"It takes all kinds to make the world."

"I always said it did myself."

The girl was used to this kind of dialogue for breakfast and more of it for dinner; sometimes they had it for supper too. When they had no guest they ate in the kitchen because that was easier. Mrs. Freeman always managed to arrive at some point during the meal and to watch them finish it. She would stand in the doorway if it were summer but in the winter she would stand with one elbow on top of the refrigerator and look down on them, or she would stand by the gas heater, lifting the back of her skirt slightly. Occasionally she would stand against the wall and roll her head from side to side. At no time was she in any hurry to leave. All this was very trying on Mrs. Hopewell but she was a woman of great patience. She realized that nothing is perfect and that in the Freemans she had good country people and that if, in this day and age, you get good country people, you had better hang on to them.

She had plenty of experience with trash. Before the Freemans she had averaged one tenant family a year. The wives of these farmers were not the kind you would want to be around you for very long. Mrs. Hopewell, who had divorced her husband long ago, needed someone to walk over the fields with her; and when Joy had to be impressed for these services, her remarks were usually so ugly and her face so glum that Mrs. Hopewell would say, "If you can't come pleasantly, I don't want you at all," to which the girl, standing square and rigid-shouldered with her neck thrust slightly forward, would reply "If you want me, here I am—LIKE I AM."

Mrs. Hopewell excused this attitude because of the leg (which had been shot off in a hunting accident when Joy was ten). It was hard for Mrs. Hopewell to realize that her child was thirty-two now and that for more than twenty years she had had only one leg. She thought of her still as a child because it tore her heart to think instead of the poor stout girl in her thirties who had never danced a step or had any *normal* good times. Her name was really Joy, but as soon as she was twenty-one and away from home, she had had it legally changed. Mrs. Hopewell was certain that she had thought and thought until she had hit upon the ugliest name in any language. Then she had gone and had the beautiful name, Joy, changed without telling her mother until after she had done it. Her legal name was now Hulga.

When Mrs. Hopewell thought of the name, Hulga, she thought of the broad blank hull of a battleship. She would not use it. She continued to call her Joy, to which the girl responded but in a purely mechanical way.

Hulga had learned to tolerate Mrs. Freeman, who saved her from taking walks with her mother. Even Glynese and Carramae were useful when they occupied attention that might otherwise have been directed at her. At first she had thought she could not stand Mrs. Freeman for she had found that it was not possible to be rude to her. Mrs. Freeman would take on strange resentments and for days together she would be sullen, but the source of her displeasure was always obscure; a direct attack, a positive leer, blatant ugliness to her face—these never touched her. And without warning one day, she began calling her Hulga.

She did not call her that in front of Mrs. Hopewell, who would have been incensed, but when she and the girl happened to be out of the house together, she would say something and add the name Hulga to the end of it, and the big spectacled Joy-Hulga would scowl and redden as if her privacy had been intruded upon. She considered the name her personal affair. She had arrived at it first purely on the basis of its ugly sound, and then the full genius of its fitness had struck her. She had a vision of the name working like the ugly sweating Vulcan who stayed in the furnace and to whom, presumably, the goddess had to come when called. She saw it as the name of her highest creative act. One of her major triumphs was that her mother had not been able to turn her dust into Joy, but the greater one was that she had been able to turn it herself into Hulga. However, Mrs. Freeman's relish for using the name only irritated her. It was as if Mrs. Freeman's beady steel-pointed eyes had penetrated far enough behind her face to reach some secret fact. Something about her seemed to fascinate Mrs. Freeman, and then one day Hulga realized that it was the artificial leg. Mrs. Freeman had a special fondness for the details of secret infections, hidden deformities, assaults upon children. Of diseases, she preferred the lingering or incurable. Hulga had heard Mrs. Hopewell give her the details of the hunting accident, how the leg had been literally blasted off, how she had never lost consciousness. Mrs. Freeman could listen to it any time as if it had happened an hour ago.

When Hulga stumped into the kitchen in the morning (she could walk without making the awful noise, but she made it, Mrs. Hopewell was certain, because it was ugly-sounding), she glanced at them and did not speak. Mrs. Hopewell would be in her red kimono with her hair tied around her head in rags. She would be sitting at the table, finishing her breakfast, and Mrs. Freeman would be hanging by her elbow outward from the refrigerator, looking down at the table. Hulga always put her eggs on the stove to boil and then stood over them with her arms folded, and Mrs. Hopewell would look at her—a kind of indirect gaze divided between her and Mrs. Freeman—and would think that if she would only keep herself up a little, she wouldn't be so bad looking. There was nothing wrong with her face that a pleasant expression wouldn't help. Mrs. Hopewell said that people who looked on the bright side of things would be beautiful even if they were not.

Whenever she looked at Joy this way, she could not help but feel that it would have been better if the child had not taken the PhD. It had certainly not brought her out any, and now that she had it, there was no more excuse for her to go to school again. Mrs. Hopewell thought it was nice for girls to go to school to have a good time, but Joy had "gone through." Anyhow, she would not have been strong enough to go again. The doctors had told Mrs. Hopewell that with the best of care, Joy might see forty-five. She had a weak heart. Joy had made it plain that if it had not been for this condition, she would be far from these red hills and good country people. She would be in a university lecturing to people who knew what she was talking about. And Mrs. Hopewell could very well picture her there, looking like a scarecrow and lecturing to more of the same. Here she went about all day in a six-year-old skirt and a yellow sweatshirt with a faded cowboy on a horse embossed on it. She thought this was funny; Mrs. Hopewell thought it was idiotic and showed simply that she was still a child. She was brilliant but she didn't have a grain of sense. It seemed to Mrs. Hopewell that every year she grew less like other people and more like herself—bloated, rude, and squint-eyed. And she said such strange things! To her own mother she had said—without warning, without excuse, standing up in the middle of a meal with her face purple and her mouth half full—"Woman! Do you ever look inside? Do you ever look inside and see what you are *not?* God!" she had cried, sinking down again and staring at her plate, "Malebranche was right: we are not our own light. We are not our own light!" Mrs. Hopewell had no idea to this day what brought that on. She had only made the remark, hoping Joy would take it in, that a smile never hurt anyone.

The girl had taken the PhD in philosophy and this left Mrs. Hopewell at a complete loss. You could say, "my daughter is a nurse," or "my daughter is a schoolteacher," or even "my daughter is a chemical engineer." You could not say, "my daughter is a philosopher." That was something that had ended with the Greeks and Romans. All day Joy sat on her neck in a deep chair, reading. Sometimes she went for walks but she didn't like dogs or cats or birds or flowers or nature or nice young men. She looked at nice young men as if she could smell their stupidity.

One day Mrs. Hopewell had picked up one of the books the girl had just put down and, opening it at random, she read, "science, on the other hand, has to assert its soberness and seriousness afresh and declare that it is concerned solely with what-is. Nothing—how can it be for science anything but a horror and a phantasm? If science is right, then one thing stands firm: science wishes to know nothing of nothing. Such is after all the strictly scientific approach to

Nothing. We know it by wishing to know nothing of Nothing." These words had been underlined with a blue pencil and they worked on Mrs. Hopewell like some evil incantation in gibberish. She shut the book quickly and went out of the room as if she were having a chill.

This morning when the girl came in, Mrs. Freeman was on Carramae. "She thrown up four times after supper," she said, "and was up twice in the night after three o'clock. Yesterday she didn't do nothing but ramble in the bureau drawer. All she did. Stand up there and see what she could run up on."

"She's got to eat," Mrs. Hopewell muttered, sipping her coffee, while she watched Joy's back at the stove. She was wondering what the child had said to the Bible salesman. She could not imagine what kind of conversation she could possibly have had with him.

He was a tall gaunt hatless youth who had called yesterday to sell them a Bible. He had appeared at the door, carrying a large black suitcase that weighted him so heavily on one side that he had to brace himself against the door facing. He seemed on the point of collapse but he said in a cheerful voice, "Good morning, Mrs. Cedars!" and set the suitcase down on the mat. He was not a bad-looking young man, though he had on a bright blue suit and yellow socks that were not pulled up far enough. He had prominent face bones and a streak of sticky-looking brown hair falling across his forehead.

"I'm Mrs. Hopewell," she said.

"Oh!" he said, pretending to look puzzled but with his eyes sparkling, "I saw 'The Cedars' on the mailbox, so I thought you was Mrs. Cedars!" and he burst out in a pleasant laugh. He picked up the satchel and under cover of a pant, he fell forward into her hall. It was rather as if the suitcase had moved first, jerking him after it. "Mrs. Hopewell!" he said and grabbed her hand. "I hope you are well!" and he laughed again and then all at once his face sobered completely. He paused and gave her a straight earnest look and said, "Lady, I've come to speak of serious things."

"Well, come in," she muttered, none too pleased because her dinner was almost ready. He came into the parlor and sat down on the edge of a straight chair and put the suitcase between his feet and glanced around the room as if he were sizing her up by it. Her silver gleamed on the two sideboards; she decided he had never been in a room as elegant as this.

"Mrs. Hopewell," he began, using her name in a way that sounded almost intimate, "I know you believe in Chistian service."

"Well yes," she murmured.

"I know," he said and paused, looking very wise with his head cocked on one side, "that you're a good woman. Friends have told me."

"Mrs. Hopewell never liked to be taken for a fool. "What are you selling?" she asked.

"Bibles," the young man said, and his eye raced around the room before he added, "I see you have no family Bible in your parlor, and I see that is the one lack you got!"

Mrs. Hopewell could not say, "My daughter is an atheist and won't let me keep the Bible in the parlor." She said, stiffening slightly, "I keep my Bible by my bedside." This was not the truth. It was in the attic somewhere.

"Lady," he said, "the word of God ought to be in the parlor."

"Well, I think that's a matter of taste," she began. "I think..."

"Lady," he said, "for a Chrustian, the word of God ought to be in every room in the house besides in his heart. I know you're a Chrustian because I can see it in every line of your face."

She stood up and said, "Well, young man, I don't want to buy a Bible and I smell my dinner burning."

He didn't get up. He began to twist his hands and looking down at them, he said softly, "Well lady, I'll tell you the truth—not many people want to buy one nowadays, and besides, I know I'm real simple. I don't know how to say a thing but to say it. I'm just a country boy." He glanced up into her unfriendly face. "People like you don't like to fool with country people like me!"

"Why!" she cried, "Good country people are the salt of the earth! Besides, we all have different ways of doing, it takes all kinds to make the world go 'round. That's life!"

"You said a mouthful," he said.

"Why, I think there aren't enough good country people in the world!" she said, stirred. "I think that's what's wrong with it!"

His face had brightened. "I didn't inraduce myself," he said. "I'm Manley Pointer from out in the country around Willohobie, not even from a place, just from near a place."

"You wait a minute," she said. "I have to see about my dinner."

She went out to the kitchen and found Joy standing near the door where she had been listening.

"Get rid of the salt of the earth," she said, "and let's eat."

Mrs. Hopewell gave her a pained look and turned the heat down under the vegetables. "*I* can't be rude to anybody," she murmured and went back into the parlor.

He had opened the suitcase and was sitting with a Bible on each knee.

"You might as well put those up," she told him. "I don't want one."

"I appreciate your honesty," he said. "You don't see any more real honest people unless you go way out in the country."

"I know," she said, "real genuine folks!" Through the crack in the door she heard a groan.

"I guess a lot of boys come telling you they're working their way through college," he said, "but I'm not going to tell you that. Somehow," he said, "I don't want to go to college. I want to devote my life to Chrustian service. See," he said, lowering his voice, "I got this heart condition. I may not live long. When you know it's something wrong with you and you may not live long, well then, lady..." He paused, with his mouth open, and stared at her.

He and Joy had the same condition! She knew that her eyes were filling with tears but she collected herself quickly and murmured, "Won't you stay for dinner? We'd love to have you!" and was sorry the instant she heard herself say it.

"Yes mam," he said in an abashed voice, "I would sher love to do that!"

Joy had given him one look on being introduced to him and then throughout the meal had not glanced at him again. He had addressed several remarks to her, which she had pretended not to hear. Mrs. Hopewell could not understand deliberate rudeness, although she lived with it, and she felt she had always to overflow with hospitality to make up for Joy's lack of courtesy. She urged him to talk about himself and he did. He said he was the seventh child of twelve and that his father had been crushed under a tree when he himself was eight year old. He had been crushed very badly, in fact, almost cut in two, and was practically not recognizable. His mother had got along the best she could by hard working, and she had always seen that her children went to Sunday School and that they read the Bible every evening. He was now nineteen year old and he had been selling Bibles for four months. In that time he had sold seventy-seven Bibles and had the promise of two more sales. He wanted to become a missionary because he thought that was the way you could do most for people. He who losest his life shall find it, he said simply, and he was so sincere, so genuine and earnest that Mrs. Hopewell would not for the world have smiled. He prevented his peas from sliding onto the table by blocking them with a piece of bread which he later cleaned his plate with. She could see Joy observing sidewise how he handled his knife and fork, and she saw too that every few minutes, the boy would dart a keen appraising glance at the girl as if he were trying to attract her attention.

After dinner Joy cleared the dishes off the table and disappeared and Mrs. Hopewell was left to talk with him. He told her again about his childhood and his father's accident and about various things that had happened to him. Every five minutes or so she would stifle a yawn. He sat for two hours until finally she told him she must go because she had an appointment in town. He packed his Bibles and thanked her and prepared to leave, but in the doorway he stopped and wrung her hand and said that not on any of his trips had he met a lady as nice as her and he asked if he could come again. She had said she would always be happy to see him.

Joy had been standing in the road, apparently looking at something in the distance, when he came down the steps toward her, bent to the side with his heavy valise. He stopped where she was standing and confronted her directly. Mrs. Hopewell could not hear what he said but she trembled to think what Joy would say to him. She could see that after a minute Joy said something and that then the boy began to speak again, making an excited gesture with his free hand. After a minute Joy said something else, at which the boy began to speak once more. Then to her amazement, Mrs. Hopewell saw the two of them walk off together toward the gate. Joy had walked all the way to the gate with him and Mrs. Hopewell could not imagine what they had said to each other, and she had not yet dared to ask.

Mrs. Freeman was insisting upon her attention. She had moved from the refrigerator to the heater so that Mrs. Hopewell had to turn and face her in order to seem to be listening. "Glynese gone out with Harvey Hill again last night," she said. "She had this sty."

"Hill," Mrs. Hopewell said absently, "is that the one who works in the garage."

"Nome, he's the one that goes to chiropracter school," Mrs. Freeman said. "She had this sty. Been had it two days. So she says when he brought her in the other night he says, 'Lemme get rid of that sty for you,' and she says, 'How?' and he says, 'You just lay yourself down across the seat of that car and I'll show you.' So she done it and he popped her neck. Kept on a-popping it several times until she made him quit. This morning," Mrs. Freeman said, "she ain't got no sty. She ain't got no traces of a sty."

"I never heard of that before," Mrs. Hopewell said.

"He ast her to marry him before the Ordinary," Mrs. Freeman went on, "and she told him she wasn't going to be married in no office."

"Well, Glynese is a fine girl," Mrs. Hopewell said. "Glynese and Carramae are both fine girls."

"Carramae said when her and Lyman was married Lyman said it sure felt sacred to him. She said he wouldn't take five hundred dollars for being married by a preacher."

"How much would he take?" the girl asked from the stove.

"He said he wouldn't take five hundred dollars," Mrs. Freeman repeated.

"Well we all have work to do," Mrs. Hopewell said.

"Lyman said it just felt more sacred to him," Mrs. Freeman said. "The doctor wants Carramae to eat prunes. Says instead of medicine. Says them cramps is coming from pressure. You know where I think it is?"

"She'll be better in a few weeks," Mrs. Hopewell said.

"In the tube," Mrs. Freeman said. "Else she wouldn't be as sick as she is."

Hulga had cracked her two eggs into a saucer and was bringing them to the table along with a cup of coffee that she had filled too full. She sat down carefully and began to eat, meaning to keep Mrs. Freeman there by questions if for any reason she showed an inclination to leave. She could perceive her mother's eye on her. The first round-about question would be about the Bible salesman and she did not wish to bring it on. "How did he pop her neck?" she asked.

Mrs. Freeman went into a description of how he had popped her neck. She said he owned a '55 Mercury but that Glynese said she would rather marry a man with only a '36 Plymouth who would be married by a preacher. The girl asked what if he had a '32 Plymouth and Mrs. Freeman said what Glynese had said was a '36 Plymouth.

Mrs. Hopewell said there were not many girls with Glynese's common sense. She said what she admired in those girls was their common sense. She said that reminded her that they had had a nice visitor yesterday, a young man selling Bibles. "Lord," she said, "he bored me to death, but he was so sincere and genuine I couldn't be rude to him. He was just good country people, you know," she said, "—just the salt of the earth."

I seen him walk up," Mrs. Freeman said, "and then later—I seen him walk off," and Hulga could feel the slight shift in her voice, the slight insinuation, that he had not walked off alone, had he? Her face remained expressionless but the color rose into her neck and she seemed to swallow it down with the next spoonful of egg. Mrs. Freeman was looking at her as if they had a secret together.

"Well, it takes all kinds of people to make the world go 'round," Mrs. Hopewell said. "It's very good we aren't all alike."

"Some people are more alike than others," Mrs. Freeman said.

Hulga got up and stumped, with about twice the noise that was necessary, into her room and locked the door. She was to meet the Bible salesman at ten o'clock at the gate. She had thought about it half the night. She had started thinking of it as a great joke and then she had begun to see profound implications in it. She had lain in bed imagining dialogues for them that were insane on the surface but that reached below to depths that no Bible salesman would be aware of. Their conversation yesterday had been of this kind.

He had stopped in front of her and had simply stood there. His face was bony and sweaty and bright, with a little pointed nose in the center of it, and his look was different from what it had been at the dinner table He was gazing at her with open curiosity, with fascination, like a child watching a new fantastic animal at the zoo, and he was breathing as if he had run a great distance to reach her. His gaze seemed somehow familiar but she could not think where she had been regarded with it before. For almost a minute he didn't say anything. Then on what seemed an insuck of breath, he whispered, "You ever ate a chicken that was two days old?"

The girl looked at him stonily. He might have just put this question up for consideration at the meeting of a philosophical association. "Yes," she presently replied as if she had considered it from all angles.

"It must have been mighty small!" he said triumphantly, and shook all over with little nervous giggles, getting very red in the face, and subsiding finally into his gaze of complete admiration, while the girl's expression remained exactly the same.

"How old are you?" he asked softly

She waited some time before she answered. Then in a flat voice she said, "Seventeen."

His smiles came in succession like waves breaking on the surface of a little lake. "I see you got a wooden leg," he said. "I think you're brave. I think you're real sweet."

The girl stood blank and solid and silent.

"Walk to the gate with me," he said. "You're a brave sweet little thing and I liked you the minute I seen you walk in the door."

Hulga began to move forward.

"What's your name?" he asked, smiling down on the top of her head.

"Hulga," she said.

"Hulga," he murmured, "Hulga. Hulga. I never heard of anybody named Hulga before. You're shy, aren't you, Hulga?" he asked.

She nodded, watching his large red hand on the handle of the giant valise.

"I like girls that wear glasses," he said. "I think a lot. I'm not like these people that a serious thought don't ever enter their heads. It's because I may die."

"I may die too," she said suddenly and looked up at him. His eyes were very small and brown, glittering feverishly.

"Listen," he said, "don't you think some people was meant to meet on account of what all they got in common and all? Like they both think serious thoughts and all?" He shifted the valise to his other hand so that the hand nearest her was free. He caught hold of her elbow and shook it a little. "I don't work on Saturday," he said. "I like to walk in the woods and see what Mother Nature is wearing. O'er the hills and far away. Picnics and things. Couldn't we go on a picnic tomorrow? Say yes, Hulga," he said, and gave her a dying look as if he felt his insides about to drop out of him. He had even seemed to sway slightly toward her.

During the night she had imagined that she seduced him. She imagined that the two of them walked on the place until they came to the storage barn beyond the two back fields and there, she imagined that things came to such a pass that she very easily seduced him and that then, of course, she had to reckon with his remorse. True genius can get an idea across even to an inferior mind. She imagined that she took his remorse in hand and changed it into a deeper understanding of life. She took all his shame away and turned it into something useful.

She set off for the gate at exactly ten o'clock, escaping without drawing Mrs. Hopewell's attention. She didn't take anything to eat, forgetting that food is usually taken on a picnic. She wore a pair of slacks and a dirty white shirt, and as an afterthought, she had put some Vapex on the collar of it since she did not own any perfume. When she reached the gate no one was there.

She looked up and down the empty highway and had the furious feeling that she had been tricked, that he had only meant to make her walk to the gate after the idea of him. Then suddenly he stood up, very tall, from behind a bush on the opposite embankment.

Smiling, he lifted his hat, which was new and wide-brimmed. He had not worn it yesterday and she wondered if he had bought it for the occasion. It was toast-colored with a red and white band around it and was slightly too large for him. He stepped from behind the bush still carrying the black valise. He had on the same suit and the same yellow socks sucked down in his shoes from walking. He crossed the highway and said, "I knew you'd come!"

The girl wondered acidly how he had known this. She pointed to the valise and asked, "Why did you bring your Bibles?"

He took her elbow, smiling down on her as if he could not stop. "You can never tell when you'll need the word of God, Hulga," he said. She had a moment in which she doubted that this was actually happening, and then they began to climb the embankment. They went down into the pasture toward the woods. The boy walked lightly by her side, bouncing on his toes. The valise did not seem to be heavy today; he even swung it. They crossed half the pasture without saying anything and then, putting his hand easily on the small of her back, he asked softly, "Where does your wooden leg join on?"

She turned an ugly red and glared at him, and for an instant the boy looked abashed." I didn't mean you no harm," he said. "I only meant you're so brave and all. I guess God takes care of you."

"No," she said, looking forward and walking fast, "I don't even believe in God."

At this he stopped and whistled. "No!" he exclaimed as if he were too astonished to say anything else.

She walked on and in a second he was bouncing at her side, fanning with his hat. "That's very unusual for a girl," he remarked, watching her out of the corner of his eye. When they reached the edge of the wood, he put his hand on her back again and drew her against him without a word and kissed her heavily.

The kiss, which had more pressure than feeling behind it, produced that extra surge of adrenalin in the girl that enables one to carry a packed trunk out of a burning house, but in her, the power went at once to the brain. Even before he released her, her mind, clear and detached and ironic anyway, was regarding him from a great distance, with amusement but also with pity. She had never been kissed before and she was pleased to discover that it was an unexceptional experience and all a matter of the mind's control. Some people might enjoy drain water if they were told it was vodka. When the boy, look- ing expectant but uncertain, pushed her gently away, she turned and walked on, saying nothing, as if such business, for her, were common enough.

He came along panting at her side, trying to help her when he saw a root that she might trip over. He caught and held back the long swaying blades of thorn vine until she had passed beyond them. She led the way and he came breathing heavily behind her. Then they came out on a sunlit hillside, sloping softly into another one a little smaller. Beyond, they could see the trusted top of the old barn where the extra hay was stored.

The hill was sprinkled with small pink weeds. "Then you ain't saved?" he asked suddenly, stopping.

The girl smiled. It was the first time she had smiled at him at all. "In my economy," she said, "I'm saved and you are damned, but I told you I didn't believe in God."

Nothing seemed to destroy the boy's look of admiration. He gazed at her now as if the fantastic animal at the zoo had put its paw through the bars and given him a loving poke. She thought he looked as if he wanted to kiss her again and she walked on before he had the chance.

"Ain't there somewheres we can sit down sometime?" he murmured, his voice softening toward the end of the sentence.

"In that barn," she said.

They made for it rapidly as if it might slide away like a train. It was a large two-story barn, cool and dark inside. The boy pointed up the ladder that led into the loft and said, "It's too bad we can't go up there."

"Why can't we?" she asked.

"Yer leg," he said reverently.

The girl gave him a contemptuous look and putting both hands on the ladder, she climbed it while he stood below, apparently awestruck She pulled herself expertly through the opening and then looked down at him and said, "Well, come on if you're coming," and he began to climb the ladder, awkwardly bringing the suitcase with him.

"We won't need the Bible," she observed.

"You never can tell," he said, panting. After he had got into the loft, he was a few seconds catching his breath. She had sat down in a pile of straw. A wide sheath of sunlight, filled with dust particles, slanted over her. She lay back against a bal, her face turned away, looking out the front opening of the barn where hay was thrown from a wagon into the loft. The two pink-speck-led hillsides lay back against a dark ridge of woods. The sky was cloudless and cold blue. The boy dropped down by her side and put one arm under her and the other over her and began methodically kissing her face, making little noises like a fish. He did not remove his hat but it was pushed far enough back not to interfere. When her glasses got in his way, he took them off of her and slipped them into his pocket.

The girl at first did not return any of the kisses but presently she began to and after she had put several on his cheek, she reached his hips and remained there, kissing him again and again as if she were trying to draw all the breath out of him. His breath was clear and sweet like a child's and the kisses were sticky like a child's. He mumbled about loving her and about knowing when he first seen her that he loved her, but the mumbling was like the sleepy fretting of a child being put to sleep by his mother. Her mind, throughout this, never stopped or lost itself for a second to her feelings. "You ain't said you loved me non," he whispered finally, pulling back from her. "You got to say that."

She looked away from him off into the hollow sky and then down at a black ridge and then down farther into what appeared to be two green swelling lakes. She didn't realize he had taken her glasses but this landscape could not seem exceptional to her for she seldom gave any close attention to her surroundings.

"You got to say it," he repeated. "You got to say you love me."

She was always careful how she committed herself. "In a sense," she began, "if you use the word loosely, you might say that. But it's not a word I use. I don't have illusions. I'm one of those people who see *through* to nothing."

The boy was frowning. "You got to say it. I said it and you got to say it," he said.

The girl looked at him almost tenderly. "You poor baby," she murmured. "It's just as well you don't understand," and she pulled him by the neck, face-down, against her. "We are all damned," she said, "but some of us have taken off our blindfolds and see that there's nothing to see. It's a kind of salvation."

The boy's astonished eyes looked blankly through the ends of her hair. "Okay," he almost whined, "but do you love me or don'tcher?"

"Yes," she said and added, "in a sense. But I must tell you something. There mustn't be anything dishonest between us." She lifted his head and looked him in the eye. "I am thirty years old," she said. "I have a number of degrees."

The boy's look was irritated but dogged. "I don't care," he said. "I don't care a thing about what all you done. I just want to know if you love me or don'tcher?" and he caught her to him and wildly planted her face with kisses until she said, "yes, yes."

"Okay then," he said, letting her go. "Prove it."

She smiled, looking dreamily out on the shifty landscape. She had seduced him without even making up her mind to try. "How?" she asked, feeling that he should be delayed a little.

He leaned over and put his lips to her ear. "Show me where your wooden leg joins on," he whispered.

The girl uttered a sharp little cry and her face was instantly drained of color. The obscenity of the suggestion was not what shocked her. As a child she had sometimes been subject to feelings of shame but education had removed the last traces of that as a good surgeon scrapes for cancer; she would no more have felt it over what he was asking than she would have believed in his Bible. But she was as sensitive about the artificial leg as a peacock about his tail. No one ever touched it but her. She took care of it as someone else would his soul, in private and almost with her own eyes turned away.

"No," she said.

"I known it," he muttered, sitting up. "You're just playing me for a sucker."

"Oh, no no!" she cried. "It joins on at the knee. Only at the knee. Why do you want to see it?"

The boy gave her a long penetrating look. "Because," he said, "it's what makes you different. You ain't like anybody else."

She sat staring at him. There was nothing about her face or her round freezing-blue eyes to indicate that this had moved her; but she felt as if her heart had stopped and left her mind to pump blood. She decided that for the first time in her life she was face to face with real innocence. This boy, with an instinct that came from beyond wisdom, had touched the truth about her. When after a minute she said in a hoarse high voice, "All right," it was like surrendering to him completely. It was like losing her own life and finding it again, miraculously, in his.

Very gently he began to roll the slack leg up. The artificial limb, in a white sock and brown flat shoe, was bound in a heavy material like canvas and ended in an ugly jointure where it was attached to the stump. The boy's face and his voice were entirely reverent as he uncovered it and said, "Now show me how to take it off and on."

She took it off for him and put it back on again and then he took it off himself, handling it as tenderly as if it were a real one. "See!" he said with a delighted child's face. "Now I can do it myself!"

"Put it back on," she said. She was thinking that she would run away with him and that every night he would take the leg off and every morning put it back on again. "Put it back on."

"Not yet," he murmured, setting it on its foot out of her reach. "Leave it off for a while. You got me instead."

She gave a little cry of alarm but he pushed her down and began to kiss her again. Without the leg she felt entirely dependent on him. Her brain seemed to have stopped thinking altogether and to be about some other function that it was not very good at. Different expressions raced back and forth over her face. Every now and then the boy, his eyes like two steel spikes, would glance behind him where the leg stood. Finally she pushed him off and said, "Put it back on me now."

"Wait," he said. He leaned the other way and pulled the valise toward him and opened it. It had a pale blue spotted lining and there were only two Bibles in it. He took one of these out and opened the cover of it. It was hollow and contained a pocket flask of whiskey, a pack of cards, and a small blue box with printing on it. He laid these out in front of her one at a time in an evenly spaced row, like one presenting offerings at the shrine of a goddess. He put the blue box in her hand. THIS PRODUCT TO BE USED ONLY FOR THE PREVENTION OF DISEASE, she read, and dropped it. The boy was unscrewing the top of the flask. He stopped and pointed, with a smile, to the deck of cards. It was not an ordinary deck, but one with an obscene picture on the back of each card. "Take a swig," he said, offering her the bottle first. He held it in front of her, but like one mesmerized, she did not move.

Her voice when she spoke had an almost pleading sound. "Aren't you," she murmured, "aren't you just good country people?"

The boy cocked his head. He looked as if he were just beginning to understand that she might be trying to insult him. "Yeah," he said, curling his lip slightly, "but it ain't held me back none. I'm as good as you any day in the week."

"Give me my leg," she said.

He pushed it farther away with his foot. "Come on now, let's begin to have us a good time," he said coaxingly. "We ain't got to know one another good yet."

"Give me my leg!" she screamed, and tried to lunge for it, but he pushed her down easily.

"What's the matter with you all of a sudden?" he asked, frowning as he screwed the top of the flask and put it quickly back inside the Bible. "You just a while ago said you didn't believe in nothing. I thought you was some girl!"

Her face was almost purple "You're a Christian!" she hissed. "You're a fine

Christian! You're just like them all—say one thing and do another. You're a perfect Christian, you're…"

The boy's mouth was set angrily. "I hope you don't think," he said in a lofty indignant tone, "that I believe in that crap! I may sell Bibles but I know which end is up and I wasn't born yesterday and I know where I'm going!"

"Give me my leg!" she screeched. He jumped up so quickly that she barely saw him sweep the cards and the blue box into the Bible and throw the Bible into the valise. She saw him grab the leg and then she saw it for an instant slanted forlornly across the inside of the suitcase with a Bible at either side of its opposite ends. He slammed the lid shut and snatched up the valise and swung it down the hole and then stepped through himself.

When all of him had passed but his head, he turned and regarded her with a look that no longer had any admiration in it. "I've gotten a lot of interesting things," he said. "One time I got a woman's glass eye this way. And you needn't to think you'll catch me because Pointer ain't really my name. I use a different name at every house I call at and don't stay nowhere long. And I'll tell you another thing, Hulga," he said, using the name as if he didn't think much of it, "you ain't so smart. I been believing in nothing ever since I was born!" And then the toast-colored hat disappeared down the hole and the girl was left, sitting on the straw in the dusty sunlight. When she turned her churning face toward the opening, she saw his blue figure struggling successfully over the green speckled lake.

Mrs. Hopewell and Mrs. Freeman, who were in the back pasture digging up onions, saw him emerge a little later from the woods and head across the meadow toward the highway. "Why, that looks like that nice dull young man that tried to sell me a Bible yesterday," Mrs. Hopewell said, squinting. "He must have been selling them to the Negroes back in there. He was so simple," she said, "but I guess the world would be better off if we were all that simple."

Mrs. Freeman's gaze drove forward and just touched him before he disappeared under the hill. Then she returned her attention to the evil-smelling onion shoot she was lifting from the ground. "Some can't be that simple," she said. "I know I never could."

SIMON RICH

Six Selected Pieces

IF LIFE WERE LIKE MIDDLE SCHOOL

JUDGE: In all my years on the bench, I have never seen a more despicable criminal. You robbed, assaulted, and tortured the victim simply for the thrill of it. Do you have anything to say in your defense before I sentence you?

CRIMINAL: Nope.

JUDGE: In that case, I hereby sentence you to forty years in a maximum security prison. I also sentence the victim to forty years in prison.

VICTIM: Wait—what? That doesn't make any sense! He attacked me!

JUDGE: I don't care who started it.

MY MOM'S ALL-TIME, TOP FIVE GREATEST BOYFRIENDS
BY JORDI STROMSON, AGE 11

5. Jason Morgan

This guy was awesome! He's by far the strongest, biggest dude I've ever met. But that's not all—he also plays for the Norfolk Admirals, my favorite minor league hockey team! My mom dated Jason for a few days last summer, and every time he came to the house he gave me a regulation Norfolk Admirals hockey puck. By the end I had five pucks! Once I ran into him in the kitchenette in the middle of the night. He was making a sandwich. I couldn't believe there was a real hockey player in my house. I wanted to say something, but I was too nervous so I just stood there. Then after a while he looked at me and said, "Hey little buddy. How's your skating?" and I said, "Fine!"

4. Igor Radulov

Igor wasn't as strong as Jason, but he was just as cool because he also played hockey for the Norfolk Admirals! He only dated my mom once so I only had one chance to talk to him. Still, it was pretty awesome. It was in the middle of the night. I couldn't sleep so I went to the kitchenette and there he was, Igor Radulov, in my house! I asked him to sign my regulation pucks and he said he would. He couldn't believe I had so many pucks! "Wow, kid," he said, "You're a real fan." He autographed all five of them and wrote "16" next to his name, which is his number!

3. Michal Barinka

This guy also played hockey for the Norfolk Admirals! He had four goals and two assists in 2006–2007, which isn't great but it was only his first year. When I asked him to sign my regulation Norfolk Admiral pucks, next to Igor's signature, he made a weird scrunched-up face and stared at my mother for a while, like he was confused. I guess he doesn't understand a lot of English because he's from the Czech Republic.

2. STEVE PASSMORE

This guy played for the Norfolk Admirals. He was an okay goalie but he had some bad luck so his save percentage was only .899. I liked him because his name has the word "Pass" in it, which is a hockey word—and he plays hockey. I only saw Steve once, in the kitchenette. I couldn't believe there was a real hockey player in my house! So I ran into my bedroom and grabbed the old cigar box I use to hold my pucks. When I came back with the box, my mother kept saying that I should go to bed. "Not now, Jordi," she started shouting, "Please!" She can be really strict. Anyway, I could tell Steve wanted to see what was in the box so I opened it. "Wow," he said, "You must be my number-one fan!" I gave him a puck and told him to sign it next to Igor and Nicolas's signature. (Nicolas was another one of my mom's boyfriends but he didn't make the top five.) At first he looked a little confused. He said something under his breath and I was scared he wasn't going to sign my pucks at all. But then he took out a pen and signed all of them! It was weird, because he didn't look at the pucks when he signed them—instead, the whole time he was staring at my mother. His signature was pretty cool—better than Nicolas's but not as good as Igor's.

1. MARTY WILFORD

This guy is great at hockey! He had forty points in the 2006–2007 season with my favorite hockey team, the Norfolk Admirals. He went out with my mom for almost two weeks. I didn't get to see him very often because my mom had made a rule that I couldn't leave my room when her boyfriends were over. Still, one night I decided to sneak out of my room and wait in the kitchenette. I mean, how many chances do you get to see a real hockey player in your own house? When I showed Marty my puck collection, he was super impressed. "What the hell is going on?" he kept saying. "What the goddamn hell is going on?" Then he looked at my mom and started to cry! It was awesome because I always feel ashamed when I cry. But I thought, if a guy like Marty Wilford can cry, an AHL all star center with thirty-five assists, then it's okay if I do too. Marty kept crying and I was so blown away that I started crying too. And when I went over to him, he hugged me with his huge arms, and it was like I had just scored a goal and he had given me the assist.

COLOMBIATOURISM.COM

Thank you for visiting ColombiaTourism.com! Here are some useful phrases for your vacation. Click on them for English-to-Spanish translations.

"Which way to the restaurant?"

"How much does it cost?"

"Where is the bathroom?

"Who are you?"

"Oh my God, where are you taking me?"

"Please do not put the rag inside of my mouth."

"My father is a wealthy man. I promise he will pay the amount you have requested, provided that you spare my life."

"I have not seen your face. If you release me, I promise, I will not be able to identify you."

"I have a family whom I love. Deep down, I am like you."

"I agree with your sentiments about America. Your philosophy is correct and very reasonable."

"I feel a strong emotional bond toward you, even though you are my captor."

"With every passing day, we are becoming better friends. Say—that is a unique gun. May I see it?"

"Thank you."

"The tables have turned!"

"Do not move while I put the chains on you. I will shoot!"

"Officer! Three men tried to kidnap me. Arrest them at once."

"What are you doing? Why are putting the handcuffs on me?"

"Oh my God, you are in league with the kidnappers. How can this be? Is there no law in this land?"

"Yes, I will stop talking."

MY FRIEND'S NEW GIRLFRIEND

My friend Jared found a girlfriend this summer, and I am so jealous. We're the two least popular kids in the ninth grade and we've always been best friends. But now Jared's always bragging about his girlfriend and how awesome she is. It makes me feel so pathetic.

I've never had a girlfriend before, but this girl sounds incredible. Her name is Tiffany Sparkle. She goes to a different school, a small modeling academy in New Brunswick. He showed me some pictures of her from magazines, and believe me, she is hot. He met her over the summer, when he was visiting his grandparents in Canada. He saved her life. She was about to get run over by a double-decker bus, when all of a sudden, he skateboarded through traffic and pushed her out of the way. There was a huge crowd of Canadians standing around, and when Jared saved Tiffany's life everybody just started cheering like crazy. Then she kissed him on the mouth. When I heard that story, I was like, "Give me a break!" because it was just about the coolest thing I had ever heard in my entire life! They spent the rest of the summer having sex all over the place in all of the different sex positions. And now they talk every night on the phone.

The amazing thing about this girl is that she isn't just hot. She also shares a lot of Jared's interests. She's totally into web design and the game Warcraft. And she's also really shy. For example, when she visited Jared over Spring break, she didn't want to meet me because she was too embarrassed. When I heard that, I was like, "Come on!" because that is so like Jared. It's kind of amazing that they found each other.

There are other similarities too. Like, he showed me a letter she wrote him last week about how she wanted to try out some new kind of sex position, and at first I thought he had written it himself because their handwritings are so similar. Tiffany also has severe bronchial asthma, which is pretty great for Jared, because now he has someone to talk to about that.

The big ninth-grade dance is in four days. I asked Jared to set me up with one of Tiffany's friends from her modeling academy, but he said that everybody there already has a boyfriend. I asked him for advice on how to find a date, but all of his suggestions involved saving girls' lives. In the end, I decided to just walk up to this girl I like named Laura and ask her point blank if she wanted to go with me. I was so nervous that my arms and legs were shaking really fast like they do in gym class when the teacher says it's my turn to lead stretches. But I asked her anyway and she said yes.

I talk to Laura on the phone every night now, which is pretty great, because Jared never has time to talk to me anymore. He's not even going to the dance! Tiffany's flying to the United States for one night only and she hates dancing so they're just going to stay home and try out new sex positions. It's amazing. I mean, don't get me wrong. My date Laura is pretty cool, and other than her leg brace, she's very attractive, but she's certainly no Canadian model. It's hard to believe that when I'm on the dance floor this Friday, trying to work up the guts to kiss her for the first time, Jared's going to be at home in his bedroom making love to the girl of his dreams. Some guys have all the luck.

LOVE COUPONS

—Brian? What are you doing here?

—I came to redeem some coupons.

—(reading) Good for one backrub… Good for one home-cooked meal… Brian, I gave these to you while we were still dating.

—There's no expiration date on the coupons.

—Brian, it's been four years. I'm married now.

—One home-cooked meal please. Then sex. Here—here's the sex one. One of the sex ones.

—Brian, I'm sorry. It's over between us.

—Coupons are coupons.

—Wow, Brian… you've really gained a lot of weight. Is everything okay?

—I've got three sex coupons. I'd like to use them all today, then the meal, then the shower. Tomorrow I'll come back with the rest of the coupons. They're all sex.

—Jesus, what happened to your nails? I can't believe I didn't notice them when I first opened the door. They're so long.

—I would like to use a sex one now please.

TIME MACHINE

As soon as my time machine was finished, I traveled back to 1890, so I could kill Hitler before he was old enough to commit any of his horrible crimes. It wasn't as gratifying as I thought it would be.

—Oh my God. You killed a baby.

—Yes... but the baby was Hitler.

—Who?

—Hitler. It's... complicated.

—Officer? This man just killed a baby.

The Conversion of the Jews

"You're a real one for opening your mouth in the first place," Itzie said. "What do you open your mouth all the time for?"

"I didn't bring it up, Itz, I didn't," Ozzie said.

"What do you care about Jesus Christ for anyway?"

"I didn't bring up Jesus Christ. He did. I didn't even know what he was talking about. Jesus is historical, he kept saying. Jesus is historical." Ozzie mimicked the monumental voice of Rabbi Binder.

"Jesus was a person that lived like you and me," Ozzie continued. "That's what Binder said—"

"Yeah?... So what! What do I give two cents whether he lived or not. And what do you gotta open your mouth!" Itzie Lieberman favored closed mouthedness, especially when it came to Ozzie Freedman's questions. Mrs. Freedman had to see Rabbi Binder twice before about Ozzie's questions, and this Wednesday at four-thirty would be the third time. Itzie preferred to keep *his* mother in the kitchen; he settled for behind-the-back subtleties such as gestures, faces, snarls, and other less delicate barnyard noises.

"He was a real person, Jesus, but he wasn't like God, and we don't believe he is God." Slowly, Ozzie was explaining Rabbi Binder's position to Itzie, who had been absent from Hebrew School the previous afternoon.

"The Catholics," Itzie said helpfully, "they believe in Jesus Christ, that he's God." Itzie Lieberman used "the Catholics" in its broadest sense—to include the Protestants.

Ozzie received Itzie's remark with a tiny head bob, as though it were a footnote, and went on. "His mother was Mary, and his father probably was Joseph," Ozzie said. "But the New Testament says his real father was God."

"His *real* father?"

"Yeah," Ozzie said, "that's the big thing, his father's supposed to be God."

"Bull."

"That's what Rabbi Binder says, that it's impossible—"

"Sure it's impossible. That stuff's all bull. To have a baby you gotta get laid," Itzie theologized. "Mary hadda get laid."

"That's what Binder says: 'The only way a woman can have a baby is to have intercourse with a man.'"

"He said *that*, Ozz?" For a moment it appeared that Itzie had put the theological question aside. "He said that, intercourse?" A little curled smile shaped itself in the lower half of Itzie's face like a pink mustache. "What'd you guys do, Ozz, you laugh or something?"

"I raised my hand."

"Yeah? Whatja say?"

"That's when I asked the question."

Itzie's face lit up. "Whatja ask about—intercourse?"

"No, I asked the question about God, how if He could create the heaven and earth in six days, and make all the animals and the fish and the light in six days—the light especially, that's what always gets me, that He could make the light. Making fish and animals, that's pretty good— "

"That's damn good." Itzie's appreciation was honest but unimaginative: it was as though God had just pitched a one-hitter.

"But making light... I mean, when you think about it, it's really something," Ozzie said. "Anyway, I asked Binder, if He could make all that in six days, and He could *pick* the six days he wanted right out of nowhere, why couldn't He let a woman have a baby without having intercourse."

"You said intercourse, Ozz, to Binder?"

"Yeah."

"Right in class?"

"Yeah."

Itzie smacked the side of his head.

"I mean, no kidding around," Ozzie said, "that'd really be nothing. After all that other stuff, that'd practically be nothing."

Itzie considered a moment. "What'd Binder say?"

"He started all over again explaining how Jesus was historical and how he lived like you and me but he wasn't God. So I said I under*stood* that. What I wanted to know was different."

What Ozzie wanted to know was always different. The first time he had wanted to know how Rabbi Binder could call the Jews "The Chosen People" if the Declaration of Independence claimed all men to be created equal. Rabbi Binder tried to distinguish for him between political equality and spiritual legitimacy, but what Ozzie wanted to know, he insisted vehemently, was different. That was the first time his mother had to come.

Then there was the plane crash. Fifty-eight people had been killed in a plane crash at La Guardia. In studying a casualty list in the newspaper his mother had discovered among the list of those dead eight Jewish names (his grandmother had nine, but she counted Miller as a Jewish name); because of the eight she said the plane crash was "a tragedy." During free-discussion time on Wednesday Ozzie had brought to Rabbi Binder's attention this matter of "some of his relations" always picking out the Jewish names. Rabbi Binder had begun to explain cultural unity and some other things when Ozzie stood up at his seat and said that what he wanted to know was different. Rabbi Binder insisted that he sit down and it was then that Ozzie shouted that he wished all fifty-eight had been Jews. That was the second time his mother came.

"And he kept explaining about Jesus being historical, and so I kept asking him. No kidding, Itz, he was trying to make me look stupid."

"So what he finally do?"

"Finally he starts screaming that I was deliberately simple-minded and a wise guy, and that my mother had to come, and this was the last time. And that I'd never get bar-mitzvahed if he could help it. Then, Itz, then he starts talking in that voice like a statue, real slow and deep, and he says that I better think over what I said about the Lord. He told me to go to his office and think it over." Ozzie leaned his body towards Itzie. "Itz, I thought it over for a solid hour, and now I'm convinced God could do it."

Ozzie had planned to confess his latest transgression to his mother as soon as she came home from work. But it was Friday night in November and already dark, and when Mrs. Freedman came through the door she tossed off her coat, kissed Ozzie quickly on the face, and went to the kitchen table to light the three yellow candles, two for the Sabbath and one for Ozzie's father.

When his mother lit the candles she would move her two arms slowly toward her, dragging them through the air, as though persuading people whose minds were half made up. And her eyes would get glassy with tears. Even when his father was alive Ozzie remembered that her eyes had gotten glassy, so it didn't have anything to do with his dying. It had something to do with lighting the candles.

As she touched the flaming match to the unlit wick of a Sabbath candle, the phone rang, and Ozzie, standing only a foot from it, plucked it off the receiver and held it muffled to his chest. When his mother lit candles Ozzie felt there should be no noise; even breathing, if you could manage it, should be softened. Ozzie pressed the phone to his breast and watched his mother dragging whatever she was dragging, and he felt his own eyes get glassy. His mother was a round, tired, gray-haired penguin of a woman whose gray skin had begun to feel the tug of gravity and the weight of her own history. Even when she was dressed up she didn't look like a chosen person. But when she lit candles she looked like something better, like a woman who knew momentarily that God could do anything.

After a few mysterious minutes she was finished. Ozzie hung up the phone and walked to the kitchen table where she was beginning to lay the two places for the four-course Sabbath meal. He told her that she would have to see Rabbi Binder next Wednesday at four-thirty, and then he told her why. For the first time in their life together she hit Ozzie across the face with her hand.

All through the chopped liver and chicken soup part of the dinner Ozzie cried; he didn't have any appetite for the rest.

On Wednesday, in the largest of the three basement classrooms of the synagogue, Rabbi Marvin Binder, a tall, handsome, broad-shouldered man of thirty with thick strong-fibered black hair, removed his watch from his pocket and saw that it was four o'clock. At the rear of the room Yakov Blotnik, the seventy-one-year-old custodian, slowly polished the large window, mumbling to himself, unaware that it was four o'clock or six o'clock, Monday or Wednesday. To most of the students Yakov Blotnik's mumbling, along with his brown curly beard, scythe nose, and two heel-trailing black cats, made of him an object of wonder, a foreigner, a relic, toward whom they were alternately fearful and disrespectful. To Ozzie the mumbling had always seemed a monotonous, curious prayer; what made it curious was that old Blotnik had been mumbling so steadily for so many years, Ozzie suspected he had memorized the prayers and forgotten all about God.

"It is now free-discussion time," Rabbi Binder said. "Feel free to talk about any Jewish matter at all—religion, family, politics, sports—"

There was silence. It was a gusty, clouded November afternoon and it did not seem as though there ever was or could be a thing called baseball. So nobody this week said a word about that hero from the past, Hank Greenberg—which limited free discussion considerably.

And the soul-battering Ozzie Freedman had just received from Rabbi Binder had imposed its limitation. When it was Ozzie's turn to read aloud from the Hebrew book the rabbi had asked him petulantly why he didn't read more rapidly. He was showing no progress. Ozzie said he could read faster but that if he did he was sure not to understand what he was reading. Nevertheless, at the rabbi's repeated suggestion Ozzie tried, and showed a great talent, but in the midst of a long passage he stopped short and said he didn't understand a word he was reading, and started in again at a drag-footed pace. Then came the soul-battering.

Consequently, when free-discussion time rolled around, none of the students felt too free. The rabbi's invitation was answered only by the mumbling of feeble old Blotnik.

"Isn't there anything at all you would like to discuss?" Rabbi Binder asked again, looking at his watch. "No questions or comments?"

There was a small grumble from the third row. The rabbi requested that Ozzie rise and give the rest of the class the advantage of his thought.

Ozzie rose. "I forget it now," he said, and sat down in his place.

Rabbi Binder advanced a seat toward Ozzie and poised himself on the edge of the desk. It was Itzie's desk, and the rabbi's frame only a dagger's length away from his face snapped him to sitting attention.

"Stand up again, Oscar," Rabbi Binder said calmly, "and try to assemble your thoughts."

Ozzie stood up. All his classmates turned in their seats and watched as he gave an unconvincing scratch to his forehead.

"I can't assemble any," he announced, and plunked himself down.

"Stand up!" Rabbi Binder advanced from Itzie's desk to the one directly in front of Ozzie; when the rabbinical back was turned Itzie gave it five fingers off the tip of his nose, causing a small titter in the room. Rabbi Binder was too absorbed in squelching Ozzie's nonsense once and for all to bother with titters. "Stand up, Oscar. What's your question about?"

Ozzie pulled a word out of the air. It was the handiest word.

"Religion."

"Oh, now you remember?"

"Yes."

"What is it?"

Trapped, Ozzie blurted the first thing that came to him. "Why can't He make anything He wants to make!"

As Rabbi Binder prepared an answer, a final answer, Itzie, ten feet behind him, raised one finger on his left hand, gestured it meaningfully towards the rabbi's back, and brought the house down.

Binder twisted quickly to see what had happened, and in the midst of the commotion Ozzie shouted into the rabbi's back what he couldn't have shouted to his face. It was a loud, toneless sound that had the timbre of something stored inside for about six days.

"You don't know! You don't know anything about God!"

The rabbi spun back towards Ozzie. "What?"

"You don't know—you don't—"

"Apologize, Oscar, apologize!" It was a threat.

"You don't—"

Rabbi Binder's hand flicked out at Ozzie's cheek. Perhaps it had only been meant to clamp the boy's mouth shut, but Ozzie ducked and the palm caught him squarely on the nose.

The blood came in a short, red spurt onto Ozzie's shirt front.

The next moment was all confusion. Ozzie screamed, "You bastard, you bastard!" and broke for the classroom door. Rabbi Binder lurched a step backward, as though his own blood had started flowing violently in the opposite direction, then gave a clumsy lurch forward and bolted out the door after Ozzie. The class followed after the rabbi's huge blue-suited back, and before old Blotnik could turn from his window, the room was empty and everyone was headed full-speed up the three flights leading to the roof.

If one should compare the light of day to the life of man: sunrise to birth; sunset—the dropping down over the edge to death; then as Ozzie Freedman wiggled through the trapdoor of the synagogue roof, his feet kicking backward bronco-style at Rabbi Binder's outstretched arms—at that moment the day was fifty years old. As a rule, fifty or fifty-five reflects accurately the age of late afternoons in November, for it is in that month, during those hours, that one's awareness of light seems no longer a matter of seeing, but of hearing: light begins clicking away. In fact, as Ozzie locked shut the trapdoor in the rabbi's face, the sharp click of the bolt into the lock might momentarily have been mistaken for the sound of the heavier gray that had just throbbed through the sky.

With all his weight Ozzie kneeled on the locked door; any instant he was certain that Rabbi Binder's shoulder would fling it open, splintering the wood into shrapnel and catapulting his body into the sky. But the door did not move and below him he heard only the rumble of feet, first loud then dim, like thunder rolling away.

A question shot through his brain. "Can this be *me?*" For a thirteen-year-old who had just labeled his religious leader a bastard, twice, it was not an improper question. Louder and louder the question came to him—"Is it me? Is it me?"—until he discovered himself no longer kneeling, but racing crazily towards the edge of the roof, his eyes crying, his throat screaming, and his arms flying everywhichway as though not his own.

"Is it me? Is it me ME ME ME ME! It has to be me—but is it!"

It is the question a thief must ask himself the night he jimmies open his first window, and it is said to be the question with which bridegrooms quiz themselves before the altar.

In the few wild seconds it took Ozzie's body to propel him to the edge of the roof, his self-examination began to grow fuzzy. Gazing down at the street, he became confused as to the problem beneath the question: was it, is-it-me-who-called-Binder-a-bastard? or, is-it-me-prancing-around-on-the-roof? However, the scene below settled all, for there is an instant in any action when whether it is you or somebody else is academic. The thief crams the money in his pockets and scoots out the window. The bridegroom signs the hotel register for two. And the boy on the roof finds a streetful of people gaping at him, necks stretched backward, faces up, as though he were the ceiling of the Hayden Planetarium. Suddenly you know it's you.

"Oscar! Oscar Freedman!" A voice rose from the center of the crowd, a voice that, could it have been seen, would have looked like the writing on scroll. "Oscar Freedman, get down from there. Immediately!" Rabbi Binder was pointing one arm stiffly up at him; and at the end of that arm, one finger aimed menacingly. It was the attitude of a dictator, but one—the eyes confessed all—whose personal valet had spit neatly in his face.

Ozzie didn't answer. Only for a blink's length did he look toward Rabbi Binder. Instead his eyes began to fit together the world beneath him, to sort out people from places, friends from enemies, participants from spectators. In little jagged starlike clusters his friends stood around Rabbi Binder, who was still pointing. The topmost point on a star compounded not of angels but of five adolescent boys was Itzie. What a world it was, with those stars below, Rabbi Binder below... Ozzie, who a moment earlier hadn't been able to control his own body, started to feel the meaning of the word *control*: he felt Peace and he felt Power.

"Oscar Freedman, I'll give you three to come down."

Few dictators give their subjects three to do anything; but, as always, Rabbi Binder only looked dictatorial.

"Are you ready, Oscar?"

Ozzie nodded his head yes, although he had no intention in the world—the lower one or the celestial one he'd just entered—of coming down, even if Rabbi Binder should give him a million.

"All right then," said Rabbi Binder. He ran a hand through his black Samson hair as though it were the gesture prescribed for uttering the first digit. Then, with his other hand cutting a circle out of the small piece of sky around him, he spoke. "One!"

There was no thunder. On the contrary, at that moment, as though "one" was the cue for which he had been waiting, the world's least thunderous person appeared on the synagogue steps. He did not so much come out the synagogue door as lean out onto the darkening air. He clutched at the doorknob with one hand and looked up at the roof.

"Oy!"

Yakov Blotnik's old mind hobbled slowly, as if on crutches, and though he couldn't decide precisely what the boy was doing on the roof, he knew it wasn't good—that is, it wasn't good-for-the-Jews. For Yakov Blotnik, life had fractionated itself simply: things were either good-for-the-Jews or no-good-for-the-Jews.

He smacked his free hand to his in-sucked cheek, gently, "Oy, Gut!" And then, quickly as he was able, he jacked down his head and surveyed the street. There was Rabbi Binder (like a man at an auction with only three dollars in his pocket, he had just delivered a shaky "Two!"); there were the students, and that was all. So far it-wasn't-so-bad-for-the-Jews. But the boy had to come down immediately, before anybody saw. The problem: how to get the boy off the roof?

Anybody who has ever had a cat on the roof knows how to get him down. You call the fire department. Or first you call the operator and you ask her for the fire department. And the next thing there is great jamming of brakes and clanging of bells and shouting of instructions. And then the cat is off the roof. You do the same thing to get a boy off the roof.

That is, you do the same thing if you are Yakov Blotnik and you once had a cat on the roof.

When the engines, all four of them, arrived, Rabbi Binder had four times given Ozzie the count of three. The big hook-and-ladder swung around the corner and one of the firemen leaped from it, plunging headlong toward the yellow fire hydrant in front of the synagogue. With a huge wrench he began to unscrew the top nozzle. Rabbi Binder raced over to him and pulled at his shoulder.

"There's no fire..."

The fireman mumbled back over his shoulder and, heatedly, continued working at the nozzle.

"But there's no fire, there's no fire..." Binder shouted. When the fireman mumbled again, the rabbi grasped his face with both his hands and pointed it up at the roof.

To Ozzie it looked as though Rabbi Binder was trying to tug the fireman's head out of his body, like a cork from a bottle. He had to giggle at the picture they made: it was a family portrait, rabbi in black skullcap, fireman in red fire hat and the little yellow hydrant squatting beside like a kid brother, bare-headed. From the edge of the roof Ozzie waved at the portrait, a one-handed, flapping, mocking wave; in doing it his right foot slipped from under him. Rabbi Binder covered his eyes with his hands.

Firemen work fast. Before Ozzie had even regained his balance, a big, round, yellowed net was being held on the synagogue lawn. The firemen who held it looked up at Ozzie with stern, feelingless faces.

One of the firemen turned his head toward Rabbi Binder. "What, is the kid nuts or something?"

Rabbi Binder unpeeled his hands from his eyes, slowly, painfully, as if they were tape. Then he checked: nothing on the sidewalk, no dents in the net.

"Is he gonna jump, or what?" the fireman shouted.

In a voice not at all like a statue, Rabbi Binder finally answered. "Yes. Yes, I think so... He's been threating to..."

Threatening to? Why, the reason he was on the roof, Ozzie remembered, was to get away; he hadn't even thought about jumping. He had just run to get away, and the truth was that he hadn't really headed for the roof as much as he'd been chased there.

"What's his name, the kid?"

"Freedman," Rabbi Binder answered. "Oscar Freedman."

The fireman looked up at Ozzie. "What is it with you, Oscar? You gonna jump, or what?"

Ozzie did not answer. Frankly, the question had just arisen.

"Look, Oscar, if you're gonna jump, jump—and if you're not gonna jump, don't jump. But don't waste our time, willya?"

Ozzie looked at the fireman and then at Rabbi Binder. He wanted to see Rabbi Binder cover his eyes one more time.

"I'm going to jump."

And then he scampered around the edge of the roof to the corner, where there was no net below, and he flapped his arms at his sides, swishing the air and smacking his palms to his trousers on the downbeat. He began screaming like some kind of engine, "Wheeeee... wheeeeee," and leaning way out over the edge with the upper half of his body. The firemen whipped around to cover the ground with the net. Rabbi Binder mumbled a few words to somebody and covered his eyes. Everything happened quickly, jerkily, as in a silent movie. The crowd, which had arrived with the fire engines, gave out a long, Fourth of July fireworks oooh-aahhh. In the excitement no one had paid the crowd much heed, except, of course, Yakov Blotnik, who swung from the doorknob counting heads. *"Fier und tsvansik... finf und tsvantsik... Oy, Gut!"* It wasn't like this with the cat.

Rabbi Binder peeked through his fingers, checked the side-walk and net. Empty. But there was Ozzie racing to the other corner. The firemen raced with him but were unable to keep up. Whenever Ozzie wanted to he might jump and splatter himself upon the sidewalk, and by the time the fireman scooted to the spot, all they could do with their net would be to cover the mess.

"Wheeeee... wheeeee..."

"Hey, Oscar," the winded fireman yelled, "What the hell is this, a game or something?"

"Wheeeee... wheeeee..."

"Hey, Oscar— "

But he was off now to the other corner, flapping his wings fiercely. Rabbi Binder couldn't take it any longer—the fire engines from nowhere, the screaming suicidal boy, the net. He fell to his knees, exhausted, and with his hands curled together in front of his chest like a little dome, he pleaded "Oscar, stop it, Oscar. Don't jump, Oscar. Please come down... Please don't jump."

And further back in the crowd a single voice, a single young voice, shouted a lone word to the boy on the roof.

"Jump!"

It was Itzie. Ozzie momentarily stopped flapping.

"Go ahead, Ozz—jump!" Itzie broke off his point of the star and coura-geously, with the inspiration not of a wiseguy but of a disciple, stood alone. "Jump, Ozz, jump!"

Still on his knees, his hands still curled, Rabbi Binder twisted his body back. He looked at Itzie, then, agonizingly, back to Ozzie.

"OSCAR DON'T JUMP! PLEASE, DON'T JUMP... please, please..."

"Jump!" This time it wasn't Itzie but another point of the star. By the time Mrs. Freedman arrived to keep her four-thirty appointment with Rabbi Binder, the whole little upside-down heaven was shouting and pleading for Ozzie to jump, and Rabbi Binder no longer was pleading with him not to jump, but was crying into the dome of his hands.

Understandably, Mrs. Freedman couldn't figure out what her son was doing on the roof. So she asked.

"Ozzie, my Ozzie, what are you doing? My Ozzie, what is it?"

Ozzie stopped wheeeeing and slowed his arms down to a cruising flap, the kind birds use in soft winds, but he did not answer. He stood against the low, clouded, darkening sky—light clicked down swiftly now, as on a small gear—flapping softly and gazing down at the small bundle of a woman who was his mother.

"What are you doing, Ozzie?" She turned toward the kneeling Rabbi Binder and rushed so close that only a paper-thickness of dusk lay between her stomach and his shoulders.

"What is my baby doing?"

Rabbi Binder gaped up at her but he too was mute. All that moved was the dome of his hands; it shook back and forth like a weak pulse.

"Rabbi, get him down! He'll *kill* himself. Get him down, my only baby... "

"I can't," Rabbi Binder said, "I can't..." and he turned his handsome head toward the crowd of boys behind him.

"It's them. Listen to them."

And for the first time Mrs. Freedman saw the crowd of boys, and she heard what they were yelling.

"He's doing it for them. He won't listen to me. It's them." Rabbi Binder spoke like one in a trance.

"For them?"

"Yes."

"Why for them?"

"They want him to..."

Mrs. Freedman raised her two arms upward as though she were conducting the sky. "For them he's doing it!" And then in a gesture older than pyramids, older than prophets and floods, her arms came slapping down to her sides. "A martyr I have. Look!" She tilted her head to the roof. Ozzie was still flapping softly. "My martyr."

"Oscar, come down, *please*," Rabbi Binder groaned.

In a startlingly even voice, Mrs. Freedman called to the boy on the roof. "Ozzie, come down, Ozzie. Don't be a martyr, my baby."

As though it were a litany, Rabbi Binder repeated her words. "Don't be a martyr, my baby. Don't be a martyr."

"Gawhead, Ozz—*be* a Martin!" It was Itzie. "Be a Martin, be a Martin," and all the voices joined in singing for Martin-dom, whatever *it* was. "Be a Martin, be a Martin..."

Somehow when you're on a roof, the darker it gets the less you can hear. All Ozzie knew was that two groups wanted two new things: his friends were spirited and musical about what they wanted; his mother and the rabbi were even-toned, chanting, about what they didn't want. The rabbi's voice was without tears now and so was his mother's.

The big net stared up at Ozzie like a sightless eye. The big, clouded sky pushed down. From beneath it looked like a gray corrugated board. Suddenly, looking up into that unsympathetic sky, Ozzie realized all the strangeness of what these people, his friends, were asking: they wanted him to jump, to kill himself; they were singing about it now—it made them that happy. And there was an even greater strangeness: Rabbi Binder was on his knees, trembling. If there was a question to be asked now, it was not "Is it me?" but rather "Is it us?... Is it us?"

Being on the roof, it turned out, was a serious thing. If he jumped, would the singing become dancing? Would it? What would jumping stop? Yearningly, Ozzie wished he could rip open the sky, plunge his hands through, and pull out the sun; and on the sun, like a coin, would be stamped JUMP or DON'T JUMP.

Ozzie's knees rocked and sagged a little under him as though they were setting him for a dive. His arms tightened, stiffened, froze, from shoulders to fingernails. He felt as if each part of his body were going to vote as to whether he should kill himself or not—and each part as though it were independent of *him*.

The light took an unexpected click down and the new darkness, like a gag, hushed the friends singing for this and the mother and rabbi chanting for that.

Ozzie stopped counting votes, and in a curiously high voice, like one who wasn't prepared for speech, he spoke.

"Mamma?"

"Yes, Oscar."

"Mamma, get down on your knees, like Rabbi Binder."

"Oscar—"

"Get down on your knees," he said, "or I'll jump."

Ozzie heard a whimper, then a quick rustling, and when he looked down where his mother had stood he saw the top of a head and beneath that a circle of dress. She was kneeling beside Rabbi Binder.

He spoke again. "Everybody kneel." There was the sound of everybody kneeling.

Ozzie looked around. With one hand he pointed towards the synagogue entrance. "Make *him* kneel."

There was a noise, not of kneeling, but of body-and-cloth stretching. Ozzie could hear Rabbi Binder saying in a gruff whisper, "...or he'll *kill* himself," and when next he looked there was Yakov Blotnik off the doorknob and for the first time in his life upon his knees in the Gentile posture of prayer. As for the firemen—it is not as difficult as one might imagine to hold a net taut while you are kneeling.

Ozzie looked around again; and then he called to Rabbi Binder.

"Rabbi?"

"Yes, Oscar."

"Rabbi Binder, do you believe in God?"

"Yes."

"Do you believe God can do Anything?" Ozzie leaned his head out into the darkness. "Anything?"

"Oscar, I think—"

"Tell me you believe God can do Anything."

There was a second's hesitation. Then: "God can do Anything."

"Tell me you believe God can make a child without intercourse."

"He can."

"Tell me!"

"God," Rabbi Binder admitted, "can make a child without intercourse."

"Mamma, you tell me."

"God can make a child without intercourse," his mother said.

"Make *him* tell me." There was no doubt who *him* was.

In a few moments Ozzie heard an old comical voice say something to the increasing darkness about God.

Next, Ozzie made everybody say it. And then he made them all say they believed in Jesus Christ—first one at a time, then all together.

When the catechizing was through it was the beginning off evening. From the street it sounded as if the boy on the roof might have sighed.

"Ozzie?" A woman's voice dared to speak. "You'll come down now?"

There was no answer, but the woman waited, and when a voice finally did speak it was thin and crying, and exhausted as that of an old man who had just finished pulling the bells.

"Mamma, don't you see—you shouldn't hit me. He shouldn't hit me. You shouldn't hit me about God, Mamma. You should never hit anybody about God—"

"Ozzie, please come down now."

"Promise me, promise me you'll never hit anybody about God."

He had asked only his mother, but for some reason everyone kneeling in the street promised he would never hit anybody about God.

Once again there was silence.

"I can come down now, Mamma," the boy on the roof finally said. He turned his head both ways as though checking the traffic lights. "Now I can come down..."

And he did, right into the center of the yellow net that glowed in the evening's edge like an overgrown halo.

RODNEY ROTHMAN

Vivian

Slow dancing with old women is not something I've ever longed to do. No offense to my grandmother, but it feels a little unnatural. That's a fact I've had to confront ever since I started attending the weekly dance of the Singles Club of West Palm Beach. The club has for years been a life preserver for South Florida senior singles. I thought it would be interesting to visit it and see for myself how senior citizens romance each other. It didn't occur to me that being the only man present under the age of seventy would be like walking around with a sign that says "Yes, I will dance with you." I am automatically a novelty, like a dangerous greaser who shows up at an ISO dance. I am dragged to the dance floor, over and over again. The women clutch me to their party dresses and, as we sway, they hum along to the swing music. They're wearing perfume that smells like tea rose. It is the first time in my life I find myself wishing somebody would start the Electric Slide.

When I first see Vivian, she is standing across the room and staring directly at me. It's jarring when you catch someone staring and she doesn't look away like most people do when they're busted. Then, Vivian is beside me. She says nothing, simply stands and waits for me to acknowledge her presence. I don't know her at all yet, but I immediately sense we are in some kind

---

This piece was originally published in Rodney Rothman's memoir, Early Bird.

of battle and decide not to give her the pleasure of an immediate greeting. I continue the boring conversation I am in and appraise her from the corner of my eye. She looks different from the rest of the older single women here. As women age they tend to start to look less distinctive. Their facial features soften and fill out, their hair becomes thinner and is coiffed into the ubiquitous old-woman Afro. Vivian, though, has somehow escaped that. Though Vivian must be in her early seventies, her hair is jet black, thick, and long. She has amazing posture. Her skin is tan and dark, her face is slim, and her features are sharp. She is the first old woman I have ever seen that I would describe as "sultry." She is possibly the sultriest older woman in South Florida.

"Aren't you going to ask me to dance?" she says. I've been the slow-dance slut of the Singles Club, but my heart starts beating fast and I feel that saying no would be the smartest thing I could do.

"I'm bad at dancing," I say, by way of an excuse.

"Yes, you are," Vivian says. "I've watched you; you don't know what you're doing."

She pulls me onto the dance floor and folds herself into my arms. Her posture is formal and bizarre-feeling. Her back is arched to an extreme. It's as if she has electricity running through her spine. As big-band music blasts from the hall's ancient speakers, I try to lead her around the dance floor, but really, she is leading. Periodically, she barks something like "Evolve! Evolve!" at me, and I have no idea what it means.

At some point, I become aware that I have an erection. The only explanation I can come up with is that I am turned on by how inappropriate it is to have an erection while dancing with an elderly woman. But that is circular logic. I have to angle my hips away from her so that she can't tell.

"I hear you are a writer," she says. "You should hear my life story. It will blow you away."

Vivian has an indeterminate Mediterranean accent that falls somewhere between Inigo Montoya and a discount electronics salesman. She is Romanian by birth.

"I am looking for somebody to write my life story," she says. "A writer like you. You are a good writer?"

"Yeah, I'm good," I say, more defensive than I want to sound.

"Just wait until you hear my life story," Vivian says. "It will blow your mind away. It has sex and love and passion. And a murder. It is better than a movie!"

Vivian hands me a business card. "This is my number," she says.

"Okay," I say.

"Good," she says. "I am looking forward to it. Maybe if you're lucky I will give you a dance lesson when you come visit me."

"Okay," I say.

She walks back into the crowd, and then I see the pairs of seniors all around, staring at me and whispering, and I feel odd and embarrassed and leave at once.

Vivian is very happy to see me, and guides me into her large condo. It's on a high floor of a prominent Palm Beach building. Her furniture is expensive-looking and large—the kind of stuff you see in luxury showrooms and wonder who actually purchases it. For instance, Vivian owns what I would call the most tasteful, most upscale leopard-skin chair I have ever seen.

"This place is really nice," I say.

"Thank you," says Vivian. "Yet it is the least impressive place I have ever lived."

She's wearing tight black slacks and open-toed shoes and bright red nail polish. Her blouse is unbuttoned several buttons.

"I'm sorry it's so hot in here," she says.

Vivian says that since she was a girl, she has always been crazy about movies, especially love stories. It's what made her want to come to America.

"My favorite movie is *Somewhere in Time*," she says, pouring some wine. "Have you seen it? It's a love story. Who was the actor in that? The one who fell off the horse?"

"Christopher Reeve," I tell her.

"No . . ." she says. "That's not him."

"Yes, it is," I say. "It's Christopher Reeve."

"No . . . It is Reeves. Christopher Reeves."

"It's Reeve."

"Reeves," she insists.

I look at Vivian for a few seconds, and then I understand that she is a woman who has never lost an argument in her life, even when she was wrong.

"You're right," I say. "Christopher Reeves."

"That's what I said," she says. "That is his name."

"When I was a child," says Vivian, "I was nothing. I was ugly and nobody cared about me. Then I turned sixteen. I went to a dance and men asked me to dance over and over again, and I knew that things would be different. There were officers there from all over the world. One man said to me, 'When you get older, you are going to break all the men's hearts.' I thought to myself: I can't wait."

As Vivian tells me stories, she grows more and more animated. She smiles and leans forward and moves her hands more and more.

"I want glamour and passion," says Vivian. "Especially passion. Always I have known that. Other people might compromise, but I do not. If I do not have what I want, I move on from where I am and get what I want."

"You sound like quite a handful," I say, then, feeling nervous, I laugh.

"Oh yes," Vivian says, "I am. I am always testing my power. Do you like the music?" Soft classical music plays on the stereo.

"It's very nice," I tell her.

"Do you recognize the composer?" she asks.

"Rachmaninoff," I guess. I have no idea what Rachmaninoff sounds like. It just seems like something she would listen to.

"Correct," she says, smiling at me, impressed. She slides off her shoes and I notice that she has young-looking feet.

Vivian married for the first time when she was nineteen, to a man who promised to take her to America. But he took her to live in rural Delaware, which is technically America, but not the place she had in mind at all. Before long she had two children.

"Imagine me," says Vivian, "in the middle of nowhere with two young children!"

Vivian forced her husband to move to Hollywood, California, despite the fact that neither had ever been there. Desperate to keep her, he agreed. Vivian soon found herself courted by several wealthy Los Angelenos. She admits that she led them on and enjoyed doing it. She and her husband grew apart. When it seemed doomed, her husband flew out a close business friend to help broker a reunion between them. They all went to dinner. That man took a liking to Vivian and stroked her leg under the table. She had a small fling with him.

"I am a femme fatale," she says, with the sort of accent that allows you to pull off a statement like that. "I have probably hurt some men in my day. I know I have. I like the chase. I am like a man that way."

Vivian takes a deep breath, and I know in that instant that she would be smoking a cigarette right now if some doctor hadn't told her to stop smoking.

"It is interesting, no?" says Vivian. "Do you think I'm interesting?"

"It all sounds like a Jackie Collins book," I say. "Or maybe Danielle Steel."

"Why do you think I'm interesting?" she says.

"I don't know," I say. "You're not really like anyone I've ever met before."

Vivian smiles and leans back. I guess I said the perfect thing.

"I like talking to you," she says. "I like having a biographer. Ask me another question."

"How many times have you been married?"

"Six times."

"Did you end all your marriages?"

"All but the last," she says. "I met him aboard Papa Doc's yacht in Haiti. And he wanted me back the next day. Too bad I changed the locks."

Vivian takes a photo out and shows me, against all probability, an image of herself as a young, beautiful, comically tan woman, aboard the lavish yacht of notorious Haitian dictator François "Papa Doc" Duvalier. Her future husband stands next to her, his arm around her, dressed in white and looking like a studly Colonel Sanders.

I had assumed she was making this stuff up.

Vivian's apartment overlooks the Intercoastal Waterway, a sliver of water that winds down the eastern side of South Florida. We are watching it as we talk; it is burnished orange by a sunset.

"After I left my first husband I supported myself," Vivian says. "In the day I taught. At night, I worked in sex."

"You did what?" I say. I'm shocked, yet not surprised. Vivian is a sultry, sexy older woman. Why wouldn't all that sultry sexiness have a dark side? I consider that, and then I begin to wonder whether I am going to end up sleeping with Vivian. Horrified, I stuff that thought away, and then it comes raging back full force. Let's face it—this woman gets what she wants, she's been coming on to me, that is unmistakable, and now I have discovered she is a former sex worker. Whether or not I sleep with her might not be up to me.

"I worked in sex," she repeats. "Why is that strange?"

"It's . . . it's not," I say.

"It's a nice store, Sex Fifth Avenue."

"Saks Fifth Avenue," I correct her.

"Yes, Sex Fifth Avenue. That's what I said. I worked in Sex for two years."

I start to laugh. "Why is that funny?" she asks.

"Have you ever been in love?" Vivian asks me. We have moved to the living room. We are sitting on leopard skin now.

"I don't know."

"You would know. Who are you dating now?"

"I'm not really with anyone. I'm really just getting back into the dating thing."

Vivian says she has been in love only twice in her life, and she married neither of those men. The last time she was in love was when she lived in Las Vegas. She fell for an ad executive. She was married at the time. In the beginning she and the executive would play chess together, and she'd beat him every time.

Eventually he invited her to his place. She began conducting an affair. She could see her lover's apartment from the regular table she and her husband sat at in their favorite restaurant. Her lover would flick his lights on and off when he knew she was eating there. Her lover was possessive and angry, convinced that Vivian was cheating on him with a third man. One time he came over and threatened her with a broken bottle.

"That turned me on," says Vivian. "I don't know why. I had the best sex with him."

"Why was it the best sex?" I ask, stammering over every word in the question. Vivian just arches her eyebrows, as if to say: If you don't know, then I feel sorry for you.

George was an American soldier who took a shine to Vivian and then proceeded to deflower her. He remained obsessed with her from that point on. He wrote her hundreds of letters. Vivian says he was the first man she ever loved, and the one she loved the longest.

"But he was never good enough," says Vivian. "He didn't have enough money or opportunities to keep me happy."

"If he did, would you have gone with him?"

"Maybe. But maybe it was less that I liked him and more that I liked that he liked me. Do you know what I mean?"

I think of every relationship that I've ever been in, and then I say, "Sort of."

One evening, Vivian invites me to visit her again. After we sit and have several glasses of wine, she asks me to read some of George's letters aloud to her. She sits back in her leopard-skin chair with her eyes closed and a half smile on her face.

"I love you," I read. "I will always love you."

"You read well," says Vivian.

"Vivian," I read, "you are like a bull in a china shop. You kick everything to bits and then you shit on the pieces."

"He was a wonderful writer, like you," says Vivian. She's never read a thing I've written.

"What happened to him?" I ask her.

"He went to jail for murder," says Vivian, "and he died ten years later."

"Oh jeez," I say.

"He loved me until the day he died," says Vivian.

"I slept with a seventy-five-year-old woman," I tell Nick, my friend in New York, over the phone.

"You did what?"

"I slept with a seventy-five-year-old woman."

I've been telling my friends I slept with Vivian. I didn't really. It's another one of my weather balloons. I get to see how they would have reacted if I actually had slept with her, without any of the guilt of having gone through with it.

It's interesting to see how young people respond. Most find the idea so ridiculous they refuse to believe me. It's just not possible. My friend Jenni just snorts and says, "You're a bad liar." In the case of Nick, his reaction is several short, sharp intakes of breath, an awkward silence, a nervous laugh, and finally a troubled stamp of approval: "Dude," he says, "that's awesome."

Other friends of mine are openly disgusted by the idea of me sleeping with an old woman, which makes me a little angry; I feel like going ahead and sleeping with Vivian just to prove a point. Old women can be sexy. I have seen it with the Peppy Purple-ites, and I have felt it with Vivian. Shouldn't we all be happy about that fact? That we are not all consigned to adorableness?

Jill, my upcoming wedding date, doesn't really react well when I tell her.

"Man," she says, "you're just lost in the Amazon down there, aren't you? With the cops, and the shuffleboard, and the Purple People Eaters or whatever."

"I didn't really sleep with her," I say. "I was only testing you."

"Yeah," she says. "Come back to us, Rodney! Come back!"

Most of the books I've been reading on health and aging make it clear that it's not just possible to enjoy an active sex life into your eighties and nineties, it's even recommended, as long as you are careful and cautious. A Duke University study found "a strong tie between the frequency and enjoyment of sexual intercourse and longevity." A more recent British study had the same result, noting lower overall rates of mortality among men who have sex more frequently than the once-a-week average. The bottom line is: People who have "frequent, loving sex tend to live longer than those who don't."

What would it be like to sleep with an old woman? The books all write about "diminished lubrication" and a "thinning of the vaginal tissue." They warn that "some of the sexual positions you enjoyed at age thirty can be difficult and even painful at the age of seventy." So I guess the Wheelbarrow position is out. Sometimes I ask Vivian questions about sex. It's easy, because it's all under the guise that I am her biographer and interviewer.

"Oh, I don't have any of those problems," she says, waving her hand to dismiss the question. "I have better sex now than ever. I didn't know how to have sex until I was older," she says.

The next time I see Vivian she has moved in to a new apartment. She no longer wanted to live in the space she shared with her fourth husband. She wanted to start fresh. Her new condo is nice, but much smaller.

We sit down on the same couch. I ask Vivian how her love life is going—we can do that now, we have broken down all those barriers. She tells me about a man who tried to pick her up in a fast-food restaurant, but all I can think as she tells me the story is: Vivian was eating in a fast-food restaurant?

Vivian's latest boyfriend is Italian, which is very Vivian, but he is the Italian American blue-collar variety, not the Milanese one.

"I hate him," she says. "He's so ignorant. I need a smart man."

Vivian acknowledges that there's something nice about the simplicity of her new relationship. "I'm still in a world of dreams," she says. "But maybe I am stupid, because you can't have perfection. Maybe that's why my marriages didn't succeed. I didn't look for the good, I looked for the glamour, you know?" Recently she brought her new boyfriend to her daughter's for dinner, and Vivian was paranoid that everyone would be stunned by how far she'd fallen. But they loved him. "My daughter said, 'Isn't it time you overcame superficial things and went for something real?'"

"That sounds like good advice," I say.

"Yes, but 'something real,' it gets on my fucking nerves," she says. "I belong with younger men now that I am older. I am like a man that way."

When we finish talking, Vivian asks me if I want another glass of wine, but I decline and tell her I need to go. We stand and say good-bye at the door. I'm feeling nervous, and can't make eye contact. Do I shake her hand? A kiss on the cheek? But where on the cheek? I decide to give her a quick kiss squarely in the middle of the cheek. I do, but my aim is off, and maybe it lands a quarter inch closer to her mouth than I expect, and maybe I linger there a bit longer than a biographer should. Vivian doesn't seem surprised. The skin is wrinkled, but softer than I expected. Then I walk out, and Vivian does look surprised.

In the elevator, on the way down, I wonder to myself: Did Vivian look surprised because of my unexpected intimacy? Did she look surprised because she wanted more? Or did she look surprised only because it was such an unfamiliar sight, a man walking away from her?

ADAM SANDLER, JAMES DOWNEY, IAN MAXTONE-GRAHAM,
TIM HERLIHY, STEVE KOREN, & LEW MORTON

Canteen Boy and the Scoutmaster

Scoutmaster............................ Alec Baldwin
Canteen Boy .... Adam Sandler
Boy Scout #1 .... Chris Farley
Boy Scout #2 .... David Spade
Boy Scout #3 .... Jay Mohr

(OPEN ON: CAMPFIRE IN THE WOODS)

(SFX: CRICKETS THROUGHOUT)

(CHRIS, DAVID, AND JAY ARE SCOUTS. ALEC, AS THE SCOUT-
MASTER, FINISHES A GHOST STORY)

SCOUTMASTER
...And hanging on the car door was a bloody hook!

(THE SCOUTS REACT)

BOY SCOUT #1
I got a ghost story, Mr. Armstrong, but I can't tell it till the Canteen

---

This sketch was originally broadcast on Saturday Night Live *on February 12, 1994.*

Boy gets back.

SCOUTMASTER

Where is Canteen Boy, anyway?

BOY SCOUT #2

Right over there.

(CUT TO: CANTEEN BOY, BY A TREE, TRANSFIXED WITH FEAR, STARING AT A BIG WOODEN OWL)

BOY SCOUT #3

Canteen Boy, come over here.

CANTEEN BOY

Hang on a sec, guys. I got a bit of a situation over here.

BOY SCOUT #2

Relax, Canteen Boy. That thing's made of wood.

CANTEEN BOY

(POKES IT TENTATIVELY)

So it is.

(GOES OVER AND JOINS THEM)

Good eye.

BOY SCOUT #1

Hey, Canteen Boy, I've got a really scary ghost story. Once upon a time there was a moron who always had a stupid canteen wrapped around his neck!

CANTEEN BOY

I think I've heard this tale before.

BOY SCOUT #1

It was a dark and stormy night, and this moron went into the woods, and a huge bear came up and ripped his head off, just 'cause he looked so stupid. The end.

(BOY SCOUTS #1, #2, AND #3 LAUGH)

CANTEEN BOY
You wanna see something really scary? Look in the mirror.

BOY SCOUT #1
Shut up, Canteen Boy.

CANTEEN BOY
You shut up.

BOY SCOUT #1
What's that?

CANTEEN BOY
Nothing.

(BOYS LAUGH AT CANTEEN BOY)

SCOUTMASTER
All right guys, lay off Canteen Boy. You can hike on back to your tents and hit the hay, let's go, move it. Not you, Canteen Boy.

(BOY SCOUTS #1, #2, AND #3 LEAVE)

SCOUTMASTER (CONT'D)
I wanted to talk to you about something. I see you take a lot of ribbing from the scouts.

CANTEEN BOY
Goes with the territory, Mr. Armstrong. Sticks and stones.

SCOUTMASTER
Attaboy.
(HE PUTS HIS ARM AROUND CANTEEN BOY)
You know, it seems like the moment you get out of the city, all your problems just kind of fade away.
(HE NUZZLES INTO CANTEEN BOY'S SHOULDER)

SCOUTMASTER (CONT'D)

I'm sorry Canteen Boy, my beard is scratchy, isn't it?

CANTEEN BOY

No harm done.

SCOUTMASTER

My beard is scratchy, but it gives good back rubs.

CANTEEN BOY

Yeah, right. I'll take a rain check on that, Mr. Armstrong.

(SCOUTMASTER TAKES HIS SHIRT OFF)

SCOUTMASTER

Whoops, my shirt fell off.

CANTEEN BOY

That's a quick fix, Mr. Armstrong, just put it back on.

SCOUTMASTER

(LAUGHS)

That's great Canteen Boy! Hey, do you like wine?

CANTEEN BOY

Actually I prefer purified water right out of the old canteen here.

SCOUTMASTER

I'm going to get us some wine.

CANTEEN BOY

All right, a little drop wouldn't kill me, I guess...

(SCOUTMASTER GOES OVER TO A PILE OF GEAR AND
RUMMAGES INSIDE)

(SFX: OWL HOOT)

CANTEEN BOY

Whoo whoo to you. Hey, owl if you're so wise why don't you go to sleep? It's the middle of the night!

(SCOUTMASTER RETURNS IN A TERRYCLOTH ROBE WITH A
BOTTLE OF WINE & 2 WINE GLASSES. HE SITS DOWN NEXT TO
CANTEEN BOY)

SCOUTMASTER

Here's to the great outdoors!

(SPILLS WINE)

Whoops, was that your sleeping bag? You better share mine. It's
extra-large.

(SCOUTMASTER GETS INTO HIS SLEEPING BAG)

CANTEEN BOY

Sure, why not, till mine dries off. Shouldn't take long, it's Gore-Tex.

(HE GETS INTO SCOUTMASTER'S DOUBLE-WIDE SLEEPING BAG
WITH HIM)

SCOUTMASTER

Canteen Boy, would you rub some bug repellent onto my chest?

CANTEEN BOY

It's, uh, February, Mr. Armstrong. I think all the bugs went down
south to hibernate, I'll be honest with you.

SCOUTMASTER

Humor me, Canteen Boy.

(CANTEEN BOY VERY TENTATIVELY RUBS SOME BUG REPEL-
LENT ON SCOUTMASTER'S CHEST)

CANTEEN BOY

There you go. No more bugs.

SCOUTMASTER

I have to apologize for my hairy chest. It can be a little scratchy.

CANTEEN BOY

My mom might like that, she's a big Tom Selleck fan.

(SCOUTMASTER LAUGHS)

(CANTEEN BOY LAUGHS ALONG)

(SCOUTMASTER CUDDLES CANTEEN BOY)

SCOUTMASTER

You're very funny, Canteen Boy. Make me laugh some more.

CANTEEN BOY

Actually, I left my joke book over in the tent, how about I go get it?

SCOUTMASTER

That's okay, Canteen Boy. Let's just lie here and look at the stars.

(HE SUCKS CANTEEN BOY'S FINGERS, ONE BY ONE, AS HE SPEAKS)

SCOUTMASTER

Do you know how to play
(SUCK)
truth or dare, Canteen Boy?

CANTEEN BOY

(FROZEN)
Uh, refresh me.

SCOUTMASTER

You choose between telling a secret
(SUCK)
or doing a dare.

CANTEEN BOY

All right, dare.

(SCOUTMASTER WHISPERS IN CANTEEN BOY'S EAR. CANTEEN BOY LOOKS SHOCKED)

CANTEEN BOY

You know what, Mr. Armstrong, let's start off with a truth.

SCOUTMASTER

I'll tell *you* a truth, Canteen Boy. You know what I hate?

(SCOUTMASTER STARTS TO WRIGGLE IN THE SLEEPING BAG)

SCOUTMASTER (CONT'D)

Underpants.

CANTEEN BOY

Jeez, I think if you're worried about bugs, underpants would be your last line of defense.

SCOUTMASTER

Problem solved.

(HE PULLS A PAIR OF SHINY BLACK BIKINI BRIEFS OUT OF THE SLEEPING BAG)

CANTEEN BOY

Your problem's solved, but I think my problem's just beginning. Hey! What the hell was that?

SCOUTMASTER

(MISCHIEVOUS)

I don't know. Must have been a bedbug.

CANTEEN BOY

That was pretty big for a bedbug.

SCOUTMASTER

Okay, it wasn't a bedbug.

CANTEEN BOY

Let's go back to saying it was a bedbug. Hey you know what? The park ranger just called, said one camper per sleeping bag. Sorry, adios amigo.

(HE STARTS TO GET OUT, BUT SCOUTMASTER PUTS HIS ARM
AROUND HIM AND LAUGHS)

SCOUTMASTER

God you make me laugh, Canteen Boy.

(HE NUZZLES UP TO CANTEEN BOY AND CLOSES HIS EYES. CAN-
TEEN BOY JUST STARES AHEAD IN TOTAL FEAR)

(FADE OUT)

(DISS TO: VT: NIGHTTIME FOOTAGE OF WOODS OR STARS)

(DISS TO: SET—MORNING. SCOUTMASTER IS STILL SLEEPING,
CANTEEN BOY STILL STARING IN FEAR, THE SAME LOOK ON
HIS FACE)

(SCOUTMASTER WAKES UP)

SCOUTMASTER (CONT'D)

I'm sorry, Canteen Boy, I fell asleep before anything happened.

CANTEEN BOY

No harm done.

SCOUTMASTER

Who's hungry? I'm going to go make us a power breakfast.

CANTEEN BOY

Okay...

(SCOUTMASTER WALKS OVER AND RUMMAGES IN A TENT.
CANTEEN BOY GETS OUT OF THE SLEEPING BAG, STANDS UP,
WHISTLES)

(CUT TO: VT: QUICK SHOT OF SNAKES COMING TO ATTENTION)

(SFX: SNAKE RATTLE)

(CUT BACK TO: CAMPSITE. CANTEEN BOY RUNS AWAY. SCOUT-
MASTER COMES BACK WITH TWO GLASSES)

SCOUTMASTER

Canteen Boy, have you ever had a mimosa? Canteen Boy?

(DOZENS OF SNAKES DROP ON SCOUTMASTER)

(<u>SFX</u>: SNAKE RATTLES)

SCOUTMASTER

Canteen Boy, you rascal!

(OUT)

DAVID SEDARIS

Go Carolina

Anyone who watches even the slightest amount of TV is familiar with the scene: An agent knocks on the door of some seemingly ordinary home or office. The door opens, and the person holding the knob is asked to identify himself. The agent then says, "I'm going to ask you to come with me."

They're always remarkably calm, these agents. If asked, "Why do I need to go anywhere with you?" they'll straighten their shirt cuffs or idly brush stray hairs from the sleeves of their sports coats and say, "Oh, I think we both know why."

The suspect then chooses between doing things the hard way and doing things the easy way, and the scene ends with either gunfire or the gentlemanly application of handcuffs. Occasionally it's a case of mistaken identity, but most often the suspect knows exactly why he's being taken. It seems he's been expecting this to happen. The anticipation has ruled his life, and now, finally, the wait is over. You're sometimes led to believe that this person is actually relieved, but I've never bought it. Though it probably has its moments, the average day spent hiding is bound to beat the average day spent in prison. When it comes time to decide who gets the bottom bunk, I think anyone would agree that there's a lot to be said for doing things the hard way.

This piece was taken from David Sedaris's book of essays, Me Talk Pretty One Day.

The agent came for me during a geography lesson. She entered the room and nodded at my fifth-grade teacher, who stood frowning at a map of Europe. What would needle me later was the realization that this had all been prearranged. My capture had been scheduled to go down at exactly 2:30 on a Thursday afternoon. The agent would be wearing a dung-colored blazer over a red knit turtleneck, her heels sensibly low in case the suspect should attempt a quick getaway.

"David," the teacher said, "this is Miss Samson, and she'd like you to go with her now."

No one else had been called, so why me? I ran down a list of recent crimes, looking for a conviction that might stick. Setting fire to a reportedly flame-proof Halloween costume, stealing a set of barbecue tongs from an unguarded patio, altering the word *hit* on a list of rules posted on the gymnasium door; never did it occur to me that I might be innocent.

"You might want to take your books with you," the teacher said. "And your jacket. You probably won't be back before the bell rings."

Though she seemed old at the time, the agent was most likely fresh out of college. She walked beside me and asked what appeared to be an innocent and unrelated question: "So, which do you like better, State or Carolina?"

She was referring to the athletic rivalry between the Triangle area's two largest universities. Those who cared about such things tended to express their allegiance by wearing either Tar Heel powder blue, or Wolf Pack red, two colors that managed to look good on no one. The question of team preference was common in our part of North Carolina, and the answer supposedly spoke volumes about the kind of person you either were or hoped to become. I had no interest in football or basketball but had learned it was best to pretend otherwise. If a boy didn't care for barbecued chicken or potato chips, people would accept it as a matter of personal taste, saying, "Oh well, I guess it takes all kinds." You could turn up your nose at the president of Coke or even God, but there were names for boys who didn't like sports. When the subject came up, I found it best to ask which team my questioner preferred. Then I'd say, "Really? Me, too!"

Asked by the agent which team I supported, I took my cue from her red turtleneck and told her that I was for State. "Definitely State. State all the way."

It was an answer I would regret for years to come.

"State, did you say?" the agent asked.

"Yes, State. They're the greatest."

"I see." She led me through an unmarked door near the principal's office, into a small, windowless room furnished with two facing desks. It was the kind of room where you'd grill someone until they snapped, the kind frequently painted so as to cover the bloodstains. She gestured toward what was to become my regular seat, then continued her line of questioning.

"And what exactly are they, State and Carolina?"

"Colleges? Universities?"

She opened a file on her desk, saying, "Yes, you're right. Your answers are correct, but you're saying them incorrectly. You're telling me that they're college*th* and univer*thitieth*, when actually they're college*s* and universitie*s*. You're giving me a *th* sound instead of a nice clear *s*. Can you hear the distinction between the two different *s*ounds?"

I nodded.

"May I please have an actual an*s*wer?"

"Uh-huh."

"'Uh-huh' i*s* not a word."

"Okay."

"Okay what?"

"Okay," I said. "Sure, I can hear it."

"You can hear what, the di*s*tinction? The contra*s*t?"

"Yeah, that."

It was the first battle of my war against the letter *s*, and I was determined to dig my foxhole before the sun went down. According to Agent Samson, a "*s*tate *c*ertified *s*peech therapi*s*t," my *s* was sibilate, meaning that I lisped. This was not news to me.

"Our goal i*s* to work together until eventually you can *s*peak correctly," Agent Samson said. She made a great show of enunciating her own sparkling *s*'s, and the effect was profoundly irritating. "I'm trying to help you, but the longer you play the*s*e little game*s* the longer thi*s* i*s* going to take."

The woman spoke with a heavy western North Carolina accent, which I used to discredit her authority. Here was a person for whom the word *pen* had two syllables. Her people undoubtedly drank from clay jugs and hollered for Paw when the vittles were ready—so who was she to advise me on anything? Over the coming years I would find a crack in each of the therapists sent to train what Miss Samson now defined as my lazy tongue. "That's its problem," she said. "It's just plain lazy."

My sisters Amy and Gretchen were, at the time, undergoing therapy for their lazy eyes, while my older sister, Lisa, had been born with a lazy leg that had refused to grow at the same rate at its twin. She'd worn a corrective brace for the first two years of her life, and wherever she roamed she left a trail of scratch marks on the soft pine floor. I liked the idea that a part of one's body might be thought of as lazy—not thoughtless or hostile, just unwilling to extend itself for the betterment of the team. My father often accused my mother of having a lazy mind, while she in turn accused him of having a lazy index finger, unable to dial the phone when he knew damn well he was going to be late.

My therapy sessions were scheduled for every Thursday at 2:30, and with the exception of my mother, I discussed them with no one. The word *therapy* suggested a profound failure on my part. Mental patients had therapy. Normal people did not. I didn't see my sessions as the sort of thing that one would want to advertise, but as my teacher liked to say, "I guess it takes all kinds." Whereas my goal was to keep it a secret, hers was to inform the entire class. It I got up from my seat at 2:25 she'd say, "Sit back down, David. You've still got five minutes before your speech therapy session." If I remained seated until 2:27, she'd say, "David, don't forget you have a speech therapy session at two-thirty." On the days I was absent, I imagined she addressed the room, saying, "David's not here today, but if he were he'd have a speech therapy session at two-thirty."

My sessions varied from week to week. Sometimes I'd spend the half hour parroting whatever Agent Samson had to say. We'd occasionally pass the time examining charts on tongue position or reading childish *s*-laden texts recounting the adventures of seals or settlers named Sassy or Samuel. On the worst of days she's haul out a tape recorder and show me just how much progress I was failing to make.

"My *s*peech therapi*s*t'*s* name is Mi*ss* Chri*ss*y Sam*s*on." She'd hand me the microphone and lean back with her arms crossed. "Go ahead, say it. I want you to hear what you sound like."

She was in love with the sound of her own name and seemed to view my speech impediment as a personal assault. If I wanted to spend the rest of my life as David Thedarith, then so be it. She, however, was going to be called Miss Chrissy Samson. Had her name included no s's, she probably would have bypassed a career in therapy and devoted herself to yanking out healthy molars or performing unwanted clitoridectomies on the schoolgirls of Africa. Such was her personality.

"Oh, come on," my mother would say. "I'm sure she's not *that* bad. Give her a break. The girl's just trying to do her job."

I was a few minutes early one week and entered the office to find Agent Samson doing her job on Garth Barclay, a slight, kittenish boy I'd met back in fourth grade. "You may wait outside in the hallway until it is your turn," she told me. A week or two later my session was interrupted by mincing Steve Bixler, who popped his head in the door and announced that his parents were taking him out of town for a long weekend, meaning that he would miss his regular Friday session. "Thorry about that," he said.

I started keeping watch over the speech therapy door, taking note of who came and went. Had I seen one popular student leaving the office, I could have believed my mother and viewed my lisp as the sort of thing that might happen to anyone. Unfortunately, I saw no popular students. Chuck Coggins, Sam Shelton, Louis Delucca: obviously, there was some connection between a sibilate s and a complete lack of interest in the State versus Carolina issue.

None of the therapy students were girls. They were all boys like me who kept movie star scrapbooks and made their own curtains. "You don't want to be doing that," the men in our families would say. "That's a girl thing." Baking scones and cupcakes for the school janitors, watching *Guiding Light* with our mothers, collecting rose petals for use in a fragrant potpourri: anything worth doing turned out to be a girl thing. In order to enjoy ourselves, we learned to be duplicitous. Our stacks of *Cosmopolitan* were topped with an unread issue of *Boy's Life* or *Sports Illustrated*, and our decoupage projects were concealed beneath the sporting equipment we never asked for but always received. When asked what we wanted to be when we grew up, we hid the truth and listed who we wanted to sleep with when we grew up. "A policeman or a fireman or one of those guys who works with high-tension wires." Symptoms were feigned, and our mothers wrote notes excusing our absences on the day of the intramural softball tournament. Brian had a stomach virus or Ted suffered from that twenty-four-hour bug that seemed to be going around.

"One of these days I'm going to have to hang a sign on that door," Agent Samson used to say. She was probably thinking along the lines of SPEECH THERAPY LAB, though a more appropriate marker would have read FUTURE HOMOSEXUALS OF AMERICA. We knocked ourselves out trying to fit in but we were ultimately betrayed by our tongues. At the beginning of the school year, while we were congratulating ourselves on successfully passing for normal, Agent Samson was taking names as our assembled teachers raised their hands saying, "I've got one in my homeroom," and "There are two in my fourth-period math class." Were they able to spot the future drunks and depressives? Did they hope that by eliminating our lisps they might set us on a different path, or were they trying to prepare us for future stage and choral careers?

Miss Samson instructed me, when forming an *s*, to position the tip of my tongue against the rear of my top teeth, right up against the gum line. The effect produced a sound not unlike that of a tire releasing air. It was awkward and strange-sounding, and elicited much more attention than the original lisp. I failed to see the hissy *s* as a solution to the problem and continued to talk normally, at least at home, where my lazy tongue fell upon equally lazy ears. At school, where every teacher was a potential spy, I tried to avoid an *s* sound whenever possible. "Yes" became "correct," or a military "affirmative." "Please" became "with your kind permission," and questions were pleaded rather than asked. After a few weeks of what she called "endless pestering" and what I called "repeated badgering," my mother bought me a pocket thesaurus, which provided me with *s*-free alternatives to just about everything. I consulted the book both at home in my room and at the daily learning academy other people called our school. Agent Samson was not amused when I began referring to her as an articulation coach, but the majority of my teachers were delighted. "What a nice vocabulary," they said. "My goodness, such big words!"

Plurals presented a considerable problem, but I worked around them as best I could; "rivers," for example, became either "a river or two" or "many a river." Possessives were a similar headache, and it was easier to say nothing than to announce that the left-hand and the right-hand glove of Janet had fallen to the floor. After compliments I had received on my improved vocabulary, it seemed prudent to lie low and keep my mouth shut. I didn't want anyone thinking I was trying to be a pet of the teacher.

When I first began speech therapy, I worried that the Agent Samson plan might work for everyone but me, that the other boys might strengthen their lazy tongues, turn their lives around, and leave me stranded. Luckily my fears were never realized. Despite the woman's best efforts, no one seemed to make any significant improvement. The only difference was that we were all a little quieter. Thanks to Agent Samson's tape recorder, I, along with the others, now had a clear sense of what I actually sounded like. There was the lisp, of course, but more troubling was my voice itself, with its excitable tone and high, girlish pitch. I'd hear myself ordering lunch in the cafeteria, and the sound would turn my stomach. How could anyone stand to listen to me? Whereas those around me might grow up to be lawyers or movie stars, my only option was to take a vow of silence and become a monk. My former classmates would call the abbey, wondering how I was doing, and the priest would answer the phone. "You can't talk to him!" he'd say. "Why, Brother David hasn't spoken to anyone in thirty-five years!"

"Oh, relax," my mother said. "Your voice will change eventually."

"And what if it doesn't?"

She shuddered. "Don't be so morbid."

It turned out that Agent Samson was something along the lines of a circuit-court speech therapist. She spent four months at our school and then moved on to another. Our last meeting was held the day before school let out for Christmas. My classrooms were all decorated, the halls—everything but her office, which remained as bare as ever. I was expecting a regular half hour of Sassy the seal and was delighted to find her packing up her tape recorder.

"I thought that this afternoon we might let loose and have a party, you and I. How does that sound?" She reached into her desk drawer and withdrew a festive tin of cookies. "Here, have one. I made them myself from scratch and, boy, was it a mess! Do you ever make cookies?"

I lied, saying that no, I never had.

"Well, it's hard work," she said. "Especially if you don't have a mixer."

It was unlike Agent Samson to speak so casually, and awkward to sit in the hot little room, pretending to have a normal conversation.

"So," she said, "what are your plans for the holidays?"

"Well, I usually remain here and, you know, open a gift from my family."

"Only one?" she asked.

"Maybe eight or ten."

"Never six or seven?"

"Rarely," I said.

"And what do you do on December thirty-first, New Year's Eve?"

"On the final day of the year we take down the pine tree in our living room and eat marine life."

"You're pretty good at avoiding those s's," she said. "I have to hand it to you, you're tougher than most."

I thought she would continue trying to trip me up, but instead she talked about her own holiday plans. "It's pretty hard with my fiancé in Vietnam," she said. "Last year we went up to see his folks in Roanoke, but this year I'll spend my Christmas with my grandmother outside of Asheville. My parents will come, and we'll all try our best to have a good time. I'll eat some turkey and go to church, and then, the next day, a friend and I will drive down to Jacksonville to watch Florida play Tennessee in the Gator Bowl."

I couldn't imagine anything worse than driving down to Florida to watch a football game, but I pretended to be impressed. "Wow, that ought to be eventful."

"I was in Memphis last year when NC State whooped Georgia fourteen to seven in the Liberty Bowl," she said. "And next year, I don't care who's playing, but I want to be sitting front-row center at the Tangerine Bowl. Have you ever been to Orlando? It's a super fun place. If my future husband can find a job in his field, we're hoping to move down there within a year or two. Me living in Florida. I bet that would make you happy, wouldn't it?"

I didn't quite know how to respond. Who was this college bowl fanatic with no mixer and a fiancé in Vietnam, and why had she taken so long to reveal herself? Here I'd thought of her as a cold-blooded agent when she was really nothing but a slightly dopey, inexperienced speech teacher. She wasn't a bad person, Miss Samson, but her timing was off. She should have acted friendly at the beginning of the year instead of waiting until now, when all I could do was feel sorry for her.

"I tried my best to work with you and the others, but sometimes a person's best just isn't good enough." She took another cookie and turned it over in her hands. "I really wanted to prove myself and make a difference in people's lives, but it's hard to do your job when you're met with so much resistance. My students don't like me, and I guess that's just the way it is. What can I say? As a speech teacher, I'm a complete failure."

She moved her hands toward her face, and I worried that she might start to cry. "Hey, look," I said. "I'm thorry."

"Ha-ha," she said. "I got you." She laughed much more than she needed to and was still at it when she signed the form recommending me for the following year's speech therapy program. "Thorry, indeed. You've got some work ahead of you mister."

I related this story to my mother, who got a huge kick out of it. "You've got to admit that you really are a sucker," she said.

I agreed but, because none of my speech classes ever made a difference, I still prefer to use the word *chump*.

PAUL SIMMS

For Immediate Release

Alex Kerner (C.E.O., C.O.O., chairman, and president of Alex Kerner's Personal Life, Inc.) announced today a wide-ranging restructuring of his imaginary company's upper management.

Tim Williams, a member of the company in varying capacities for five years, has been promoted to Best Friend, and he will report directly to Kerner in all friendship-related matters.

"Tim has proved himself to be a solid guy who's always up for whatever," Kerner says. "During the past five years, I've watched him excel in every position he's occupied. From Mere Acquaintance to Periodic Dinner Companion (In Groups of Four or More People) to Frequent Midweek Business-Lunch Cohort, Tim has consistently shown himself to be just the kind of person we're looking for in a Best Friend.

"Tim's willingness to charge midweek lunches to his expense account represents just one element in a strategic alliance that will be an asset for both of us far into the future."

The former holder of the Best Friend position, Lou Solomon, will not be leaving the organization but, rather, will be transitioning into the newly created post of Independent Phone Acquaintance.

"As my Best Friend for the past few years, Lou has shepherded our outfit through more than a few successful endeavors," Kerner says. "He was our point man on the Night I Puked in a Cab. He was a sage adviser on the Night I Lost One Shoe. And he was indispensable in quickly assembling a crisis-response team on the Night I Lost My Phone But Then We Found It in His Futon.

"Lou also pioneered the 'poison pill' defense, whereby we pretended to be Mutual Friends with Tom Monroe, a known dick, thus staving off a hostile-takeover attempt by Jack Houlihan & Friends, L.L.C.

"Drinking and Puking and Losing Things will always be a core part of our business," Kerner says. "But, as we focus on diversifying into Non–Drinking and Puking and Losing Things–related areas, we feel that Lou's skills can be put to better use elsewhere. Regardless, I look forward to speaking to Lou every once in a while on the phone if I'm not too busy for many years to come."

Also affected in the restructuring is Solomon's girlfriend, Kay Madison, who was increasingly involved in all of Kerner and Solomon's activities, despite the fact that she technically reported solely to Solomon.

"I wish Kay all the best in her future endeavors," Kerner says. "I know she was often frustrated by her lack of direct access to me—except through Lou—but I doubt that she'll be without a solid friendship position for long, as there are many organizations out there looking for a bold, brassy, loud, and opinionated woman who is hell-bent on finding a way to insert herself into every aspect of the friendship structure."

In a reshuffling move unrelated to the current streamlining, former Best Platonic Female Friend Lisa Mayberry has been summarily terminated from the organization for malfeasance involving telling Kerner's ex-girlfriend details about Kerner's current girlfriend.

"We hold all our employees—from Best Friend for Life, Emeritus, on down to 'Hey, How You Doing, We Don't Know Each Other's Names, But We Live in the Same Building'–level Elevator Companions—to a strict standard of conduct," Kerner says. "And there's simply no room in this organization for a yappy gossip who I suspect was always just waiting for me to be between girlfriends and depressed so she could try to trick me into sleeping with her."

Kerner is also exploring a possible merger with a onetime competitor, the Bill Schofield Group. Schofield's assets include fairly good Knicks season tickets and at least one semi-famous friend.

"We're not looking to steal Bill's old college buddy Dan Abrams from him," Kerner says. "But, if we could become friends with him as part of the bargain, that would represent a win-win for all involved."

Also, Ahmed Humza—a seven-year veteran in the Friendly But Nameless Newsstand Operator post—has been promoted to the newly created position of Ahmed.

"I've been going to that same newsstand every day for seven years," Kerner says. "I don't know why, but recently I finally asked the guy what his name is. Though I doubt Ahmed will ever rise to the 'You're Allowed in My Apartment' level of upper management, he will serve as a significant rhetorical asset to be used in arguments about terrorism when the other person says, 'Okay, but I bet you don't even have any Arab friends.'"

Finally, despite rumors to the contrary, Kerner has reaffirmed that Tom Monroe will continue to fill the post of That Dick.

"I found myself standing next to Tom at a party recently, and we had a cordial conversation," Kerner says. "But anyone who says that we're Friends— or even Mutual Tolerators—is sorely mistaken. I want nothing to do with that dick."

Lookwell

A TV Pilot

Ty Lookwell	Adam West
Det. Kennery	Ron Frazier
Hyacinth	Ann Weldon
Jason	Todd Field
Ben	John Riggi
Alex	Brian Bradley
Suzanne	Molly Cleator
Alberti	Bart Braverman
Rental Agent	Chris Barnes
Desk Sergeant	Jeff Austin
Phil	John Capodice
Manny	Sal Lopez
Racing Official	Terry Beaver
Actor #1	Steve Schubert
Actor #2	Brick Karnes

Lookwell *was produced for NBC in 1991. The Sunday night it was broadcast the tape machine malfunctioned, causing a staggered effect throughout the show. The pilot was not picked up. Only one episode exists.*

ACT ONE

FADE IN:

EXT. MOVIE STUDIO LOT—ESTABLISHING—DAY

CUT TO:

INT. CASTING DEPT. WAITING AREA—CONTINUOUS

ACTOR #1 approaches a RECEPTIONIST. ACTORS in the background are studying their sides.

ACTOR #1

I'm here to audition for "Happy Days: The Next Generation."

RECEPTIONIST

Right over there.

The actor takes a card and walks to the end of the room. The camera pans a long line of casually dressed actors waiting their turn. The camera stops on TY LOOKWELL, a middle-aged, well-preserved actor. He's dressed in a complete fifties greaser outfit: black pompadour wig, T-shirt, leather jacket, and rolled-up jeans. Lookwell is in the midst of lecturing ACTORS #1 & #2.

LOOKWELL

...Yes, I learned long ago that a casting director only has so much time to make a choice. The thinking actor knows he must use every edge to make that choice a forgone conclusion.

ACTOR #2

Wow, I guess I blew it.

LOOKWELL

Perhaps... but you never fail when you learn from your mistake.

ACTOR #1

You know, I recognize you. Aren't you Ty Lookwell?

> LOOKWELL

Yes, but until the audition is over I prefer to be addressed as "Buzz McCool."

> ACTOR #1

Well, it's nice to meet you. I still remember "Banacek." That was a great show.

> LOOKWELL

I wasn't Banacek. You're thinking of George Peppard. My show was "Bannigan."

> ACTOR #2

"Brannigan?"

> LOOKWELL

No, that was Hugh O'Brian. I was "Bannigan."

> ACTOR #1

Oh, right, you had a black secretary.

> LOOKWELL

No, that was "Mannix." I had a sheep dog.

> ACTORS #1 & 2

Right!

A CASTING DIRECTOR emerges.

> CASTING DIRECTOR

Sorry, people, it looks like we have everyone we need. But thanks for coming down. We appreciate it.

The actors start to file out.

> ACTOR #2
> (sarcastic)

That's just great.

LOOKWELL

Their loss, my friend.

CUT TO:

EXT. MOVIE STUDIO PARKING LOT—LATER

Lookwell and the two actors are walking to their cars. Lookwell is now wearing his traditional blazer and turtleneck and is carrying a garment bag over one shoulder. In his hands he holds the pompadour wig.

LOOKWELL

...We could have done a fourth season, but I felt my character had said all that he had to say.

ACTOR #1

How did the network feel?

LOOKWELL

Similar.

LOOKWELL gets into a vintage Italian sports car.

LOOKWELL (CONT'D)

Well, best of luck to both of you.

ACTOR #2

That's a beautiful car, Mr. Lookwell.

LOOKWELL

(tapping his temple and winking)

Remember, the "thinking" actor.

Lookwell proudly drives off.

Lookwell proudly drives down the street, outside the studio. Suddenly, he turns left.

CUT TO:

EXT. "ALBERTI E-Z LUXURY CAR RENTAL" PARKING LOT— CONTINUOUS

Lookwell pulls up to the "check-in" area. The RENTAL AGENT in a booth takes his rental agreement.

RENTAL AGENT
Alright, sir, that's two hours, so it comes to fifty dollars plus tax.

LOOKWELL
Hmmm, by my watch I was only out for an hour and forty-five.

RENTAL AGENT
We round off to the closest hour, sir. It's in your agreement.

LOOKWELL
Look, I didn't want to bring this up, but the blinker makes a "click-click" sound.

RENTAL AGENT
It's supposed to, sir.

LOOKWELL
Alright, here's a twenty. Let's agree to disagree.

A police car with a flashing siren passes Lookwell and drives up to the main offices of Alberti E-Z Luxury Car Rental, where other police cars have already congregated.

LOOKWELL (CONT'D)
What's that about?

RENTAL AGENT
We had a car stolen last night, sir.

LOOKWELL
Sounds like trouble. Better take a look.

Lookwell speeds away, up toward the police cars. The owner of the rental agency, MR. ALBERTI, is being questioned by SEVERAL PATROLMEN. Lookwell hurries out of his car and approaches the group.

POLICEMAN #2

What was the license plate number, Mr. Alberti?

ALBERTI

(upset)

I don't have it. It was only written on the keychain.

LOOKWELL

What seems to be the problem, officers?

POLICEMAN #1

We're handling it, sir, could you please step back?

LOOKWELL

I don't think you understand. I used to be a detective.

POLICEMAN #2

Oh yeah, he was "Bennigan."

LOOKWELL

No, that was George Kennedy. I was "Bannigan."

ALBERTI

Could we get back to this, please!?

POLICEMAN #1

We'll do what we can, sir. But this is the fifth lot to have a classic car stolen this week.

LOOKWELL

It sounds to me like a string of classic car thefts. You boys better check it out. As Shakespeare reminds us, "How oft the sight of means to do ill deeds makes ill deeds done."

The policemen seem confused.

ALBERTI

Would you get lost!

> LOOKWELL

Well, I'll leave it to you gentlemen for now. (TO ALBERTI) And as for you, sir, it wouldn't hurt to be more careful about the kind of scum you rent your cars out to.

Lookwell gets into his car, a Chevy Nova, and drives away.

> CUT TO:

EXT. LOOKWELL'S HOUSE—CONTINUOUS

The house is a Spanish-style in the Hollywood Hills. Lookwell parks his car and walks inside.

> CUT TO:

INT. LOOKWELL'S HOUSE—CONTINUOUS

It's a comfortable Hollywood home that Lookwell's been living in for twenty years. The decor is dominated by memorabilia from his acting career. HYACINTH, Lookwell's longtime black housekeeper, supportive and unflappable, cheerfully greets him.

> HYACINTH

Hey, Lookwell!

> LOOKWELL

Hello, Hyacinth.

> HYACINTH

How'd that audition go?

> LOOKWELL

Quite well, but these things take time. Did you do that shopping I asked you to do?

> HYACINTH

I tried, but the store said they don't make that hairspray anymore.

> LOOKWELL

Maybe if you called the company...

> HYACINTH

I think they're just going to tell us the same thing.

> LOOKWELL
> (muttering)

Those fools...

> HYACINTH

Oh, I washed your nephew's clothes. He said he might want to stay a few extra days.

> LOOKWELL

Hmmm. Matt must be enjoying himself. Ah, youth.

Lookwell pushes a button on his answering machine.

> LOOKWELL (V.O.)

Hello. If you'd like to leave a message for Ty Lookwell, or for the Ty Lookwell Actor's Workshop, or for Matt Conway, do so at the beep. I'll get back to you shortly.

SFX: BEEP

Lookwell starts lightly slapping the bottom of his chin to keep it taut.

> VOICE #1 (V.O.)

This is for Matt Conway. Matt, this is Carol Harris at CBS. We liked your audition very much. Please give me a call.

Lookwell picks up an actor's 8 × 10" of MATT'S handsome face.

SFX: BEEP

> VOICE #2 (V.O.)

Hey, Matt, this is Rick. Francis Coppola wants to meet with you tomorrow at three-thirty. Let me know if you can make it.

Lookwell walks to his refrigerator and takes a box of ice cream bars out of the freezer. The box reads, "Firm-Pops. The frozen treat that tightens your skin."

SFX: BEEP

VOICE # 3 (V.O.)
Hi, Matt. You may not remember me. My name's Jenni. I met you at a party last week. I'll try again later.

Lookwell sits down next to the machine, munching his Firm-Pop.

SFX: BEEP

Hyacinth, embarrassed for Lookwell, sneaks out of the room.

VOICE #2 (V.O.)
It's Rick again. Listen, I was just talking to Don Bavak at George Lucas's studio and they really want you to...

Lookwell presses the fast-forward button, stopping occasionally to check the message and then presses it again.

VOICE #2 (V.O.) (CONT'D)
...eebydeebee eebydeebee eebydeebee eebydeebee Spielberg project and eebydeebee eebydeebee eebydeebee you and Costner. So let me know. I'll be...

LOOKWELL
(musing to himself over message)
It's good to see Matt get a lot of lucky breaks. I hope he sticks with it.

VOICE #2 (V.O.)
...Oh, and one other thing. That "Happy Days" audition. I told them to forget it. It turned out to be this big losers' cattle call.

The answering machine clicks and starts to rewind itself.

LOOKWELL
Good, no calls to make. I can kick back and enjoy some television.

Lookwell opens a large cabinet which contains an extensive video library. As he runs his finger along the tapes, it is revealed that all of them are "Bannigan" episodes with different dates. He selects one and pops it into his VCR.

CUT TO:

"BANNIGAN" OPENING CREDITS—DAY

On television screen, we see the opening credits, with theme music, of an early seventies crime drama. Lookwell watches with pride.

CUT TO:

EXT. SMALL HOLLYWOOD CHURCH—DAY

"Bannigan" theme music continues.

Tighten to sign on side door. The sign has Lookwell's picture on it and reads, "Ty Lookwell's Acting Workshop—downstairs, second door on the left." A sign next to it reads, "Lamaze Seminar—downstairs right."

CUT TO:

INT. CLASSROOM—CONTINUOUS

The "Bannigan" episode is being projected on the wall.

"BANNIGAN" EPISODE—DAY

A darker-haired Lookwell is holding a gun on an extravagant seventies PIMP. A POLICE OFFICER stands nearby.

> LOOKWELL
> He's all yours, officer.

> PIMP
> You ain't got nothin' on me, Bannigan. I want my lawyer!

> LOOKWELL
> You can call the Supreme Court for all I care. You're gonna do time, Leron. Hard time. (TO POLICE OFFICER) Get him out of my sight.

FREEZE FRAME.

The music builds to a crescendo.

INT. CLASSROOM—CONTINUOUS

BEN, a balding, thirtyish member of the class, turns off the projector as LOOKWELL addresses his class.

> LOOKWELL
>
> "You're gonna do time, Leron. Hard time." In those lines, I had to convey both anger and triumph.

As Lookwell continues, the camera pans his admiring, attentive students, including JASON, a young, average-looking member of the class; ALEX, a male model with a huge jaw who tries to emulate Lookwell; SUZANNE, a ratty-haired brunette; and MISS ROYSTER.

> LOOKWELL (CONT'D)
>
> A sense of disgust for Leron and all he represented, as well as reaffirmation that the balance of nature had been restored. I served, if you will, as both magistrate and messenger.

> JASON
>
> So the pimp was actually funneling money through the disco?

> LOOKWELL
>
> Uh, yes. That's right. But allow me to get back to my point. Acting is resolving conflict. Now, taking what we're just learned, let's try that resolution scene from "King Lear" again. Alex? Suzanne?

Suzanne and Alex get up.

> ALEX
>
> O, my good master!

> SUZANNE
>
> Prithee away!

> ALEX
>
> 'Tis noble Kent, your friend.

> LOOKWELL
>
> Alright, stop right there. Which actor is conveying the dichotomy we saw in my "Bannigan" episode?

Miss Royster raises her hand.

                    LOOKWELL (CONT'D)
Yes, Miss Royster?

                    MISS ROYSTER
I kinda thought, like, both of them?

                    LOOKWELL
                    (flirtatious)
A provocative answer, Miss Royster. One worth... further examination.

                    BEN
                    (self-satisfied)
I think Alex has a good sense of his "who," kind of like Patrick did.

                    LOOKWELL
A worthy observation, Ben, but I'm afraid the others don't know who
Patrick is. (TO OTHERS) Ben has taken the class before. Alex?

                    ALEX
                    (sucking up)
Well, sir, I was attempting to summon my life experiences and transport them to the Earl of Kent's situation. As you yourself taught us...

                    LOOKWELL
                    (hitting on something)
Wait a minute. What did you say?

                    ALEX
I was just talking, sir, about my technique...

                    LOOKWELL
No, no, transport. The stolen cars are being "transported"... to another country...

                    SUZANNE
Mr. Lookwell?

                    LOOKWELL
                    (his wheels turning)

Sorry... used to... play... detective... mind... can't... help... but make... deductions... Class, I might have to step away for a bit. Ben, why don't you run the group until I'm back.

BEN
Want me to put them through the emotional tag exercise?

LOOKWELL
Whatever you like. Right now I'm going to pay a little visit to my friends at the police station.

The students look at each other, impressed.

CUT TO:

<u>EXT. POLICE HEADQUARTERS—ESTABLISHING—DAY</u>

CUT TO:

<u>INT. POLICE HEADQUARTERS—CONTINUOUS</u>

Lookwell is talking to a DESK SERGEANT.

DESK SERGEANT
Your name is what?

LOOKWELL
(impatient)
Lookwell. Ty Lookwell.

DESK SERGEANT
And you're a what?

LOOKWELL
I'm an honorary member of the force.

Lookwell whips out a badge encased in a lucite block and places it firmly on the sergeant's desk.

LOOKWELL (CONT'D)
This was given to me in 1972.

DESK SERGEANT
(reading)
"Presented to Ty Lookwell, TV's 'Brannigan'…"

LOOKWELL
"Bannigan." Hugh O'Brian was "Brannigan."

DESK SERGEANT
Who's Hugh O'Brian?

LOOKWELL
Exactly.

DESK SERGEANT
(reading)
"Honorary Crimestopper—1972." I don't know, Mr. Lookwell.

LOOKWELL
(indignant)
That was presented to me at a formal ceremony in Television City.

DETECTIVE KENNERY enters.

DET. KENNERY
Sergeant, when they post the watch schedule, I want you to…

LOOKWELL
Detective Kennery!

DET. KENNERY
(slightly embarrassed)
Oh. Hi, Lookwell.

DESK SERGEANT
Don't worry, Detective, I was just getting rid of this guy.

DET. KENNERY
No, no, Sergeant, he's with me.

> LOOKWELL
> (smug)
> (TO SERGEANT) Detective Kennery was the technical advisor on my show. Perhaps if you watched a little more television, you'd be better at your job.

CUT TO:

11 INT. KENNERY'S OFFICE—CONTINUOUS

Lookwell is pacing dramatically.

> LOOKWELL
> Detective, I think I've got a break on those classic car robberies.

> DET. KENNERY
> Well, that's great, Ty, and we appreciate your enthusiasm. But I thought we had a talk about how you weren't really needed around here.

> LOOKWELL
> Believe me, I wish I weren't. But the hard fact is those thieves are still at large and, with all due respect, I did three episodes on this kind of thing.

Detective Kennery reacts wearily.

> LOOKWELL (CONT'D)
> Now, consider this. What we're dealing with are cars which are stolen, or, as we say in the force, "hot." So hot, in fact, that they would have to be transported out of the country. Inspect the waterfront, Detective. You'll find that these cars are being shipped.

> DET. KENNERY
> Lookwell, these cars are imports. They'd fetch a higher price here than anywhere else. We're fairly certain these thieves are altering the cars quickly and then storing them somewhere to be resold later.

> LOOKWELL
> "Imported cars?" Well, perhaps if the police were to share these

nuggets of information with their honorary crimestoppers, we could work together more efficiently.

The desk sergeant peeks his head in.

DESK SERGEANT

The commissioner wants to see you.

DET. KENNERY

Tell him I'll be right there.

DESK SERGEANT

He knows who you're with and he says he'd like you to join him in reality.

DET. KENNERY

Uh, we'll talk later, Ty. Alright?

LOOKWELL

Very well, then I'll be out of your way. But remember this, gentlemen. I have a lot of free time.

FADE OUT.

END OF ACT ONE

ACT TWO

EXT. L.A. RESTAURANT/BAR—ESTABLISHING—NIGHT

CUT TO:

INT. RESTAURANT/BAR—CONTINUOUS

Lookwell is holding court at his favorite booth with Jason, Alex, Suzanne, Ben, and Miss Royster. Among the signed 8 × 10"s hanging on the wall is Lookwell's own. Lookwell holds a newspaper with the headline, "Seventh Stolen Car Outruns Police."

LOOKWELL

...And yet, they're still at large. The police are obviously baffled, but they're too proud to ask for my help.

ALEX
Wow. Well, did they tell you anything?

LOOKWELL
They say the cars are being altered.

SUZANNE
You mean, like painting them?

LOOKWELL
(deducing)
Exactly. And I wouldn't be surprised if those cars are being painted at an auto painting shop.

STUDENTS
(impressed)
Hmmmmmmmm.

LOOKWELL
Alex, get me a Yellow Pages.

Alex, sitting between Lookwell and Miss Royster, awkwardly climbs over her to get out.

ALEX
Yes, sir... excuse me, sorry...

As soon as Alex exits, Lookwell slides closer to Miss Royster.

JASON
I don't know. Isn't an auto painting shop way too obvious?

BEN
They never learn, Mr. Lookwell.

LOOKWELL
Remember what Shakespeare said, Jason. "How oft the sight of means to do ill deeds makes ill deeds done."

Alex returns with the Yellow Pages and hands it to Lookwell.

                    LOOKWELL (CONT'D)
Thank you, Alex.

He starts to flip through the pages.

                    LOOKWELL (CONT'D)
Now I'm going to pay a visit to a certain auto painting shop. One that's close enough to the crimes and large enough to tuck away a stolen car or two without anyone noticing.

                    MISS ROYSTER
What are you going to do there?

                    LOOKWELL
Let's just say a little acting... (WITH A TWINKLE IN HIS EYE) ...a little undercover acting.

                                        CUT TO:

EXT. CARL SCHWAB'S AUTO PAINTING SHOP—ESTABLISHING—DAY

We hear Phil, the manager of the shop.

                    PHIL (V.O.)
Okay, we're gonna start you out on this Cutlass over here.

                                        CUT TO:

INT. CARL SCHWAB'S AUTO PAINTING SHOP—CONTINUOUS

PHIL, a white-haired, portly man, and MANNY, a Mexican employee, are showing Lookwell a car. Both Phil and Manny are wearing paint-stained coveralls. Lookwell is dressed in a sparkling white "Man from Texaco" outfit, complete with cap, gloves and bow tie. He speaks with his regular voice, although he thinks he's playing a character.

                    PHIL
So you've painted Uni-body frames before, right?

LOOKWELL

Ah, yes, the Uni-body. A lighter-weight alternative frame introduced by Detroit in the mid-seventies.

PHIL

Huh, well, you seem to know your stuff.

LOOKWELL

Why, of course. My father was a car painter, as was his father and his father before him.

PHIL

Alright, this here's Manny. He'll sand the cars before you paint 'em.

Lookwell picks up a paint gun.

LOOKWELL

It's nice to meet you, Manny.

Lookwell starts to casually spraypaint the bumper of the car.

MANNY

Don't paint the bumper, man.

LOOKWELL
(covering)

Oh, alright. It's all the rage in... Minnesota.

PHIL

Look, we better get going here. We only charge sixty bucks to paint these things, so we like to move 'em in and out pretty quick.

LOOKWELL
(slyly)

Heh-heh, I bet you do.

PHIL

Okay, you guys, get to it.

LOOKWELL

Oh, and Phil, if there's anything "else," you'd care for me to "do," just let me know.

PHIL

Huh? What do you mean?

LOOKWELL

Oh, you know. Any "special" jobs that need "extra attention."

MANNY

(PRIVATELY TO PHIL) Is he gay?

PHIL

Hey, it don't matter if he does a good job.

LOOKWELL

Just give me the signal and I'll deliver.

MANNY

Look, man, we're not into that stuff.

LOOKWELL
(grinning slyly)
That's not what I've heard.

WIPE TO:

INT. CLASSROOM—DAY

Lookwell is wearing sunglasses and has a few bandages on his face. The class is assembled.

SUZANNE

How did you get beat up, Mr. Lookwell?

LOOKWELL

I'm not exactly sure, Suzanne. The working-class mind is strange and unpredictable.

ALEX

So you didn't find out anything.

LOOKWELL

On the contrary. While they thought I was unconscious, I rummaged through their office files. There was no evidence of wrongdoing.

JASON

So the shop's not involved with the ring of thefts?

LOOKWELL
(with a twinkle in his eye)
Glad to see you've caught up with the rest of us, Jason.

Jason looks skeptical.

LOOKWELL (CONT'D)

Now, let's resume with our soliloquies.

Miss Royster gets up in front of the class.

MISS ROYSTER
(impassioned)
"I won't answer that question. I only know that Elbert Loevborg had the courage to live according to his principles. And now, he's done something big! Something beautiful!"

LOOKWELL

Your Hedda Gabler is quite powerful, Miss Royster. And, may I add, most enchanting.

Miss Royster smiles coyly.

BEN

Excuse me, Mr. Lookwell.

LOOKWELL

Yes, Ben?

> BEN

Do you think it would be faster if I demonstrated the transformation technique for the class?

> LOOKWELL
> (hitting on something)

Wait a minute... Faster...

> BEN

Sir?

> LOOKWELL

Fast. Race. There's an auto race in town, isn't there?

> ALEX

That's right, sir. The LA Grand Prix is here Sunday.

> LOOKWELL
> (his wheels turning)

Hmmmm. Car thieves... keep outrunning police... high speeds. Expert drivers... attracted to... Grand... Prix.

> JASON

Mr. Lookwell, are you okay?

> LOOKWELL

Jason, how do you feel about portraying a pit crew mechanic?

> JASON

What do you mean, Mr. Lookwell?

> LOOKWELL

Let's just say that you and I are going to do a little Grand Prix auto racing.

WIPE TO:

EXT. RACE TRACK—DAY

Lookwell and Jason are standing next to a chain-link gate, talking to a RACING OFFICIAL. A SECURITY GUARD stands by. A sign on the gate reads, "Race Personnel and Pit Crew Only." Jason is dressed as a pit crew mechanic and Lookwell is dressed as a dashing turn-of-the-century racer with goggles, scarf, high boots, etc.

> RACING OFFICIAL
> No, you can't come in. You're not in the race.

> LOOKWELL
> Tell him my name is Dash Carlysle and I'm a world-renowned auto racer.

> JASON
> He's Dash Carlysle, and...

> RACING OFFICIAL
> No, you're not! You're not on the list and there's no such person. Now, I'm tired of talking to you. Get out of here.

Lookwell and Jason turn and start to leave.

> LOOKWELL
> That was a good effort, Jason. You just need to work on your physicalization.

> JASON
> What do we do now, Mr. Lookwell?

> LOOKWELL
> Not to worry. Every good undercover man has a Plan B.

Suddenly, Lookwell turns, runs back, and tries to scale the fence quickly.

> RACING OFFICIAL
> Hey, get down from there!

SECURITY PERSONNEL rush in from all directions and start to pull Lookwell off the fence.

DISSOLVE TO:

INT. JAIL CELL—LATER

Lookwell is sitting on a cot, gazing intensely at something off-camera.

Widen to reveal TWO BURLY ASIAN JAIL THUGS, casually tossing a limp Jason back and forth between them.

> LOOKWELL
> (calling out)
> Alright, relax, Jason! Stay loose, it's going well!

Suddenly, Lookwell stands.

> LOOKWELL (CONT'D)
> Okay, that's enough for now.

The two thugs stop tossing Jason.

> LOOKWELL (CONT'D)
> You see how it works? The person in the middle puts his complete trust in his fellow actors. Now, let's try it with Kam in the middle.

Detective Kennery and guard enter. The guard opens the cell door.

> DET. KENNERY
> Okay, Lookwell, you made bail. You and your friend are free to go.

> LOOKWELL
> (TO THUGS) Work on those exercises. You've got Forrest Tucker quality.

> KAM
> Me?

> LOOKWELL
> Both of you.

The camera follows Detective Kennery, Jason, and Lookwell as they walk down the hallways of the police station.

> DET. KENNERY
> Ty, I've talked to the track officials and they've agreed not to press charges if you promise not to bother them again.

LOOKWELL

Sorry, Detective. I was merely about to capture our elusive car thief in his guise as a Grand Prix competitor.

DET. KENNERY

Well, actually, during the race two more cars were stolen.

JASON

So we were just wasting our time?

LOOKWELL

You never waste time, Jason. Time wastes you.

Detective Kennery and Jason look confused.

DET. KENNERY

Well, anyway, I hope you realize now that this kind of thing isn't worth your trouble.

Lookwell whips out the lucite-encased badge.

LOOKWELL

Detective, maybe Bob Conrad didn't take his honorary badge seriously, but I do.

Detective Kennery shrugs wearily.

HYACINTH (O.C.)

Lookwell!

Hyacinth enters.

LOOKWELL

Thanks for posting my bail, Hyacinth. I'll remunerate you by the first of the month.

They start to walk out of the police station.

HYACINTH

No problem, Lookwell.

LOOKWELL

You're always there for me, Hyacinth. By the way, how much was it?

HYACINTH

A thousand dollars.

LOOKWELL

Really? If I could just see a receipt, not that I don't trust you.

HYACINTH
(cheerfully)

Right here. (Hands him the receipt) I had it notarized.

LOOKWELL
(resigned)

Yes. Good.

HYACINTH

You okay, Lookwell?

LOOKWELL

I'm fine, Hyacinth. It's just these car thefts. Until I solve them, I'm still a prisoner.

HYACINTH

Mmm-hmm. Yes.

DISSOLVE TO:

EXT. L.A. PARK—DAY

MUSIC: MELANCHOLY

Lookwell walks dejectedly through the park.

CUT TO:

Lookwell glumly feeds some squirrels.

CUT TO:

Lookwell sadly looks into a pond. He notices his reflection and starts to primp his hair and lightly slaps the bottom of his chin as before.

CUT TO:

A clearing in the park. Lookwell enters and thoughtfully looks up at a statue of William Shakespeare.

                    LOOKWELL
                    (meaningfully)
Hello, old friend. It's a beautiful day, isn't it? Or, as you would put it, "How oft the sight of means to do ill deeds makes ill deeds done." (SIGH) If only the rest of us had your insight. Still, when all seems lost, it's comforting to know that I can come to this place, think of your words, and sort out the puzzle that is life.

CUT TO:

Lookwell paces in front of the statue.

                    LOOKWELL (CONT'D)
Now, we know the cars aren't leaving the country and yet none have been spotted on the road. Of course, Detective Kennery says...

CUT TO:

The statue's inanimate face

                    LOOKWELL (V.O.)
...the cars are being hidden. But how can you hide such unusual cars...

CUT TO:

Lookwell paces.

                    LOOKWELL
...without attracting attention? Unless the cars... aren't being... stolen... at all. Of course! Owners... stealing... own cars... collecting insurance... Alberti's Car Rental... He didn't even know the license number...

CUT TO:

The statue's face.

LOOKWELL (V.O.)

Follow Alberti, prove his guilt, expose the whole conspiracy. It's all so perfect.

CUT TO:

Lookwell.

LOOKWELL

Thank you, William. As always, you've shown me the way. Now, if you'll excuse me.

Lookwell dashes off through some bushes.

CUT TO:

EXT. MUSEUM—ESTABLISHING—NIGHT

CUT TO:

INT. MAIN HALL OF MUSEUM—CONTINUOUS

COUPLES in formal eveningwear chat over drinks under a banner that reads, "Santa Monica Foundation for the Homeless—'They're Everybody's Problem.'" The camera finds ALBERTI chatting with some partygoers.

PARTYGOER

As Always, Mr. Alberti, your generosity is most appreciated.

ALBERTI

Well, I'm just happy to be a part of it.

The camera pans to the door, where a DOORMAN receives Miss Royster and Lookwell. She is dressed in an elegant evening gown. Lookwell is dressed as a cartoonish tramp in baggy, patched clothing and is carrying a long stick with a handkerchief full of his "belongings" tied to the back.

DOORMAN

Good evening, Miss...?

MISS ROYSTER

Vanderhaven. Eloise P. Vanderhaven. Maybe you've heard of my father,

Thaddeus Vanderhaven, who built himself a vast fortune from nothing.

DOORMAN

I see.

MISS ROYSTER

This is Willie, the homeless person whom I'm sponsoring.

LOOKWELL
(in his regular voice)
Good evening. I live in the streets.

The doorman nods and they enter.

LOOKWELL (CONT'D)

(TO MISS ROYSTER) Well done. I knew you were right for this.

MISS ROYSTER

What do we do now?

LOOKWELL

I want you to mix and mingle, get a feel for the room. I've got a rat to catch. A rat named Alberti. Alberti the rat...

Suddenly, Lookwell notices that Miss Royster has left him to mingle. So he forges into the crowd, interacting with puzzled partygoers.

LOOKWELL (CONT'D)

Good evening, I haven't a home. Hello, nice to be indoors. Hi there, the sidewalk is my pillow...

CUT TO:

Alberti, chatting with some partygoers.

ALBERTI

I just feel that we have to remember these are real people with real lives.

Suddenly, Lookwell enters holding a glass of white wine.

LOOKWELL

Good evening, quite a little fundraiser, isn't it?

ALBERTI

Yes, it is.

LOOKWELL

(coy)

Well, Mr. Alberti. Pity about your stolen car.

ALBERTI

Yes...

LOOKWELL

I don't suppose you'll ever see it again. Or will you?

ALBERTI

What are you talking about?

LOOKWELL

Oh, pay no attention. I'm just a crazy old vagabond. Now, if you'll excuse me.

Lookwell exits.

ALBERTI

(TO GROUP) Who was that?

CUT TO:

Lookwell joins Miss Royster.

MISS ROYSTER

How did it go?

LOOKWELL

Too well, I'm afraid. Alberti tried to play dumb, but he's no actor.

MISS ROYSTER

Wow.

LOOKWELL

Jason's waiting for us outside. We've got no time to lose. (SEES SOMETHING) Damn!

MISS ROYSTER
What's the matter?

LOOKWELL
Robert Wagner's here.

CUT TO:

ROBERT WAGNER is working his way through the crowd.

LOOKWELL (CONT'D)
If he sees me, my cover will be blown.

Robert Wagner walks by, gives Lookwell a glance as if to say, "What's with this guy?" and keeps going.

LOOKWELL (CONT'D)
Good man, he played along. Let's go! (THEY HEAD FOR THE EXIT) Excuse me, homeless coming through... Pardon me, eat out of a trash can...

CUT TO:

EXT. MUSEUM PARKING LOT—CONTINUOUS

Jason, dressed as a valet parking attendant, is standing beside a board of car keys. Lookwell and Miss Royster rush in, still dressed in their costumes.

LOOKWELL
Pssst... Jason!

JASON
Yes?

LOOKWELL
Don't be alarmed. It's me, Ty Lookwell.

JASON
(tolerating)
I know.

LOOKWELL
Do you remember which car Alberti came in?

JASON
Yeah, a dark green Jaguar.

LOOKWELL
Okay, bring the keys. Let's go!

The three of them run down a hill and stop at a black sports car. Lookwell opens the car door.

JASON
(nervously)
Look, are you sure this guy is guilty?

LOOKWELL
As guilty as Miss Royster is beguiling.

Lookwell and Miss Royster share a look.

MISS ROYSTER
Be careful, Mr. Lookwell.

LOOKWELL
Don't worry, I'm just going to hide in the backseat.

Lookwell starts climbing into the backseat.

LOOKWELL (CONT'D)
Within a few hours, Alberti will lead me right to where the stolen car is hidden.

Lookwell curls up on the floor.

LOOKWELL (CONT'D)
Oh, and if I don't see you two again, remember what Shakespeare said…

CUT TO:

Alberti, standing at the top of the hill.

> ALBERTI
> (shouting)
> Hey, what the hell's going on down there!?

CUT TO:

The car.

> LOOKWELL
> Get in!

> JASON
> What?

> LOOKWELL
> Change in plans, both of you get in the car!

Jason and Miss Royster get in the front seat of the car. Jason is behind the wheel.

CUT TO:

Alberti runs down the hill.

> ALBERTI
> They're in my car!

CUT TO:

The car.

> LOOKWELL
> Start the car, Jason.

> JASON
> Mr. Lookwell!

> LOOKWELL
> I know what I'm doing. Now, drive!

They peel out and rocket down a two-lane road.

> MISS ROYSTER
> (panicked)

Why do I have to be in the car?

LOOKWELL

Stay calm, Miss Royster.

JASON

What do we do now?

LOOKWELL

We improvise, Jason. It's one of the most important tools an actor has at his disposal.

MISS ROYSTER
(angry)
You know something, you're an idiot!

LOOKWELL

Indeed. Idiotic like a fox.

JASON

I think some cars are chasing us!

LOOKWELL

Perfect. Alberti's band of thugs. We'll lead them right to police headquarters.

Suddenly, sirens blare and the flashers from several police cars appear in the rear window. Jason and Miss Royster react.

MISS ROYSTER

It's the police!

LOOKWELL

Speed up!

JASON

What?

LOOKWELL

Trust me, I've got another idea.

CUT TO:

CAR CHASE MONTAGE—CONTINUOUS

Several police cars are chasing Lookwell and his students. Lookwell is gesturing directions from the backseat. Shots are fired from the pursuing police cars.

JASON

They're shooting at us!

LOOKWELL

I'll handle this.

Lookwell sticks his head out the window as bullets whiz past.

LOOKWELL (CONT'D)

I'm not a car thief, I'm an actor. Now follow me!

The POLICEMEN continue to fire.

CUT TO:

EXT. "ALBERTI E-Z LUXURY CAR RENTAL" PARKING LOT— CONTINUOUS

Jason crashes through the front gate and swerves into the lot at high speed, slamming into the car rental sign. The police cars follow close behind.

CUT TO:

Policemen pull Jason, Miss Royster, and Lookwell out of the smashed car. As they emerge, they are handcuffed. Detective Kennery talks to a distraught Alberti. The rental agent approaches.

LOOKWELL

I'll accept your apologies for arresting me in advance, gentlemen. Inspect the premises and you'll find that Alberti's your man.

DET. KENNERY

We're sorry about this, Mr. Alberti.

LOOKWELL

Detective, is it police policy now to apologize to the criminal?

DET. KENNERY

Ty, please...

LOOKWELL

You're going to do time, Alberti. Hard time.

DET. KENNERY

Ty, he was helping us! His car was part of a sting operation tonight!
Of course, that's all ruined now.

LOOKWELL

Sting operation?

DET. KENNERY

The museum lot was targeted as a prime strike zone, and his car was bait.

LOOKWELL
(absorbing)

Prime strike zone...

DET. KENNERY

Look, we don't have time for this!

ALBERTI

(TO RENTAL AGENT) Hey, you! This guy crashed through my gate
and my alarm didn't go off.

RENTAL AGENT

It must be a malfunction, sir. I'll have it checked in the morning.

ALBERTI

It's a new system! And what are you doing here after hours?

LOOKWELL
(still absorbing)

Alarm system...

RENTAL AGENT
(nervous)

Well, I was just... doing some inventory.

DET. KENNERY

(TO ALBERTI) Wait a minute. Did he know we were staking out the museum tonight?

ALBERTI

Sure, I told him.

The rental agent tries to run away, but is grabbed by a policeman.

LOOKWELL

There's your man.

DET. KENNERY

Take him in. I bet these have all been inside jobs. (TO ALBERTI) Good work.

LOOKWELL

Well, Detective, I guess our little drive led you right to the criminal himself. I'm just glad my unique blend of talents could play a role.

POLICEMAN #3

(ASIDE TO KENNERY) Detective, he was accusing the owner.

DET. KENNERY

Please, just let it go. It's not worth it.

LOOKWELL

Gentlemen, it's been a pleasure working with you. If you need me again, here's my head shot.

Lookwell hands an 8 × 10" to a policeman as he is led away.

Widen.

FADE OUT

END OF ACT TWO

EPILOGUE

INT. CLASSROOM—DAY

Lookwell is holding court among his students. Jason and Miss Royster are absent.

> LOOKWELL
>
> After I located the first criminal, the police were able to find the rest. Jason and Miss Royster were very brave. Unfortunately, because they were driving and in the front seat, they'll be in jail a bit longer. In the meantime, we have two new students.

CUT TO:

The two oriental thugs from the prison sit cross-legged on the floor.

> LOOKWELL (CONT'D)
>
> I trust you'll all make them feel welcome. Yes, Alex?

> ALEX
>
> I'm sorry, sir, but if you thought Alberti had stolen his own car, and it turned out to be some other guy, does that mean you were wrong?

> LOOKWELL
>
> Alex, I'd be delighted to talk crime with you at length, but the last time I checked this was an acting class. Now, if you'll hit the lights, Ben...

Lookwell produces a "Bannigan" cassette.

> LOOKWELL (CONT'D)
>
> ...there's a scene in this next episode which merits our attention.

Widen.

FADE OUT.

THE END

More Selected Poems

SUICIDE SONG

But now I am afraid I know too much to kill myself
Though I would still like to jump off a high bridge

At midnight, or paddle a kayak out to sea
Until I turn into a speck, or wear a necktie made of knotted rope

But people would squirm, it would hurt them in some way
And I am too knowledgeable now to hurt people imprecisely

No longer do I live by the law of me
No longer having the excuse of youth or craziness

And dying you know shows a serious ingratitude
For sunsets and beehive hairdos and the precious green corrugated

Pickles they place at the edge of your plate
Killing yourself is wasteful, like spilling oil

At sea or not recycling all the kisses you've been given
And anyway, who has clothes nice enough to be caught dead in?

Not me. You stay alive, you fool,
Because you haven't been excused

You haven't finished though it takes a muleish stubborness
To chew this food

It is a stone it is an inconvenience it is an innocence
And I turn against it like a record

Turns against the needle
That makes it play.

HARD RAIN

After I heard *It's a Hard Rain's a-Gonna Fall*
played softly by an accordion quartet
through the ceiling speakers at the Springdale Shopping Mall,
I understood there's nothing
we can't pluck the stinger from,

nothing we can't turn into a soft drink flavor or a T-shirt.
Even serenity can become something horrible
if you make a commercial about it
using smiling, white-haired people

quoting Thoreau to sell retirement homes
in the Everglades, where the swamp has been
drained and bulldozed into a nineteen-hole golf course
with electrified alligator barriers.

"You can't keep beating yourself up, Billy"
I heard the therapist say on television
                            to the teenage murderer,
"About all those people you killed—
You just have to be the best person you can be,
                            one day at a time—"

And everybody in the audience claps and weeps a little,
because the level of deep feeling has been touched,
and they want to believe that
the power of Forgiveness is greater
than the power of Consequence, or History.

Dear Abby:
My father is a businessman who travels.
Each time he returns from one of his trips,
his shoes and trousers
    are covered with blood—

but he never forgets to bring me a nice present;
Should I say something?
                    Signed, America.

I used to think I was not part of this,
that I could mind my own business and get along,

but that was just another song
that had been taught to me since birth—

whose words I was humming under my breath,
as I was walking thorough the Springdale Mall.

AT THE GALLERIA SHOPPING MALL

Just past the bin of pastel baby socks and underwear,
there are some 49 dollar Chinese-made TVs;

one of them singing news about a far-off war,
one comparing the breast size of an actress

from Hollywood to the breast size
of an actress from Bollywood.

And here is my niece Lucinda,
who is nine and a daughter of Texas,

who has developed the flounce of a pedigreed blonde
and declares that her favorite sport is shopping.

Today is the day she embarks upon her journey,
swinging a credit card like a scythe

through the meadows of golden merchandise.
Today is the day she stops looking at faces,

and starts assessing the price of purses;
So let it begin. Let her be dipped in the dazzling bounty

and raised and wrung out again and again.
And let us watch.

As the gods in olden stories
turned mortals into laurel trees and crows
                          to teach them some kind of lesson,

so we were turned into Americans
to learn something about loneliness.

"POOR BRITNEY SPEARS"

is a sentence
I never expected to say in this lifetime

If *she* wants to make a career comeback
so her agent gets a spot on the MTV awards show
but she can't lose the weight beforehand

so looks a little chubby in a spangled bikini
before millions of fanged, spiteful fans and enemies
and gets a little drunk beforehand
so misses a step in the dance routine

making her look, one critic says,
like a "comatose piglet,"

well, it wasn't by accident, was it?
that she wandered into the late twentieth century glitteratti party
of striptease American celebrity?

First we made her into an object of desire,
then into an object of contempt,
Now we want to turn her into an object of compassion?

Are you sure we know what the hell we're doing?

Is she a kind of voodoo doll
onto whom we project
our vicarious fantasies of triumph and humiliation?

Is she a pink, life-size piece of chewing gum
full of non FDA approved additives
engineered by the mad scientists
of the mainstream dream machine?

Or is she nothing less than a gladiatrix
who strolls into the coliseum

full of blinding lights and tigers

with naught but her slim javelin of talent
and recklessly little protective clothing?

Oh my adorable little monkey,
prancing for your candy,

with one of my voices I shout, "Jump! Jump, you little whore!"
With another I say,

in a quiet way that turns down the lights,
"Put on some clothes and go home, Sweetheart."

WINDCHIME

She goes out to hang the windchime
in her nightie and her workboots.
It's six-thirty in the morning
and she's standing on the plastic ice chest
tiptoe to reach the crossbeam of the porch,

windchime in her left hand,
hammer in her right, the nail
gripped tight between her teeth
but nothing happens next because
she's trying to figure out
how to switch #1 with #3.

She must have been standing in the kitchen,
coffee in her hand, asleep,
when she heard it—the wind blowing
through the sound the windchime
wasn't making
because it wasn't there.

No one including me especially anymore believes
till death do us part,
but I can see what I would miss in leaving—
the way her ankles go into the workboots
as she stands upon the ice chest;
the problem scrunched into her forehead;
the little kissable mouth
with the nail in it.

PHONE CALL

Maybe I overdid it
when I called my father an enemy of humanity.
That might have been a little strongly put,
a slight overexaggeration

an immoderate description of the person
who at that moment, two thousand miles away,
holding the telephone receiver six inches from his ear,
must have regretted paying for my therapy.

What I meant was that my father
was an enemy of my humanity
and what I meant behind that
was that my father was split
into two people, one of them

living deep inside of me
like a bad king or an incurable disease—
blighting my crops,
striking down my herds,
poisoning my wells—the other
standing in another time zone,
in a kitchen in Wyoming,
with bad knees and white hair sprouting from his ears.

I don't want to scream forever,
I don't want to live without proportion
like some kind of infection from the past,

so I have to remember the second father,
the one whose TV dinner is getting cold
while he holds the phone in his left hand
and stares blankly out the window

where just now the sun is going down
and the last fingertips of sunlight
are withdrawing from the hills
they once touched like a child.

I HAVE NEWS FOR YOU

There are people who do not see a broken playground swing
as a symbol of ruined childhood

and there are people who don't interpret the behavior
of a fly in a motel room as a mocking representation of their thought
process.

There are people who don't walk past an empty swimming pool
and think about past pleasures unrecoverable

and then stand there blocking the sidewalk for other pedestrians.
I have read about a town somewhere in California where human beings

do not send their tuberous feeder roots
deep into the potting soil of others' emotional lives

as if they were greedy six-year-olds
sucking the last half inch of milkshake up through a noisy straw;

and other persons in the Midwest who can kiss without
debating the imperialist baggage of heterosexuality.

Do you see that creamy, lemon-yellow moon?
There are some people, unlike me and you,

who do not yearn after fame or love or quantities of money as
        unattainable as that moon;
Thus, they do not later
        have to waste more time
heatedly defaming the object of their former ardor.

Or consequently run and crucify themselves
in some solitary midnight Starbucks Golgotha.

I have news for you—
there are people who get up in the morning and cross a room

and open a window to let the sweet breeze in
and let it touch them all over their faces and bodies.

COMMERCIAL FOR A SUMMER NIGHT

That one night in the middle of the summer
when people move their chairs outside
and put their TVs on the porch
so the dark is full of murmuring blue lights.

We were drinking beer with the sound off,
watching the figures on the screen—
the bony blondes, the lean-jawed guys
who decorate the perfume and the cars—

the pretty ones
the merchandise is wearing this year.

Alex said, I wish they made a shooting gallery
        using people like that

Greg said, *That woman has a PhD in Face.*
Then we saw a preview for a movie

about a movie star who is
        having a movie made about her,
and Boz said, This country is getting stupider every year.

Then Greg said that things were better in the sixties
and Rus said that Harold Bloom said
that Neitzsche said Nostalgia
is the blank check issued to a weak mind,

and Greg said,
        They didn't have checks back then, stupid,
and Susan said it's too bad you guys can't get
Spellcheck for your brains.

Then Greg left and Margaret arrived
and a breeze carried honeysuckle fumes across the yard,

and Alex finished his quart of beer
and Boz leaned back in his chair

and the beautiful people on the TV screen
moved back and forth and back,
looking very much now like shooting gallery ducks—

and we sat in quiet pleasure on the shore of night,
as a tide came in and turned and carried us,
folding chairs and all,

far out from the coastline of America

in a perfect commercial for our lives.

JON STEWART

Lenny Bruce: The Making of a Sitcom

DATE: Dec. 3, 1960
FROM: F. Silverman, Prod. Asst.
TO: J. Aubrey, VP Programming, ABC
RE: Talent Search—The Crescendo in Hollywood

Saw the Four Freshmen at the Crescendo. Thought they might make for a funny high school sitcom, but found out they weren't actually freshmen. Opening act was interesting. Lenny Bruce. Hilarious. Didn't see him perform but word at the club is he won't be there long. And this was only his first night! I guess he's a comer. Better jump before NBC or CBS gets him. Could be our answer for Danny Thomas or Benny.

DATE: Jan. 23, 1961
FROM: F. Silverman, Prod. Coordinator
TO: L. Goldenson, President ABC; J. Warner, President Warner Bros.;
   J. Aubrey VP Programming, ABC; D. Lewine, VP Programming, ABC
RE: Minutes of the Jan. Meeting on the Lenny Bruce Sitcom development
   project

Bruce meeting went very well. I do believe this is our guy. Not crazy about Lenny's original suggestion of a show about a Jewish Davy Crockett with a coonskin yarmulke, although we could give further consideration to the marketing aspects. My opinion is that kids won't buy coonskin yarmulkes, even if we call them beanies, as Mr. Bruce suggested.

Jack Warner's suggestion of a sitcom to reflect Lenny's reality is a winner. Audiences buy it because it's real. Aubrey's idea of playing up the war veteran angle of Bruce's life is also a winner. We haven't seen a funny Audie Murphy yet, so the timing could be perfect. Especially if we set the show in Nebraska and add three-year-old twins as Mr. Goldenson said.

I think Lenny was won over. Especially when he found out the kind of talent we can surround him with here at ABC. I told him in the hallway that we've got producer Hal Roach Jr. and designer Edith Head under contract. He said if we could get him a Roach and Head, or even just Head, he'd be a happy camper.

I also checked into Mr. Warner's concern about Lenny's itching and nodding off during the meeting. Mr. Bruce's personal physician, a Dr. Slats Finnegan of Miami, assured me the symptoms would disappear after adjusting Mr. Bruce's allergy medicine. Still looking for that tape of Mr. Bruce's act. His agent, Jack Sobel, said he sent it over but I have yet to track it down.

DATE: April 11, 1961
TO: L. Bruce
FROM: F. Silverman, VP Programming Development, ABC
RE: Lenny Bruce project pilot script

First off, Mr. Bruce, let me congratulate you on the punctual delivery of your pilot script. Some of the cocktail napkins weren't entirely legible, but we were able to get the general idea. It's very funny, although the *Make Room for Daddy* writers we assigned to the project said it was not exactly the same script as the one they thought was being turned in. Irregardless of the high quality of your work, the "suits," as always, have a couple of nitpicks we should go over.

THE TITLE: Because the show is to take place in Nebraska, we feel it's best to go back to Jack Warner's original idea for a title, *Have a Heartland.* We felt the title *Schmucks* doesn't brand a clear enough image of the warmth and humor we all know this show will possess. Besides, a quickie poll of the gals in the secretarial pool showed a good 85 percent thought schmucks was a breakfast food.

YOUR CHARACTER: We applaud the "up-and-coming comedian" aspect to your character. It's real and gives the audience a chance to identify with and root for the underdog in all of us. In the pilot, however, your character never deals with this very fertile area. We never see him at work or even talking about work.

Also, your character has no visible or legal means of supporting the family while pursuing this worthwhile dream. Your character's dialogue (on the second "Hungry I" napkin), "Here I am digging the priest scam. A Jew boy from Brooklyn conning old Catholic gals out of their pensions on the promise of an eternal bliss without liver spots. But it's only enough scratch for a taste" is a start. Rather than a con artist, however, we thought your character could be an elementary school teacher. Remember, these suggestions are just food for your brain.

YOUR BEST FRIEND: This idea leads into the next character, your best friend, "Flat Foot Jackson—an uptown sax hipster who could blow cheese that made the Virgin Mary cum in her golden panties." Although jazz is certainly gaining in popularity, we thought perhaps this character might work better at the elementary school, as its wise yet sometimes overlooked custodian. And while we appreciate that Flat Foot's character is the best cook in Harlem, we'd prefer if there is to be cooking on the show, that your wife do it. And what exactly is a Dilaudid casserole with Methedrine sprinkles?

YOUR WIFE: Given only your character description of "a sweet-faced shiksa dancer, with big tits and magnificent pink nipples," we agree that Angie Dickinson could work. We need, however, more description. Two other things. What kind of dancer is she? And although we love the endearing quality of you referring to her as "Honey," at some point in the process, we'll need to know her actual name.

YOUR DAUGHTER: We love the idea of the daughter character. We want to see more of her. Actually, we would like to see any of her. Why, if she is your daughter, does she live with your mother? We can all appreciate that "pimps and whores do not playmates make" but perhaps our school idea will solve that riddle, and the daughter can come home. Also, why do you and your wife live in a flophouse?

THE PLOT: We don't, under any circumstances, think you should cheat on your wife in the pilot episode, especially when she's just been arrested. We agree that her character is certainly in the wrong after "copping my ten grand and turning on every freak in Hollywood," and agree that she seems to treat you "like shit." This still doesn't justify your character's indifference to her arrest as stated on the third "Playboy Club" napkin, "That fucking hillbilly whorehouse junkie bitch can feast on prison cuisine. Dyke sandwiches for everyone!"

We were thinking that instead of the episode centering around Honey's betraying you and her second-act arrest on prostitution and drug charges, perhaps she could be nagging you for a new car. But you've got your eyes on a state-of-the-art television set.

Also, the B story involving the character of "White Man" could be tweaked. It's an amusing runner to have him constantly making sure that the "sheeny and negro promise not to put it to my sister," but we thought maybe he just wants to borrow your lawnmower. Also we thought it would be nice to give him a name other than "White Man." Ned, perhaps. And he shouldn't be drinking.

Overall I think we're off to a great start. We're all really excited about this project and believe with some integration of a few of the abovementioned notes, we have a real winner here. Look forward to your thoughts.

DATE: April 14, 1961
FROM: F. Silverman, Vice President, ABC
TO: L. Bruce
RE: Script notes and rewrite

Let me begin, Mr. Bruce, by saying how surprised and pleased we all were here at the American Broadcasting Company by the alacrity of your response to our script notes. Contractually you were not required to tender a second draft of your pilot script until June, yet you seem to have turned one around in less than twenty-four hours. So . . . Bravo!

On the other hand, your redraft seems not to address a few of our concerns. While we may have appeared overly critical in our notes concerning your first draft, our intent was to help you continue polishing that effort. The emerging view of your current work is that you are now working on a completely different project. And while we can agree this new project is quite entertaining, we were wondering what happened to all the other characters and plot points we had originally discussed.

If we are correct in piecing together the balled-up cigarette papers this draft was submitted on, it seems you are now working on a pilot script entitled *The Lone Ranger Is a Fag.* If that is correct, Mr. Bruce, I must make you aware of ABC's strenuous objection. A masked man fighting crime as the Lone Ranger is a wonderful idea, but unfortunately one that already exists—first on radio and then as a very successful television program. The legal eagles here at ABC have asked me to make it clear that we do not condone plagiarism in any form. We must officially state that if you are committed to this *Lone Ranger Is a Fag* script, we will no longer be able to continue our involvement in the project.

If you would, however, permit us to change the name of the lead character from the Lone Ranger to the "Single Horseman," we might have interest in pursuing this new script. We all very much liked the crime-fighting angle. Also we would prefer if you would change this Single Horseman character into a heterosexual. This small change would fix the Single Horseman's currently problematic relationship with his partner in crime fighting, the Indian Tonto. Whom we would now like you to call Ronto.

Again, Mr. Bruce, please just take these suggestions as bricks to help you build . . . buildings.

Oh, and before I forget: You mistakenly enclosed a grainy black-and-white photograph in the envelope with your script. It is, I believe, a picture of a woman checking her dog's genitals for ticks, using what appears to be her mouth. The scribbled inscription says, "Greetings from Miss America," and also that the dog's name is Fred. I am sending it back to you with the hope that its disappearance caused you no worry, as I imagine it may have sentimental value.

DATE: May 11, 1961
FROM: F. Silverman, President, ABC
TO: Jack Sobel, agent and attorney for L. Bruce
RE: The incident

It is with great regret we must inform you of the termination of Mr. Bruce's contract with the American Broadcasting Company. We understand he had some issues with the creative process, but we don't feel it was handled appropriately. The circus atmosphere he created by showing up at our offices naked made it nearly impossible to focus on his grievances. We do apologize for his untimely fall from our third-floor window. Our security can be overly zealous.

I can also assure Mr. Bruce that I was not spawned from an unholy tryst involving Senator McCarthy and Mother Cabrini. My people are actually from Massapequa. Good luck in your future endeavors.

*   *   *

The untitled Lenny Bruce project was subsequently sold to CBS. It was assigned to Sheldon Leonard and on October 3, 1961, it debuted as The Dick Van Dyke Show. *Lenny Bruce died on August 3, 1966. At the time of his death, he was working on a pilot for a children's show about the perils of our legal system called* Uncle Lenny's Guide to All Things Penal. *The show was set for a fall slot on ABC.*

TOBIAS WOLFF

Hunters in the Snow

Tub had been waiting for an hour in the falling snow. He paced the sidewalk to keep warm and stuck his head out over the curb whenever he saw lights approaching. The fall of snow thickened. Tub stood below the overhang of a building. Across the road the clouds whitened just above the rooftops, and the whiteness seeped up the sky. He shifted the rifle strap to his other shoulder.

A truck slid around the corner, horn blaring, rear end sashaying. Tub moved to the sidewalk and held up his hand. The truck jumped the curb and kept coming, half on the street and half on the sidewalk. It wasn't slowing down at all. Tub stood for a moment, still holding up his hand, then jumped back. His rifle slipped off his shoulder, clattering on the ice, and a sandwich fell out of his pocket. The truck went careening past him and stopped at the end of the block.

Tub picked up his sandwich and slung the rifle and walked down to the truck. The driver was bent against the steering wheel, slapping his knees and drumming his feet on the floorboards. He looked like a cartoon of a person laughing. "Tub, you ought to see yourself," he said. "You look just like a beach ball with a hat on. Doesn't he, Frank?"

The man beside him smiled and looked off.

"You almost ran me down," Tub said. "You could've killed me."

"Come on, Tub," said the man beside the driver. "Be mellow. Kenny was just messing around." He opened the door and slid over to the middle of the seat.

Tub took the bolt out of his rifle and climbed in beside him. "My feet are frozen," he said. "If you meant ten o'clock, why didn't you say ten o'clock?"

"Tub, you haven't done anything but complain since we got here," said the man in the middle. "If you want to piss and moan all day you might as well go home and bitch at your kids. Take your pick." When Tub didn't say anything he turned to the driver. "Okay, Kenny, let's hit the road."

Some juvenile delinquents had heaved a brick through the windshield on the driver's side, so the cold and snow funneled right into the cab. The heater didn't work. They covered themselves with a couple of blankets Kenny had brought along and pulled down the flaps on their caps. Tub tried to keep his hands warm by rubbing them under the blanket, but Frank made him stop.

They left Spokane and drove deep into the country, running along black lines of fences. The snow let up, but still there was no edge to the land where it met the sky. Nothing moved in the chalky fields. The cold bleached their faces and made the stubble stand out on their cheeks and along their upper lips. They stopped twice for coffee before they got to the woods where Kenny wanted to hunt.

Tub was for trying someplace different; two years in a row they'd been up and down this land and hadn't seen a thing. Frank didn't care one way or the other, he just wanted to get out of the goddamned truck. "Feel that," he said, slamming the door. He spread his feet and closed his eyes and leaned his head back and breathed deeply. "Tune in on that energy."

"Another thing," Kenny said. "This is open land. Most of the land around here is posted."

"I'm cold," Tub said.

Frank breathed out. "Stop bitching, Tub. Get centered."

"I wasn't bitching."

"Centered," Kenny said. "Next thing you'll be wearing a nightgown, Frank. Selling flowers out at the airport."

"Kenny," Frank said, "you talk too much."

"Okay," Kenny said. "I won't say a word. Like I won't say anything about a certain babysitter."

"What babysitter?" Tub asked.

"That's between us," Frank said, looking at Kenny.

Kenny laughed.

"You're asking for it," Frank said.

"Asking for what?"

"Hey," Tub said, "are we hunting or what?"

They started off across the field. Tub had trouble getting through the fences. Frank and Kenny could have helped him; they could've lifted up the top wire and stepped on the bottom wire, but they didn't. They stood and watched him. There were a lot of fences and Tub was puffing when they reached the woods.

They hunted for two hours and saw no deer, no tracks, no sign. Finally they stopped by the creek to eat. Kenny had several slices of pizza and a couple of candy bars; Frank had a sandwich, an apple, two carrots, and a square of chocolate; Tub ate one hard-boiled egg and a stick of celery.

"You ask me how I want to die today," Kenny said, "I'll tell you burn me at the stake." He turned to Tub. "You still on that diet?" He winked at Frank.

"What do you think? You think I like hard-boiled eggs?"

"All I can say is, it's the first diet I ever heard of where you gained weight from it."

"Who said I gained weight?"

"Oh, pardon me. I take it back. You're just wasting away before my very eyes. Isn't he, Frank?"

Frank had his fingers fanned out on the stump where he'd laid his food. His knuckles were hairy. He wore a heavy wedding band and on his right pinkie another gold ring with a flat face and an "F" in what looked like diamonds. "Tub," he said, "you haven't seen your own balls in ten years."

Kenny doubled over laughing. He took off his hat and slapped his leg with it.

"What am I supposed to do?" Tub said. "It's my glands."

They left the woods and hunted along the creek. Frank and Kenny worked one bank and Tub worked the other, moving upstream. The snow was light but the drifts were deep and hard to move through. Wherever Tub looked the surface was smooth, undisturbed, and after a time he lost interest. He stopped looking for tracks and just tried to keep up with Frank and Kenny on the other side. A moment came when he realized he hadn't seen them in a long time. The breeze was moving from him to them; when it stilled he could sometimes hear Kenny laughing—nothing more. He quickened his pace, breasting the drifts, fighting away the snow. He heard his heart and felt the flush on his face but never once stopped.

Tub caught up with Frank and Kenny at a bend of the creek. They were standing on a log that stretched from their bank to his. Ice had backed up behind the log. Frozen reeds stuck out.

"See anything?" Frank asked.

Tub shook his head.

There wasn't much daylight left and they decided to head back toward the road. Frank and Kenny crossed the log and they all started downstream, using the trail Tub had broken. Before they'd gone very far Kenny stopped. "Look at that," he said, and pointed to some tracks going from the creek back into the woods. Tub's footprints crossed right over them. There on the bank, plain as day, were several mounds of deer shit. "What do you think that is, Tub?" Kenny kicked at it. "Walnuts on vanilla icing?"

"I guess I didn't notice."

Kenny looked at Frank.

"I was lost."

"You were lost. Big deal."

They followed the tracks into the woods. The deer had gone over a fence half buried in drifting snow. A NO HUNTING sign was nailed to the top of one of the posts. Kenny wanted to go after him but Frank said no way, the people out here didn't mess around. He thought maybe the farmer who owned the land would let them use it if they asked. Kenny wasn't so sure. Anyway, he figured that by the time they walked to the truck and drove up the road and doubled back it would be almost dark.

"Relax," Frank said. "You can't hurry nature. If we're meant to get that deer, we'll get it. If we're not, we won't."

They started back toward the truck. This part of the woods was mainly pine. The snow was shaded and had a glaze on it. It held up Kenny and Frank but Tub kept falling through. As he kicked forward, the edge of the crust bruised his shins. Kenny and Frank pulled ahead of him, to where he couldn't even hear their voices any more. He sat down on a stump and wiped his face. He ate both his sandwiches and half the cookies, taking his own sweet time. It was dead quiet.

When Tub crossed the last fence into the road the truck started moving. He had to run for it and just managed to grab hold of the tailgate and hoist himself into the bed. He lay there, panting. Kenny looked out the rear window and grinned. Tub crawled into the lee of the cab to get out of the freezing wind. He pulled his earflaps low and pushed his chin into the collar of his coat. Someone rapped on the window but Tub wouldn't turn around.

He and Frank waited outside while Kenny went into the farmhouse to ask permission. The house was old and paint was curling off the sides. The smoke streamed westward off the top of the chimney, fanning away into a thin gray plume. Above the ridge of the hills another ridge of blue clouds was rising.

"You've got a short memory," Tub said.

"What?" Frank said. He had been staring off.

"I used to stick up for you."

"Okay, so you used to stick up for me. What's eating you?"

"You shouldn't have just left me back there like that."

"You're a grown up, Tub. You can take care of yourself. Anyway, if you think you're the only person with problems I can tell you that you're not."

"Is something bothering you, Frank?"

Frank kicked at a branch poking out of the snow. "Never mind," he said.

"What did Kenny mean about the babysitter?"

"Kenny talks too much," Frank said.

Kenny came out of the farmhouse and gave the thumbs-up and they began walking back toward the woods. As they passed the barn a large black hound with a grizzled snout ran out and barked at them. Every time he barked he slid backwards a bit, like a cannon recoiling. Kenny got down on all fours and snarled and barked back at him, and the dog slunk away into the barn, looking over his shoulder and peeing a little as he went.

"That's an old-timer," Frank said. "A real graybeard. Fifteen years if he's a day."

"Too old," Kenny said.

Past the barn they cut off through the fields. The land was unfenced and the crust was freezing up thick, so they made good time. They kept to the edge of the field until they picked up the tracks again and followed them into the woods, farther and farther back toward the hills. The trees started to blur with the shadows and the wind rose and needled their faces with the crystals it swept off the glaze. Finally they lost the tracks.

Kenny swore and threw down his hat. "This is the worst day of hunting I ever had, bar none." He picked up his hat and brushed off the snow. "This will be the first season since I was fifteen I haven't got my deer."

"It isn't the deer," Frank said. "It's the hunting. There are all these forces out here and you just have to go with them."

"You go with them," Kenny said. "I came out here to get me a deer, not listen to a bunch of hippie bullshit. And if it hadn't been for Dimples here I would have, too."

"That's enough," Frank said.

"And you—you're so busy thinking about that little jailbait of yours you wouldn't know a deer if you saw one."

"Drop dead," Frank said, and turned away.

Kenny and Tub followed him back across the fields. When they were coming up to the barn Kenny stopped and pointed. "I hate that post," he said. He raised his rifle and fired. It sounded like a dry branch cracking. The post splintered along its right side, up toward the top. "There," Kenny said. "It's dead."

"Knock it off," Frank said, walking ahead.

Kenny looked at Tub. He smiled. "I hate that tree," he said, and fired again. Tub hurried to catch up with Frank. He started to speak but just then the dog ran out of the barn and barked at them. "Easy, boy," Frank said.

"I hate that dog." Kenny was behind them.

"That's enough," Frank said. "You put that gun down."

Kenny fired. The bullet went in between the dog's eyes. He sank right down into the snow, his legs splayed out on each side, his yellow eyes open and staring. Except for the blood he looked like a small bearskin rug. The blood ran down the dog's muzzle into the snow.

They all looked at the dog lying there.

"What did he ever do to you?" Tub asked. "He was just barking."

Kenny turned to Tub. "I hate you."

Tub shot from the waist. Kenny jerked backward against the fence and buckled to his knees. He knelt there with his hands pressed across his stomach. "Look," he said. His hands were covered with blood. In the dusk his blood was more blue than red. It seemed to belong to the shadows. It didn't seem out of place. Kenny eased himself onto his back. He sighed several times, deeply. "You shot me," he said.

"I had to," Tub said. He knelt beside Kenny. "Oh God," he said. "Frank. Frank."

Frank hadn't moved since Kenny killed the dog.

"Frank!" Tub shouted.

"I was just kidding around," Kenny said. "It was a joke. Oh!" he said, and arched his back suddenly. "Oh!" he said again, and dug his heels into the snow and pushed himself along on his head. Then he stopped and lay there, rocking back and forth on his heels and head like a wrestler doing warm-up exercises.

"Kenny," Frank said. He bent down and put his gloved hand on Kenny's brow. "You shot him," he said to Tub.

"He made me," Tub said.

"No, no, no," Kenny said.

Tub was weeping from the eyes and nostrils. His whole face was wet. Frank closed his eyes, then looked down at Kenny again. "Where does it hurt?"

"Everywhere," Kenny said, "just everywhere."

"Oh God," Tub said.

"I mean where did it go in?" Frank said.

"Here." Kenny pointed at the wound in his stomach. It was welling slowly with blood.

"You're lucky," Frank said. "It's on the left side. It missed your appendix. If it had hit your appendix you'd really be in the soup." He turned and threw up onto the snow, holding his sides as if to keep warm.

"Are you all right?" Tub said.

"There's some aspirin in the truck," Kenny said.

"I'm all right," Frank said.

"For me," Kenny said.

"We'd better call an ambulance," Tub said.

"Jesus," Frank said. "What are we going to say?"

"Exactly what happened," Tub said. "He was going to shoot me but I shot him first."

"No sir!" Kenny said. "I wasn't either!"

Frank patted Kenny on the arm. "Easy does it, partner." He stood. "Let's go."

Tub picked up Kenny's rifle as they walked down toward the farmhouse. "No sense leaving this around," he said. "Kenny might get ideas."

"I can tell you one thing," Frank said. "You've really done it this time. This definitely takes the cake."

They had to knock on the door twice before it was opened by a thin man with lank hair. The room behind him was filled with smoke. He squinted at them. "You get anything?" he asked.

"No," Frank said.

"I knew you wouldn't. That's what I told the other fellow."

"We've had an accident."

The man looked past Frank and Tub into the gloom. "Shoot your friend, did you?"

Frank nodded.

"I did," Tub said.

"I suppose you want to use the phone."

"If it's okay."

The man in the doorway looked behind him, then stepped back. Frank and Tub followed him into the house. There was a woman sitting by the stove in the middle of the room. The stove was smoking badly. She looked up and then down again at the child asleep in her lap. Her face was white and damp; strands of hair were pasted across her forehead. Tub warmed his hands over the stove while Frank went into the kitchen to call. The man who'd let them in stood at the window, his hands in his pockets.

"My friend shot your dog," Tub said.

The man nodded without turning around. "I should have done it myself. I just couldn't."

"He loved that dog so much," the woman said. The child squirmed and she rocked it.

"You asked him to?" Tub said. "You asked him to shoot your dog?"

"He was old and sick. Couldn't chew his food any more. I should have done it myself."

"You couldn't have," the woman said. "Never in a million years."

The man shrugged.

Frank came out of the kitchen. "We'll have to take him ourselves. The nearest hospital is fifty miles from here and all their ambulances are out already."

The woman knew a shortcut but the directions were complicated and Tub had to write them down. The man told them where they could find some boards to carry Kenny on. He didn't have a flashlight but said he'd turn the porch light on.

It was dark outside. The clouds were low and heavy-looking and the wind blew in shrill gusts. There was a screen loose on the house and it banged slowly and then quickly as the wind rose again. Frank went for the boards while Tub looked for Kenny, who was not where they had left him. Tub found him farther up the drive, lying on his stomach. "You okay?" Tub said.

"It hurts."

"Frank says it missed your appendix."

"I already had my appendix out."

"All right," Frank said, coming up to them. "We'll have you in a nice warm bed before you can say Jack Robinson." He put the two boards on Kenny's right side.

"Just as long as I don't have one of those male nurses," Kenny said.

"Ha ha," Frank said. "That's the spirit. Ready, set, *over you go*," and he rolled Kenny onto the boards. Kenny screamed and kicked his legs in the air. When he quieted down Frank and Tub lifted the boards and carried him down the drive. Tub had the back end, and with the snow blowing into his face he had trouble with his footing. Also he was tired and the man inside had forgotten to turn the porch light on. Just past the house Tub slipped and threw out his hands to catch himself. The boards fell and Kenny tumbled out and rolled to the bottom of the drive, yelling the whole way down. He came to rest against the right front wheel of the truck.

"You fat moron," Frank said. "You aren't good for diddly."

Tub grabbed Frank by the collar and backed him hard up against the fence. Frank tried to pull his hands away but Tub shook him and snapped his head back and forth and finally Frank gave up.

"What do you know about fat," Tub said. "What do you know about glands." As he spoke he kept shaking Frank. "What do you know about me."

"All right," Frank said.

"No more," Tub said.

"All right."

"No more talking to me like that. No more watching. No more laughing."

"Okay, Tub. I promise."

Tub let go of Frank and turned away. His arms hung straight at his sides.

"I'm sorry, Tub." Frank touched him on the shoulder. "I'll be down at the truck."

Tub stood by the fence for a while and then got the rifles off the porch. Frank had rolled Kenny back onto the boards and they lifted him into the bed of the truck. Frank spread the seat blankets over him. "Warm enough?" he asked.

Kenny nodded.

"Okay. Now how does reverse work on this thing?"

"All the way to the left and up." Kenny sat up as Frank started forward to the cab. "Frank!"

"What?"

"If it sticks don't force it."

The truck started right away. "One thing," Frank said, "you've got to hand it to the Japanese. A very ancient, very spiritual culture and they can still make a hell of a truck." He glanced over at Tub. "Look, I'm sorry. I didn't know you felt like that, honest to God I didn't. You should've said something."

"I did."

"When? Name one time."

"A couple hours ago."

"I guess I wasn't paying attention."

"That's true, Frank," Tub said. "You don't pay attention very much."

"Tub," Frank said, "what happened back there, I should've been more sympathetic. I realize that. You were going through a lot. I just want you to know it wasn't your fault. He was asking for it."

"You think so?"

"Absolutely. It was him or you. I would've done the same thing in your shoes, no question."

The wind was blowing into their faces. The snow was a moving white wall in front of their lights; it swirled into the cab through the hole in the windshield and settled on them. Tub clapped his hands and shifted around to stay warm, but it didn't work.

"I'm going to have to stop," Frank said. "I can't feel my fingers."

Up ahead they saw some lights off the road. It was a tavern. Outside in the parking lot there were several jeeps and trucks. A couple of them had deer strapped across their hoods. Frank parked and they went back to Kenny. "How you doing, partner?" Frank said.

"I'm cold."

"Well, don't feel like the Lone Ranger. It's worse inside, take my word for it. You should get that windshield fixed."

"Look," Tub said, "he threw the blankets off." They were lying in a heap against the tailgate.

"Now look, Kenny," Frank said, "it's no use whining about being cold if you're not going to try and keep warm. You've got to do your share." He spread the blankets over Kenny and tucked them in at the corners.

"They blew off."

"Hold on to 'em then."

"Why are we stopping, Frank?"

"Because if me and Tub don't get warmed up we're going to freeze solid and then where will you be?" He punched Kenny lightly in the arm. "So just hold your horses."

The bar was full of men in colored jackets, mostly orange. The waitress brought coffee. "Just what the doctor ordered," Frank said, cradling the steaming cup in his hand. "Tub, I've been thinking. What you said about me not paying attention, that's true."

"It's okay."

"No. I really had that coming. I guess I've just been a little too interested in old number one. I've had a lot on my mind. Not that that's any excuse."

"Forget it, Frank. I sort of lost my temper back there. I guess we're both a little on edge."

Frank shook his head. "It isn't just that."

"You want to talk about it?"

"Just between us, Tub?"

"Sure, Frank. Just between us."

"Tub, I think I'm going to be leaving Nancy."

"Oh, Frank. Oh, Frank." Tub sat back and shook his head.

Frank reached out and laid his hand on Tub's arm. "Tub, have you ever been really in love?"

"Well— "

"I mean *really* in love." He squeezed Tub's wrist. "With your whole being."

"I don't know. When you put it like that, I don't know."

"Then you haven't. Nothing against you, but you'd know it if you had." Frank let go of Tub's arm. "This isn't just some bit of fluff I'm talking about."

"Who is she, Frank?"

Frank paused. He looked into his empty cup. "Roxanne Brewer."

"Cliff Brewer's kid? The babysitter?"

"You can't just put people into categories like that, Tub. That's why the whole system is wrong. And that's why this country's going to hell in a rowboat."

Tub shook his head. "But she can't be more than— "

"Sixteen. She'll be seventeen in May." Frank smiled. "May fourth, three twenty-seven p.m. Hell, Tub, a hundred years ago she'd have been an old maid by that age. Juliet was only thirteen."

"Juliet? Juliet Miller? Jesus, Frank, she doesn't even have breasts. She's still collecting frogs."

"Not Juliet Miller. The *real* Juliet. Tub, don't you see how you're dividing people up into categories? He's an executive, she's a secretary, he's a truck driver, she's sixteen years old. Tub, this so-called babysitter, this so-called sixteen-year-old has more in her little finger than most of us have in our entire bodies. I can tell you this little lady is something special."

"I know the kids like her."

"She's opened up whole worlds to me that I never knew were there."

"What does Nancy think about all this?"

"She doesn't know."

"You haven't told her?"

"Not yet. It's not so easy. She's been damned good to me all these years. Then there's the kids to consider." The brightness in Frank's eyes trembled and he wiped quickly at them with the back of his hand. "I guess you think I'm a complete bastard."

"No, Frank. I don't think that."

"Well, you ought to."

"Frank, when you've got a friend it means you've always got someone on your side, no matter what. That's how I feel about it, anyway."

"You mean that, Tub?"

"Sure I do."

"You don't know how good it feels to hear you say that."

Kenny had tried to get out of the truck. He was jackknifed over the tailgate, his head hanging above the bumper. They lifted him back into the bed and covered him again. He was sweating and his teeth chattered. "It hurts, Frank."

"It wouldn't hurt so much if you just stayed put. Now we're going to the hospital. Got that? Say it—I'm going to the hospital."

"I'm going to the hospital."

"Again."

"I'm going to the hospital."

"Now just keep saying that to yourself and before you know it we'll be there."

After they had gone a few miles Tub turned to Frank. "I just pulled a real boner," he said.

"What's that?"

"I left the directions on the table back there."

"That's okay. I remember them pretty well."

The snowfall lightened and the clouds began to roll back off the fields, but it was no warmer and after a time both Frank and Tub were bitten through and shaking. Frank almost didn't make it around a curve, and they decided to stop at the next road-house.

There was an automatic hand-dryer in the bathroom and they took turns standing in front of it, opening their jackets and shirts and letting the jet of hot air blow across their faces and chests.

"You know," Tub said, "what you told me back there, I appreciate it. Trusting me."

Frank opened and closed his fingers in front of the nozzle. "The way I look at it, Tub, no man is an island. You've got to trust someone."

"Frank?"

Frank waited.

"When I said that about my glands, that wasn't true. The truth is I just shovel it in. Day and night. In the shower. On the freeway." He turned and let the air play over his back. "I've even got stuff in the paper towel machine at work."

"There's nothing wrong with your glands at all?"

Frank had taken his boots and socks off. He held first his right foot, then his left up to the nozzle.

"No. There never was."

"Does Alice know?" The machine went off and Frank started lacing up his boots.

"Nobody knows. That's the worst of it, Frank. Not the being fat, I never got any big kick out of being thin, but the lying. Having to lead a double life like a spy or a hit man. I understand those guys, I know what they go through. Always having to think about what you say and do. Always feeling like people are watching you, trying to catch you at something. Never able to just be yourself. Like when I make a big deal about only having an orange for breakfast and then scarf all the way to work. Oreos, Mars bars, Twinkies. Sugar Babies. Snickers." Tub glanced at Frank and looked quickly away. "Pretty disgusting, isn't it?"

"Tub. Tub." Frank shook his head. "Come on." He took Tub's arm and led him into the restaurant half of the bar. "My friend is hungry," he told the waitress. "Bring four orders of pancakes, plenty of butter and syrup."

"Frank— "

"Sit down."

When the dishes came Frank carved out slabs of butter and just laid them on the pancakes. Then he emptied the bottle of syrup, moving it back and forth over the plates. He leaned forward on his elbows and rested his chin in one hand. "Go on, Tub."

Tub ate several mouthfuls, then started to wipe his lips. Frank took the napkin away from him. "No wiping," he said. Tub kept at it. The syrup covered his chin; it dripped to a point like a goatee. "Weigh in, Tub," Frank said, pushing another fork across the table. "Get down to business." Tub took the fork in his left hand and lowered his head and started really chowing down. "Clean your plate," Frank said when the pancakes were gone, and Tub lifted each of the four plates and licked it clean. He sat back, trying to catch his breath.

"Beautiful," Frank said. "Are you full?"

"I'm full," Tub said. "I've never been so full."

Kenny's blankets were bunched up against the tailgate again.

"They must've blown off," Tub said.

"They're not doing him any good," Frank said. "We might as well get some use out of them."

Kenny mumbled. Tub bent over him. "What? Speak up."

"I'm going to the hospital," Kenny said.

"Attaboy," Frank said.

The blankets helped. The wind still got their faces and Frank's hands but it was much better. The fresh snow on the road and the trees sparkled under the beam of the headlight. Squares of light from farmhouse windows fell onto the blue snow in the fields.

"Frank," Tub said after a time, "you know that farmer? He told Kenny to kill his dog."

"You're kidding!" Frank leaned forward, considering. "That Kenny. What a card." He laughed and so did Tub. Tub smiled out the back window. Kenny lay with his arms folded over his stomach, moving his lips at the stars. Right overhead was the Big Dipper, and behind, hanging between Kenny's feet in the direction of the hospital, was the North Star, polestar, Help to Sailors. As the truck twisted through the gentle hills the star went back and forth between Kenny's boots, staying always in his sight. "I'm going to the hospital," Kenny said. But he was wrong. They had taken a different turn a long way back.

ABOUT THE CONTRIBUTORS

James Agee was born in Tennessee in 1909. After graduating from Harvard, he became a feature writer for *Time* and *The Nation*. His first book, the poetry collection *Permit Me Voyage*, was published in 1934. His renowned story of Alabama sharecroppers during the Depression, *Let Us Now Praise Famous Men*, appeared in 1941. Agee was also known for his movie reviews and screenplays, and he wrote the scripts for such film classics as *The African Queen* and *The Night of the Hunter*. He died in 1955, two years before his major work of fiction, *A Death in the Family*, was published and won the Pulitzer Prize.

Jonathan Ames is the author of eight books, including *Wake Up, Sir!* and *The Alcoholic*. His novel *The Extra Man* is now a film, starring Kevin Kline and Paul Dano. Mr. Ames is also the creator of the HBO show *Bored to Death*, starring Jason Schwartzman, Ted Danson, and Zach Galifianakis.

Judd Apatow wrote and directed the films *Funny People*, *Knocked Up*, and *The 40-Year-Old Virgin* (co-written with Steve Carell). He produced the films *Anchorman*, *Superbad*, *Walk Hard*, *Pineapple Express*, and *Get Him to the Greek*. For television he was a writer and director on *The Larry Sanders Show*, created *Undeclared* and *The Ben Stiller Show* (with Ben Stiller), and was the executive producer of *Freaks and Geeks*.

Amy Bloom is the author of two novels, three collections of short stories, and a nominee for both the National Book Award and the National Book Critics Circle Award. Her stories have appeared in Best American Short Stories, Prize Stories: The O. Henry Awards, and numerous anthologies here and abroad. She has written for the *New Yorker*, the *New York Times Magazine*, and the *Atlantic Monthly*, among many other publications, and has won a National Magazine Award. Her most recent novel, *Away*, an epic story about a Russian immigrant. Her new collection of short stories, *Where the God of Love Hangs Out*, just came out. She lives in Connecticut and is Wesleyan University's Writer-in-Residence.

Raymond Carver was born in Clatskanie, Oregon in 1938. His first collection of stories, *Will You Please Be Quiet, Please?* (a National Book Award nominee in 1977), was followed by *Beginners, What We Talk About When We Talk About Love, Cathedral* (nominated for the Pulitzer Prize in 1984), and *Where I'm Coming From* in 1988, when he was inducted into the American Academy of Arts and Letters. He died in August of that year, shortly after completing the poems of *A New Path to the Waterfall*.

Michael Chabon lives in Berkeley with his wife, Ayelet Waldman, and their four children.

Dan Chaon is the author, most recently, of the national bestseller *Await Your Reply*, as well as the short story collection *Among the Missing*, (a finalist for the 2001 National Book Award), and the novel *You Remind Me of Me*. Dan's fiction has appeared in many journals and anthologies, including Best American Short Stories, The Pushcart Prize, and The O. Henry Prize Stories. Dan teaches at Oberlin College, where he is the Pauline M. Delaney Professor of Creative Writing and Literature.

Hugleikur Dagsson was born in northern Iceland in 1977 and raised in Reykjavik from the age of six. He graduated from the Iceland Academy of the Arts in 2002, and that same year started self-publishing his cartoons. Since then he has written/drawn seventeen books. Three of his collections have been published in English: *Should you be laughing at this?*, *Is this supposed to be funny?*, and *Is this some kind of joke?*. He is also a playwright and a TV writer. He is currently working on more books and plays.

James Downey—veteran comedy writer—has been with *Saturday Night Live* for most of its thirty-five-year run. Joining the show in 1976, fresh from his time at the *Harvard Lampoon*, where he was president, Downey has contributed countless memorable sketches to the show's canon—most notably the show's political satire.

Andre Dubus (August 11, 1936–February 24, 1999) was an American writer. Born in Lake Charles, Louisiana, Dubus attended McNeese State College there before joining the Marines and studying at the Iowa Writers'

Workshop. From 1966 to 1984, Dubus taught at Bradford College (U.S.) in Massachusetts. Dubus was mainly known as a writer of short fiction and novellas. His collections include: *Dancing After Hours: Stories*, *Adultery & Other Choices*, and *Finding a Girl in America: A Novella and Ten Short Stories*. His writing awards included the PEN/Malamud Award and NEA and MacArthur Foundation Fellowships. There are several writing awards named after him.

Dave Eggers is the author of seven books, including *What Is the What* and *Zeitoun*. He is the founder and editor of McSweeney's and co-founder of 826 Valencia, a nonprofit writing and tutoring center for youth in the Mission District of San Francisco. Local communities have since opened sister 826 centers in Chicago, Los Angeles, Brooklyn, Ann Arbor, Seattle, Boston, and Washington D.C.

Nora Ephron is a journalist, novelist, playwright, screenwriter, and director. Her credits include *Heartburn*, *When Harry Met Sally*, *Sleepless in Seattle*, *You've Got Mail*, and the play *Imaginary Friends*. She received three Oscar nominations for screenwriting. Her books include *Crazy Salad*, *Scribble*, and *Heartburn*. Her latest book, *I Feel Bad About My Neck: And Other Thoughts on Being a Woman*, was a number-one bestseller. Her latest film is *Julie & Julia*, starring Meryl Streep and Amy Adams. Her play *Love, Loss and What I Wore*, written with her sister Delia Ephron, is currently running off-Broadway at the Westside Theater. Nora lives in New York City.

Paul Feig is the creator of the long-ago-canceled TV series *Freaks and Geeks*, as well as the author of the books *Kick Me: Adventures in Adolescence* and *Superstud: Or How I Became a 24-Year-Old Virgin*. He is also the author of the young adult sci-fi book series *Ignatius MacFarland: Frequenaut!* He also directs movies and TV but has resisted the urge to list out all of these credits for fear that it will make him look too desperate in front of the much better authors in this book.

Faye Fiore is a national correspondent for the *Los Angeles Times* in Washington D.C. She has been a reporter for thirty years, twenty of them at the *Times* and fifteen of those in Washington, where she covers politics, the homefront, and anything else the news shovels up. She is also raising two teenaged sons and is tired. Occasional humor writing keeps her from walking outside and killing herself.

F. Scott Fitzgerald was born in St. Paul, Minnesota, in 1896, attended Princeton University, and published his first novel, *This Side of Paradise*, in 1920. That same year he married Zelda Sayre, and the couple divided their time between New York, Paris, and the Riviera, becoming a part of the American expatriate circle that included Gertrude Stein, Ernest Hemingway, and John Dos Passos. Fitzgerald was hailed early on as a major new voice in American fiction; his other novels include *The Beautiful and Damned* and *Tender Is the Night*. He died of a heart attack in 1940 at the age of forty-four, while working on *The Love of the Last*.

Jonathan Franzen is the author of four novels—*The Twenty-Seventh City*, *Strong Motion*, *The Corrections*, and *Freedom*—a collection of essays, *How to Be Alone*, and a personal history, *The Discomfort Zone*. He is also a regular contributor of journalism and essays to the *New Yorker*. He lives in New York City and Santa Cruz, California.

Ian Frazier was born in Cleveland, Ohio, in 1951. He received his B.A. from Harvard in 1973 and became a staff writer at the *New Yorker* just one year later. He is the author of ten books, including *Great Plains*, *The Fish's Eye*, *On the Rez*, and *Family*, as well as *Coyote vs. Acme*, and *Lamentations of the Father*. His most recent book, *Travels In Siberia,* is forthcoming in October from Farrar, Straus and Giroux. A frequent contributor to the *New Yorker*, he lives in Montclair, New Jersey with his wife and two children.

Tom Gianas has written and directed for *Saturday Night Live*, *The Adventures of Tenacious D*, *Human Giant*, *The Awful Truth with Michael Moore*, and *Mr. Show with Bob and David* (director). He is currently writing and directing the Comedy Central series *Nick Swardson's Pretend Time* and the FX pilot *Them's My Peeps* with Bob Odenkirk. *Strippers and Babies*, the screenplay he co-wrote with Sarah Silverman, has been optioned, and Tom is also writing the first adult puppet show for the Henson Company.

Jack Handey is the author of the bestselling *Deep Thoughts* series of books. He was a longtime staff writer on *Saturday Night Live*, where he wrote such sketches as "Toonces the Cat," "Deer Heads," "Anne Boleyn," and "Happy Fun Ball," in addition to writing and narrating "Deep Thoughts." His humor pieces have appeared in the *New Yorker*, *Outside*, *Playboy*, and elsewhere, and are collected in his latest book, *What I'd Say to the Martians*. He lives in Santa Fe with wife Marta, one dog, three cats, and a pack rat, Squeaky.

Ernest Hemingway was born in Oak Park, Illinois in 1899. He served in the Red Cross during World War I as an ambulance driver and was severely wounded in Italy. He moved to Paris in 1921, devoted himself to writing fiction, and soon become part of the expatriate community, along with Gertrude Stein, F. Scott Fitzgerald, Ezra Pound, and Ford Maddox Ford. He revolutionized American writing with his short, declarative sentences and terse prose. He was awarded the Nobel Prize for Literature in 1954, and his classic novella, *The Old Man and the Sea* won the Pulitzer Prize in 1953. Known for his larger-than-life personality and his passions for bullfighting, fishing, and big-game hunting, he died in Ketchum, Idaho on July 2, 1961.

Tim Herlihy is a comedy writer and producer. He has been nominated for an Emmy and a Tony, losing both by presumptively substantial margins. He lives in Connecticut.

Tony Hoagland's latest book of poems, *Unincorporated Persons in the Late Honda Dynasty*, was published by Graywolf in January. His recognitions include the Jackson Poetry Prize, the O.B. Hardisson Award, and the Mark Twain Award. His previous collection, *What Narcissism Means to Me*, was a finalist for the National Book Critics Award in poetry in 2004. He teaches in the writing program at the University of Houston. In 2005 his book of essays about poetry and craft, called *Real Sofistakashun*, was brought out from Graywolf.

Miranda July is a filmmaker, artist, and writer. Her videos, performances, and web-based projects have been presented at sites such as the Museum of

Modern Art, the Guggenheim Museum, and in two Whitney Biennials. July wrote, directed, and starred in her first feature-length film, *Me and You and Everyone We Know* (2005), which won a special jury prize at the Sundance Film Festival and the Caméra d'Or at the Cannes Film Festival. Her fiction has appeared in the *Paris Review*, *Harper's*, and the *New Yorker*, and her collection of stories, *No One Belongs Here More Than You* (Scribner, 2007), won the Frank O'Connor International Short Story Award. In 2002 July founded the participatory website, Learning to Love You More (*learningtoloveyoumore.com*), with artist Harrell Fletcher, and a companion book was published in 2007 (Prestel). For the 2009 Venice Biennale she created an interactive sculpture garden, *Eleven Heavy Things*. Raised in Berkeley, California, she currently lives in Los Angeles, where she is making her second feature film, *The Future*.

Steve Koren began his writing career by handing jokes to Dennis Miller and David Letterman in the hallways of the real 30 Rock in Manhattan, where he worked as a tour guide. This led to a writing position with *Saturday Night Live*, earning him several Emmy nominations. Steve eventually entered the sitcom world, working as a writer/producer on *Seinfeld*. In the motion picture world, Steve's screenplay credits include *A Night at the Roxbury*, *Superstar*, *Bruce Almighty*, *Click*, and the upcoming *A Thousand Words*. Currently, Steve is writing the upcoming *Jack and Jill* starring Adam Sandler.

John Lahr is the senior drama critic of the *New Yorker*, where he has written about theatre and popular culture since 1992. Among his eighteen books are *Notes on a Cowardly Lion: The Biography of Bert Lahr* and *Prick Up Your Ears: The Biography of Joe Orton*, which was made into a film. He has twice won the George Jean Nathan Award for Dramatic Criticism. Lahr, whose stage adaptations have been performed around the world, received a Tony Award for co-writing *Elaine Stritch at Liberty*, the first critic ever to be so honored. He is currently working on a biography of Tennessee Williams.

Steve Martin, the multi-talented Grammy and Emmy award-winning actor/ comedian/musician and bestselling author, has proven his star power as one of the most diversified performers in the entertainment industry today. Notable film credits include *The Jerk, Roxanne, Dirty Rotten Scoundrels, Father of the Bride, Sgt. Bilko, Bowfinger, Cheaper by the Dozen, Shopgirl* (the screenplay to which he adapted from his bestselling novella of the same name), and *The Pink Panther*. In 2008 Martin released his *New York Times* bestselling autobiography *Born Standing Up*, which chronicles his early years as a standup comic. Most recently Martin has experienced a successful foray into the music world with the release of his first bluegrass album, *The Crow: New Songs for the Five-String Banjo*. His children's book *Late For School* will be published in September 2010 and his forthcoming book, *An Object of Beauty* will be published in November 2010.

Ian Maxtone-Graham has been a writer for *The Simpsons* since 1995. He wrote for *Saturday Night Live* from 1992 to 1995.

Carson McCullers was the author of numerous works of fiction and nonfiction, including *The Heart is a Lonely Hunter, The Member of the Wedding, Reflections in a Golden Eye*, and *Clock Without Hands*. Born in Columbus, Georgia on February 19, 1917, she became a promising pianist and enrolled in the Juilliard School of Music in New York when she was seventeen, but lacking money for tuition, she never attended classes. Instead she studied writing at Columbia University, which ultimately led to *The Heart Is a Lonely Hunter*, the novel that made her an overnight literary sensation. On September 29, 1967, at age fifty, she died in Nyack, New York, where she is buried.

Adam McKay is a writer, director, and producer who has previously done the movies *Anchorman, Talladega Nights*, and *Step Brothers*, which he cowrote with Will Ferrell. He is a former head writer of *Saturday Night Live* and one of the founding members of the Upright Citizens Brigade. Other past credits include writing for Michael Moore's show *The Awful Truth* and cofounding the comedy website *Funny or Die*. He has also produced the hit HBO comedy series (which is going into its second season) *East Bound and Down*, through his production company with Will Ferrell, Gary Sanchez Productions. Most recently he directed the Tony-nominated Broadway show *You're Welcome America: A Final Night with George W. Bush*, as well as finished production on a new movie he wrote, produced, and directed called *The Other Guys*, starring Will Ferrell and Mark Wahlberg.

Lorrie Moore was born in Glens Falls, New York and attended St. Lawrence and Cornell universities. She is the author of the story collections *Birds of America*, *Like Life*, and *Self-Help*, as well as the novels *Anagrams*, *Who Will Run the Frog Hospital?* and *A Gate at the Stairs*, which was a finalist for the PEN/Faulkner Award and the Orange Prize. Her stories, reviews, and essays have appeared in the *New Yorker*, the *New York Review of Books*, the *New York Times*, the *Paris Review*, the *Yale Review*, and elsewhere. John Updike selected one of her stories for inclusion in *The Best American Short Stories of the Century*. She has been the recipient of The Irish Times Prize for International Literature, the Rea Award for the Short Story, the PEN/Malamud Award, the O. Henry Award, and a Lannan Foundation literary fellowship. She has been inducted into the American Academy of Arts and Letters and is currently a professor at the University of Wisconsin, in Madison, where she lives with her son.

Lew Morton has written for such TV shows as *Saturday Night Live*, *NewsRadio*, *Futurama*, and *Undeclared*. Most recently, he created *Big Lake* for Comedy Central.

Alice Munro grew up in Wingham, Ontario and attended the University of Western Ontario. She has published eleven story collections—*Dance of the Happy Shades*; *Something I've Been Meaning to Tell You*; *The Beggar Maid: The Moons of Jupiter*; *The Progress of Love*; *Friend of My Youth*; *Open Secrets*; *The Love of a Good Woman*; *Hateship, Friendship, Courtship, Loveship, Marriage*; *Runaway*; and a volume of selected stories, as well as a novel, *Lives of Girls and Women*. She is the recipient of many awards and prizes, including three of Canada's Governor General's Literary Awards and two of its Giller Prizes, the National Book Critics Circle Award, and the Edward MacDowell Medal in Literature. Her stories have appeared in the *New Yorker*, the *Atlantic Monthly*, the *Paris Review*, and other publications, and her collections have been translated into numerous languages.

Conan O'Brien has been hailed by the *Washington Post* as "modest, wry, self-effacing, and demonstrably the most intelligent of the late-night comics." Earning the title "Late Night's King of Cool" from *Entertainment Weekly*,

O'Brien hosted NBC's *Late Night* program for sixteen years. During his tenure at *Late Night*, O'Brien was honored with multiple Emmy nominations for Outstanding Comedy-Variety Series and Outstanding Writing in a Comedy or Variety Series. Additionally, O'Brien and the *Late Night* writing staff received six Writer's Guild Awards for Best Writing in a Comedy/Variety Series, including two consecutive wins in 2002 and 2003, and twelve nominations overall. O'Brien moved to Los Angeles upon graduation from Harvard and joined the writing staff of HBO's *Not Necessarily the News*. In 1989, O'Brien began a three-and-a-half-year run as a writer for *Saturday Night Live*, earning an Emmy Award for Outstanding Writing in a Comedy or Variety Series in his first year, and producing such recurring sketches as "Mr. Short-Term Memory" and "The Girl Watchers" (first performed by Tom Hanks and Jon Lovitz). In 1991 he signed on as a writer/producer for the Fox series *The Simpsons*, where he later became the show's supervising producer.

Flannery O'Connor was born in Savannah, Georgia in 1925, the only child of Catholic parents. In 1945 she enrolled at the Georgia State College for Women. After earning her degree she continued her studies at the University of Iowa's writing program, and her first published story, "The Geranium," was written while she was still a student. Her writing is best known for its explorations of religious themes and Southern racial issues, and for combining the comic with the tragic. After university, she moved to New York, where she continued to write. In 1952 she learned that she was dying of lupus, a disease which had afflicted her father. For the rest of her life, she and her mother lived on the family dairy farm, Andalusia, outside Millidgeville, Georgia. For pleasure she raised peacocks, pheasants, swans, geese, chickens, and Muscovy ducks. She was a good amateur painter. She died in the summer of 1964.

Simon Rich is the author of two humor collections, *Free-Range Chickens* and *Ant Farm*, which was a finalist for the Thurber Prize for American Humor. He's written for the *New Yorker*, *Saturday Night Live*, and other places. His first novel, *Elliot Allagash*, was published by Random House in May 2010.

Philip Roth won the Pulitzer Prize for *American Pastoral* in 1997. In 1998 he received the National Medal of Arts at the White House, and in 2002 the highest award of the American Academy of Arts and Letters, the Gold Medal in Fiction. He has twice won the National Book Award and the National Book Critics Circle Award. He has won the PEN/Faulkner Award three times. In 2005 *The Plot Against America* received the Society of American Historians' prize for "the outstanding historical novel on an American theme for 2003–2004." Recently Roth received PEN's two most prestigious prizes: in 2006 the PEN/Nabokov Award, and in 2007 the PEN/Saul Bellow Award for achievement in American fiction. Roth is the only living American writer to have his work published in a comprehensive, definitive edition by the Library of America.

Rodney Rothman most recently served as producer for the film *Get Him to the Greek* and as an Executive Producer on *Forgetting Sarah Marshall*. He is a former head writer for the *Late Show with David Letterman* and was a writer and a supervising producer for the television show *Undeclared*. His writing has appeared in the *New York Times*, the *New York Times Magazine*, the *Best American Nonrequired Reading*, the *New Yorker*, *McSweeney's*, and *Men's Journal*. He is also the author of *Early Bird: A Memoir of Premature Retirement*.

Adam Sandler has enjoyed phenomenal success as an actor, writer, producer, and musician. His films have grossed over $3 billion worldwide and include box office smashes such as *Funny People*, *The Longest Yard*, *Anger Management*, *50 First Dates*, and *The Wedding Singer*, among many, many others. Sandler's comedy albums on Warner Bros. Records have gone multi-platinum and his production company, Happy Madison, is one of the most successful in Hollywood. As a five-year regular on *Saturday Night Live*, he created many memorable characters, including Canteen Boy. Sandler currently lives in Los Angeles with his wife and two beautiful daughters.

David Sedaris is the author of *Barrel Fever* and *Holidays on Ice*, as well as collections of personal essays, *Naked*, *Me Talk Pretty One Day*, *Dress Your Family in Corduroy and Denim*, and *When You Are Engulfed in Flames*, each of which became a bestseller. There are a total of seven million copies of his books in print and they have been translated into twenty-five languages. He was the editor of *Children Playing Before a Statue of Hercules: An Anthology of Outstanding Stories*. Sedaris's pieces appear regularly in the *New Yorker* and have twice been included in *The Best American Essays*. His newest book, a collection of fables entitled *Squirrel Seeks Chipmunk: A Modest Bestiary* (with illustrations by Ian Falconer), is due out in fall 2010.

Paul Simms writes for television (*Late Night with David Letterman*, *The Larry Sanders Show*, *NewsRadio*, *Flight of the Conchords*) and for the *New Yorker*.

Robert Smigel's years at *Saturday Night Live* yielded "Da Bears," "Schmitt's Gay," and "The Sinatra Group," and also included frequent collaborations with his friend Conan, leading to his favorite job, as original head writer and producer of *Late Night with Conan O'Brien*. There he created "In the Year 2000" and "Triumph the Insult Comic Dog," whose rear end he inhabits to this day. He returned to *Saturday Night Live* to create the TV Funhouse cartoons, including "The Ambiguously Gay Duo." He has written filthy, Grammy-nominated songs for Triumph and Adam Sandler, with whom (and Judd) he wrote *You Don't Mess with the Zohan*. While he continues to chase success, he is nearly as proud of his many, many, many failures.

Jon Stewart is one of America's top social and comedic figures. As host of Comedy Central's *The Daily Show with Jon Stewart*, Stewart has interviewed such political luminaries as former Presidents Jimmy Carter and Bill Clinton, Senators Hillary Clinton, Barack Obama, John McCain, and John Edwards, and celebrities Tom Cruise, Tom Hanks, and George Clooney. As the *New York Times* bestselling author of *America (The Book): A Citizen's Guide to Democracy Inaction*, Stewart is also the cocreator and executive producer of the Emmy award-winning Comedy Central show *The Colbert Report*. Stewart and *The Daily Show with Jon Stewart* have received twenty-eight Emmy Award nominations and won thirteen. In 2001 and 2005, the show received the Peabody Award for its campaign coverage of "Indecision 2000" and "Indecision 2004." In addition to gracing the cover of *Newsweek*, *Rolling Stone*, and

GQ, Stewart was *Entertainment Weekly*'s "Entertainer of the Year" and *Variety*'s "New York Entertainer of the Year" in 2004. He was named to *Time* magazine's inaugural Time 100 list of the world's most influential people.

Tobias Wolff's books include the memoirs *This Boy's Life* and *In Pharaoh's Army: Memories of the Lost War*; the short novel *The Barracks Thief*; the novel *Old School*; and four collections of short stories: *In the Garden of the North American Martyrs, Back in the World, The Night in Question*, and, most recently, *Our Story Begins: New and Selected Stories*. He has also edited several anthologies, among them *Best American Short Stories 1994, A Doctor's Visit: The Short Stories of Anton Chekhov*, and *The Vintage Book of Contemporary American Short Stories*. His work is translated widely and has received numerous awards, including the PEN/Faulkner Award, the *Los Angeles Times* Book Prize, both the PEN/Malamud and the Rea Award for Excellence in the Short Story, the Story Prize, and the Academy Award in Literature from the American Academy of Arts and Letters. He is the Ward W. and Priscilla B. Woods Professor of English at Stanford.

PERMISSIONS

"A Mother's Tale" by James Agee. Copyright © 1930, 1931, 1952 by the James Agee Trust, reprinted with permission of The Wylie Agency, LLC.

"No Contact, Asshole!" from *I Love You More Than You Know.* Copyright © 2006 by Jonathan Ames. Used with permission of Grove/Atlantic, Inc.

"How I Got Kicked Out of High School" by Judd Apatow. Copyright © 2000 by Judd Apatow. Originally appeared in the *Los Angeles Times* (April 23, 2000). Reprinted with permission of Judd Apatow. All rights reserved.

"Love Is Not a Pie" from *Come to Me* by Amy Bloom. Copyright © 1993 by Amy Bloom. Reprinted by permission of HarperCollins Publishers.

"Elephant" by Raymond Carver, originally published in the *New Yorker*, currently collected in *Where I'm Coming From* by Raymond Carver. Copyright © 1986 by Raymond Carver, reprinted with permission of The Wylie Agency, LLC.

"Ocean Avenue" from *A Model World* by Michael Chabon. Copyright © 1991 by Michael Chabon. Reprinted by permission of HarperCollins Publishers.

"I Demand to Know Where You're Taking Me" from *Among the Missing* by Dan Chaon. Copyright © 2001 by Dan Chaon. Used by permission of Ballantine Books, a division of Random House, Inc.

Ten illustrations from *Should You Be Laughing at This?* by Hugleikur Dagsson. Copyright © 2006 by Hugleikur Dagsson. Reprinted by Permission of HarperCollins Publishers.

Four illustrations from *Is This Some Kind of Joke?* by Hugleikur Dagsson (first published as *Fylgio okkur* by JPV Publishers Iceland, 2006, Michael Jospeh, 2008). Copyright © Hugleikur Dagsson, 2008.

Seven illustrations from *Is This Supposed to be Funny?* by Hugleikur Dagsson (first published by JPV Publishers Iceland, Michael Jospeh, 2007). Copyright © Hugleikur Dagsson, 2006.

"All the Time in the World" from *Dancing After Hours* by Andre Dubus. Copyright © 1995 by Andre Dubus. Reprinted by permission of Alfred A. Knopf, a division of Random House, Inc.